THE OXFORD HISTORY OF
MODERN CHINA

JEFFREY N. WASSERSTROM is the Chancellor's Professor of History at the University of California, Irvine, where he also holds courtesy appointments in Law and in Literary Journalism. He has written, co-written, edited, or co-edited a dozen books on topics ranging from human rights and revolutions to gender in Chinese history. His most recent books are, as author, *Vigil: Hong Kong on the Brink* (2020), and, as coauthor, the third edition of *China in the 21st Century: What Everyone Needs to Know* (2018). He is a past editor of the *Journal of Asian Studies* (2008–2018) and a past Associate Editor of the *American Historical Review*. He is a member of the editorial board of *Dissent* Magazine and is the advising editor for China for the *Los Angeles Review of Books*. In addition to writing for scholarly periodicals, he often contributes to newspapers (including the *New York Times*, the *Wall Street Journal*, the *Guardian*, and the *Hindu*) and magazines (such as the *TLS*, the *Atlantic*, *Internazionale*, and the *American Scholar*). He has spoken at literary festivals in Europe, Asia, and the United States and served as a consultant on "The Gate of Heavenly Peace," a prize-winning documentary film about the Tiananmen protests and June 4th Massacre.

T0002835

The fifteen specialists who contributed to the *Oxford History of Modern China* are all distinguished authorities in their field. They are:

ROBERT BICKERS, University of Bristol

WILLIAM A. CALLAHAN, London School of Economics and Political Science

JAMES CARTER, Saint Joseph's University

TIMOTHY CHEEK, University of British Columbia

EMILE DIRKS, University of Toronto

DIANA FU, University of Toronto

ANNE GERRITSEN, University of Warwick

IAN JOHNSON, Council on Foreign Relations

RICHARD CURT KRAUS, University of Oregon

KATE MERKEL-HESS, Penn State University

RANA MITTER, University of Oxford

STEPHEN R. PLATT, University of Massachusetts, Amherst

S. A. SMITH, University of Oxford

JEFFREY N. WASSERSTROM, University of California, Irvine

PETER ZARROW, University of Connecticut

THE OXFORD HISTORY OF MODERN CHINA

EDITED BY
JEFFREY N. WASSERSTROM

OXFORD
UNIVERSITY PRESS

OXFORD
UNIVERSITY PRESS

Great Clarendon Street, Oxford, OX2 6DP,
United Kingdom

Oxford University Press is a department of the University of Oxford.
It furthers the University's objective of excellence in research, scholarship,
and education by publishing worldwide. Oxford is a registered trade mark of
Oxford University Press in the UK and in certain other countries

Published in the United States of America by Oxford University Press
198 Madison Avenue, New York, NY 10016, United States of America

British Library Cataloguing in Publication Data
Data available

Library of Congress Control Number: 2021942855

ISBN 978-0-19-289520-2

Printed and bound by
CPI Group (UK) Ltd, Croydon, CR0 4YY

PREFACE TO THE 2018
REPUBLICATION OF THE
ILLUSTRATED EDITION

THE origins of this book lie in late 2012 and early 2013. This was a notable moment in China's history, as it was just then that Xi Jinping, the current leader of the People's Republic of China (PRC), was being chosen first to become head of the Chinese Communist Party (CCP) and then serve as President as well, posts that he was expected to hold for ten years before relinquishing them to his successor toward the end of 2022 and the beginning of 2023, respectively. While a changing of the guard was taking place in Beijing, I was inviting a variety of experts in modern Chinese history, each of whom had demonstrated mastery of a particular period and shown a flair for communicating with general readers as well as fellow specialists, to join me in carrying out a kind of literary relay race across more than four centuries of China's past. More specifically, I asked these scholars, most of them trained as historians but with some political scientists mixed in as well, to help me tell the tale of China's modern period, which I was choosing to define as beginning in the final years of the Ming Dynasty (1368–1644), for reasons explained below in my "Introduction" to this volume.

The finish line in this relay would be the aftermath of the 2008 Beijing Olympics, an event that continues to stand out as a major turning point in the PRC's rise to global prominence. After all these main chapters, though, the baton would be handed off one more time, for a victory lap of sorts, carried this time by historically minded journalist Ian Johnson. My brief to him was to write a "Coda" devoted to the "Presence of the Past" in an era that finds the CCP presenting itself as an organization that draws on the wisdom of Confucius while staying true to the traditions of Marx, Lenin, and Mao Zedong (1893–1976)—a tricky balancing act when we remember that the last of these considered the first a "feudal" thinker whose beliefs had long hindered China's pursuit of modernity.

The hardback edition of the book was published midway through 2016, just a year-and-a-half ago. Given that so little time has passed since then, the text has not been updated except for the correction of a few errors. In ordinary times, it might seem unnecessary to comment in a Preface such as this about what has transpired since the original version of the book appeared. Some-times, though, things that occur in an eighteen-month period can do enough to alter the domestic situation within a country, the way it is viewed by people living in other places, its standing in the international order, or all of these things to justify at least a brief discussion of recent events. As later chapters will show, for example, in the case of China, a book initially published in the middle of 1910 and then reissued in 1912 would certainly have benefitted from prefatory remarks on the intervening end of dynastic rule, and even though China's political system was not altered by the protests and massacre of 1989, it would have been important to preface a 1990 paperback edition of a 1988 work with comments on the tragedy of the previous June.

Nothing as monumental as the 1911 Revolution has taken place since the middle of 2016. It is also too soon to tell if the events of the last year-and-a-half will come to stand out as a counterpart to other decidedly lesser but still significant turning point moments, which left the political system in place while altering other things. There is a good case to be made, though, that the brief period since the hardback edition appeared has been so extraordinary when it comes to Chinese domestic politics and, even more so, China's place in the world, that an effort to take stock briefly of the current context is in order.

Let's begin with what recent months have revealed or underscored about Xi. When the original edition was published, he was already being described as the most powerful figure China had seen since Mao, who ruled the PRC from its founding in 1949 until his death in 1976, and Deng Xiaoping, his most influential successor. There were not yet, though, academic centers devoted to the study of "Xi Jinping Thought," as there now are. Nor had Xi, his eponymous set of ideas, and even the main international policy associated with him, the "Belt and Road Initiative," been formally proposed for inclusion in China's Constitution. Only Mao, who held power from 1949 until his death twenty-seven years later, had seen his name and creed invested with this sort of sacred status while he was still alive, as even Deng, who was the most powerful person in China from the late 1970s until his death in 1997, only received it posthumously.

More generally, in 2016, it was still the norm to break the history of the PRC into two main chunks of time, with the brief rule by Mao's immediate successor, Hua Guofeng, treated as a transitory interregnum. There were the Mao Years, which ended in 1976, and a Reform Era, which had begun at the end of 1978 or start of 1979 and was assumed to still be underway. At the 19th Party Congress in October 2017, however, Xi pronounced that a "New Era," a third PRC epoch, had begun. Another important thing happened—or, rather, did not happen—during that Party Congress. While the CCP conformed to recent tradition by formally announcing the foregone conclusion that Xi would be appointed for a second five-year term as the organization's head, they did not make it clear who would succeed him when the next Congress was held. This has fueled speculation that Xi may diverge from the pattern set by Jiang Zemin and Hu Jintao, his immediate predecessors, and stay in control of the country for more than ten years. He might well, some say, as only a few were suggesting as recently as mid-2016, take a page from Vladimir Putin's playbook and find a way to stay in power.

Will the idea of 2017 marking the start of a "New Era" gain traction in the coming years or fade away? Only time will tell. Some future historians may argue for continuity stretching from Deng's time to the end of Xi's days in power, whenever that comes. Others may insist that a third epoch has started, but claim it began at the moment Xi took power or earlier still. After all, the ratcheting up of controls on civil society that are among the hallmarks of the Xi era can be traced back as far as the midpoint in Hu's decade in power, and while China's current leader has shown greater proclivity for quoting the classics than any previous one, the wave of renewed reverence for Confucius began around the turn of the millennium and made its mark on the Opening Ceremonies of the 2008 Beijing Games. Still, regardless of just how large they end up looming in future works of history, the recent domestic developments associated with Xi noted above deserve mention here.

If these were the only significant political events that had taken place since the middle of 2016, however, writing this Preface would have been merely optional, not essential. What makes it feel crucial to include it is something that occurred across the Pacific from the PRC, which may have profound implications for the trajectory of Chinese history. At this writing, the unexpected election of Donald J. Trump to the presidency of the United States seems to have provided Xi with new opportunities in the international arena, and distracted global scrutiny of the ongoing moves to silence opposition within the PRC, that in another period would have gotten more attention from foreign commentators and observers. The broader slide of America's global reputation, and, in Asia at least, doubts about its full commitment to treaty obligations, has been a political gift for Xi. This has led to seismic shifts in the world order that make the centuries-long trajectory of China's decline from, and return to, international prominence feel differently than it did in mid-2016. Then, the PRC was a country that had surged ahead economically in extraordinary ways, but which still seemed more of a regional than a truly global power, a secondary rather than primary player in some key international spheres. Now, this is no longer the case.

One way to put this issue into perspective is to ponder the question of which world leaders at different periods of time have been credible candidates for the title of most powerful individual on earth. China's emperor might have been a good candidate for this position at various points in the distant past, but thanks to the military and diplomatic defeats that the country experienced during the final decades of rule by the Qing Dynasty (1644–1912), no one would have thought of asserting that any Chinese leader of the 1830s through the early twentieth century was the most powerful person on the planet. During much of the late Qing era and the entire Republican period (1912–1949), in fact, thanks to Japan's surge, China's top leader was not even the most influential individual in Asia.

Even in mid-2016, it was still assumed that when China's top leader met the President of the United States, the most that could be said of the former was that this person might be a fairly close second in influence and clout to the latter. By the fall of 2017, by contrast, *The Economist* was describing the Xi-Trump summit in Beijing as one in which the more "powerful" individual was the one playing host. The magazine was not alone in this assessment.

Eighteen months is a very short period when it comes to the centuries-long view of China's past provided in the chapters that follow, let alone within the much longer sweep of Chinese history as a whole. In addition, if history is any guide, one thing we can be sure of is that Xi and Trump, a pair of strongman leaders who share important traits even while the restrained speaking style of the former and bombastic one of the latter are a study in contrasts, will be viewed differently than they are today, both within their own countries and globally. Still, there is no question that, thanks in part to these two men, the international order is not the same now as it was a year-and-a-half ago. And the changes that have taken place have implications for not just the present and the future but also, in less obvious ways, for how the past is viewed and understood. Coincidentally or not, Xi and Trump both like to tell simplistic stories about history to present themselves as leading grand missions to revive past glories. This book strives to show the value of taking a longer and more nuanced view, which emphasizes, along with other things, how politically charged stories about the past are themselves one of the results—but not the only result—of complex historical processes.

JEFFREY N. WASSERSTROM,
January 2018

CONTENTS

LIST OF MAPS

A GUIDE TO PRONOUNCING ROMANIZED CHINESE (WADE-GILES AND PINYIN)

SINCE Chinese uses characters rather than an alphabet, many different systems of romanization have been developed over the years to help Americans and Europeans learn to pronounce the Chinese characters. Until the establishment of the People's Republic of China in 1949, the **Wade-Giles system** had been the predominant system, and it is still used as the official romanization system in Taiwan. In their attempts to simplify the Chinese language and to increase literacy among the Chinese people, the People's Republic of China (PRC) developed a new system, known as the **pinyin system**. This system is now used by US newspapers and many book publishers.

The following are a few tricks to pronouncing Chinese words which are romanized using pinyin:

The letter	is pronounced as...	Some examples
c	ts, as in "its"	cai (pronounced "ts-eye"; n. vegetable)
q	ch, as in "check"	Qing Dynasty is pronounced "Ching" Dynasty
x	sh, as in "she"	Deng Xiaoping is pronounced "Deng Shiaoping"
zh	"j"	Zhou Enlai is pronounced "Joe Enlai";
		Zhou Dynasty is pronounced "Joe Dynasty"

All other sounds can be pronounced as they are written.

Wade-Giles	Pinyin	Pronunciation in English
		ch
ch' (aspirated)	q	(The name of Mao's widow is written "Chiang Ch'ing" in Wade-Giles, "Jiang Qing" in pinyin, and would be pronounced "Jiang Ching.")
		j
ch (unaspirated)	j or zh	("Chou Enlai" in Wade-Giles is spelled "Zhou Enlai" in pinyin and would be pronounced "Joe Unlie.")
		k
k' (aspirated)	g	("Hua Kuofeng" in Wade-Giles has become "Hua Guofeng" in pinyin)
k (unaspirated)	g	g
p' (aspirated)	p	p
		b
p (unaspirated)	b	(The capital of Taiwan is no longer written Taipei but Taibei.)
t' (aspirated)	t	t
		d
t (unaspirated)	d	(The t in Mao's name changes to d: Mao Zedong.)
ts' and tz' (aspirated)	c	ts
ts and tz (unaspirated)	z	a or ds
		(ds as in "woods")
		sh
hs	x	(The first part of Deng Xiaoping changes from Hsiao to Xiao.)
		French j plus r
j	r	(no exact English equivalent)

a	a	a (as in star)
e	e	e (as in set)
i	i	e (as in he) or i (as in machine)
ou	ou	o (as in over)
u	u	oo (as in too)
en	en	un (as in under)
ih	i	ir (as in bird—no exact English equivalent)
u	u	German u (no exact English equivalent)
ai	ai	ie (as in lie) or i (as in i)
ei	ei	ay (as in day)
ao	ao	ow (as in now)
uo	uo	oo (as in too) plus ou (as in ought)
ui, uei	ui	oo (as in too) plus ay (as in day)
ung	ong	oo (as in book) plus ng (as in thing)

Chart courtesy of TEXPERA (Texas Program for Educational Resources)
Taken from Asia for Educators website: <http://afe.easia.columbia.edu>

Introduction

JEFFREY N. WASSERSTROM

WHEN asked to free associate about China as a country, many people will begin by referring to it as a large place with a giant population. They may also describe it as a nation that in recent years has been transformed by an economic boom, seen its status in the global order rise dramatically, and now is home to some of the world's most massive and polluted cities. Some will mention the irony of it still being governed by a Communist Party, but by one that curiously accepts capitalists into its ranks. They may also bring up the fact that parts of it now look strikingly modern yet it remains a country strongly shaped by its past. One thing that many will stress is that China has an incredibly long history, meaning that to make sense of its present, it is crucial to keep in mind enduring cultural traditions that began in the era of the country's great axial age sage Confucius (551–479 BCE). It is common to assume that the contemporary country needs to be seen as the product of ideas, beliefs, institutions, and practices that go back to Confucius or even further. A phrase that has recently assumed mantra-like qualities via its appearance in everything from textbooks and newspaper editorials to speeches by leaders is that "5,000 years of Chinese civilization" lie behind and inform what goes on in the People's Republic of China (PRC). For those who teach and write about modern Chinese history for a living, such as the stellar array of specialists in different recent periods responsible for the chapters that follow, the set of widely believed ideas about China just described, especially the notion of China's massive size and the longevity of its "civilization," are both a blessing and a curse.

They are a blessing because the assumption that the country is important and shaped by history means that we do not have to work as hard to justify our interest in and passion for our subject as some of our colleagues working on other places. They are a curse because, when taken together, the constellation of notions just outlined distorts important things about both the kind of country China was in previous centuries and the kind of place the PRC is now.

Consider, for example, the way that a fascination with China's great size, when combined with a belief in the shaping power of something called "Chinese civilization" stretching back in supposedly continuous form for many millennia, can warp the geographical imagination. Many people inside and outside of the country find it natural to assume that when they see a map of the PRC, which was founded in 1949, it portrays a country that may have grown a bit over time but nevertheless always looked something like it does now. In terms of the location of its borders, this kind of thinking goes, surely they are not so different from what they were back when the ruler of the Han Dynasty (206 BCE–220 ACE) held power—while the

Roman emperor Hadrian was building a wall at the other end of Eurasia. Or further back still, when the first emperor of the short-lived Qin Dynasty (221–206 BCE), the celebrated and infamous unifier (as closely associated with the Great Wall as Hadrian is with his eponymous one), brought together smaller warring states to form a single great country. Perhaps, many will acknowledge, the specific locations of some borders were once not quite the same, but surely the differences were minor rather than fundamental or just a matter of a specific territory, such as Taiwan in recent times, being politically part of or separate from China proper.

At least, this powerful though inaccurate logic goes, there are basic things about China's territorial spread that have been constant. Is it not true, for example, that the country has long been and is still defined in terms of the flow through it of three great rivers: the Yellow River that moves across its northern plain and takes its name from the color of the rich loess soil that lines it; the Yangzi River that bisects the PRC of today and connects inland provinces such as Sichuan to the Pacific Ocean via the great port of Shanghai; and the Pearl River in the South that ends in a delta region that includes both Guangzhou (Canton) and Hong Kong? And since the first emperor's day, hasn't the Great Wall he built defined the northern edge of China proper, with land just beyond it alternately being claimed by the Chinese ruler and by nomadic groups of Mongol and Manchu dwellers on the steppes? The problem is that "no" is the right answer to both of these questions.

This is because, in reality, what we now think of as "China" has been of wildly varying sizes and shapes in different eras—and not just because Taiwan has not always been part of it and that some regions to the far west that are now part of the PRC (such as Tibet in the far west and north of that Xinjiang) have sometimes, like Mongolia and Manchuria, been outside of Chinese control. The "China" of some emperors was many times smaller than that outlined on today's maps, in some cases containing only a handful of the more than a dozen provinces that make up the PRC. Even to speak of a "China" of Confucius' day is misleading, since that foreign term and its Chinese language variants would not be coined for centuries, but if one *is* said to have existed, only the Yellow River flowed through it. Conversely, during the last century-and-a-half of the Song Dynasty (960–1279), Chinese emperors governed the ports that lined the Yangzi and Pearl rivers and their deltas but held no sway over the Yellow River's fertile loess plateau.

There are equally significant problems with thinking of the first emperor's Great Wall as a symbol of continuity and a marker of an enduring border. The first emperor was obsessed with large projects, as the massive army of terra cotta warriors built to accompany him into the afterlife suggests, and he was responsible for the erection of major fortifications. What we see labeled on maps now as "The Great Wall," however, does not trace the location and length of his creations, even if in legend and lore those are described as having been kept up by each ruler who followed him. Rather, some of his successors maintained or extended and others ignored the Qin Dynasty walls. And the lines that read "Great Wall" on current maps trace the path of this famous barrier not as it has been for more than 2,000 years but as it has been for roughly half-a-millennium. Similarly, the images of the Great Wall that flashed on

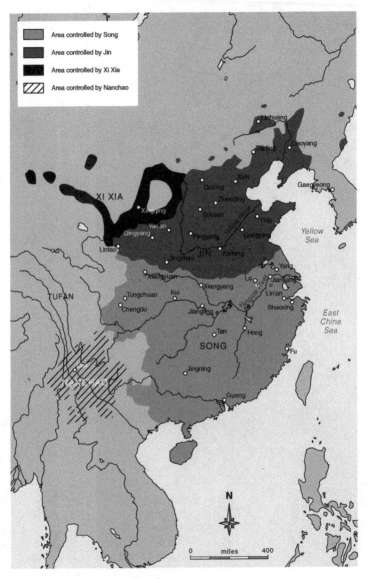

1. China during the Song dynasty (960–1279).

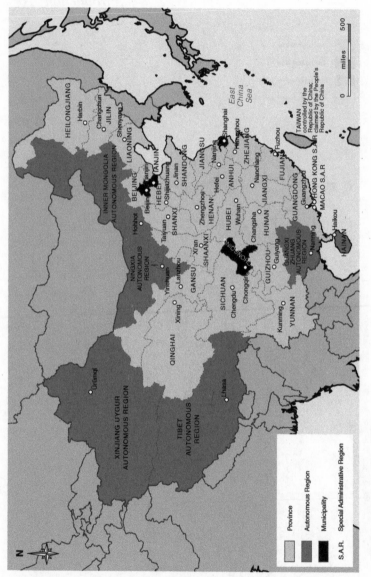

2. The People's Republic of China.

television screens around the world to introduce segments of the 2008 Beijing Games, while sometimes accompanied by commentaries that described it as a symbol of China's ancient past, showed an object that only began to look the way it does now once more than a dozen centuries had passed since the first emperor had died.

One challenge in writing an overview of Chinese history, as this brief summary of issues of continuity over time suggests, is when to begin the story—when to say that "China" in any meaningful use of that term began. One option is to start with a very early dynasty, the Xia, which is mentioned in documents of two millennia ago as having existed more than a millennium before the documents themselves were written. Perhaps better thought of as rooted in myth than provable fact, allusions to it are folded into comments about "five thousand years" of Chinese history. We are on firmer ground in the Shang Dynasty, which is famous for its oracle bones, even if there are disputes over figuring out just when it existed, with some saying it fell around 1122 BCE and others placing its demise almost a century-and-a-half later in 1046 BCE. Via different logics, one could begin with the time of Confucius and other sages of the sixth through third centuries BCE, or with the first emperor of the Qin. The issue here, fortunately, is not finding a time to begin the history of China, though noting how difficult it is to do that is useful, but rather finding a beginning for *modern* China. Even here, however, there are many places that such a more chronologically circumscribed narrative might begin. Some scholars, including Naito Konan (1866–1934), arguably the most important Japanese Sinologist of all time, have made strong cases for thinking of China's modern age beginning during the Song Dynasty (960–1279), a time of great economic and technological breakthroughs. Another tradition, which informs many PRC histories and is tied to Marxist ideas of class struggle and a progression from "feudal" to "bourgeois" to "socialist" eras, sees China's *modern* period beginning after the first Opium War (1839–42), a violent clash discussed in detail in the second chapter of this book, and ending with the lead-up to the founding of the Chinese Communist Party (CCP) in 1921. PRC textbooks refer to this period as bringing a close to a long era of "feudal" rule in China, and present the era that follows as best characterized as *contemporary* times. Here, we opt for a third alternative: that of locating the origins of the modern age rather imprecisely in the period when the fortunes of the Ming Dynasty (1368–1644) began to decline to the south of the Great Wall, while to the north of it, the Manchu groups who would eventually found the new Qing Dynasty (1644–1911) were gaining in strength.

One attraction of this starting point for an account of modern China is that, while many things that happened earlier continue to exert an influence on China today, this is the era when some key symbols of China's "five thousand years of civilization" came into existence or at least took their most familiar form. The case of the Great Wall has already been cited. It is, moreover, by no means the only famous edifice that is often presented as a symbol of continuity with ancient times but really should be associated with the Ming. The Forbidden City is another such case in point: a site that is indeed hundreds of years old, but one that television viewers are often encouraged to assume is far older than it really is.

It is not only buildings that make a starting point near to the Ming–Qing transition attractive for an account of modern China. The varied ideas and practices that come to mind now when "Confucianism" is mentioned can be traced back to many points in the past, but recent work stresses the important role of late Ming encounters between Chinese scholars and Jesuits from the West in what historian Lionel Jensen has dubbed the "manufacturing" of a Confucian creed that began to seem comparable in some ways to what Westerners referred to as a religion. And it is no accident that the standard term for a valuable piece of Chinese pottery is "Ming Vase," for as the next chapter stresses, the period marked an inflection point in the production and global spread of China's justly famed porcelain.

Another attraction of starting with the fall of the Ming and rise of the Qing is that recent generations of scholars have shown that, as important as the coming of the West was in shifting the course of Chinese history, demographic and other developments that preceded the Opium War were also crucial in putting strains on the imperial system that helped account for its eventual demise. There is no magic moment when China became "modern," but to understand many of the phenomena and dilemmas that have been crucial parts of the Chinese story during the country's event-filled last two centuries, including the revolutions that established first the Republic of China (in 1912) and then the PRC (in 1949), starting several hundred years earlier makes sense.

A final point worth making about the value of beginning our tale in the late Ming/early Qing era is that it was then that some of the most enduring works of Chinese popular culture were created. Two pervasively significant Chinese novels, with characters whose names remain as widely known in China as Shakespearean creations are in many parts of the world, date from that time. One is *Hong Lou Ming* (The Dream of the Red Chamber—also sometimes translated as The Story of the Stone), an eighteenth-century work that has inspired sequels and spin-offs, films and television series, and even theme parks that recreate the large family compound and elaborate gardens that are the setting for its scenes of elite life.

Another famous novel from the time, *Xi You Ji* (*Journey to the West*), incorporates animals with magical and allegorical sides into the historically based tale of the monk, Xuanzang, who brought key Buddhist texts from India to China. Its beloved characters, such as the mischievous Monkey King, also live on now in many formats, making appearances in animated films and inspiring toys and computer games.

There is a great value in placing these two works side by side at the start of an account of modern Chinese history, for the differences between them draw our attention to a final distorting assumption that many people unfamiliar with China's past bring to a book like this, especially at a time when Beijing's current leaders are emphasizing the need to ensure that the country adheres to "Chinese values," as if a singular, unified cultural tradition has existed since the days of Confucius. China, some readers may be tempted to assume, has long been a place where order is prized and chaos feared, where family relations are at the heart of all important stories, where reverence for seniority, respect for ritual, and the pursuit of harmony are woven into the fabric of daily life.

Only in truly exceptional moments, such as the wildest days of Maoist extremism, this logic suggests, have these characteristics of "Chineseness" been temporarily forgotten, to terrible effect.

If the only great novel from late Ming/early Qing times that remained known and had proved steadily popular were *Hong Lou Meng*, then fiction could be invoked to support this misleading idea. The fact is, though, that *Xi You Ji*, which celebrates disruption and a form of playfulness far removed from staid ritual, has been and continues to be enjoyed by the same populace that is drawn to the placidity and wistfulness of *Hong Lou Meng*. Just as any account of Western civilization that pays attention to Greece but not to Rome is bound to be flawed, so, too, the reader should keep in mind that Chinese civilization has always had more than one strand. Readers should proceed through the chapters to come ready to encounter a China of varying sizes and shapes, which has a cultural heritage that has been marked by change as much as by continuity and which has room for not just Confucian solemnity but also the mischievous irreverence of the Monkey King.

1. *From Late Ming to High Qing, 1550–1792*

ANNE GERRITSEN

THE early life experiences of a man named Zhu Yuanzhang (1328–98) had a lasting impact on the dynasty that would become known as "Great Brightness" (Da Ming) and lasted from 1368 to 1644. Also known as the Hongwu emperor after the first reign period (1368–98) of the dynasty he founded, Zhu Yuanzhang came from a poor peasant background. As a youth, he spent time in a Buddhist monastery, and later joined a religious-inspired rebel force that eventually spelled the end of the preceding Mongol-Yuan dynasty (1297–1368). His first-hand experience of poverty and the hardships of peasant life, together with his understanding of the potential power of temple organizations, religious groups, and rebel armies, shaped the policies he formulated. Under the guidance of scholarly advisers, the Hongwu emperor established a political regime that made agriculture the mainstay of the economy and sought to impose strict controls over temples and monasteries. He tolerated no opposition, and ruthlessly exterminated all critics, rebels, and their extended families. The laws and institutions of the Ming, some inherited from previous dynasties, some formulated under the authoritarian regime of its first emperor, remained in place, more or less unchanged until the end not only of the Ming dynasty but also the Qing dynasty, which lasted from 1644 to 1911.

The legal and institutional continuity between the Ming and Qing dynasties, to some extent the legacy of Zhu Yuanzhang's early life experiences, is one of the reasons why the period under discussion in this chapter, sometimes referred to simply as "late imperial China," is usually described as a single epoch. The period begins with the economic growth and socio-cultural developments of the late sixteenth century. It covers the fall of the Ming, the transition to the Qing, and ends in the late eighteenth century. Despite the very significant changes that took place during this period, including the shift from Han Chinese to Manchu leadership and the roughly tripling in size of both population and territory under the empire's control, the legal and institutional foundations laid by Zhu Yuanzhang remained more or less intact.

It is important to understand the implications of that institutional continuity. Take for example the size of the administration. Zhu Yuanzhang determined the number of provinces in which the Ming empire should be divided, the number of prefectures in which each province should be divided, and the number of counties in each prefecture, with a single centrally appointed administrator at the head of each unit. Territorial expansion under the Qing regime meant that a few new provinces were created, but despite the very substantial growth of the population, especially in the pre-existing provinces, the number of units and the size of the administration remained unchanged. In other words, by the late eighteenth century, county governors ruled over far larger populations than their predecessors had in the fourteenth century. Similarly, the standardized examination system and the classic Confucian texts it was based on, which served to select the administrators of the empire, remained in place for the duration of the Ming and Qing empires, despite the fact that the late thirteenth-century civil servants were confronted with an entirely different geopolitical reality from those of the late eighteenth.

During his reign as first emperor of the Ming, Zhu Yuanzhang changed his vision of government numerous times and his laws were subject to constant revisions. Throughout the reigns of his immediate successors, however, the social and legal instructions of the "first emperor" became institutionalized. Zhu had divided the population into separate social groups; families had to register as farming or military families, as craftsmen or as scholars. That registration conferred a precise social status, but also identified a family unit's address as well as its tax and labor duties. The system of taxation throughout the empire was based on agricultural production, and most of the population paid taxes in kind (e.g. in bushels of grain and bolts of silk). It was not until the last decades of the Ming that the system was adjusted to allow single tax payments in silver instead of the complex combinations of silk, grains, and labor duties.

While Zhu Yuanzhang's palace had been in Nanjing, in the south of the empire, one of his sons, who would become known as the Yongle emperor, shifted his capital to the north, to Beijing. There he established a palace complex surrounded by high walls, where he housed an extensive palace bureaucracy, populated by numerous palace women and a vast staff of eunuchs. The palace grounds were out of bounds for the general population, and it henceforth became known as the Forbidden City. Its hierarchically organized spaces, where the emperor ruled hidden behind closed walls, located in the far north of the empire, served as the seat of political power throughout the Ming and Qing regimes. Together with the thousands of miles of the Great Wall, erected in brick to the north of Beijing, along pre-existing lines of defense against the threat of invading nomadic forces, the Forbidden City came to symbolize what was assumed to be the political character of the Ming and Qing dynasties: autocratic, seemingly isolated, static, and unresponsive to the changes that were happening in the wider empire and in the world.

It will become clear from what follows, however, that these characteristics and continuities coexist with dynamic changes, social diversity, and political openness. It is precisely by the start of our period, the late Ming dynasty, or around 1550, that significant changes began to shake the foundations laid by the first Ming emperor. While the political center of the empire remained located in Beijing in the north, the economic growth was all located in the southern parts of the empire. Economic growth was especially vibrant in the region known as Jiangnan, a highly fertile region in the southeast of the empire, where the Yangzi River forms a delta and flows into the East China Sea. It was here, in what became the economic heart of the empire, that the old taxation and status registration systems of the early Ming completely broke down. Despite Zhu Yuanzhang's vision for an agricultural land-empire, the economic growth in the south came from manufactures, interregional trade, and export. Market towns became flourishing urban centers, small-scale manufactures became near-industrial size production centers, and the mercantile activities of late Ming traders grew to encompass trade and exchange patterns that circumnavigated the entire globe. In the south, well beyond the reach of the imperial administrators, many of those previously registered as peasants or scholars opted to participate in the far more lucrative manufacture and trade activities, leading to a social blurring on a scale never seen before. Where farming or a life devoted to study might have seemed a safe option before, opportunities for making money tempted people away from stability, lured them into towns and away from their family networks, and opened vast swathes of the population to the benefits but also the risks of trade and business. And while Zhu's vision had been for a dynasty ensconced behind a Great Wall, safe from invaders and protected from foreign visitors, the presence of foreigners became ever more noticeable in the late Ming. Missionaries became a regular presence, on the southern coast, but also in Beijing, and foreign traders hovered in each coastal port and on each accessible island off the southern coast, keen to access the wealth of manufactures produced in the empire. And again, far from the watchful eye of the governing powers in the capital, southern administrators and residents both participated actively in this trade.

Late Ming social and cultural life

So what did life in late Ming China look like? To us distant observers, it seems that much of it played out in the public domain. The multitude of travel records, personal accounts and diaries, visual representations on paintings and scrolls, novels and short stories of the late Ming help us to visualize this world. Imagine a large city, with streets and canals, densely populated with boats, carts, sedan chairs, and pedestrians, travelling to and from theatres, temples offering a variety of religious services, and shops with advertising banners and displays of the goods and services for sale. There were goods for sale everywhere, not just in shops but also along the roads and in specialized markets. Markets were regular events: daily for vegetables, fruit, and meat from the local farms, weekly for goods sold in larger bulk such as grains and bolts of textiles, and slightly less frequently for clothing, art and antiques, and other consumer goods such as books, ink and paper, tea, and furniture. Such markets punctuated urban life, at intervals set by the rhythms of regional markets, travelling salesmen, and religious festivals, which were always occasions for large-scale buying and selling as well as theatrical performances and ritual ceremonies.

The late Ming was a time known for its lack of distinctions, its social blurring, and its dynamic interactions. The significance of the markets in late Ming social and cultural life can hardly be exaggerated. They were occasions where people of all social backgrounds mingled in public. From peasants selling daily vegetables in the street to big businessmen conducting major transactions behind closed doors, and from scribes offering to write up complaints to learned scholars with experience of the examination system, high and low status blended together on the street. Similarly, men and women mingled on the occasions of markets and fairs, deities' birthdays, and the numerous festivals in the moon calendar. The prescriptive record may well stress the social distinctions between different social groups, the proper distances between high and low, and the appropriate separation of men and women, but the social practice was completely different.

When men and women of all ages and backgrounds encountered each other in the street, fashionable appearances were one way of flagging up distinctions. Fashion and clothing mattered, perhaps precisely because other social distinctions had become so much less visible. There were numerous silks and cottons in vibrant colors and patterns to choose from, there were styles of clothing to select and accessories to flaunt. Fashion was, then as now, about creating identities, showing personal style, and presenting an image of the self to the outside world. Houses and gardens were similarly subject to fashion and ostentation. By selecting the right pieces of furniture, combined with a few scrolls of fine paintings or calligraphy and a porcelain vase, and thereby creating the outward appearance of a scholarly studio, anyone could own what looked like the status of a scholar. By investing in the right plants and rocks, one could make a garden fit with the latest fashion in garden design. And for those with new wealth and little understanding of how to make the right choices and distinctions, there were etiquette handbooks, collectors' guides, and manuals with samples of letters.

Behind the scenes of all this conspicuous urban consumption and social blurring was of course the vast majority of the population concentrated on the supply side to meet the demand. The growing rural population continued to intensify the agricultural output, but large parts of the population in the Jiangnan region also worked in the manufacturing of silks, cottons, and porcelains. These were in demand not only throughout the empire, but throughout the world. Chinese porcelains had long been exported to Japan, Korea, and Southeast Asia, but from the sixteenth century onwards, they found their way to the homes of Portuguese and Flemish nobles, Dutch burghers, and via Manila to Spanish colonial homes in New Spain. It was this manufacturing and export on a vast scale that brought enormous wealth to the Ming empire, mostly in the form of Spanish silver. If the laws of the first emperor of the Ming dynasty had allowed for the flexibility to apply taxes to the wealth generated by overseas trade, the imperial coffers would not have suffered as heavily from the draining costs of maintaining an ever-growing palace household and staving off invading forces. As it was, however, those costs came to cripple and eventually topple the Ming state.

In 1644, 276 years of Ming rule came to an end when the Qing, who would rule until 1911, created a new political unity. Unsurprisingly, the dramatic chain of events that took place in that year tells only a small part of the story. The decline of the Ming dynasty had started long before 1644, when several related social, economic, and political developments had begun to weaken the regime and seriously threatened its longevity. Similarly, for the Manchu who founded the Qing dynasty, 1644 was the endpoint of a longer period of growth that originated in the steppe lands north of the Great Wall. The Manchu started as a small association of diffuse and mobile nomads unified under different charismatic military leaders. These units then became a loose federation of military troupes, which operated across a wide territory under a single leader. Gradually, this group emerged as a political organization with the ambition to establish a sedentary base in the southern agricultural lands occupied by Han Chinese peasants. From their base in these lands (which would become known as Manchuria), their forays into Ming territory only gradually began to pose a credible threat to the incumbent rulers. The Ming leadership sent out armed forces to try to stop the advances of the Manchu in the north, but their attention was divided by a simultaneous second threat emerging in the south: the rebel forces led by Li Zicheng.

Li Zicheng was born in Shaanxi in 1606, in humble circumstances and, as legend has it, with a spirit of resistance against the ever-increasing tax demands the Ming rulers and their local representatives imposed on the rural population. When famine struck, Li was able to marshal the anti-Ming sentiments of the alienated peasant population into a rudimentary military force. His dual aims of dividing the land and returning it to the peasants, and abolishing the abusive grain taxes all peasants had to pay attracted the peasantry, especially after the flooding caused by the breaking of the banks of the Yellow River in 1642. Li Zicheng and his rebel army invaded the capital in 1644, after which the ruling emperor known as the Chongzhen emperor committed suicide. But precisely at that moment, the Manchurian forces were strengthened by the defection of a high-level Ming military leader, a man named Wu Sangui. When Wu Sangui and the Manchu army defeated the rebel army, Li Zicheng fled the capital, leaving the door open for the Manchu to take possession of the palace.

For the Manchu invaders, 1644 formed the beginning of a steep learning curve and a period of rapid growth.

It was necessary for the new Qing rulers to transition first from a small mobile military power to a civil government, and second from a polity that ruled within a Manchu cultural context to one that governed using Han Chinese institutions. These transitions were made rather effortlessly as the Qing had begun a process of transition prior to their invasion of Ming China, which included establishing and administering institutions similar to those of the dynasty they would soon replace. Most notable of their new institutions was the banner system. This was a hereditary registration system that divided the population into "banners," territorial units with a mixture of military and agricultural duties. Each of these units, identified by a distinct plain-colored or bordered banner, had its own identity, sometimes on the basis of an ethnic background (groups of Manchu, but also Mongols and Han Chinese), sometimes on the basis of geographical location (such as the banner with responsibilities in border defense). But mostly, the Manchu created a combined or dual system that drew heavily on pre-existing (i.e. Ming) institutions, with the appointment of dual administrators, one Han Chinese and one Manchu, so as to marshal the expertise of the Han Chinese while safeguarding Manchu political superiority.

The Han Chinese population, most notably the elite men, had to make a fundamental choice: to stay loyal to the Ming or switch allegiance to the Qing. In the early years after the founding of the new regime, Ming loyalists had the moral high ground. They stayed true to the system they had worked so hard to join through the acquisition of Confucian learning and the passing of examinations by choosing to end their lives, or by withdrawing entirely from public

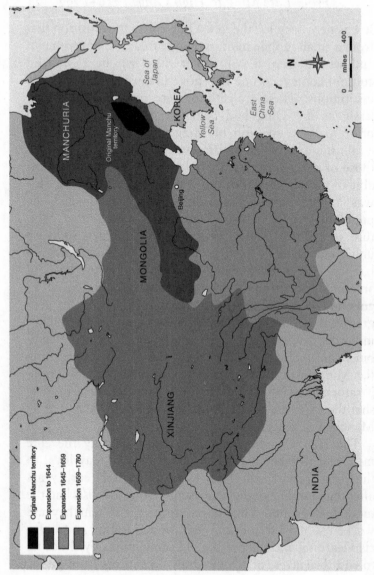

3. Expansion of imperial control during Ming and Qing times.

life, only professing their loyalty to the Ming in secret. But as time went on, and the Qing rulers became more Confucian in their outward appearance, many switched allegiance and began to participate in the new regime.

The three emperors: Kangxi, Yongzheng, Qianlong

The three emperors that ruled Qing China between the mid- to late seventeenth century and the end of the eighteenth century presided over a highly successful dynasty. By the time the Kangxi emperor (1654–1722) came to the throne in 1661, the chaotic transitional period from late Ming to early Qing had come to an end, and war and unrest began to be replaced by peace and stability. During the long-lived reigns of these three men, Qing China flourished: the political regime was largely stable, supported by a well-funded military; the economy grew, as did the population and the territory under Qing control. This period, known as the High Qing, is famous for its stability, growth, and numerous outstanding cultural achievements,. Of course the three emperors faced different challenges and their responses were shaped not just by the changing circumstances, but also by their different personalities. On the whole, however, the continuities justify our treatment of the three regimes as a single period.

The Kangxi emperor's main challenge was the Three Feudatories Rebellion between 1673 and 1681. The rulers of three southern provinces threatened the authority of the Qing regime and proposed a re-establishment of the Ming dynasty, posing enough of a challenge to occupy half of the territory under Qing rule. The Kangxi emperor and the imperial armies were ultimately victorious, but it reinforced the emperor's belief in the need for the continued strengthening and legit-imization of Qing rule. One of the administrative innovations that followed from this rebellion was the establishment of a secret palace memorial system, whereby provincial officials could communicate directly with the emperor, without the intervention of other officials. The legitimization of Qing rule had to come mostly from the Han Chinese elite, so Kangxi invested heavily in cultural projects that drew Confucian scholars to his side. The compilation of a large dictionary of the Chinese language, known as the Kangxi dictionary, the appointment of a large team of scholars to write the history of the preceding Ming dynasty, and the issuing and widespread distribution of a short tract with moral advice for the ordinary population known as the Kangxi Edict can all be seen as emerging from Kangxi's desire to increase the legitimacy of his regime. Finally, Kangxi was open-minded to what foreign visitors to the empire might have to offer, and appointed the Flemish Jesuit missionary Ferdinand Verbiest (1623–88) to share his knowledge about medicine, map-making, astron-omy, and armaments including canons. He also relied on Jesuit missionaries in his negotiations with the Russians when a border conflict threatened stability in what is now Siberia. The Treaty of Nerchinsk, signed in 1689, is signifi-cant not only for Kangxi's appointment of Jesuits to the role of mediators and translators, but for Kangxi's willingness to recognize the sovereignty of another political entity existing outside the realm under Qing control.

Kangxi's successor, the Yongzheng emperor, was born in 1678, but only came to the throne in 1722, and only ruled for fourteen years until 1735. The most important political innovation of his rule came in 1733, when he established a Privy Council of personal advisers that would outstrip the importance of the Grand Secretariat, and thus became known as the Grand Council. It was this small team of close advisers that met with the emperor behind closed doors that would determine all policy until the end of the dynasty in 1911. Yongzheng continued the expansion of territory into the northwest that had started under the rule of Kangxi, leading to a substantial increase in the size, power, and budget of the military that continued under his successor, the Qianlong emperor. Contacts with foreigners, however, decreased during this period, with the Yongzheng emperor forbidding the Manchu from converting to Christianity.

The expansion of the territory by vast military campaigns and the declining fortunes of Christianity under Qing rule continued under the extended reign of the Qianlong emperor. Born in 1711, he reigned supreme over the largest population and territory of all the pre-modern land-based empires until 1799, although he officially seceded from the throne in 1796 to make way for his son, so as not to challenge the record length of rule set by his grandfather. The Qianlong emperor was not merely interested in being an emperor, and ruling over an empire that was "great" in terms of its size and population, its economy, technology, and cultural achievements; he was interested in being visible and perceived as such. He embarked on extensive military campaigns, and had himself painted as victorious military leader; he employed thousands of scholars to gather and select a complete anthology of Chinese literary texts, and promulgated its existence widely; he collected the finest examples of paintings, calligraphy, and decorative art, and added his own poems, stamps, and signatures to mark his connoisseurship; he held inspection tours throughout the realm, and had court artists record each of these events. He understood the importance of symbols of power, and manipulated these to the very best of his ability.

The Qing empire of the eighteenth century was both an extremely successful imperial regime, and, ultimately, a victim of that same success. Economically speaking, the empire flourished under Qianlong's rule. As new territories were incorporated into the empire, new lands became available to support a growing population. The human waste of that population (also known as night soil) was used to fertilize that land, so that its output increased. During much of the eighteenth century, there was enough elasticity in the system to accommodate both a growing population and the intensification of agriculture. It was a precarious balance, and when it was lost, the pendulum swung hard in the other direction. From the late eighteenth century onwards, and especially during the nineteenth century, as we will see in subsequent chapters, the growth of the population was both unstoppable and unsustainable, with overpopulated regions suffering from an increasing shortage of land and resources, which in turn led to widespread famine and peasant unrest. But for much of Qianlong's reign, population growth was a strength that allowed for dynamic urban centers, with large-scale manufacturing for domestic use and for export, and active networks of trade connecting far-flung regions.

One of the most significant strengths of the regime that the Qianlong emperor had inherited from his predecessors was the so-called dual system of administration. The structure itself was largely unchanged from the Ming dynasty: officials were appointed on the basis of civil service examination success, they served in provincial, prefectural, and county-level posts in areas that were not their own, to avoid the risk of favoritism, or in the capital, and rotated on a regular basis. As mentioned above, the novelty of the Qing system was that each position was held jointly by a Manchu official and a Han Chinese one. By serving together, they held each other in check, making sure both interests were served. For the Han Chinese officials, what mattered were continuities with the Ming legal structure, legitimization through Confucian values, and at least the semblance of fair taxation for the general population. The Manchu appointees, however, were there not merely to ensure loyalty to the Manchu, but to safeguard the distinct qualities of the Manchu. Through the use of Manchu language in official documentation, the imposition of the Manchu hairstyle on all officials, the separation of the population through an inter-cultural marriage ban, and ongoing training in the martial arts, Manchu identity was continuously reconstructed and reinforced. The effectiveness of this dual appointment system, and the institutional recognition of the different cultural identities, that included not only Han and Manchu but also Mongol socio-cultural groups, both lend this Qing political system an air of sophistication.

By the end of the eighteenth century, the elasticity that had until then accommodated the ever-growing population had begun to disappear. One of the most significant events to challenge the authority of the Qianlong emperor towards the very end of his regime is the White Lotus rebellion, a movement with its roots in popular religion that will be discussed in more detail in the next chapter. The crucial point to note here is simply that the overall cost of its suppression, both in terms of finance and human life, seriously weakened the

Qing state, and is often seen as marking a turning point in the fortunes of the dynasty.

Women and gender

For many decades, students of China with an interest in women and gender have relied on a small number of texts to inform them about the role of women in society. These were either Confucian tracts about propriety and hierarchical distinctions in all social relations, or educational texts for women aimed specifically at the inculcation of moral values. Some of these dated from before the Han dynasty (206 BCE–220 CE), so we may well ask how relevant they were in the social world of the late Ming and Qing dynasties. The complex system of texts, ideas, and values we refer to as Confucianism does identify a specific role for women; in contrast to men, women are to operate within the realm of the home, they should take responsibility for the care of the elders and children, and they should espouse values like modesty and loyalty. For far too long, women in China were depicted as helpless victims of an oppressive system that restricted their freedom, not just spiritually but physically by binding their feet. A woman with tightly bound feet, unable to walk freely, came to represent the inequalities of late imperial Chinese society.

But ideals, prescriptions, and philosophical values can only ever tell a small part of the story. Confucianism itself underwent major changes, emerging from its classical foundations before the Han dynasty as Neo-Confucianism in the Song dynasty (960–1279), and becoming more focused on the individual and the self in the late Ming dynasty. More importantly, the social context within which women's roles took shape had changed fundamentally, especially in the economically vibrant Jiangnan region, where wealth, leisure, urban culture, and social fluidity created more freedoms and opportunities than before, especially for women.

Perhaps unsurprisingly, it makes a very significant difference which sources one uses for understanding women's lives. While Confucian prescriptions restricted women to the concerns of the household, managing the affairs of that household by the late Ming also meant taking responsibility for the business transactions of that household and making consumer choices in the market. Paintings and scrolls from the late Ming depict vibrant urban scenes where men and women both participate in the social, economic, and cultural activities that take place in the street. Even more important for understanding women are not materials written *about* women, but sources produced *by* women themselves. We have large quantities of stories and plays, poems and letters written by women and shared between extensive networks of women. These sources have opened our eyes to the extensive presence of women in the records of the past. Their level of education, the sophistication of their literary output, the geographical reach of their epistolary networks, and the political importance of their associations have fundamentally challenged the depiction of women as victims of an oppressive system. Even the practice of footbinding has been rethought, shifting the emphasis away from suffering to the cultural context in which women assigned meaning to the practice. Through writing about bound feet, exchanging elaborately made silk embroidered shoes, and celebrating shared ideals of female beauty, women appropriated the practice as their own and used it to create and strengthen shared bonds.

The transition from late Ming to early and High Qing did make a difference in terms of the official rhetoric about women. With the establishment and gradual legitimization of the Manchu regime, adherence to Confucian morals took on a different significance. To seem more Confucian and morally upright than their predecessors, Qing administrators sought ways to restrict some of the freedoms women had claimed in the late Ming. The so-called chastity cult, which had its origins in the Yuan dynasty (1271–1368), flourished particularly in the eighteenth century. The imperial state used the chastity cult to extol women's virtue in a variety of ways: by assigning high cultural status to women who preserved their chastity by not remarrying after the death of their husbands, by awarding plaques and erecting arches to celebrate female virtue publicly, and by compiling extensive lists of such virtuous women in local gazetteers. On the basis of such plaques, arches, and lists, together with the extensive body of regulations that clarified who qualified for the status of virtuous women, and who transgressed against the regulations for behavior, we might argue that the mid-Qing was a time in which severe moral restrictions shaped women's lives. Arguably, however, the chastity cult points less to restrictions and more to the anxieties caused by the blurring of divisions along social and gendered lines that economic development had brought. The chastity cult mattered during this period, precisely because women had claimed greater freedoms than before, precisely because women played such active roles in the social and cultural realms, and precisely because greater wealth had brought consumption, fashion, and leisure to women's lives.

Art and material culture at the Qing court

Consumption, fashion, and leisure shaped not only the social but also the material world of the High Qing. Of course the art and material culture collected at the imperial court by no means adequately represent the wider world of goods produced during the Qing dynasty. Arguably, the most significant change that occurred during the Qing was in the extraordinarily wide range of goods for sale in the markets and shops throughout the empire. But the imperial court played an important role: in the workshops of the imperial court, some of the most skilled craftsmen from within and beyond the empire worked with the finest materials to produce the luxury goods the emperors demanded. The Qianlong emperor, for example, appointed one of his trusted advisers to serve as superintendent of the porcelain production to supervise the manufacture of the finest porcelains. On the instigation of the emperor, the potters worked with new glazes and colors to create porcelains with dazzling hues, coated to look like bronze, jade, or wood, and in the shape of birds, dogs, and lions, as well as making the finest blue-and-white vases ever seen. Unlike some of his predecessors, the Qianlong emperor was not concerned if the less successful items ended up for sale by local merchants, thereby boosting the quality and design of the goods in circulation throughout the empire.

The porcelain industry was located in the southern province of Jiangxi, where the white clays were found that made Chinese porcelain famous in the first place. But that was unusual; most of the imperial workshops were located within close reach of the emperor's private quarters in the Forbidden City. The workshops for metalwork, for example, were there, as were the jade carvers, the furniture makers, the silk embroiderers, and the kilns that fired the tiles for the palace roof. The Qing emperors all had different preferences: the Kangxi emperor was interested in new technologies and materials, and worked closely with the artisans he appointed to overcome challenges and obstacles, the Yongzheng emperor had a collector's approach, and appointed court painters to document his favorite antiquities in the imperial collection, while the Qianlong emperor saw himself not only as a great patron of the arts but on a par with the great artists and connoisseurs of the past, adding his own calligraphies to their work. Another of his interests was to recreate certain antiquities in different materials: he had ancient bronzes made in carved bamboo, and the soft feathers of a bird or the unctuous quality of jade made in porcelain. The palace collection also contains some of the finest works of painting and calligraphy, both those inherited from the collection of the preceding Ming dynasty, and those commissioned by the Qing emperors. Some of the imperially appointed painters and calligraphers worked with long-standing models of landscape art or imitated the great calligraphers of the Song and Yuan dynasties, others brought in eccentric and individual perspectives, including those who used their paintings to profess an undying love for the Ming dynasty. Zhu Da, for example, was a descendent of the Ming imperial family who painted some of the greatest early Qing paintings in the guise of a crazy monk under the name of Bada Shanren.

Imperial interest and support lifted the skill levels of the artisans and their knowledge of materials to unprecedented heights. Artisans were brought in from the far corners of the empire, including from newly appropriated territories like Tibet and Xinjiang, to work within the imperial work-shops and palace buildings. Architectural specialists from Tibet were brought to the capital, for example, to oversee the building of the Buddhist temples in Beijing, and Islamic and Tibetan carpet makers worked in the palace work-shops to produce the woolen carpets that adorned the palace floors as seen in some of the imperial portraits of the Qing emperors. The art and material culture in the collections of the Qing imperial palace, now held in the Palace Museum collections in Beijing and Taiwan, may not have been representative for the art and material culture of the High Qing as a whole, but it served the palace well in representing itself to the outside world as a culturally sophisticated, highly skilled, and technologically advanced Confucian institution.

The Qing and the Nanyang

The Qing code known as the "*Da Qing lüli*" ("Laws and precedents of the Great Qing"), largely based on the Ming code, strictly prevented any interaction between the Qing population and overseas visitors. Anyone who proceeded either by land or by water through a barrier station would be given a punishment of eighty blows, unless they had a license to do so, and those who avoided the regular barrier stations and sought to leave the boundaries of the empire via unpatrolled roads or creeks would be punished by ninety blows. Far worse punishments were in store for those who not only left Qing lands but then proceeded to communicate with such foreigners as might be lurking in the waters and islands off the Qing coast: confinement, followed by death by strangling. Exporting goods by sea or across the land boundaries was also punished severely, especially when it concerned horses, cattle, iron-work capable of being wrought into military weapons, copper coin, silks, gauzes, or satins. Finally, anyone who had left the boundaries of the Qing and settled elsewhere was forbidden from ever returning home, once again on punishment of death.

Such were the laws, valid throughout the Qing dynasty, as they had been throughout the Ming, formulated by the first emperor of the Ming and his Confucian advisers. The aim of these laws was to support the self-sufficiency of the empire and its agricultural foundations, to protect the boundaries and keep the population safe within the boundaries. Implementing these laws effectively, however, was an entirely different matter. This had been a serious problem under the Ming regime, but became an even less tenable position under the Qing regime.

In part, this was because as the population grew, there was a severe shortage of land, especially in the mountainous coastal provinces along the southern seaboard, pushing a high percentage of the population into other occupations such as trade and smuggling, and into the search for new lands beyond the Qing boundaries. The landless found opportunities for trade and settlement in places like Taiwan, the Philippines, and throughout Southeast Asia. Widespread emigration from mainland China, and the formation of overseas Chinese communities in turn supported the growth of extensive trade links that connected the coastal provinces of the Qing to the islands, kingdoms, and port cities in the South China Sea and the Indian Ocean. The lands to the south and southeast of the Qing (now Malaysia, Singapore, Thailand,

Vietnam, Cambodia, Myanmar, Laos, the Philippines, and Indonesia), referred to as Nanyang (literally "southern ocean"), may have been closely connected to the Qing through migration and trade, but the Qing regime did not officially recognize the ethnically Chinese population that resided here as its responsibility. On a number of occasions, violent clashes occurred here, leading to the brutal massacre of thousands of overseas Chinese, without any response from the imperial government.

In part, however, the lack of implementation of laws that sought to prevent the Qing population from trading with foreigners was due to the fact that the number of officials stationed in the coastal regions was far too small to patrol the coast effectively. More importantly, perhaps, the cost of bypassing an official was more than compensated for by the profits that could be made from supplying the foreign merchants with goods manufactured inland. Corruption was widespread, not least because the official salary of a lower-order official in the employ of the state was far too low, and the expectation was that an official would supplement his salary with a range of other benefits. In the late Ming, when the patterns of migration and overseas trade first began, and up to the middle of the Qing, foreign merchants wanted far more from the Chinese than the other way around. There was intense global demand for the silk, tea, and porcelain that was produced mostly in the southern provinces, and most of these goods had to be paid for in silver. Of course the Chinese also wanted goods: precious woods, fragrances and incense, spices, plants and animals with medicinal qualities, much of which came from the islands and forested lands of Southeast Asia. But on the whole, the balance of trade was in favour of the

Chinese, and silver, sourced mostly from the mines in South America, flowed freely into China. This situation created a great deal of wealth for both the empire and the southern population while it lasted. That it would change was inevitable; how it changed will be explored in a later chapter.

Christianity in Ming and Qing China

During the course of the sixteenth century, the landscape of Christianity in Europe changed profoundly. Where the Catholic Church had once more or less held sway over all aspects of the visible and invisible realm, the Reformation (i.e. the split between Catholic and Protestant religion) meant that the Catholic Church felt it had lost a large part of its followers. In response to this, the Catholic Church decided to seek souls to convert beyond the boundaries of the European "old world," and bring the Christian faith to the new world. The order of the Jesuits, founded in 1534, prepared missionaries for their work overseas not only by giving them a religious education, but also by providing them with a sophisticated understanding of the sciences such as cartography, mathematics, and astronomy. Many other missionary orders, such as the Benedictines, Dominicans, and Franciscans, were also involved in delivering Christianity to the far corners of the earth, but in China, it was the Jesuits who had the greatest impact. In part, this was because the approach of the Jesuits was to acquire in-depth knowledge of the country they were trying to convert. As such, famous Jesuit missionaries in China were both fluent in Chinese and presented themselves to the emperor in the outward guise of Chinese scholars. Their aim was to convert the Chinese emperor, or at the very least high imperial officials, so that the followers of the emperor would then automatically follow. This top-down approach, combined with a very accommodating attitude to the existing religious terminology and patterns of practice, would ultimately earn the Jesuits a great deal of criticism, including from the Pope in Rome. Ironically, it was the critique of the Pope, and the strife between the different religious orders, that did the most severe damage to the overall success of the Christian missionary enterprise in China. In 1724, the Yongzheng emperor banned the Manchu population from converting to Christianity, and in 1737, the Qianlong emperor outlawed Christianity in China altogether.

Throughout the long seventeenth century, from the arrival of the first Jesuit in Macau in 1582, to the diminished role the Jesuits played at Qianlong's court in the first half of the eighteenth century, numerous Jesuits played high-profile roles in China. Matteo Ricci (1552–1610) was not only the first but probably the most widely known. After he successfully predicted a solar eclipse, the Wanli emperor appointed him to the position of special adviser in the Forbidden City, an honour no Westerner had achieved before him. The legacy of Matteo Ricci includes not only Chinese writings and extensive letters introducing the Chinese empire to his European readers, but also the first world map that brings together European cartography and Chinese knowledge of the realm. Instead of placing Jerusalem in the middle of the map, as was the tradition in Western mapmaking, the *Kunyu Wanguo quantu*, produced by Matteo Ricci first in 1584, and reprinted in 1602 at the behest of the Wanli emperor, placed the Chinese empire at the centre.

The Wanli emperor offered patronage to Ricci, but the two men never met. The Kangxi emperor, patron to the Flemish Jesuit Ferdinand Verbiest (1623–88), entertained a very close relationship to this missionary, appointing him to an official position as chief astronomer and mathematician of the Qing empire and demanding personal instruction in the Western sciences. Neither the Yongzheng emperor nor Qianlong were as interested as the Kangxi emperor was in the acquisition of knowledge about the wider world. The Qianlong emperor did, however, appreciate the knowledge and skills of missionary painters, and used these very effectively to help promulgate his vision of the Qing empire abroad. An Italian missionary by the name of Giuseppe Castiglione (1688–1766) served as court painter under Qianlong, and made numerous famous portraits of the emperor, combining European painting skills with the ideals and practices of Chinese imperial court painting.

Despite the high positions awarded to select Jesuits, and the tireless work of numerous lower-profile missionaries in seventeenth- and eighteenth-century China, Christianity did not reach a very large part of the Chinese population, in part because of imperial sanctions against conversions, and in part because of the refusal of the Christian Church leadership to tolerate the coexistence of Christianity with the family-based ritual practices and popular religions that shaped the this-worldly and other-worldly views of the Chinese.

Jesuits and technology in late imperial China

Arguably, the contribution of the Christian missionaries to Chinese science and technology, and especially the exchange of scientific knowledge between China and

Europe, is greater than to the spread of Christianity in China. The Jesuits saw the "arts," such as mathematics, astronomy, and mnemonics (memorization techniques) as additional tools for attracting the Chinese and convincing them of the glory of their Christian God. For the Chinese emperors, however, that glory was less significant than their own position. They were keen to capture the Jesuits' skills for their own purposes. The Shunzhi emperor (1638–61), who ruled when the Qing was founded in 1644, appointed the German Jesuit Adam Schall von Bell (1592–1666) to advise him on matters related to astronomy and religion, and the two are said to have spent a great deal of time together. We already saw that the Jesuit Verbiest, too, had a close relationship to the emperor, serving in an official position in the imperial bureaucracy under Kangxi. In his role as Director of the Imperial Observatory, Verbiest rebuilt the institution and equipped it with armillary spheres, globes, sextants, and other instruments for measuring the size and distance of celestial bodies and predicting their trajectories. The early Qing emperors were keen to marshal the powers of these astronomers for the empire, and happy to employ European specialists for the purpose.

In 1687, a group of French missionaries arrived in China. The party included Louis-Daniel le Comte (1655–1728) and five other Jesuit scientists. He remained only for three years: in 1691, he had been assigned the task of returning to France to inform his superiors that the mission near Beijing was struggling financially. During his time in China, he travelled from Shanxi where his original assignation was to Xi'an, where he spent two years, and later on to Canton. Like Matteo Ricci and the many missionaries after Ricci, Le Comte sent long letters back to

Europe, describing the features of life in China that struck him as noteworthy, but while Ricci's letters were full of admiration and wonder about the marvels of this sophisticated empire, Le Comte's letters are more critical. In the seventeenth century, the Jesuits felt that although China lacked Christianity, the Europeans had a great deal to learn from the Chinese, and common ground could be found, both in religious belief and in scientific thinking. By the end of the seventeenth century and during the course of the eighteenth century, especially when the so-called scientific and industrial revolutions in Europe began to transform all aspects of life in Europe, European thinkers and visitors to China started to focus on what they considered to be an absence of scientific thought and a lack of technological development in China.

The critical attitudes in writings about China by eighteenth-century European missionaries and merchants can to some extent be explained by the continued failures they faced: lack of freedom to proselytize seriously hampered the missionaries' chances to convert the population of China, and the lack of access to the interior meant that traders were reduced to visiting certain ports, at set times of the year, through a small group of imperially appointed, designated merchants. But their criticisms of Chinese science and technology, and their description of the Chinese empire in the eighteenth century as stagnant, would leave a lasting impression on views held by Chinese and Western scholars on the High Qing. Only in recent decades have scholars begun to pay more attention to the ways in which Chinese science and technology did develop in the eighteenth century, and to evaluate Chinese scientists "on their own terms," as historian Benjamin Elman has described it.

The High Qing was a period of growth and dynamic development: the population grew, the territory under Qing control increased, a more sophisticated multi-cultural and multi-lingual administration than ever before was in operation, Chinese manufactures increased and tea, silk, and porcelain were exported all over the world and in larger quantities than ever before. And even if there were not as many scientific innovations during the Qing as there had been during the Song dynasty, they were still numerous. The use of Western armament technologies in the Qing imperial army, the use of Western cartography in mapping the empire, the use of perspective in the paintings commissioned by the imperial court, the use of colored enamels to make imperial porcelains reveal that particularly for the purpose of strengthening the imperialist ambitions of the emperors and their administrators, collaborations between Western and Chinese scientists also thrived as never before during the High Qing.

2. New Domestic and Global Challenges, 1792–1860

STEPHEN R. PLATT

IN the autumn of 1792 when Britain's first diplomatic mission to China set sail, the Qing dynasty was at its peak. In terms of power, stability, and extent, its empire was almost unrivalled in Chinese history. Its territory was double the size of the old Ming empire, its economy was thriving and largely self-sufficient, and it was the pre-eminent military power in Asia, facing no serious threats on its extensive borders. The visit of a British ambassador, Lord Macartney, was thus treated by officials in the Qing court as something of an amusing novelty—a chance to accept tribute from the distant British while impressing them with the grandeur and hospitality of the Qianlong emperor.

The British, however, had more concrete goals in mind. Industrialists in northern England were agitating for greater markets for their products, especially woolen textiles. But since 1760 all British trade in China had been restricted by the emperor to the southern port of Canton, which had a warm climate and little or no market for wool products. Macartney had come to ask China to open new ports for British trade, to give the British preferential tariff rates, and to allow them to station a permanent ambassador in Beijing to resolve any disputes that might come up between the two countries or their subjects. To impress the Qing emperor with Britain's newfound technological might, Macartney brought along a shipload of gifts—600 crates and packages containing cutting-edge scientific instruments, a room-sized planetarium, giant lenses, a hot-air balloon, a diving-bell, and modern weaponry including a 12-pound howitzer with ammunition.

However, much to the disappointment of the British ambassador and the 100-strong retinue of artists, technicians, servants, musicians, and various gentlemen who accompanied him, those gifts from Great Britain were marked as "tribute" when they arrived in China. Furthermore, it was made clear to Macartney that if he hoped for an audience with the Qing emperor he should show subservience in the same manner as ambassadors from other tribute states like Korea and Siam. Specifically, he would have to perform what the British called the "kowtow"—a ritual series of three kneelings and nine prostrations to acknowledge the emperor's superiority. Macartney refused to do this, reasoning that since he would never perform such abasements before his own sovereign he could not do so before the emperor of China. After some negotiation he was, in the end, allowed to honor Qianlong after his own fashion—by kneeling, as he would do before his own king—and the imperial audience went on as planned. But soon afterwards, although Macartney had hoped to winter over in Beijing for sustained negotiations with the emperor, Qianlong dismissed the entire British embassy from Beijing and sent them back to England with no concessions whatsoever. He refused all of Macartney's requests for opening new ports and stationing an ambassador in Beijing. To add insult to injury, at least in the eyes of the British, he also wrote a famous edict addressed to King George III in which he even dismissed the gifts Macartney had brought, writing: "As your ambassador can see, we possess all things. I set no value on objects strange or ingenious, and have no use for your country's manufactures."

Macartney's refusal to perform the kowtow—a refusal that would be repeated, conspicuously, in another failed British embassy in 1816—became a rallying-point for the British. It was taken as proof of the Qing emperor's arrogance and Chinese ignorance of Britain's strength. As the logic went, by demanding the kowtow Qianlong had refused to acknowledge the equality of the British empire. Macartney's refusal to indulge him thus became a bold defense of Britain's national pride. For skeptics, however—such as Napoleon, who declared in 1817 that if *he* had sent an ambassador to Beijing he would have let him perform any ceremony whatsoever that was traditional to that court—Macartney's inflexibility towards Qing courtly custom was blamed as the reason the mission had failed. Both sides, however, lost track of the key fact that the Qing court had, in fact, allowed Macartney to kneel as per his own custom, and they did not refuse him an imperial audience on that basis. More importantly, those who blamed the mission's failure on the kowtow—and they would be legion by the time of the Opium War in the late 1830s—seem not to have understood that even if Macartney *had* performed the expected kneelings and prostrations, it was just as unlikely Qianlong would have granted any of Britain's unprecedented demands.

Macartney left China in anger, and later wrote in dark resentment that the power and grandeur of China was in fact nothing more than an illusion. Up close, he claimed, the façade of strength gave way to foundations that were rotting from beneath. "I often perceived the ground to be hollow under a vast superstructure," he wrote, "and in trees of the most stately and flourishing appearance I discovered symptoms of speedy decay." He predicted that the Chinese subjects of the Qing dynasty would soon rise up against their Manchu (or "Tartar") overlords. The Chinese "are awaking from the political stupor they had been thrown into by the Tartar impression," he claimed, "and begin to feel their native energies revive. A slight collision might elicit fire from the flint, and spread the flames of revolt from one extremity of China to the other."

Macartney would turn out to be more correct than he had any right to be. Quite unknown to Macartney and his entourage, the Qianlong emperor at the time of their visit was already beginning to lose control over his government. To them he appeared clear-eyed and sound of mind, but in fact he was verging on senility after nearly six decades on the throne. And though he had, in his earlier years, been a forceful and active administrator given to lavish displays of power and ego, by the 1790s Qianlong was entering his senescence and relinquishing ever more power to his advisers. Nowhere was this more apparent than in the rise of his favorite minister, a former Manchu guardsman by the name of Heshen, who had first caught the emperor's fancy in 1775 and had, by the mid-1790s, married his son to the emperor's favorite daughter and assumed to himself a stunning level of power within the government. Heshen oversaw a vast system of patronage through official appointments that funneled huge sums of embezzled government funds into his own pockets. And though his corruption was well known to more conscientious officials at court, to attack him was to attack the emperor's own judgment in trusting him. Equally dangerous, criticizing him risked bringing to light the dangerous forces of disunity and factionalism at court, and so his critics remained largely silent and Heshen himself remained untouchable.

At the end of his sixtieth year of rule, in 1796, Qianlong formally abdicated the throne. However, the abdication was little more than an over-the-top display of filial piety, a public declaration that he would not try to outdo his grandfather, Kangxi, who had spent sixty-one years on the throne from 1661 to 1722 and was the longest reigning emperor in China's history. In reality, after the abdication Qianlong continued to wield power just as he had before, and his son—who reigned as the Jiaqing emperor (1796–1820)—lived in Qianlong's shadow for the following three years, serving in little more than a symbolic role. But Qianlong's mental abilities continued to decline as he aged. A Korean ambassador in 1794 reported that Qianlong ordered breakfast immediately after having finished it; another, in 1798, wrote that in the evening the emperor could no longer remember what had happened in the morning. As Qianlong declined, Heshen's power and corruption rose in proportion.

It was only in 1799 when Qianlong finally died that Jiaqing assumed real power and control over the administration, and one of his very first acts was to have Heshen arrested and put to death after a rapid trial in which he was found guilty of a long list of corruption-related crimes. There were many gradations of capital punishment in imperial China and Heshen, because he had been favored by Jiaqing's father, was granted the privilege of strangling himself with a silk cord. Heshen's stolen belongings were confiscated—sprawling mansions, hundreds of thousands of acres of farmland, millions of ounces of silver and gold bullion, entire storehouses of precious gems—but in practical terms his arrest and execution served mainly as a sign that the new emperor was aware of the decline that had begun in his father's final years. Slowing that decline, however, would prove far more difficult than merely punishing a corrupt minister.

China had enjoyed great prosperity during most of Qianlong's reign in the eighteenth century, a period largely free from internal wars in which China enjoyed a thriving economy underpinned by a steady supply of silver from foreign trade. By measures such as consumption of luxury goods, the wealthy regions of eastern China rivaled or surpassed the quality of life in Western Europe. But such prosperity fostered a dramatic increase in the empire's population, and by the end of Qianlong's reign the empire's population was fully double what it had been under the late Ming dynasty. The introduction of new-world crops such as corn, peanuts, and sweet potatoes helped fuel this growth in China's population, because they could be cultivated on formerly unused land such as hillsides hostile to more traditional Chinese crops. By the end of the eighteenth century there were more people in China than in all of Europe, and the overall population of roughly 300 million Qing subjects represented nearly a third of the world.

However, the government was unable to expand in kind to meet the needs of controlling such a large population. Qianlong's grandfather Kangxi, late in his reign in 1711, had issued an edict promising never to raise the land taxes that formed about 80 percent of the government's income (the rest coming primarily from a salt monopoly, mining in the southwest, and foreign trade). The decree was a sign of confidence in the dynasty's government at the time—that it *could* avoid raising the land tax—as well as a means of placating wealthy Chinese landowners and purchasing their loyalty to the Manchu rulers. But it was not beneficial to later generations. For Qianlong to overturn his grandfather's act would have been unfilial, and so the government in the late eighteenth century had to make do with a very slowly rising budget at a time of fast population growth. The result—which would hold enormous significance for the future—was that the bureaucracy could not expand as needed. The lowest level of imperial officials found themselves with larger and larger populations under their immediate jurisdictions, and it became proportionally more difficult to judge court cases, collect taxes, and mobilize labor for public works, to say nothing of providing security. The effects were particularly demoralizing for the masses of scholars who devoted their lives to preparing for the civil service exams in hopes of gaining positions as government officials, for even as their numbers grew, the quotas for how many were allowed to pass did not. By the end of the eighteenth century, there were only about 20,000 government positions available for more than a million degree-holders. Even a scholar who passed the notoriously difficult provincial-level examinations might have to wait twenty years for a position to become available.

The dilution of the empire's attention and the increasing difficulty of the landless classes of Chinese to carve out an existence amid a rising population were especially hard felt in regions of China that were late to be settled, where land rights were tenuous. In one especially mountainous region of Hubei province known as the Han River Highlands, new migrants had multiplied the local population six times over during the course of the eighteenth century, most of them refugees squeezed out from more prosperous and longer-settled regions. These transplants made their livings as hired laborers, charcoal-makers, and tenant farmers. They were by nature unsettled and transitory, and in the absence of a strong imperial presence in the region, disputes were often settled with violence. Many turned to informal groups in search of mutual protection and—in the face of a life that was difficult and held few opportunities—moral guidance.

They were ideal recruits for a new form of an old religion, the White Lotus strain of millennial Buddhism, already mentioned in passing in Chapter 1, which preached a coming apocalypse in which traditional society and the Qing government would be destroyed. Believers, especially those who helped to bring about the revolution that was to come, were told they would be rewarded in the new world. Itinerant teachers converted peasants who had little to look forward to in their precarious lives, telling them that if they believed in the White Lotus doctrines they should chant the proper sutras and begin stockpiling weapons. Those who helped overthrow the corrupt government of the Manchus, they were told, would receive great rewards in the new world that was to come. Those who did not, would be swept away in the apocalypse.

The White Lotus uprisings began in 1796, at a time when most of the local Qing military forces in the Han River Highlands had been transferred south to neighboring Hunan province to fight a separate uprising of the Miao minority group. As the religious groups in Hubei province began to rebel—individual cells acting in almost complete independence of one another, typically numbering in the hundreds or low thousands, looting villages and setting up blockades on the roadways—most counties in the province had no more than a few dozen soldiers on hand to stop them.

Chinese governments had a long history of dealing with religious uprisings, but the White Lotus proved almost impossible to contain. By 1799 the rebellion had spread beyond the borders of Hubei and embroiled five provinces in a wildfire of sectarian violence. A confluence of factors hampered the government's attempt to stop them—a shortage of soldiers meant hasty recruitment of local militias, many of which proved even more destructive than the rebels themselves. Qianlong, for his part, refused to send the elite banner troops from the Beijing region, insisting instead that local military leaders must suppress the White Lotus with local forces. What the government *did* do, was to lavish the officers in charge of the White Lotus campaigns with nearly all the funds they asked for from the central government.

It was here that Heshen's pyramid of corruption made itself felt most severely, for he himself was in charge of the campaigns, and his chosen henchmen supervised the fighting on the ground. An unheralded level of graft entered the military campaigns. By the peak of the war, officers were reporting (and demanding salaries for) over one million militia troops, many of which didn't actually exist— their salaries were going directly into the pockets of the military leaders themselves, with hefty kickbacks to Heshen besides. Even worse, the generals in charge of fighting the White Lotus appear to have prolonged the conclusion of the war for several years after it might have otherwise have ended, allowing the fighting to go on so they could ensure a constant flow of funding from the government.

In the end it was only Qianlong's death, and Jiaqing's execution of Heshen, that allowed a new direction in the White Lotus campaign. Commanders were replaced. A new strategy of building fortified villages to protect loyal peasants and using scorched-earth to destroy the areas controlled by the sectarians finally proved effective in starving the rebels into submission. But by the time the campaigns came to an end in 1804 they had all but bankrupted the government, costing the once-flush Qing treasuries 120 million taels of silver—an amount equal to several years' worth of imperial revenue. Harsh cutbacks in military spending followed, as reprisal for the corruption of the White Lotus campaign, and China thus moved forward into the nineteenth century with a demoralized military and exceptionally stringent limits on military spending that all but ensured that the empire's soldiers would be poorly trained, underpaid, and have no new weapons or equipment. The aftermath of the White Lotus campaigns would leave the dynasty all the more vulnerable to the conflicts with European powers and even larger internal uprisings that were to come a generation later.

Separately from the ongoing issue of sectarian rebellion, the other major source of trouble for the dynasty was, at least as it appeared in the early 1800s, an unlikely one: the flourishing trade with Britain and other Western countries that went on at Canton. It was unlikely precisely because the trade was so valuable to all concerned. Since 1760, Qianlong had restricted all Western trade with China to the southern port of Canton, where the East India Company—which the British government had granted a monopoly on imports from China to England—purchased vast quantities of tea and silk for resale back home. Second to the British were the Americans, who since 1784 had sent ships from Salem, Boston, and New York to load up on tea for their own markets.

Canton was a provincial capital city with a population of roughly one million people, where the British and other Western traders were allowed to reside during the trading season in a small district just outside the city proper, on a lot only 300 yards wide and 200 yards deep that contained the so-called "factory" buildings (which contained offices, living quarters, and warehouses, and were owned by the Chinese merchants). In the off season, the foreigners had to leave Canton and repair to the nearby Portuguese settlement at Macao. The small size of the factory district, however, belied its importance to international trade. Hundreds of thousands of Chinese were employed in various capacities growing, processing, packing, and transporting the tea, silk, and porcelain that went out from Canton to supply the needs of European and American markets. For their part, the foreign traders brought in textiles, furs, ginseng, quicksilver, sandalwood, and dozens of other minor commodities to trade at Canton. But in the end, none of those commodities could generate enough of a demand in China to offset the tea and silk that was going out, and so foreign traders had to make up the imbalance in silver. The British, at least, had Indian cotton and Lancashire textiles to make up some of the difference, while the Americans, for the most part, were reduced to sending ships to China loaded with chests of silver.

The value of this trade to both Great Britain and China was enormous. The British government's tax on the East India Company's tea imports ranged at various times from 12 percent to upwards of 100 percent, providing an enormous stream of reliable income to the British government that comprised one tenth of its entire yearly revenue. China likewise profited enormously from the trade at Canton, and the taxes levied on the Chinese traders made for a hefty revenue stream at a time of declining Qing government fortunes. Huge "contributions" of millions of taels were exacted from the Canton merchants to help underwrite the Qing empire's campaigns in the far west and the suppression of the White Lotus rebellion. Meanwhile, the high tariffs imposed at Canton also formed a direct revenue stream for the emperor himself, and paid most of the expenses of maintaining his family and household. By the 1830s, one of the leading Chinese merchants at Canton, known to the foreigners as Houqua, was thought to be the richest man in the world.

Until the early nineteenth century the balance of trade at Canton favored the Chinese merchants, with a net inflow of millions of silver dollars per year coming into the country from foreign trade. Indeed, from the sixteenth century up to the nineteenth China was the largest net importer of silver in the world. But global shifts began making it more difficult for the British to continue procuring such large amounts of silver to offset their tea purchases. In 1776 the American Revolution (sparked in part by the Tea Act that allowed the East India Company to ship its tea directly to the colonies in North America) stanched the flow of new-world silver to England. Then the early nineteenth-century revolutions in Peru and Mexico, which provided most of the world's silver and gold, destabilized their mining industries and caused a worldwide shortage of silver that ultimately drove the British to settle on a different way to balance their trade in China.

The solution to Britain's trade imbalance was opium. Grown and processed under monopoly in the East India Company's territories of eastern India, the British could ship the drug to Canton (and, after its trade was banned in Canton proper, to an island sixty miles away where Chinese smuggling ships retrieved the foreign cargo). As non-medicinal opium had been illegal in China since 1729, the Company carefully avoided carrying any on its own ships into Canton, instead selling the drug at auction in Calcutta to so-called "country" traders—Parsis and independent British merchants—who took the real risk of shipping the drug to China. When the country traders sold their opium to Chinese merchants they would receive silver in exchange (since it was a clandestine trade) which they then paid into the East India Company's treasury at Canton to cover the original auction price of the drug or to purchase bills of exchange. The Company then had plenty of silver available in Canton to purchase its tea.

Opium in smokable form caught on in China in a way few could have anticipated. Beginning with wealthy courtiers and bored Manchus, it came down in price as the trade expanded, taking root at all levels of society—farmers, peddlers, soldiers, monks, officials, and students joined the ranks of its users. As usage spread, the wholesale demand for foreign opium at Canton increased dramatically. By 1823 opium surpassed cotton as the primary British import from India into China. By 1828 the trade reached a balance overall, with the opium and cotton from India matching the value of the tea and silk that went out from Canton. But then the balance kept shifting in Britain's favor and China's long-standing advantage slipped away completely. In the first decade of the nineteenth century China had still enjoyed a net inflow of 26 million silver dollars from foreign trade. But by the century's third decade 34 million silver dollars were shipped *out* of China. Up into the 1850s, China would continue to lose an average of 8 million silver dollars per year to its foreign trade.

Even so, as long as the East India Company maintained its monopoly over British trade between China and England, as well as control over the production of opium in its Indian territories, there was at least some kind of rational accounting behind the foreign opium traffic, cold as it may have been. However, so-called "Malwa" opium shipped from Bombay, which was produced in regions of western India outside of the Company's control, emerged as strong competition for the "Patna" variety controlled by the Company, which drove down prices overall and increased supplies. Then, in response to free-trade lobbying in England, the British Parliament terminated the East India Company's monopoly on British trade with China in 1833. By 1834 the Canton trade was opened up as a free-for-all where any private British firm with a ship to send to Canton could claim a piece of the lucrative trade, and the market quickly became oversaturated.

Meanwhile, the less scrupulous of the private merchants, such as the Scots William Jardine and James Matheson, began sending ships secretly up the coast of China to probe for new markets where they could conduct their trade. Whereas the East India Company had overseen the import of about 4,500 chests of opium per year earlier in the early 1800s, by 1830 with aggressive smuggling by private traders the total amount had more than tripled to about 15,000 chests. After the Company's monopoly ended in 1834, the figures continued to rise: more than 20,000 chests in 1835, then passing 30,000 in 1836–37. At 133 pounds per chest, that was 2,000 tons of the drug, enough to supply what some estimated to be more than a million habitual users.

In South China, even families that housed no opium users and had no connection to the inland smuggling trade felt severe effects from what was happening at Canton and along the coast. China had two metallic currencies: silver ingots known as taels, and copper coins known as cash. Under normal circumstances one tael of silver was worth 1,000 cash. But with the loss of silver to foreign trade, exacerbated by the global shortage of the metal, its value in relation to copper rose steeply and the exchange rate followed. By the 1830s, depending on location, it could take 1,500 or 1,600 copper cash to purchase one tael of silver, sometimes as much as 2,600. Peasants, for the most part, lived their lives in the copper currency but the land tax quotas were figured in silver. Thus, their effective taxes and rents rose as the copper coinage they possessed lost its value relative to the silver they owed. Independently of the health or moral effects of the opium trade, the currency imbalance caused many families and landowners in south China to slip into poverty as their money became worth less and less, until it was no longer sufficient to meet their heavy tax burdens.

The British were hardly unaware of the moral implications of their illegal drug trade in China. Missionaries led the way in attacking the "accursed traffic," which they deemed a disgrace to the very country that considered itself a beacon of freedom and humanity after banning the institution of slavery in 1834. Not all missionaries, however, were in agreement; one, a Prussian missionary named Karl Gutzlaff, worked for Jardine and Matheson as an interpreter, rationalizing that their smuggling ships were the best way to sneak Chinese-language bibles into the country. The opium traders themselves argued that the Chinese weren't serious about the illegality of the drug—the very ease with which they could unload their cargoes, and the eagerness of Chinese buyers to make purchases from them, they pointed out, were proof enough that the trade was, de facto, an acceptable one in China. Some affected a stance of cultural relativism, arguing that the smoking of opium was a Chinese custom on which Westerners were not qualified to pass judgment. Others claimed that opium use in China was no more or less harmful than the scourge of gin in England.

By the late 1830s, high-level Chinese officials were entering into serious debate about how the government should address the rising tide of opium smuggling, and—at least as pressing—the drain of silver that went along with it. Some argued in favor of legalization, recommending that the government allow the trade but establish a monopoly. They reasoned that it was proving impossible to stamp out opium usage domestically, but legalization would remove the corruption that surrounded the drug trade, and, by bringing it into the open, stem the flood of silver leaving the country. Further, it could be taxed to create a new source of badly needed government revenue. From the other side, however, more militant scholars who viewed China's position as one of relative strength vis-à-vis the foreign merchants argued that the emperor should take aggressive measures to shut down the traffic completely before it could cause greater harm to the country.

In the end, the Daoguang emperor (1820–50) settled in favor of suppression. In December of 1838 he sent Lin Zexu, a talented official with impeccable moral credentials and a history of anti-opium crusading, to Canton to shut down the illegal trade. Attacking the foreign trade at its source seemed the only viable strategy for controlling opium. Despite several years of high-level anti-opium campaigns and moral exhortations from the emperor and his officials, at the ground level many if not most Chinese didn't see opium trafficking or the use of the drug as a serious crime. When officials tried to crack down, villagers tended to protect their own. Furthermore, the internal traffic of opium in China encompassed a vast network of criminal gangs, fleets of fast boats crammed with oars, corrupt officials, and bribed police. In contrast, the small foreign compound at Canton provided a conveniently focused node at which to throttle the trade completely.

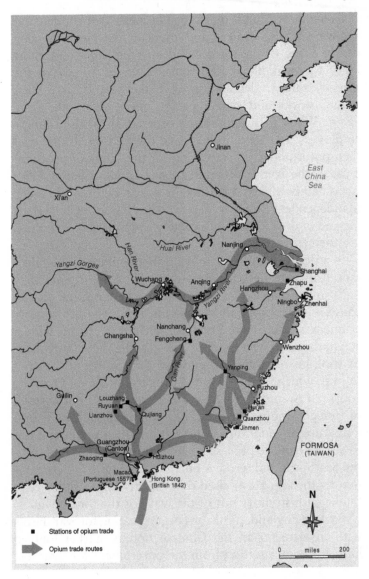

4. How opium was brought into China in the nineteenth century.

Arriving in March of 1839, Lin Zexu first took action against Chinese dealers and users in the city, arresting nearly 2,000 of the former and opening sanitaria for the latter to break their addictions. Then he turned to the British traders, demanding that they hand over their opium stocks and sign a pledge never to sell the drug again. When they refused, he ordered all of the Chinese employees and servants to leave the factory district and then put it under siege. Fearing for the safety of his countrymen, the British superintendent of trade Charles Elliot (who had been stationed there to supervise the wide range of independent British traders who had come to China since the end of the East India Company's monopoly) negotiated a settlement.

In a deeply significant move, Elliot convinced the reluctant British traders to hand over all of the opium they had—more than 1,300 tons in all, packed in some 20,283 chests—in exchange for a guarantee that the British government would make good for their loss. Faced with a stagnating and oversupplied market, the merchants readily took his offer and surrendered their stores of the drug to him, which he then handed over to Lin Zexu. Over the course of twenty-three days, Lin Zexu had the entire stock of foreign opium destroyed, his workers dissolving it into a mixture of water, lime, and salt and then washing it out to sea. When the process began, Lin offered a sacrifice to the Sea Spirit and wrote a poem to apologize for contaminating the sea. He advised that the creatures of the ocean might wish to move out of the way for the time being.

Back in England, the drums began beating for war. Firms with investments in the Chinese opium market lobbied hard for compensation from the government for their lost merchandise, while others pushed the foreign minister Lord Palmerston for action to punish what they saw as Lin Zexu's reckless endangerment of British subjects in China (by laying siege to the factory district) and his insult to British national honor. Others induced him to think of the great advantages to trade that could be had if the British should win a war against China and make them sign a treaty—a feat that the war's proponents believed would be nearly effortless. Others, however, warned that even if a victory of British naval forces on the Chinese coast might be a simple matter, if it caused the Chinese government to shut down trade with Britain in retaliation and cut off all supplies of tea, the results could be catastrophic.

The moral issues were clear enough to the British public. The cynical name of "Opium War" was coined by none other than *The Times*, which initially decried the "reckless negligence and gross incapacity of the Queen's ministers" in starting it and described the situation in China as "the case of a lawless and accursed traffick [*sic*], to be bolstered up by a flagitious and murderous war." (Later, however, once the launching of the war was a fait accompli, *The Times* would come fully on board.) In a lengthy speech in Parliament denouncing those who supported what he saw as a war on behalf of drug dealers, the young William Gladstone charged that "if [the British flag] were never to be hoisted except as it is now hoisted on the coast of China, we should recoil from its sight with horror." But in the end, economic interests won over moral ones by a hair's breadth. By a margin of only nine votes, out of more than 500 cast, the House of Commons defeated a motion of censure against Palmerston and the other ministers of government, effectively giving them a parliamentary endorsement of their war in China.

It was a one-sided war, for the Qing dynasty had always faced its most serious threats on land and it possessed no navy to speak of. A British war fleet of sixteen naval vessels, four armed steamers, twenty-seven transports, and 4,000 soldiers from Ireland, Scotland, and India arrived in the South China Sea in June of 1840. The British first blockaded Canton, then made war up the coast, capturing the island of Zhoushan and fighting their way all the way up to the Dagu Forts which guarded the way to Beijing. Blaming Lin Zexu for provoking an unwanted war, the emperor had him stripped of rank and sent into exile, replacing him with a more conciliatory negotiator who settled an initial peace agreement in January of 1841. Unfortunately, the agreement satisfied neither side—the Chinese felt they had granted too much and the British felt they hadn't demanded enough—and so the war resumed again, with 10,000 more British troops being brought in from India. In February of 1841 the British laid siege to Canton, which was ransomed for six million silver dollars (paid mostly by the Chinese merchants of the city). The British continued to fight their way up the coast, then up the Yangzi River, and finally threatened the major city of Nanjing, at which point the Chinese finally surrendered and signed a treaty on August 29, 1842 to end the war.

The Treaty of Nanjing dismantled the Canton system, opening that city along with four others (Xiamen, Fuzhou, Ningbo, and Shanghai) as "treaty ports" where the British could live year-round, rent property, build homes, offices, and warehouses, station consuls, and largely govern themselves. Britain also took Hong Kong as a full-fledged colony. Tariffs were made more consistent, and British citizens were granted extraterritoriality—that is, while in the treaty ports they would be subject only to British law. Finally, China had to pay a massive indemnity of 21 million silver dollars, both as compensation for the opium Lin Zexu had destroyed in 1839 and as payment for Britain's costs in mounting the war. Over the next few years China would sign similar treaties with the Americans and French giving them the same rights as the British in China and guaranteeing them status as most-favored nations, hoping (in vain, as it would turn out) to avoid further conflict with the Western powers.

All of the favorable terms in the Treaty of Nanjing were on the British side, with no concessions to the Chinese, for which reason it—along with the other treaties like it that were to come—would be known as the "unequal treaties." The one conspicuous absence from the Treaty of Nanjing, however—a convenient one, given the ignominy with which the opium trade was viewed back in Britain—was that it did not legalize the selling of opium. That would come later, as a quiet supplement to a treaty in 1860 that set an official tariff rate for the drug, but in 1842 when the Opium War ended, the British side was able to claim that the war had been entirely about the ostensibly nobler issues of free trade and protection for British citizens overseas, not for the protection of drug dealers.

In the aftermath of the Opium War, it was southern China that bore the full economic brunt of the Treaty of Nanjing. Foreign firms eagerly moved much of their operations northwards up the coast to the more advantageous port of Shanghai, which stood at the mouth of the Yangzi River along which much of China's tea and silk were produced. Canton's fortunes declined once it no longer held an imperial monopoly on foreign trade, and local merchant houses began going bankrupt. Hundreds of thousands of poor laborers in south China were put out of work by the decline in foreign trade, compounded by general economic malaise and natural disasters as the region suffered floods and famine in the mid-1840s. Some southern Chinese sought their fortunes abroad, taking passage to other countries in Southeast Asia or to the west coast of America after the Gold Rush of 1849. Others remained rooted but looked to new sources of security as imperial control weakened and social disorder continued to rise.

Several different kinds of social organization competed with the empire for subjects' loyalties at this time. There were secret societies, often referred to as Triads, that were often heavily involved in opium smuggling and which promised mutual protection to their members as they traveled along rivers and between towns. Minority ethnic ties were important as well, as tensions between the majority Han and other groups became especially fierce in hard times. As neighboring villages fought over land and water rights, minority groups relied on their own family and clan bonds to provide the security that government forces could not give them. And as with the White Lotus groups in the late eighteenth century, many peasants turned to informal religious groups, led by charismatic teachers who promised their followers improved health and, in the case of the millennial sects, survival of a coming apocalypse and rewards in the new world it would usher in. All of these groups had in common that they easily drew the suspicions of imperial authorities. They also had in common that when the government acted on its suspicions, trying to suppress them or arrest their leaders, they were likely to turn against the dynasty itself. It was a vicious cycle that repeated many times over in which informal social networks built on mutual aid might, under pressure from the government, metastasize into full-blown rebellions.

The largest rebellion of all, which would bring the Qing dynasty to the edge of collapse, began humbly enough with a candidate for the civil service by the name of Hong Xiuquan. He was a member of the Hakka minority, many of whom lived in south China, and he was a talented scholar who competed for years at the difficult Confucian examinations that formed the sole gateway into an official career in China. After failing the exams repeatedly in the 1830s, he suffered a nervous breakdown, from which—after reading some translated Christian scriptures prepared by foreign missionaries—he emerged with the belief that he was the son of God, brother of Jesus Christ, and sent to earth to build a new Christian kingdom in China and destroy the Manchus.

Like the White Lotus teachers, Hong Xiuquan promised his converts salvation and positions of power in a new world to come. In the early 1840s he envisioned a future Heavenly Kingdom of Great Peace in which believers who helped him destroy the Manchus and the old Confucian civilization would be rewarded. This Heavenly Kingdom would be free of oppression and degradation, and it would be morally puritanical: opium, footbinding, slavery, prostitution, and gambling would all be forbidden. Everyone's needs would be provided for, and the people would live together in communal, utopian peace, worshipping the Christian God in Protestant churches. It was a powerful message to poor, disenfranchised imperial subjects at a time of economic depression and weak government control. And when an epidemic ravaged his home province in 1850, rumors spread that those who had prayed to Hong Xiuquan's God had been spared, a rumor believable enough to convince large numbers of new recruits to join his sect.

The Taiping Rebellion, as Hong Xiuquan's uprising would be known, began formally on January 11, 1851 when he proclaimed the advent of the Heavenly Kingdom and called on his followers to make war on the Manchus. Beginning with an army of 10,000 believers wielding home-made weapons, the rebel movement proved wildly success-ful at drawing in large numbers of new followers as it gained momentum and moved north, conquering a series of walled cities and collecting weapons and treasure as it went. Imperial troops were caught unprepared, in part because military budgets had been cut to the bone for nearly fifty years as a result of the corruption of the White Lotus campaigns. By January of 1853 the Taiping had captured the major Yangzi entrepôt of Wuchang—the linchpin of central China—at which point they numbered half a million soldiers and followers. That March they went on to capture Nanjing, the original capital of the Ming dynasty, where they slaughtered the entire Manchu popu-lation. Renaming the city their "Heavenly Capital," they dug in at Nanjing for a ten-year civil war that would, by its end, kill at least 20 million people by warfare, disease, and starvation.

At first, the foreign powers kept a wary distance from the rebellion. Nanjing was only 200 miles up the Yangzi from Shanghai, where the British and other foreign traders had just moved many of their investments from Canton. With little knowledge of what was actually happening at Nanjing, the Westerners were torn between fear of a Taiping attack on Shanghai that might destroy their trade, and hope that the rebels might turn China into a Christian country that would be friendlier to the West than the Qing dynasty had been. At the outset some outsiders welcomed the Taiping as the liberators of the Chinese people from the Manchus while missionaries would eventually turn on them, charging that the rebels were merely destructive zealots who had perverted the doctrines of Christianity by presuming their leader to be the son of God.

The Taiping communal utopia never took root, and was all but abandoned by the late 1850s—it simply proved too difficult for the rebels to change habits and social practices that had been ingrained into the Chinese population for centuries. Nevertheless, the rebel movement continued to pose a grave military threat to the dynasty. By 1859 a new government was formed under Hong Xiuquan's cousin Hong Rengan, who had lived in Hong Kong with foreign missionaries and spoke English. Among other proposals, he called for equal diplomacy with Westerners, free trade, and the development of railroads and steamship lines in China. He also launched a new offensive against Qing forces that met with remarkable success. By 1860 the vast rebel armies had surged eastward from Nanjing to conquer most of the Yangzi delta provinces, controlling a population of tens of millions. Meanwhile, in the vacuum of imperial power as the Qing tried helplessly to contain the Taiping, other rebellions broke out all over China, including a major Muslim revolt in the southwest and a bandit rebellion in north China with a roving army of 40,000 soldiers on horseback. The empire was coming apart at the seams.

Although the British initially maintained neutrality in the civil war between the Qing dynasty and the Taiping rebels, the empire's troubles did not prevent them from making demands to revise the Treaty of Nanjing. The British wanted more treaty ports and were angry that Canton had not been opened as agreed. They therefore launched a renewed war against China right on top of all of the rebellions the dynasty was facing at the same time. Known as the Arrow War, or Second Opium War, its ignominious *casus belli* was that in 1856 Chinese authorities had boarded the *Arrow*, a Chinese smuggling ship flying the British flag, and allegedly struck its colors. This was taken as an insult to Britain and justification to attack Canton.

This time, Parliament staunchly opposed another war in China. Palmerston, however, simply called new elections—dubbed the "Chinese Elections" by the British press—in which the pro-war politicians were returned to power in a popular landslide. A joint expedition was launched with the French under Lord Elgin and Baron Gros, which occupied Canton in 1857. In 1858 the joint force fought its way past the Dagu Forts and to Tianjin, a stepping-stone to Beijing, where the Chinese capitulated. Among other concessions, the new treaty opened ten more treaty ports—no longer just on the coast but inland up the Yangzi as well—and it finally granted Macartney's long-deferred request by allowing the British to station a permanent minister in Beijing.

The treaty was brought back to England for ratification, and a year later Elgin's younger brother (who was slated to be the British minister in Beijing), returned to China to exchange signed copies with the emperor. By this time, however, the emperor had decided to refuse the treaty.

Qing forces sprang a surprise attack on the British fleet when it arrived at the Dagu Forts, sinking several of the ships and killing or wounding more than 400 British marines and sailors. It was a deeply humiliating loss for the British, and surely enough, the passage of another year saw the return of Elgin himself at the head of a massive British and French fleet, one of the largest ever assembled, on a mission of pure revenge. The new fleet smashed its way through the coastal defenses at Dagu and its land forces swept past Tianjin, then marched on Beijing to force the emperor to sign the treaty.

As the British and French army approached, the young Xianfeng emperor (1850–61)—grandson to Jiaqing and great-grandson to Qianlong—abandoned his capital and fled north, leaving his brother behind to make peace. But by the time Lord Elgin reached Beijing, he had decided that there was far more at stake than just a treaty; the emperor needed to be taught a lesson. On the excuse of reprisal for the Manchus having kidnapped and tortured a small band of British and French personnel during the fighting, Elgin ordered his forces to destroy the emperor's Summer Palace.

The Summer Palace of the Qing emperors was considered one of the wonders of the world in the nineteenth century, a gorgeous and sprawling 800-acre complex of ornate palaces and gardens just a few miles outside of Beijing. Macartney had stayed there during the embassy of 1793. It was in one of the Summer Palace's halls that his technician had assembled the great planetarium and lenses with which he hoped in vain to impress the Qianlong emperor. But whereas the British had come to the palace then as guests and supplicants, seeking audience with an emperor at the climax of his power, in 1860 they came

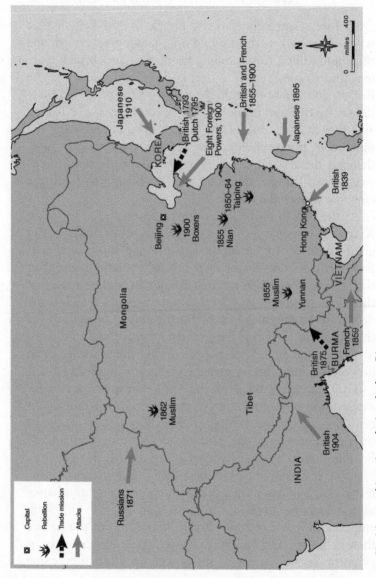

5. Uprisings and invasions during the late Qing.

instead as destroyers. Over the course of three days in October, British forces looted the buildings of the Summer Palace (uncovering, along the way, several gifts left by Macartney nearly seventy years earlier). Then they burned everything they could to the ground.

Broken by internal rebellions and now crushed decisively by European forces, the Qing dynasty at the end of 1860 was on the verge of collapse. Xianfeng, the young emperor who fled into hiding, would never return to the capital. He would die a year later, leaving a mere child, his only son, to rule in his stead. The treasuries were bankrupt, the Taiping rebels ascendant, the imperial palace a smoking ruin. When the dynasty was first founded in Beijing in 1644, there were widely publicized divinations that predicted the Qing would rule for 200 years—an optimistic figure at the time, predicting a reign to rival some of the most glorious dynasties of the past. But by 1860 even the dynasty's supporters were beginning to realize that those two centuries had now passed. "A ruling house of two hundred years, endangered in an instant," wrote the scholar Zhao Liewen, heartbroken, when he heard the news from Beijing. "I never imagined the end would come so soon."

3. *Restoration and Reform, 1860–1900*

ROBERT BICKERS

WITH the 1858 Treaty of Tianjin, ratified by the 1860 Convention of Peking, Qing China was exposed to a bumptiously confident and increasingly widespread and diverse foreign presence. Foreigners came to serve even at the heart of the state; overseas nationals took their trading or proselytizing enterprises across the realm; treaty ports increased in number, size, and sophistication; information about China was collated and circulated as never before; subjects of the Qing migrated overseas as free or indentured labor. To counter this new wave of concessions to foreign powers—or at least to manage it adequately—new offices of state were created, foreign skills and knowledge were sought, and arsenals and shipyards were built. It is known that in many ways the victory of the British in the first "Opium War" had not greatly disturbed Qing bureaucrats. But by the end of the nineteenth century, despite a program of "self-strengthening" and reform, discussion of the possibility of the extinction of China at the hands of foreign aggressors was being widely discussed both within and outside the state. These discussions took place in a range of new public forums that had not existed in 1860. With so much change and innovation, how had this come to pass: why were many Chinese still predicting an imminent apocalypse?

With the cessation of hostilities against the British and French, the Qing could turn back to concentrate on the Taiping and the congeries of other revolts that they faced. Unlikely as it seemed, officials now found the Europeans, their recent opponents, intent on becoming their allies. While foreign observers had once greedily explored the possibilities that a Han Chinese Christian revolt seemed to offer, the Taiping were now largely deemed to be people that no one could do business with, and a greater menace to foreign ambitions than the Qing. Moreover, while the rebels had proved too weak to win, they were still too strong to be defeated. In the aftermath of the victory in north China, foreign diplomats and officials, while maintaining (generally) a formal policy of public neutrality, nevertheless indirectly supported military action against the rebels, especially in the Shanghai region. The recruitment of units of foreign-trained and foreign-led Chinese soldiers was approved, and on occasion foreign forces engaged the Taiping directly. The greatest contribution came in the form of a cadre of foreign nationals serving in the rapidly developing Imperial Maritime Customs Service, which delivered to the Qing a steadily increasing revenue stream that allowed the state to invest in particular in acquiring new military technology to defend itself against internal and external threats.

Taiping strategy, and their lingering hopes of foreign interest in displacing the Qing (or at least their hopes of foreign neutrality), were dashed most notably at Ningbo in

May 1862, when British forces dislodged the rebels who had seized the city six months previously (and who many foreign observers thought had administered it quite irreproachably). It was, however, the devolution of military and revenue-raising responsibilities to provincial administrators, notably the Hunanese official Zeng Guofan and his acolytes, such as Li Hongzhang, which ultimately proved decisive in defeating the Taiping rebels. This devolution of responsibilities led to the raising and deployment of new armies that by the summer of 1864 had re-conquered most Taiping-held territory. In July of that year they besieged and captured Nanjing, the capital of the rump Heavenly Kingdom of Great Peace. Few of those remaining in the city survived its fall. Hong Xiuquan had died six weeks earlier. His son and other leaders who escaped were hunted down, and by the end of the year had been captured and killed. Central and eastern China had been devastated by the fourteen-year civil war. Estimates of the scale of the impact of the rebellion have ranged as high as 100 million (and this for just five of the affected provinces): 70 million dead from war, hunger, or disease, and a 30 million depression of expected population figures as a result of all the destruction and turmoil. Many cities and towns never recovered; others took decades. And the devolution of military power from the center that had been central to Qing victory was to have bloody and destabilizing consequences for its successor state in the twentieth century. Although the rebels were annihilated, and nearly all traces of their kingdom were effaced, the legacy of the Taiping rebellion was to prove long lasting.

The Qing state was emboldened by the defeat of the rebels. It was also stronger at the center now, for in

November 1861 the regency appointed by the late Xianfeng emperor to guide his son and heir was deposed in a *coup d'état* that saw the public execution of the Grand Councilor Shusun. Power was now lodged in the hands of Xianfeng's brother Yixin—Prince Gong—and his widow, best known in the West as Cixi (Tzu-hsi, the Empress Dowager), as well as his senior consort Cian. Prince Gong and Cian would eventually be sidelined, and court politics would be dominated for much of the remainder of the century by Cixi, an adept at political manoeuver, and in the balancing coalitions of often mutually hostile factions. Under the banner of a "Restoration," the child Qixiang emperor's reign (1861–75) was renamed "Tongzhi": "return to order." Restoration meant restoring state capacity, and where that required institutional or other innovation this was in many instances undertaken. Debate would continue within the Qing administration about the relative merits of different approaches to building state power in an era of new threats and an unwelcome international environment. How far and in what ways might indigenous learning and thinking have to adapt to a world in which the Qing was threatened by foreign power (and by the legal, political, ideological, and organizational foundations on which it was based)? A formulation that would later become common was in all practical ways already being deployed: "ti/yong" (essence/use). Chinese learning would provide an intellectual foundation on and through which Western learning would be used. But this pragmatic approach also had its entrenched opponents.

At the heart of the restoration initiative was a new central state office for dealing with foreign relations, known in short as the Zongli Yamen. This was less a "foreign office"—though this was how foreigners often referred to it—than a coordinating bureau for dealing with foreign matters, which would include for example initiatives in the fields of technology transfer, the acquisition of foreign expertise, and the employment of foreign experts. The existing central state Board structure was not affected by the establishment of this new office, and its leading officials generally held concurrent posts elsewhere in the administration as well, but it became the core focus of the postwar consolidation of state capacity. The Zongli Yamen was the body that oversaw the establishment and development of new shipyards and arsenals; the creation of the Tongwenguan (the interpreters' college); the dispatch abroad for education of a small cohort of students (whose impact in many areas far outweighed their numbers); the sending overseas of investigation and diplomatic missions, translation and information gathering projects; and the wide range of activities undertaken by the Foreign Inspectorate of the Maritime Customs Service. The revenue for much of this activity was delivered by the Customs Service, and in essence the Foreign Inspectorate of the Maritime Customs Service became the operational arm of the Zongli Yamen. Through the Foreign Inspectorate and the enterprises that it helped oversee and fund, a cadre of useful foreign nationals now came to serve at the heart of the Qing state, and their impact was highly significant.

Effectively leading the Customs Service from 1861 onwards was a man Prince Gong was heard to describe as "Women de Hede"—"Our Hart"—Ulster native Robert Hart, a 26-year-old former British consular officer, who had joined the Foreign Inspectorate in 1859. Hart's linguistic and cultural skills were to underpin the very good relationships he built up with key figures in the Zongli

Yamen. The Irishman was initially one of two officials acting for fellow Briton Horatio Nelson Lay, a much more brittle personality, who had failed to demonstrate any understanding that either he or his office were subordinate to his Qing superiors, preferring instead to present himself as some sort of independent power in the land. Robert Hart, however, parlayed his sensitive handling of interpersonal relations with officials into establishing a position of great trust and autonomy that turned the Customs Service into the single most important institution in Qing foreign relations down to the end of the century. Money also talked, and while a China trade bubble burst in the aftermath of the end of the Taiping rebellion—and of the American Civil War—the Customs facilitated a steady increase in Sino-foreign trade that brought in the resource that paid for self-strengthening. It did this through rationalizing procedures, collating and disseminating data and information, initiating infrastructural projects such as aids to navigation and coastal lighting systems, meteorological work, and organizing the representation of China at international exhibitions. There was little it seemed that the rapidly increasing number of foreign nationals brought to China by Hart's organization did not get involved in, and Hart would joke privately in his diary about becoming "Inspector General of Everything." His most important skill, however, lay in remembering his subordinate place in the Qing state, and in fostering within the Customs Service an ethos that made loyal servants of China—in most cases—out of his polyglot recruits.

Significant tensions between the Qing and the foreign powers remained, but a new era appeared to have commenced, and the disaster of 1860 was to recede. Foreign diplomats established their legations in Peking, at the heart of the empire, and China was increasingly better understood overseas. Through its extensive publication program—which included a series of medical reports, and even a monograph on Chinese music—the Customs made a great range of knowledge about Chinese society, culture, trade, and politics accessible in English, as well as raw scientific data about the lands of the Qing. In these endeavors, Hart and his leading associates were important interlocutors for and interpreters of Western interests and ambitions to the Zongli Yamen, often acting as a foil to the less trusted foreign diplomats in the capital. The ambiguities of his position were considerable, however, and even at his death in 1911, there were foreign observers not reconciled to the vision of a British national so smoothly serving his "Asiatic" masters.

Almost comically central to the new treaties signed in 1858 and ratified in 1860 was a pedantic foreign insistence that the Qing recognize the foreigners as equals. This accorded with developing and strengthening notions of the formal relationship between states in the international order, but it also had a long history in foreign representations of Qing attitudes towards outsiders. The issue of Macartney and the "kowtow" in 1793 remained live, and would continue to do so for decades yet. The new treaties also enjoined the Qing to forgo any use of the term "yi" to describe foreigners, even in internal communications. The British and others interpreted this as meaning "barbarian," and could not be shaken from this view. Its meaning remains today a source of scholarly dispute, but this is somewhat irrelevant: this is how it was understood by the foreign powers at the time, and the British—for all that they sought to establish relations on the basis of mutual equality—aimed to do so by intervening in the internal procedures of the Qing and imposing their understandings of the meaning of the term. The agreements also stipulated the precise and equal relationship between different ranks of foreign diplomats and Qing officials. This also created a further source of friction, as the diplomats, having secured their legations in the heart of Peking, next lobbied to be formally presented to the emperor, in conformity with accepted practice in the European world. It was another thirteen years before this was granted, and even then it was concluded by foreign observers that an insulting sleight of hand meant that the diplomats had not secured their audience with the emperor in precisely the appropriate place. A readiness to find offence and complain officially about it characterized the world of the foreign diplomats at Peking.

The foreign establishment in China was now spreading far beyond the initial five opened ports and Hong Kong. The opening of the Yangzi River to foreign trade and navigation was accompanied by the establishment of Hankou, Jiujiang, and Zhenjiang as treaty ports. In north China, Yingko (Niuzhuang) and Tianjin were opened, as were ports in the southeast and Taiwan. Foreign traders, who had been pushing for an extended range of ports, rapidly established new offices and businesses. This increase in geographical reach was accompanied by developments in the internal administration of the opened ports, and a steady increase in the numbers of foreign residents and firms, as well as in the diversity of their operations. The treaty ports were not formal colonial possessions, and foreign residents largely administered their own affairs, bringing a touch of European and North American local government practices and assumptions to cities in the heart of Qing China. They built sewers, established police forces, and enacted regulations to prevent cruelty to animals. By the end of the century local government reformers in cities as diverse as Shanghai and Chengdu would look for inspiration to the practices and structures of the foreign concessions.

While industrial manufacturing was to remain prohibited until 1895, foreign entrepreneurs established shipyards, brewed beer, established service industries and banks, newspapers and recreation clubs. Most treaty ports looked largely indistinguishable from formal colonies in south and Southeast Asia. All of this was undertaken in collaboration with Chinese partners, and often using Chinese capital. Initially this came via collaborations mediated between foreign firms and their compradors (their Chinese partners and agents). From the early 1860s, notably in Shanghai, it also came through the formation of joint stock companies incorporated under English company law and operating through what became the Shanghai Stock Exchange. While land speculation had always been a factor in the laying out and development of a treaty port, the flight of refugees from civil war irrevocably turned the settlements at Shanghai and other treaty ports into sites of significant Chinese residence, and of a Chinese market for land and property, and also for services to support that community and deploy its capital to potentially profitable or other use. These included newspapers: a functional "Shipping List and Advertiser," *Shanghai xinbao*, began publication in 1863, and in 1872 two Britons, Ernest and Frederick Major, began publication with Chinese partners at Shanghai of a much more ambitious Chinese newspaper,

Shenbao (Shanghai News), which was to become a hugely influential vehicle for the development of Chinese public debate and opinion forming. Thereafter, new titles began to be established across China and in Hong Kong.

As in 1842, opium was not explicitly mentioned in the treaties that brought to an end the second of the wars that bears its name. That was left to a subsidiary tariff conference in 1858, which legalized and set tariffs for a range of goods whose import or export had hitherto been prohibited. As with the Tianjin Treaty itself, the provisions accorded the British were largely copied into treaties subsequently negotiated with the United States. Most agreements embedded "most favored nation" clauses into their text, so that in most respects all foreign powers securing a treaty with the Qing were accorded very similar rights. The opium trade, in which American firms had also always been involved, was no exception. The legalization of imports heralded the onset of a decade in which the opium trade was at its most profitable. Imports soared and were to peak in 1879, but in fact rising costs, and steadily increasing competition from domestic production, resulted in firms such as Jardine, Matheson & Co. diversifying their operations and moving to other business areas. Nevertheless, consumption of opium continued to rise. Current estimates put the proportion of adult males who in any fashion consumed the drug at about one in five, but most of these used it moderately. Probably only a very small percentage were heavy users. The perceived evils of opium and its impact on society and on individuals remained a constant, however, in the minds of foreign critics of either British policy, or Chinese culture, or both. A missionary-dominated Society for the Suppression of the Opium

Trade was established in Britain in 1874, and lobbied constantly for a change in policy. It would succeed eventually in prompting the convening of a Royal Commission to investigate the trade in 1893–95, but this simply concluded that the drug, especially in the way it was actually consumed, was mostly harmless—and the evidence then, as now, largely supports the view—and that its importance in the finances of the Government of India was such, that unless there were sound practical grounds for discontinuing the trade, it might as well continue. An international movement would continue to grow to suppress the trade, but the British and others, however, simply shifted ground. What was the point of suppressing the trade, they argued, when China produced so much of its own opium? If the Qing were to suppress domestic cultivation, then and only then would they curtail imports from India.

A more effective drug on which to hook the Qing proved to be finance. Jardine, Matheson & Co. pioneered the provision by foreign firms of private loans to the Qing Court. The Hongkong & Shanghai Bank—one of a number of new institutions established after 1860 to service the increasingly sophisticated market—floated the first public loan to the Chinese government on the London market in 1874, to raise funds during the crisis caused by the Japanese intervention in Taiwan. The Imperial Maritime Customs provided the obvious security for such loans, for its efficiency was seen in the eyes of foreign lenders to be guaranteed by the fact that it was led and staffed by their fellow foreign nationals. As conflicts with foreign powers began to take on a quite predictable course, it was to become routine for the Qing to borrow to finance development of their military capacity, as well as the use of it during a crisis, and then payment of an indemnity afterwards. The ease with which finance was raised was also to underpin the issuing of loans for other purposes as well, not least in the 1890s for railway development. The international politics of financing development loans to China was to become quite fraught. Banks and dedicated finance combines formed part of the repertoire of tools used by different powers jockeying for advantage in China. Even a small power like Belgium could attain an influential position through the growth of its financial interests in the Qing empire. But the surrender of sovereignty that this financial securitization represented proved increasingly politically problematic for the Qing. For instance, the assigning of China's railways as security for loans outraged widening circles of public opinion, while also fueling what would be termed "rights recovery" agitation.

The embedding of the Qing yet more deeply in internationalized circuits of diplomacy, finance, and trade was not simply a product of foreign action. Many expatriate Chinese had also come back to the domain of the Qing as foreign colonial subjects, thereby being both protected by and benefiting from the principle of extraterritoriality. This provided flashpoints for diplomatic controversies well into the twentieth century, but the commercial and later the cultural, educational, and political activities of these "Overseas Chinese" would come to be significant elements in China's development. Conversely, Chinese merchants used the new infrastructure underpinning regional interconnections to move out themselves, settling or sojourning in the treaty ports opened in Japan after 1858, and in Korea. People, goods, and ideas flowed in all directions. The role of the treaty ports in modern China's development has been the subject of some controversy, ranging from views of them as central drivers in China's emerging modern economy, to being simply irrelevant to the broader picture, mere flies on an elephant's back in one view. Hostile political criticism has viewed them as bridgeheads of foreign invasion, although their leading interests were characteristically quite insecure about their relationship to the formal worlds of imperial power. Shanghai, for example, was never marked red on maps of the reach of the British empire.

It should be remembered here that Britain loomed much larger as a factor in Chinese history than China did in Britain's. The relationship was always asymmetrical. China was for the most part, most of the time, a minor factor in the global interests of Britain, the United States, France, Russia, or other powers. A more accurate assessment of the treaty ports would highlight the diverse range of influences they had on China (which were out of all proportion to their size), as well as their minor share of the overall Chinese economy of the time (though not, of course, their near-monopoly of what might be termed the "modern" economy: overseas trade, manufacturing). It would also acknowledge, moreover, that the treaty ports were in fact places of collaboration between Chinese and foreigners. Sino-foreign collaborations in various forms shaped their functions, despite what most foreign nationals thought and claimed to the contrary. Foreign enterprise alone did not deliver the gains demonstrated through the developments of the treaty ports. Foreign legal systems and other practices were vital, but these provided the basis upon which Sino-foreign collaboration and enterprise flourished.

The global context was important. Developments in China remained inextricably bound up with broader changes internationally; not least the steady growth of various inter-twined processes of globalization in the latter half of the nineteenth century. Technological innovation delivered faster and more programmable communications—shipping and the telegraph bound Qing China more closely into faster and more intense global flows of goods, information, and people. Maritime safety initiatives, hydrographic surveys, and the spread of British naval power in particular, as well as piracy suppression initiatives, helped make trans-oceanic and regional maritime highways much more secure. While it would take hostile foreign observers decades yet to accept the fact, Chinese from all walks of life, in the rapidly growing treaty ports and far from them in the countryside, would happily adopt most imported innovations. The steamship and the telegraph are a case in point. The purchase and dismantling by Qing officials in 1877 of the first railway line built in China was undertaken not because of any resistance to foreign technology, but as a matter of principle. No permission had been sought for its construction, let alone granted. While it ran, Shanghai residents eagerly took rides on the line, which ran from the city to the port of Wusong, in the same way that they made use of other new inventions such as steamships and the telegraph. Once dismantled, the Shanghai track and equipment were shipped to Taiwan, and there left to rust. Railway lines would start to be developed on a small scale, however, within less than a decade after this inauspicious start. Qing officials also experimented with a new strategy to lessen the stranglehold that foreign firms quickly established on internal transport communications: the China

Merchants Steam Navigation Company. This represented an innovative form of state enterprise, known as the *Guandu Shangban* system, in which merchant management was combined with official supervision. Although beset with a range of problems, such initiatives were emblematic of the range of experiments adopted by some leading officials to deal with the challenges the Qing faced.

A further local consequence of wider global developments was the growth of an evangelical Christian missionary presence across China. This too had specific origins in the treaties of 1858/60, as these permitted the purchase of land or buildings anywhere in China by foreigners from the signatory powers, and free travel (subject to consular permission) throughout the country. They also removed Qing prohibitions against the practice and proselytizing of Christianity. At the same time, the Protestant Evangelical movement in Europe and North America provided the "Christian soldiers"—the hymn itself was composed in 1865—who shaped and staffed the increasing number and variety of missionary initiatives across the non-Christian globe. The new treaty provisions delivered the legal grounds upon which missions already active in China, and new arrivals—notably the evangelical China Inland Mission (Zhongguo neidi hui) led by James Hudson Taylor—penetrated into cities, towns, and counties that had no previous settled foreign presence.

Since 1843, and the arrival of the first Congregationalist missionaries under the banner of the London Missionary Society, evangelists had been persistent in pushing beyond the geographical bounds laid down by locally agreed regulations at the treaty ports. They had also developed a range of medical and educational activities to attract potential converts, as well as straightforwardly evangelical tactics. The last proved slow-going, but there was an appetite for some elements of foreign medicine and education, and missionary societies of all stamps found it relatively easy to interpolate themselves into circuits of charity, social welfare provision, or disaster relief. Some of these activities were to have a profound impact on elements of rural as well as urban Chinese society. But the politics of the missionary presence remained potentially explosive. The French had identified themselves with the protection of the historic Roman Catholic communities in China—their involvement in the second "Opium War" was based on the murder of a French priest in Guangxi province—and the identification in Chinese official and popular minds of foreign missions with foreign power was to prove troublesome. This was not least the case for British diplomats, who were largely anti-pathetic to the mission enterprise, on the grounds of *realpolitik*, as well as simple snobbery—for missionaries did not on the whole emerge from the same strata of society as they did. Nevertheless, in spite of this, consuls on the ground found themselves compelled to support the rights and interests of their nationals wherever these were protected by treaty.

Mission problems proved essentially threefold. As they moved to new locales missionaries needed to acquire sites, and this often quickly led to conflicts with local elites and officials (as happened to James Hudson-Taylor's China Inland Mission at Yangzhou in 1869). Secondly, conversion involved the rupture of relations between individuals and their family, and with their local communities. In one sense this was quite routine, for a revolution of the person lay at the heart of Christian conversion. But as was the case in other areas of encounter between Christianity and indigenous societies, most missionaries proved hostile to the cultural and social norms that glued communities together: shared involvement in annual rituals around temples and local deities, and filial expectations and responsibilities. Converts essentially removed themselves from society; and their behavior in relation to perceived responsibilities towards existing norms and expectations often seemed shockingly heterodox. This sometimes had paradoxical consequences: in more than a few instances, already-marginalized groups and individuals found succor and power, as well as new identities, through conversion. Thirdly, social welfare initiatives, and medicine, could be disastrously misunderstood. Orphanages were to suffer from an eagerness, for example, to baptize young children (which could mean in practice taking in the dying to allow their salvation to be guaranteed). They also suffered from low standards of care and poor hygiene. Death rates could consequently be high in such institutions; but even if they were not, the power of rumor and fear of difference could be potent. Underlying all of this (as well as more than a few instances of the aggressive assertion of missionary rights) was the poisonous legacy of the Taiping rebellion, and the propaganda war against these indigenous Christians. In Hunan province, in particular, anti-Taiping pamphlets and ideas found continuing life in anti-Christian and anti-mission activity.

In this wider context of tension, the Yangzhou incident led to the British Consul at Shanghai securing a Royal Navy show of force at the mouth of the Grand Canal, then still the conduit for Peking's grain supplies, which passed through the city. And at Tianjin in June 1870 fear and rumor around the activities of the French Association de la Sainte Enfance (Holy Childhood Association) and the impetuous and violent response of the French Consul led to a serious riot, the killing of sixty foreign nationals and Chinese Christians, and the burning down of the newly built Roman Catholic cathedral. Qing and other officials feared war, and only the more pressing problems that France brought on itself in July 1870 (with Napoleon III's declaration of war against Prussia and resulting rapid defeat) took the edge off the dispute. The Tianjin Massacre was only the most dramatic of the steady procession of "incidents," missionary and otherwise, disputes, riots, and disagreements that kept the diplomatic temperature hot. A sort of predictable script developed, and all knew their parts. A foreign national somewhere outside the treaty ports was killed; the circumstances would be ambiguous enough for both Qing officials and his own diplomats to both feel that they were on firm ground in their representations of it; the foreigners demanded redress, and punishment of the allegedly guilty. Dire consequences would be threatened; sometimes, as in the 1875 crisis (known, after the murdered British consular officer involved, as the "Margary Affair"), the foreign ambassador would withdraw from the capital. Foreign naval vessels were likely to be dispatched along the coast or rivers to the site. A commission of enquiry might eventually convene, including foreign representatives, and a report was often issued. Those guilty, or near enough guilty, or unluckily close to hand at the wrong time, might be punished. But foreign diplomats proved consistent in their habits of extracting new concessions from the Qing with every unhappy incident—another treaty port, for example, a change in this regulation or that one.

Learning the rules of the foreign diplomatic game was a priority for the Qing; but the foreign powers concerned were inconsistent in how they abided by these. Robert Hart and others encouraged the Zongli yamen to consider posting representatives overseas, or sending missions, and this started to happen. Facilitated by the Customs, Qing officials went on missions to investigate the conditions of expatriate Chinese labour in Cuba, and in South America in 1873–75; consuls would be appointed in the Dutch East Indies and in San Francisco in 1878, reflecting the pattern of the distribution of Chinese overseas; and Ministers (ambassadors) were sent abroad after 1877 to a number of European countries, starting with Britain, as well as the United States and Japan. But the realities of an asymmetrical and unpredictable power relationship were highlighted by the intense negotiations with British Minister Sir Rutherford Alcock that led to the signing in Beijing of the 1869 "Alcock Convention," which included various measures reforming the 1858 treaty, and codifying some agreements made in the period since. The draft convention was rejected by London after a great deal of lobbying by British commercial and missionary interests, who felt that it did not go far enough. Qing officials had negotiated in good faith in the ways expected of them by British diplomats like Alcock, but found that even this was to no avail. Many foreign interests were not interested in actually treating the Qing as diplomatic equals after all: they saw the empire as a site in which to make new gains at China's expense. "Foreigners are unreasonable," concluded one Chinese ambassador, Zeng Jize, during an 1878 audience with Cixi befre his departure to take up his post, "while Chinese are ignorant of current events and circumstance." The sentiments might be formulaic, but they were not inaccurate, and the combination remained an unhealthy one.

The assumptions underpinning the Qing view of the world were also unsettled further by the arrival on the scene of a new and awkward power, Japan. The Meiji restoration in 1868 heralded an intense program of Westernization within Japan, which affected the diplomatic sphere no less than many others. It was the Japanese foreign minister Soejima Taneoni who arrived in Peking in June 1873 to take precedence over all the Western diplomats in the capital at the first formal audience with the 17-year-old Tongzhi emperor. This took the diplomats aback as well. Arising from discussions held during this visit was the Japanese military expedition to the southeast coast of Taiwan in May 1874. Ostensibly the objective was to "punish" Taiwanese indigenes who had attacked and killed shipwrecked Okinawan sailors, but it was in fact a practice run for empire building. The discussions in 1873 between Soejima and Li Hongzhang had included what the Japanese felt were the ambiguities of the status of Chosŏn Korea, Okinawa (one of the islands known as the Ryukyus), and Taiwan. The Qing mobilized for war over the Taiwan expedition; the Japanese were persuaded to leave, having extracted suitable punishment (though at great cost, mostly through disease, of their forces), and in the aftermath the Qing reformed and strengthened their administrative presence in Taiwan. The apparently "ambiguous" status of relations between the Qing and their neighbors, most of whom had recognized some form of at least nominal subordinate relationship to Peking in the past, was now exploited and "clarified" by the foreign powers. The British moved to assert control over Burma; the French over Annam; the Russians, having quietly secured an enormous tract of maritime northeast Asia in 1858, asserted themselves in central Asia. There were a number of crises that threatened war—in Taiwan and in Xinjiang with the Russians—and a crisis that actually led to war with France in 1884–85.

In that military conflict, barring the sinking in seven minutes of a Chinese fleet of Western-style vessels at Fuzhou as the war commenced, the Qing and their allies largely fought the French to a standstill, although they had failed to counter a naval blockade and the seizure of the Penghu islands and Taiwan ports. But if they did not lose the war, they did not win the peace. The diplomatic result in the 1885 Treaty of Tianjin allowed the French free rein in northern Vietnam, and paved the way for a full colonial occupation there. Moreover, during the war the Japanese engineered a coup in Korea to further their own interests. The destruction of the fleet on August 23, 1884, and of the French-built shipyard and arsenal at Fuzhou, however, was a sharp blow to the self-strengthening movement. Tensions over strategy in the face of the steadily widening range of foreign pressures had already frayed the entire project. The influence of Prince Gong had been steadily whittled away by Empress Dowager Cixi over the previous two decades, and the defeat set the seal on his fall from power. Simple technology transfer—the acquisition of the means to construct modern warships, for example—had proved insufficient. For some, this meant that such initiatives needed to be greatly expanded and intensified, and backed up with new techniques and institutional initiatives to underpin them. For others, it exposed "Westernization" as a fallacy, and pointed to the need to seek an alternative strategy for strengthening the Qing that was more strongly rooted in Chinese norms. Those "norms" themselves came under intense scrutiny. A Cantonese scholar, Kang Youwei, deeply troubled by the failure to counter Western aggression, and especially aggrieved (as were many others) at the 1885 settlement, put forward bold claims in a series of books published in the 1890s that examined the texts underpinning Qing state practice and ideology. Kang argued that there was no unmediated classical canon, and that Confucius himself was an innovator and reformer. Where some found the prompt for wholesale reform in the crisis of the present alone, Kang found his mandate for dramatic institutional change in the past. This was a critical intellectual intervention, which was to directly influence one of the most dramatic political episodes of the 1890s.

In the meantime, concern about the foreign challenge was not confined to the court or to students and scholars. Grassroots tensions over the foreign presence continued to find sporadic expression in violent confrontations. There were occasional clashes in the treaty ports—a riot in the British concession at Zhenjiang in 1889 over policing for example, and violent agitation against a tax on wheelbarrows in Shanghai's international settlement in 1894 (these were a popular and cheap form of urban transport). Missionaries, more vulnerable, and more embedded in localities in which they aimed to effect change, remained a source of disputes. One noticeable new development was demonstrated in 1891 with a series of anti-foreign riots targeting missionaries in several Yangzi towns and cities.

Still-circulating anti-Taiping propaganda was a factor there, but so was anti-Qing activism. A secret anti-dynastic organization, the Gelaohui (Elder Brother Society), organized and led the attacks, and the events highlighted the slow but steady growth of an incipient and violent resistance to the Qing.

Of course, most of the time, in most places, there was no conflict. This was not only because lower-level administrators did their best to bring disputes to a quick resolution, to avoid internationalizing local disputes that threatened to escalate their way up through chains of reporting to the Zongli Yamen and foreign diplomats in the capital, and thereby to draw unwanted attention to themselves from on high. There were also more positive reasons why conflict was the exception rather than the norm. To view relations between *all* Chinese and *all* foreigners as suffused with tension, with imperialist arrogance and attitudes on the one hand and nationalistic zeal on the other, is simply ahistorical. It is a picture that does still retain a hold on understandings of Sino-foreign relations, but it is important to remember in spite of this that most interactions between Chinese and foreigners remained peaceable and of largely mutual benefit.

But the "foreign" certainly remained conspicuous. The distinction people routinely made between foreign and domestic, or foreign and "Chinese" remained strong, rooted as it was in a confident cultural insularity and patterns of thinking based on such binary assumptions as "inner" and "outer" (*nei* and *wai*). Yet while remaining conspicuous, the "foreign" was increasingly on display in a steadily increasing number of treaty ports, and at mission stations—in terms of architecture for example—and more widely through the circulation of foreign goods, many of which were adopted with alacrity by Chinese consumers. The "foreign" was also increasingly widely represented in print, in both image and text. This process of integration was steady and persistent, even if tensions obviously remained. It also served to generate new questions, which began to be asked about Han Chinese identity, and the place of the people of the Qing in the world more widely. A visitor could as a matter of easy routine enter most treaty port concessions or settlements, and see on display there electric or gas-lit builtscapes that would not be out of place in British or American towns and cities. As new communities of foreign nationals grew and asserted their own identity, Russian, or Italian or German architecture might be viewed as well. The world of the West was on permanent display in Chinese cities.

A visitor would find himself in a new soundscape as well. Macadamized roads changed the sounds that might be expected to be heard in cities from carriages and horses. Church bells and police whistles, as well the horns of ships, added new sounds to the auditory environment. There were public performances of Western music in the open air at city parks in summer. There were private performances at circuses (which Chinese urban audiences readily took to) and at foreign theatres (which they did not). Drilled troops or police marched along the roads, often led by military brass bands. A new machine, the rickshaw (which was invented in Japan and added Western-style wheels to the sedan chair, dispensing with the rear shafts), spread rapidly across Asia after the late 1860s. The padding of the rickshaw puller's feet added yet another dimension. A small cannon was fired every day at noon in Shanghai, for mariners to check their timepieces. On the coast, powerful lighthouse fog-horns could disturb the air. Much of this was intensely foreign, and equally as intensely absorbed into the evolving urban culture of late imperial China. The brass band, for example, was rapidly appropriated, and elaborate funerals in Shanghai's streets often boasted as many bands as the organizers could afford. They did not play in step with each other: this will have been a novel and singular auditory experience for all concerned.

A new commercialized urban leisure culture evolved, and in places grew quite rapidly. Sites of commercial activity were also sites of conspicuous consumption. Shanghai often led, but other cities also followed, or moved quickly in line. "Traditional" forms of leisure evolved to suit new tastes and market demands, and were often at least inflected by their foreign equivalents. Ideas about what was "Chinese" or "traditional"—areas as diverse as music and medicine—came often to be driven by comparison or contrast to their foreign equivalents. New sites of leisure and interaction also emerged, such as the hotel, the theatre, the opium house, the carriage promenading on a public road, steamships, and railways. A new butt for jokes, or target for social criticism, arrived: the "foreignized" comprador, near-illiterate in his own language (at least, in the caricature) and a slave to foreign fashions and fads. Few societies have ever liked the *nouveaux riches*, and Qing China was no exception. But a wider tranche of urban society participated in the creation of this new urban culture and the spaces in which it was played out than simply those Chinese working with foreign firms, and it was intensely permeated by new goods and practices from overseas: clocks, watches, and photography amongst them.

This diverse new range of goods and practices permeated far beyond the towns and cities. Missionaries would deploy photography, for example, through the medium of magic lantern shows, to drum up crowds for proselytizing. Although there was an increasing commercialization of agriculture during the nineteenth century, China overwhelmingly remained an agrarian society. Work on the land remained generally labor intensive, and was supplemented by handicraft production and seasonal migration to find other work. There were significant developments, such as the rise of silk production—for some decades after 1887 silk was China's leading export commodity by value—but evidence of any shattering and destructive impact on the rural economy arising from imports of foreign manufacturers remains elusive. China's population continued to grow, and it also largely continued to feed itself, expanding the acreage of land that was cultivated. Migration took place internally, notably into Manchuria from Shandong, and of course into the areas devastated by the Taiping war. Despite the formal prohibition on emigration remaining in force until 1893, large numbers of people did move overseas to work, or to settle.

Rural life remained vulnerable to the vicissitudes of the weather, or in north China to the unpredictable and ultimately unmanageable Yellow river. The El Niño cycle of climate change delivered a debilitating drought to north China in the years 1875–79 that led to successive crop failures and a famine that took an estimated 9.5 million lives, despite the efforts of state and private relief initiatives, in which foreign missionaries and others played a role.

The state's preparedness to counter famine had been weakened, as it had diverted resources over recent decades to counter rebellion and foreign threats. This was not lost on the newly emerging forums of public discussion that revolved around such newspapers as *Shenbao*, which was to play a critical role in disseminating information about the disaster and in mobilizing relief. The idea of China as a "land of famine" came to have a powerful hold on the foreign imagination, but the evidence suggests that China's agrarian economy largely remained robust, and that life in the countryside was not set in any static, unchanging mode. One significant transformation, for example, came through the rapid spread of the use of imported kerosene to light houses, even of the very poor. Nonetheless, rural life could be hard (but urban life could be hard, too). The population continued to increase, and famine was the contingent exception, not a rule.

The rise of Shanghai also subverted the geography of power in China, as did the growth in influence of provincial power-holders such as Li Hongzhang. Existing relationships and hierarchies more widely were definitively reshaped by the power of capital, and this caused intense cultural anxiety. But some of these traditional relationships were themselves questioned by critics who saw them as impediments to any process of cultural or political rejuvenation which might help counter the existential threat posed by foreign power. One area in which there was debate and activism was around the status of women, and one site of controversy was foot-binding. This once-elite practice had penetrated all levels of Han Chinese society. A group of emerging reform-minded scholars, such as Kang Youwei and Liang Qichao, were amongst those who formed groups to encourage the discontinuation of the practice. There was support for this from missionaries but at the same time contrary arguments were advanced by foreign cultural relativists who opposed interference in "traditional" Chinese practices. The movement was to build some momentum and secure notable high-level endorsements throughout the 1890s. It was notable also that it placed the position of China's treatment of women at the heart of thinking about reform, and about the nation. Foreign observers would routinely factor in a society's treatment of women as emblematic of its level of "civilization." Setting aside the inconsistencies and hypocrisies this involved, it formed a powerful discourse, and it was one that increasingly mirrored the thinking of China's own home-grown critics. And the number of these continued to grow.

Self-criticism was also prompted by the indignities of colonialist attitudes and practices amongst foreign residents in China. A visitor to a treaty port would find that his status as a Chinese excluded him from any full enjoyment of the benefits of residence in a place like Shanghai's International Settlement. For all that it was grounded fundamentally on a coalition with Chinese interests, Chinese residents found themselves excluded from its representative institutions, treated separately through its taxation regime, and prohibited from enjoying such facilities as its parks or riverside laws. As early as 1881, elite Chinese residents complained formally about such treatment, but while some concessions were made, in general this pattern of racist discrimination was to continue. It was later to generate moments of intense and sometimes violent conflict locally, but it also served to spark reflection on the place of the Chinese and of China in a world dominated by foreign empires.

The world of those empires grew more brittle throughout the last three decades of the nineteenth century. The rise of Prussia and its unification of Germany after its defeat of France in 1870–71 brought on to the scene an ambitious new power. A general acceleration of European colonial expansion was accompanied by challenges to the existing order from both Japan and the United States. For the Qing this came to a head in 1894–95 when Japanese ambitions in Korea (in which the Qing had been reasserting its presence) led to war, and to victory for Tokyo. This defeat was yet more appalling for the Qing because of Japan's still recent subordinate status in the scheme of regional relationships within which the Qing worked. It marked a further failure of the modernized armies and navy of the empire to counter foreign aggression. A land campaign fought in Korea and Manchuria, and in the province of Shandong, which came to threaten the capital, led the Qing to sue for peace.

The terms of the Treaty of Shimonoseki were shocking: Korea was definitively removed from the orbit of the Qing; Taiwan was surrendered to Japanese colonial control; the Penghu islands and part of the Liaodong Peninsula were transferred to Japan; a large indemnity was demanded; new treaty ports on the Yangzi, and Hangzhou and Suzhou were to be opened. The Japanese triumph led to an imperialist feeding frenzy. Russia, France, and Germany cooperated in a "Triple Intervention" to demand that Japan surrender its Manchurian acquisition. For much of the rest of the decade the powers went knocking on China's door: in 1898 Germany seized on a routine pretext—a fatal missionary incident—to seize Jiaozhou Bay in Shandong province, and established a colony there. Russia itself took the Liaodong Peninsula. The British expanded their territory at Kowloon by acquiring the "New Territories," and took their own port in Shandong province (Weihai). The French established a new leased territory west of Canton at Guangzhouwan. Only Italy failed in its attempt to gain territory. The broader context was provided by the "New Imperialism" generated by the rise of German ambition, and of Russo-British antagonism, and by the emergence of notions of declining nations and "races" derived from vulgar understandings of Social Darwinism. The question of the "break-up of China" seemed to be one of "when," not "if." Popular resistance to the new developments was not entirely new. At the very least, Chinese populations in newly opened treaty ports had at times passively resisted the newly arriving foreigners. But in the New Territories, in the countryside around Jiaozhou Bay, and most defiantly in Taiwan, where a short-lived republic was proclaimed, there was violent (if unsuccessful) struggle. More was to come. Meanwhile reform newspapers and study groups spread rapidly.

Defeat in 1895, and then the rapacity of the "scramble for concessions" after the German seizure of Jiaozhou, prompted an extraordinary moment of frenetic but ultimately defeated reform at the heart of the Qing state. The Tongzhi emperor had died in 1874, and the Empress Dowager Cixi chose as his successor her nephew, a boy barely 3 years old, who was given the reign-title Guangxu (1875–1908). This was problematic, for it was contrary to succession rules for the emperor's successor to come from the same generation, and it exacerbated problems of legitimacy posed by Cixi's female regency. In June 1898

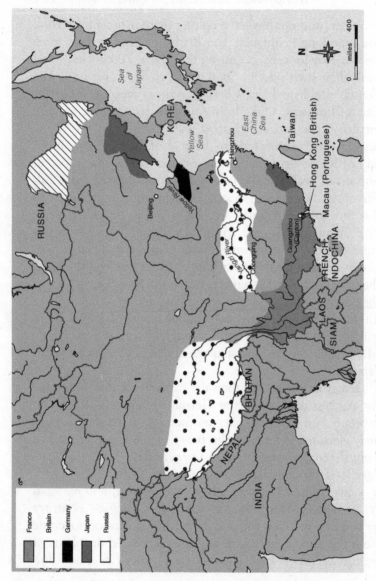

6. Foreign spheres of influence during the late Qing.

Guangxu, having now assumed his majority, seized his day, and issued a stream of decrees that outlined a break with the past that was all the more revolutionary for being so rapidly proclaimed. Education, the military, and the structure of government were to be reformed; the reform-minded were promoted, opponents dismissed. Commerce and industry were to be encouraged. The influence at Guangxu's court of a group of scholars centering around the Cantonese scholar Kang Youwei lay at the heart of this "Hundred Days" reform, and Kang himself drafted many of the decrees. But this was too much, too quickly, for more conservative elements, and Cixi stepped out of formal retirement and with conservative allies struck back. The emperor was seized, numbers of his new advisers were arrested and executed, and the decrees annulled. Many of those had been ignored anyway by many provincial governors. Kang Youwei escaped, evading capture with British help, to take up a banner of loyal opposition to the Qing overseas, travelling the world to raise support amongst overseas Chinese communities for his Baohuang hui (Society to Protect the Emperor).

The influence of Kang's brand of loyalist, constitutional monarchy was steadily to be supplanted by more radical thinkers, however, such as Sun Yat-sen, outraged at the weakness of the Qing, and the failure of reform. The Guangxu emperor lived out his days under close house arrest, and, at least according to rumor, was murdered at his aunt's orders as she herself lay dying in 1908. This was all high political drama of a type that could hardly have been better scripted. The most significant legacy of the Hundred Days, however, was that it took place in public, and was debated and discussed in the new press, and in debating clubs and circles. There had now evolved in China a public opinion that nestled wherever a newspaper circulated and scholars and students gathered. It was increasingly national in form and reach, and also clearly transnational. China had partly been turned inside out by the internationalizing changes of the previous four decades, and the movement of its people across the seas. From Japan, from Hong Kong, from Southeast Asia, the United States, and elsewhere, expatriate Chinese took note of what was happening to their nation, and felt involved in its survival during a time of great weakness and danger. The next great shock delivered to the Qing, however, came not from the scholars or expatriate reformers, but out of the rural heartlands and from communities that had barely encountered the foreign threat directly. In these areas, it was rumor, fear, and a sense of the world turned upside down that prevailed. The consequence was cataclysmic.

4. *Felling a Dynasty, Founding a Republic*

PETER ZARROW

As the nineteenth century drew to a close and court factions in the Forbidden City engaged in murderous struggles, flood, followed by drought, stalked the north China plains. Landless young men prepared themselves through martial arts and spirit possession to purify the realm. The Yihequan—Boxers United in Righteousness ("boxers" referring to martial arts practices)—performed rituals designed to give them invulnerability in battle. The "Boxers," as they have been called for short in Western writings since the spring of 1900, were not an organized uprising, but across hundreds of communities loosely affiliated groups of angry young peasants sprang up. Their goal was to restore the moral order in the face of real and perceived threats to community solidarity. At the head of those threats were foreign missionaries and Chinese Christians.

The Boxer movement had much in common with countless traditional peasant uprisings, including the White Lotus rebellion discussed in Chapter 2. The original Boxer groups sought as much to protect property from outside attack in a time of great troubles as to aggrandize their power. But a pattern of Boxer clashes with Catholic missionaries emerged in Shandong province in the mid-1890s. Missionaries had been spreading across the countryside since the 1860s and had often gained a reputation for interfering in local governance. Missionaries made relatively few converts, and though in some villages relations between Christians and non-Christians were amiable, relations were particularly disturbed in Shandong, where a set of German Catholic missionaries closely tied themselves to the growing German military presence. As a second and third year of natural disasters unfolded with no help from officials, the Boxer movement was suppressed in Shandong but then spread to neighboring provinces. Over the winter of 1899–1900, destitute peasants and drifters moved through thousands of square miles in the provinces of Zhili, Shanxi, and Henan, and even into the northeast, attacking Western missionaries and Christian communities. Gaining the approval of a few key officials and now called the Yihetuan (militia united in righteousness), Boxers fought under the banner of "Support the Qing, destroy the foreign." Women Boxers organized independently in units called Red Lanterns. They burned churches and looted houses. Several foreign diplomats were killed as Boxers began to infiltrate the cities. The Boxers' own explanations for their actions were diverse, but a typical piece of doggerel condemned Christians:

> They proselytize their sect,
> And believe in only one God,
> The spirits and their own ancestors

Are not even given a nod....
No rain comes from Heaven.
The earth is parched and dry
And all because the churches
Have bottled up the sky.

The Christians' magic was especially feared. Christians, it was said, practiced incest, poisoned wells, created armies out of paper figures, used human organs to make magic, and scattered blood to make people go mad. Above all, they refused to join in community prayers to the village gods to make it rain: they angered the gods.

What separated the Boxers from traditional peasant rebels was not the support they often received from local gentry, but their target. What turned the uprising into an international war was the ability of missionaries to get help from their home countries. In the wake of the debacle of the 1898 Reform Movement (discussed in the Chapter 3), the Qing court had purged suspected reform sympathizers and moved the most competent of the high Chinese officials, Li Hongzhang, out of the north to become governor-general in the far south. Manchu–Chinese relations worsened. Many Chinese suspected the Empress Dowager Cixi of plotting to kill the emperor, and she was generally seen as having usurped his powers. Long-standing prejudice against women in government further damaged the court's legitimacy. The failure of the court's assassins to kill the escaped reformers Kang Youwei and Liang Qichao, who had successfully fled abroad, made the court look weak as well as vindictive. Ultra-conservatives—Manchu aristocrats, Bannermen (the mostly Manchu hereditary military caste), and Chinese officials—were left without challenge in the court itself, but they felt increasingly besieged by the world outside. Their anti-foreignism reached new heights.

On June 21, 1900 Cixi issued an edict effectively declaring war on all the foreign powers. This remarkable, even bizarre decision to take on more powerful nations from around the world was made as war was breaking out anyway. Seeing the Boxer movement spread, by June foreign troops had already moved into Beijing and Tianjin, and clashes broke out among the foreign troops, Boxers, and Qing soldiers. The court finally had to decide whether to support or to suppress the Boxers. There had been clashes between Qing troops and the Boxers through May. However, on the whole, officials in north China found themselves too weak to deal firmly with widespread social disorder, and the official view of the Boxers was ambiguous. Several high-ranking Manchu officials were sympathetic at least with the Boxers' anti-foreignism, although it is hard to believe many officials of any rank enthusiastically supported uncontrollable roving bands of violent men (and women). Nonetheless, as the foreign legations in Beijing summoned more troops to their support, the Qing court gambled on war. Not without justification, Cixi's edict stated, "The foreigners have been aggressive towards us, infringing upon our territorial integrity, trampling our people. They oppress our people and blaspheme our gods. The common people suffer greatly at their hands, and each one of them is vengeful."

Notwithstanding official and popular anti-foreignism, Qing attacks on foreigners were less than wholehearted. Provincial military commanders stayed entirely aloof, and key Beijing commanders understood the need for restraint. (In the south, Li Hongzhang not only guaranteed the safety of foreigners but ignored orders to send troops to the north.) The foreign legations in Beijing, as well as foreign communities in Tianjin and Harbin, held out until relief came in August. Certain officials in Beijing had even hedged their bets by helping to smuggle food and supplies into the besieged legations. This is not to say there was no fighting. There were major battles as the "Eight-Power Expedition" marched from Tianjin on the coast to Beijing. This army then sacked Beijing and spread out across the north China countryside to find "Boxers" and punish them. The force consisted of troops from Britain (including Gurkhas and Punjabi cavalry), Germany, Russia, France, Italy, the United States (including Afro-American cavalry), the Austro-Hungarian Empire, and Japan. Of these eight invaders, Japan provided the largest number of troops and cemented its role as one of the imperialist powers. They took no prisoners. Mopping up operations, largely led by Germans, indiscriminately killed alleged Boxers through the rest of the year. The Chinese death toll was in the tens of thousands; Boxers had killed over 200 foreigners and several thousand Chinese Christians; Qing soldiers probably killed several hundred more foreign troops. The loot seized by foreign troops was tremendous, and continues to enrich museums and private collections around the world to this day.

Even so, most Boxers were able to blend back into the general population, while Cixi, the Guangxu emperor, and high court officials fled west to Xi'an. Cixi ordered Li Hongzhang to return north to negotiate surrender terms, which were harsh. The powers demanded that officials who cooperated with the Boxers be executed, apology missions sent abroad, foreign troops stationed in north China, and an indemnity of 450 million taels of silver (US$333 million) be paid over thirty-nine years at 4 percent interest: an unprecedented sum that further crippled a government that was already broke and whose annual revenues ran to about 250 million taels. Though obsessed with "punishment," most foreigners did not want the Qing to fall lest the ensuing power vacuum draw the Western powers and Japan into fatal competition. Financial interests, including governments, needed a functioning Chinese government to recoup their investments. In the end, the Boxer debacle confirmed that "spheres of influence" would mark the informal colonization of China. Russian power expanded in the northeast, Britain in the Yangzi Valley, France in the southeast, Japan in Fujian across from its colony of Taiwan as well as southern Manchuria and Korea, and Germany in Shandong—but the outright division of China was avoided.

Several other features of the Boxer movement and the Boxer War were unprecedented as well. Imperialist aggression designed to inflict punishment through razing villages; declaring open seasons on killing, raping, and looting; and imposing indemnities were not new. But international cooperation against China on such a vast scale, and including Japanese even in the face of Western racist contempt for "Asiatics," set a new pattern. Claims to represent civilization in the face of barbarism and talk of the "Yellow Peril" reached new heights, even while a few Western critics of imperialism wondered who were the civilized and who the barbarian. In America, Mark Twain commented, "We do not allow Chinamen to come here, and I say in all seriousness that it would be a graceful thing to let China decide who shall go there." The Boxer War was one of the first "world events" the news of which was disseminated quickly, and even before the era of the transoceanic telegraph, faked newsreels of Boxer depredations were shown in the new cinemas of Western nations. For later generations of Chinese, the Boxers became a symbol of superstition, of backwardness, and of the decadence of an official class just as ignorant as peasants. Equally, however, the Boxers became a symbol of the potential of popular resistance and, indeed, righteousness.

From Guangdong—a somewhat peripheral province far to the south from Beijing's point of view but a corner of the empire that had long enjoyed foreign contacts and that produced most of China's overseas merchants—arose a small revolutionary movement dedicated to the outright overthrow of the dynasty. But although Sun Yat-sen and a few southerners had attempted to rouse popular revolt against the Manchus in the late 1890s, it was only after the Boxer disaster that a segment of leading reformers turned against the dynasty. A few intellectuals from China's wealthy central provinces such as Zhang Binglin (who also wrote under the name of Zhang Taiyan) began to denounce the Qing as a foreign, inherently oppressive dynasty. Zhang even cut off his queue, symbol of submission to Qing rule. For a time, the distinction between reform and revolution remain blurred, perhaps because reformers wished to restore Guangxu to the throne at the expense of Cixi. And the Qing continued to proscribe "constitutionalist" writings that advocated a constitutional monarchy as vigorously as it proscribed revolutionary screeds. In August 1900, Tang Caichang, a follower of Kang Youwei, led an uprising in Guangxu's name. Although this uprising was nipped in the bud, it suggested that constitutionalists who sought to reform the monarchy and revolutionaries who sought to overthrow it could still find some common ground. The two groups also cooperated with Chinese merchants in 1905 to boycott American goods in protest against the exclusion laws that prohibited Chinese immigration to the United States. With most of the organization and funds coming from Overseas Chinese supporters of Kang Youwei, the movement, brief as it was, foreshadowed the alliances between radicals, students, and merchants of the 1920s.

But the constitutionalists and revolutionaries soon drifted apart. An incident that helped clarify the meaning of revolution occurred in 1903. Russian troops that were originally part of the Eight-Power Expedition had remained in Manchuria instead of withdrawing as the Boxer treaty had stipulated. A group of radical students and teachers—partly protected by living in the foreign concessions in Shanghai—published polemics against the Qing in the *Subao* newspaper. Zou Rong, then 18 years old, wrote a pamphlet called "The Revolutionary Army" that almost hypnotically chanted, "To sweep away the despotism of these thousands of years, to cast off the servile nature bred in us over these thousands of years, to exterminate the five million and more of the furry and horned Manchu race, to expunge the humiliation of our 260 years of harsh and unremitting pain, to cleanse the great land of China, and to make the descendants of the Yellow Emperor all become Washingtons ... The most exalted and incomparable aim is Revolution! How imposing a thing is revolution! How magnificent a thing is revolution!" Zou's ardent republicanism was based on the premise that the Han Chinese needed to free themselves of the incubus of their Manchu overlords. Zhang Binglin criticized Kang Youwei's reformism in a long attack, incidentally using the personal name of the emperor and calling him a "little clown." The Qing government had had enough. It sought the deaths of the radicals associated with *Subao*. But British authorities in the Shanghai concession, operating with some adherence to free speech principles, refused to turn them over. The Qing's prolonged efforts to extradite men it wanted to behead as traitors simply highlighted its vindictiveness and, worse, its weakness. That the Qing was falling apart is also shown by the actions of those officials who warned the radicals to escape, which some did, although Zhang and Zou decided to remain. Eventually the two men were sentenced to brief jail terms for lèse-majesté. Zou died in prison but Zhang was released a revolutionary hero in 1906.

At the same time—in the wake of the Boxer debacle—the court under a chastised Cixi began a series of "New Policy" reforms. These reforms were extensive but largely reflected the very ideas that the court had so violently rejected in 1898. The government was to be streamlined and modernized. Military reformers worked to build a better equipped, more disciplined, and even more educated army. Educational reformers began to build a new state school system. The number of schools gradually grew, especially in major cities, not incidentally providing employment for educated men and a few women and customers for publishers of textbooks and magazines. Money was found to send students abroad, especially to Japan where as many as 7,000 students were studying in mostly short-term legal and military courses by 1905 (some students were self-funded).

Even before Japan's astonishing victory over Russia in 1905, which inspired all of Asia, Chinese intellectuals and leaders looked to Japan as a model of modernization, and Japanese advisers and teachers were brought to China. The age-old Confucian examination system, producing the officials of the empire for over 800 years, was abolished in 1905.

Another reform was "local self-government," though this was actually a policy to bring local leaders into the central bureaucratic system and was enormously disruptive to traditional patterns of rural authority. The most far-reaching reform, at least on paper, was the Qing promise of a constitution. A small team of Manchu aristocrats and high Chinese officials was appointed to study the issue. After an initial delay caused by a revolutionary's assassination attempt, a delegation left to study the constitutions of Japan, Europe, and the United States in 1906. Imperial edicts over the following years set up timetables to implement a constitution and further streamline the administrative structure. A draft constitution was promulgated that followed the model of the Meiji Constitution of Japan, keeping all sovereignty and most powers in the emperor's hands. It was never fully implemented, but provincial assemblies were elected in 1909, giving local elites a new kind of political voice. These constitutional promises gave hope to Chinese reformers and scared the revolutionaries, who insisted the Qing was just trying to cheat the Chinese people.

In the event, the reforms, sincere or not, came too late to save the dynasty. The late Qing reforms were not in vain—they formed a basis for the state-building projects of the generation that followed—but they actively undermined the Qing in the short run. Modernization projects were expensive, and peasants resented tax increases, such as those which paid for schools whose new curriculum seemed to depart from traditional moral concerns while offering nothing of practical use to farmers. That beloved temples might be forcibly turned into schools that only rich children could attend added salt to the wound. The abolition of the examination system was also destabilizing. Though elites were quick to turn to modern schooling for their children, men whose lives had revolved around study of the Confucian classics felt abandoned by a court that suddenly seemed to have no use for them. The exams had not been a mere institutional device to recruit officials but were integral to the Confucian integration of the dynastic realm.

The new educational system of course taught loyalty, but in practice schools became sites where radical students and teachers came together to protest every incident of Qing pusillanimity in the face of imperialist aggression. Perhaps most importantly of all, although suffrage was limited to wealthy and highly educated elites, the new provincial assemblies offered such men new ways to pressure the Qing court on a range of issues from taxes to the pace of constitutional reform. The assemblies reflected and fostered a new kind of national elite: largely based in the wealthy cities of the Jiangnan region (centered on Shanghai) but concerned with national rather than provincial issues. Furthermore, beyond the court's purview, reform-minded Chinese were setting up a variety of political organizations: antifootbinding societies, opium suppression societies, "citizen's martial societies," constitutional study societies, and the like.

Over the first decade of the twentieth century, constitutionalist and revolutionary organizations took root among

Chinese students and merchants living abroad, most importantly in Tokyo. In normal times, these organizations would have remained marginal to events in China, but this was not a normal time. Overseas communities were by no means divorced from China—all of the students and many of the merchants had intimate business and family ties with the new national elites, and their writings evaded censorship to circulate widely in China itself. The "brush-war" between constitutionalists and revolutionaries was fierce, and sometimes involved shouting down and even attacking the enemy's meetings. Emotions ran high, especially on the revolutionary side. In the first decade of the twentieth century a series of doomed uprisings, mostly reflecting Sun Yat-sen's feckless faith that a spark would start a prairie fire, resulted in the deaths of hundreds in the southeast. Several students committed suicide to demonstrate the sincerity of their ideals and inspire comrades to continue the struggle. Others engaged in assassinations. Take the case of Qiu Jin. Abandoning her fairly wealthy family, including a husband and two children, she travelled to Japan to pursue her studies in 1904. A prolific author of classical poetry and vernacular political proclamations, Qiu argued both for women's rights and Han Chinese nationalism. "Unbinding my own feet to undo the poisoned years | Arousing the souls of a hundred flowers to passionate movement," she wrote on her way to Japan. Upon her return to China in 1906, she became a teacher. When her involvement in a plot to kill Manchu officials was discovered in 1907, she was executed. Much of Qiu's life foreshadowed the actions of women revolutionaries in the ensuing decades.

The heart of the revolutionaries' case lay in virulent anti-Manchuism. Zou Rong's *Revolutionary Army* began with the command "Kill, kill, kill." Zhang Binglin and Liu Shipei, both classical scholars, demonstrated that the Manchus were an alien and barbarian group from time immemorial. But the "Han race" was descended from conquering clans occupying China since ancient times. In the modern language of nationhood and race, therefore, Manchu rule over China was inherently illegitimate. As a hereditary military caste living in garrisons and separate urban districts, Manchus represented daily injustice. According to the revolutionaries, the Chinese were wretched today because their natural evolution into a strong nation had been suppressed by the Manchus. As "slaves of slaves" the Chinese had to throw off Manchu rule before they could stand up for themselves in the world. Accounts of the trauma of the bloody Manchu conquest of the seventeenth century aroused calls for ancestral revenge.

In 1905 in Tokyo, small and disparate revolutionary groups were brought together in an umbrella organization, the National Alliance or *Tongmenghui*, under Sun Yat-sen's leadership. An activist and money-raiser more than an intellectual, Sun was able to loosely unite revolutionary students around the principles of anti-Manchuism (nationalism), republicanism, and the "equalization of land rights" or a vaguely socialist sentiment. France and the United States stood as examples of the patriotic energies engendered by republicanism, and revolutionaries tended to argue that republicanism represented universal human values seen, at least in embryonic form, in China as well as the West. They trusted that representative institutions would strengthen China, not weaken it. Indeed, they argued that since all persons were aware of the evils of the absolute monarchy, it would be easier to carry out a republican revolution than to pursue constitutional reforms under a hopelessly recalcitrant dynasty. They linked the idea of revolution (*geming*, an ancient term referring to the change of dynasties) to restoration (*guangfu*): the recovery of China by the Han people.

Socialism won Chinese adherents by promising a practical path toward economic development. Intellectuals who studied Western socialism concluded that China lacked the class conflict that was roiling Europe and America. They certainly understood that some Chinese were richer than others, but they saw the task before them as enriching society as a whole, not sharing the poverty. Sun Yat-sen was particularly attracted to the single-tax proposal of Henry George—that a tax be levied on the appreciation of land prices, an idea popular at the time but with little relevance to Chinese economic conditions.

The National Alliance's support for land nationalization was not designed to "free" peasants but to forestall future class conflict as well as provide the basis for future state development programs. Only a handful of anarchists advocated full-scale "social revolution." Two groups of Chinese anarchists, one in Tokyo and one in Paris, called for the abolition of the state entirely, though not necessarily through mass violence. The Paris group advocated "revolutionary education" as a means to promote "free association." The Tokyo group spoke of a revolution of the "whole people." The institutions of republicanism, in their view, were no less oppressive than those of monarchism. Anarchists also advocated cultural revolution, criticizing the Confucian "Three Bonds" that reinforced an entire social hierarchy in the model of the relationships of parent–child, ruler–subject, and husband–wife. The traditional morality of filial piety was to be replaced with equality, freedom, and rights. Anarchists demanded that respect be paid to traditionally despised groups: peasants, workers, women, and youth.

The main spokesman for the constitutionalist reformers was Liang Qichao, and it was Liang's innovative journalism that introduced many Chinese, including his revolutionary opponents, to Western political doctrines. In the 1890s, Liang had criticized the Manchus for their reactionary and sclerotic leadership, their refusal to tear down the boundaries separating Manchu and Han, and indeed their "racial backwardness," in the parlance of the era. But in the early 1900s his fear of revolution was greater than his distrust of the Qing court. Revolution, Liang claimed, would bring disorder and could well weaken China to the point that the foreign powers would take it over entirely. He distrusted republicanism, at least for the foreseeable future, as inherently less stable than constitutional monarchism. Pointing to Britain and Japan, Liang saw in constitutional monarchism a recipe for steady progress, giving the people a voice in government while providing overarching institutions to resolve conflicts among the people. He foresaw that by building up a civic culture gradually, the Chinese state would be defined by active citizens rather than "racial solidarity." Liang contrasted the "narrow nationalism" of an "ethnically pure" Han China to "greater nationalism," or "the unity of all groups belonging to the national territory to resist all foreign groups." In racial terms, the Han and the Manchus shared a common enemy: the Whites. In political terms, institutions mattered less than raising the ability of the Chinese to cooperate among themselves and identify with the state. Given the people's current backwardness, Liang said, republicanism was bound to fail.

For Liang, the nation-state was the only effective unit of struggle in a Social Darwinist world. The nation was not a biological given but an artifice of state-building. The strong survived while the weak perished. China's contemporary crisis, in Liang's view, had deeper historical roots than the Manchu conquest or Qing policies. Rather, although Liang was occasionally enticed by the notion of "enlightened absolutism," he blamed China's weakness on its long failure to progress out of an era of central imperial rule. This failure rested on two factors: first, the sclerotic institutions of absolute monarchy; and second, China's long dominance in East Asia, which meant the state had not faced the kind of competition that would have forced it to evolve. Liang called for all Chinese to become citizens—members of the national community bearing rights and duties—because he saw this as the basis for strengthening the state. The people depended on the state and the state on the people. But ultimately state interests had to come first for Liang. He had no use for the revolutionaries' advocacy of popular sovereignty, remained suspicious of egalitarianism, and despised cosmopolitanism (which threatened to weaken commitment to the nation's struggle for survival). While some revolutionaries advocated women's rights and free marriage on the grounds of natural justice, for example, Liang argued that women should be educated essentially in order that they could raise better citizens of the future.

In an influential stream of articles published over the first decade of the twentieth century Liang did much to create public opinion in China itself. Publishing houses and the schools formed the institutional basis for public opinion. Not coincidentally, the late Qing saw a profusion of fiction-writing and translation, much of which was designed to foster patriotic sentiments. Potentially seditious public opinion included the notions that the Qing dynasty was not the same as China and ultimate loyalty was owed only to the latter; that a new basis of the legitimacy of rulers lay in some kind of consent of the citizens; and that citizens constituted a political community that belonged to its members. Even officials used Liang's words to talk about reform. When the National Assembly met in late 1910 it demanded to be treated as a legislative body, not the advisory role it was assigned in law. Some of the controversies that poisoned the relationship between assembly-men and the Qing court involved finances and official appointments. Some were symbolic, such as demands to abolish the queue and to pardon Kang and Liang for their role in the 1898 reforms.

Assemblymen were no radicals, though some of their sons and daughters were. Rather, they were frustrated by a court that was seemingly incapable of change. Since the deaths of Cixi and Guangxu in 1908 and the ascension of a 2-year-old to the throne, the Manchu regents' commitment to reform faltered. Worse, the regency had cashiered prominent Han Chinese officials such as the military leader Yuan Shikai. Behind the clashes between the assemblymen and the Qing court lay the issue of how far power was going to be centralized—and whether it was going to be centralized in the hands of the imperial clan.

The political culture of urban elites was transformed at the beginning of the twentieth century, but the countryside was sinking further into stagnation. The gap between urban and rural China would continue to grow throughout the twentieth century, and it was in fact cemented into place by Maoist policies from the 1950s through the 1970s. Throughout the first decades of the century the rumble of rural unrest never ceased, and peasants resisted new tax impositions whenever they could. Such movements were local and less class-based than they were community-based. To speak of "peasants" is to include not only farmers but a range of men and women from drifters and beggars to petty merchants and lower gentry. An important group in much of rural China might be called "lumpen gentry": tradition-ally educated men of some but not great or even secure property whose status in the community—and chances of upward mobility—had been disrupted by the abolition of the exams. Some of this group lost property and status in the course of the late Qing reforms, but others were able to make themselves into a new type of community leader by organizing armed bands of supporters.

Whole villages might band together to resist outside impositions or to struggle with neighboring villages over scarce resources like water. Rioting peasants would seize government buildings and grain storehouses. They often attacked the new schools and police offices, which not only demanded new taxes but expropriated temples and land. They knew nothing of democratic theory, though they possessed a strong sense of morality based on the mutual obligations of kin and community. Peasants often belonged to religious sects and secret societies. These were fraternal organizations, sometimes Mafia-like robbery and extortion rings, but mostly dedicated to self-defense. Such organizations could number their adherents in the tens of thousands and sometimes were headed by men of considerable wealth and power. Officials increasingly found themselves working with secret societies, the existence of which was obviously not secret, though some of their rituals and practices were. And the lines between peasants taking collective action, the formation of local militia, and the government's regular soldiers were often blurry. Many men divided their time among their family's fields, soldiering, and banditry, depending on the season and circumstances. Bands of beggars also roamed the land. Revolutionaries in the years before 1911 looked to secret societies for support. However, the revolutionaries' national perspective clashed with the secret societies' dedication to local interests. Rural unrest contributed to the revolution in mostly indirect ways, forcing elites to ask themselves who would control the peasants if officialdom failed to do so.

In 1910 the attempt to conduct a new national census provoked an explosion of opposition. Officials thought of the census as part of the new electoral system and the modernization of China; peasants thought of it as a means of imposing new taxes. As long as provincial elites backed the Qing, rural unrest delayed modernization plans but was politically irrelevant. Conflicts between the court and gentry leaders, however, were rising. Take railroads: enormously expensive and disruptive, requiring the government to borrow money and expropriate land, offering the opportunity of profit for a few, and involving the most sensitive issues of national sovereignty. Foreign investment in railway construction had become the norm, and gave foreigners rights to mine natural resources along the tracks as well. "Railway rights recovery" movements sought to gain control over the railroads for Chinese investors. But the court opposed local railway projects, and its insistence on nationalizing private railway companies after 1908 seemed to many provincial elites to be a sell-out to foreign interests. Of course, such men also saw that their own interests were at stake. The plan for a line from Hankou to Chengdu in Sichuan promised the exciting possibility of opening up the entire southwest to development. Sichuanese backers were enthusiastic, even though they themselves were divided into competing groups and even though a good deal of their money was lost to corruption and bad investments. At any rate, they agreed on opposition to court efforts to nationalize their companies—not least because the government was planning to use a foreign loan to do so—and street protests started in the spring of 1911. Student and merchant strikes crippled Chengdu, and peasants and secret societies attacked police and tax bureaus all through the region. Local militia clashed with soldiers over the following months, and revolutionaries became involved. The scale of the violence was extreme in Sichuan, but the issues were national.

Just as these events were unfolding in Sichuan, the Wuchang Uprising broke out down the Yangzi River in central China on October 10, 1911. Tensions in the area, reflecting the disturbances upriver, had been running high. Student radicals, some but not most affiliated with the National Alliance, had worked hard since at least 1904 to recruit New Army soldiers to the revolutionary cause. Of

18,000 troops in the area, about a third were members of various revolutionary organizations by 1911. On the night of October 9 revolutionary bomb-makers suffered an accidental explosion, and Qing officials began to make arrests, seizing key membership lists. Surviving revolutionaries realized they could not go underground: they had to resist, and the rebellion got under way the following morning. The Manchu governor-general and the top military commander both fled, and the rebels found themselves with a local victory. The rebels convinced a reluctant colonel to lead them. This man, Li Yuanhong, had prestige among the troops, spoke some English, and was familiar to the elites of central China. The Qing response was to send in military reinforcements and to ask Yuan Shikai to return to official service. Yuan, however, did not accept his new command until he had placed men loyal to him in critical positions. Meanwhile, although the Wuchang revolutionaries were bottled up, revolution broke out in other cities over the last ten days of October: in the provinces of Shanxi, Hunan, Jiangxi, and Yunnan. By the end of November, central and southern China had in effect seceded from the Qing empire, along with Shanxi and Shaanxi in the north. Cities with major Qing garrisons were taken by the revolutionaries, sometimes after fierce fighting and even massacres of Manchus. Still, all-out civil war did not occur. In some places that the Qing lost, the military took control; in others urban elites worked with the military; in a few places revolutionaries held power. But Qing forces held in the north, and a stalemate ensued. In December Yuan Shikai sent a representative to conduct negotiations with the revolutionaries in Shanghai. It may be that Yuan thought the Qing could be turned into a genuine constitutional monarchy, with a new parliament and himself as prime minister.

Such was not to be the case. When the Wuchang Uprising broke out, Sun Yat-sen was in Denver, from whence he travelled to Europe seeking the powers' neutrality and, if possible, loans. He arrived back in China at the end of the year and, though loan-less, was elected provisional president of the Chinese republic in Nanjing on January 1, 1912. Sun was something of a compromise candidate, but at least he represented long-term dedication to the cause of revolution. The founding of the Republic of China (ROC) was in itself a considerable blow to the Qing. Symbolizing its break from the imperial past and its membership in the world of modern nation-states, the ROC adopted the solar calendar and proclaimed Year One of the Republic.

Yet not until February 12 did the Qing actually abdicate, bringing the dynasty to an end after 260 years. The deal was this: as the revolutionaries wanted, China would become a republic; as Yuan Shikai wanted, Sun would resign as president, turning the post over to Yuan; as the imperial house wanted, or at least as Empress Dowager Longyu was willing to accept, the court would be given an allowance and certain privileges, such as temporarily remaining in the Forbidden City. Yuan became the ROC's second provisional president, and Li Yuanhong became his vice-president.

The 1911 Revolution did little to affect class relations or the rural–urban gap. It did nothing to challenge imperialism. It even left many of the old provincial power-holders in place, if with new titles. The conservative aspects of the revolution are thus clear. Yet the revolution established fundamentally new political principles, and Yuan continued the battered reform policies of the late Qing: modernizing the military, building up the infrastructure, supporting new schools, and, not least, using foreign advisers and taking out foreign loans. The revolution demolished forever the right of any one family to claim the rule of the empire; it instilled the principle that legitimate power rested on the sovereignty of the people; and it created China as a modern state, claiming distinct borders to mark its territories and position in the world.

Backed by the power of the gun, Yuan Shikai formally became president in 1913 and remained in office until his death in 1916. His was not a happy presidency. Over the four years from 1912 to 1916 the liberal constitutional order dreamed of by reformers and revolutionaries alike was demolished to make way for Yuan's autocracy, and self-destructive autocracy at that. Yuan had the support of the military, though only up to a point, as he was to learn. Anti-Manchuism did not disappear, but it diminished with the passing of the dynasty. In fact, it disappeared so quickly that we may wonder how important a factor it really was in the revolution. At any rate, by 1912, revolutionaries agreed with Yuan that China was to be the "republic of five races"—Han, Manchu, Mongol, Hui (Muslim, Uighur), and Tibetan. The ROC flag consisted of five stripes of red, yellow, blue, white, and black, symbolizing the five races. Such multi-ethnic nationalism was the basis for the ROC's claim to the territory of the old Qing empire, a territory much larger than the Ming had governed. With considerable skill, Yuan's government was able to maintain Chinese sovereignty over the non-Han borderland regions, with the exception of what became Mongolia under Russian sponsorship.

In 1912, while a rump Qing court remained in the Forbidden City, the Imperial City just to the west became the new presidential palaces (and it remains the Communist Party headquarters today). Yuan inherited the vast debts of the Qing. The land tax was in disarray. Tariffs were collected by the foreign-controlled Maritime Customs Service, but these were used to pay off indemnities and the interest on old loans. Yuan's first task was to gain foreign recognition of the new government and a new loan. The foreign powers saw in Yuan the one man who might hold China together and protect their investments, and he duly received a loan to the tune of £25 million.

Parliamentary elections were held. The right to vote was broadened to include adult males with some property and education: about 40 million men or 10 percent of the population qualified. National political parties were formed, another demonstration of the new national consciousness. With Sun Yat-sen's support, the revolutionaries coalesced around Song Jiaoren at the head of a newly organized Nationalist Party (Guomindang—ancestor to but distinct from the Nationalist Party founded at the end of the decade in a different political climate). Song promoted a strong cabinet system, which would have the effect of limiting Yuan's powers as president. Song abandoned the revolutionaries' socialism and rejected a role for women in politics. These moves were designed to appeal to voters who might otherwise support the Progressive Party, headed by Liang Qichao, or even more conservative parties. They paid off, with the Nationalist Party able to form a working majority of the new parliament in 1913. Song himself, however, was assassinated on his way to Beijing. Evidence pointed to Yuan as the culprit, but the case was never proved. Over the course of 1913 Yuan moved against the Nationalist Party and dismissed its members from parliament. Sun attempted to organize a "second revolution" against Yuan, but Yuan easily put it down and Sun's men fled again to Japan.

Yuan has thus come down in history as a traitor to the republic. The charge is fair, but Yuan's devotion to state-building was genuine. In effect, Yuan continued the Qing's "New Policy" reforms that he had originally helped to put into place. Unfortunately, he implemented them as top-down impositions on local society, and they continued to arouse popular opposition. Yuan's efforts to suppress opium had some success, but his attempt to rationalize tax collection contributed to an alarming rise in rural banditry. At the same time, school-building and even prison reform gave Yuan's rule an aura of modernity. Yuan's habit of appearing in his generalissimo uniform, while not democratic, expressed the new China's determination to strengthen itself. Late Qing intellectuals had already criticized traditional Chinese contempt for soldiers, and now Yuan embodied the ideal of a militarized society. Military parades dominated the anniversary celebrations of "Double Ten"—commemorations of the Wuchang Uprising of October 10. Schools turned physical education classes into military drills. Children were taught a new sense of bodily discipline, posture, and punctuality. This may have had roots in traditional concern for health seen in the kind of martial arts rituals practiced by the Boxers. But it rested on a new scientific understanding of childhood development. Schools preached endlessly about standards of hygiene, and demanded that students line up before and after class, defecate once a day on schedule, and generally abide by standards of "civilized" behavior. Notions of "civilized behavior" and bodily discipline deeply affected Chinese culture. New Republican citizens abandoned the kowtow in favor of shaking hands. Sun Yat-sen, among others, was to complain about Chinese who farted and blew their noses in public. Signs in Chinese cities to this day link proper spitting and urination to civilization. Queues were forcibly cut and anti-footbinding drives gained further momentum. New regulations stipulated that officials were to wear formal Western clothing on certain occasions.

The economy under Yuan benefited greatly from the European war that broke out in 1914. Western imports contracted, benefiting Chinese manufacturers, and foreign demand for Chinese resources rocketed up. Like America, China initially remained neutral, though Britain's ally Japan took over the German concessions in Shandong. In January 1915 Japan presented Yuan with its "Twenty-One Demands," mostly insisting on special Japanese economic rights in the north and in Fujian Province (opposite its colony of Taiwan). A final set of demands would have brought Japanese police and administrators into the central government itself. Yuan deliberately leaked the demands to the press, and predictable popular opposition was loud and swift. An anti-Japanese boycott dwarfed that of the anti-American boycott ten years earlier. This is perhaps the one occasion Yuan tried to work with—or at least use—public opinion and bottom-up politics. Finally, Japan issued an ultimatum, and Yuan had no choice but to agree to all but the most draconian of the demands on May 25, which became National Humiliation Day in future Chinese calendars. A sense of humiliation was to become a core element of

Chinese nationalism in the 1920s and persists to this day. This was not merely an aggrieved charge of wrongs done to the Chinese people from the Opium War on, but a deeply embedded historical narrative. Every schoolchild came across "humiliation maps" in history and geography text-books detailing when and where particular instances of imperialist aggression and territorial loss occurred.

In the immediate wake of the Twenty-One Demands, Yuan moved to make himself emperor of a new dynasty. This radical move was not entirely unexpected, and it seems probable that Yuan thought that the Chinese people wanted the return of an emperor to restore order. He may also have thought it would placate the monarchy across the sea, Japan. But he miscalculated on both counts. Public opinion—urban and educated—was aghast, and top army officers, hitherto loyal, were dismayed. Yuan's traditional-ism was long-standing. He had consistently demanded that Confucianism remain a major part of the school curricu-lum, though he resisted the demands of Kang Youwei and others that Confucianism be made the state religion. In December 1914 he had revived the ancient imperial prac-tice of making sacrifices to Heaven at the winter solstice. The next year Yuan began to implement an elaborate—but perfectly transparent—hoax of supposedly popular peti-tions and elections demanding that he become emperor. He promised that his would be a constitutional monarchy, not the absolutist dynasties as of old. In this way Yuan tried to combine disparate forms of legitimization: the trad-itional will of Heaven and the new democratic notions of popular sovereignty. But in neither role he was convincing.

Yuan lost the support of all the social forces in China that mattered. The ordinary people were irrelevant, and most peasants had no knowledge of these events in Beijing. But of elites, even monarchists were dismayed, since most of them favored a restoration of the Qing. More representative of the various strands of urban sentiment, the rivals Liang Qichao and Sun Yat-sen alike denounced Yuan in the harshest terms. Provinces in the southwest were the first to declare their independence, armies were raised, within three months Yuan cancelled the monarchy, and within another three months he was dead of uremia and mortification.

Thus began the "warlord era" and further descent into political chaos. Li Yuanhong assumed the presidency and recalled parliament. But real power shifted into the hands of regional militarists large and small. In Beijing, Yuan's top generals Duan Qirui and Feng Guozhang attempted to share power, but the government broke down in a welter of factional struggles. One result was that another general, one who believed in the restoration of the Qing, was able to briefly take the city in July 1917 and put the boy emperor Puyi back on his throne. That lasted not quite two weeks. Meanwhile, the Japanese government made further, secret loans to the Beijing militarists, in return for which the Japanese were allowed to station police and army troops in Mongolia, Manchuria, and Shandong. The foreign powers continued to recognize the Beijing government diplomatically, and a skeletal civil service continued to work in the areas of foreign affairs, education, and the legal system. It even managed to convince the powers to raise tariffs to 5 percent. But the unified polity was broken with Yuan's death, if indeed it had not already disintegrated with the fall of the Qing.

The failures of Yuan's monarchy in 1916 and of the Qing restoration in 1917 showed that what had been broken could not be put back together again. China, at least urban China, had moved on. By the 1910s, urban groups showed little nostalgia for the imperial order. Merchants were organized into Chambers of Commerce, skilled workers into guilds (unskilled workers might be members of gangs or secret societies), and students and young women insisted on being heard. All these groups were learning to speak in the name of the nation, progress, and civilization. If they had conflicting goals, they could also unite around shared causes such as the anti-Japanese boycott of 1915. The question facing politically minded Chinese was how to understand the failure of liberal constitutionalism and the ongoing weakness of their country.

One answer was to critically examine Chinese culture for the causes of political failure. In this view, autocracy and monarchism were the symptoms, not the cause of the disease. It followed that the cure lay not in political action but cultural change. And by cultural change, certain intellectuals meant to tear out Confucianism root and branch. The New Culture Movement popularized the radically democratic and anti-Confucian sentiments first broached by a few thinkers in the late Qing. This is not to say most Chinese—even most young, educated Chinese—agreed that there was nothing at all good in Confucianism. Most people continued to have some respect for the values of filial piety, benevolence, and loyalty. But not if such notions conflicted with new values of democracy, egalitarianism, and science. New Culture intellectuals were cosmopolitans. Chen Duxiu, for example, praised the French Revolution. He had no more respect for the nationalism and imperialism of Western nations than he had for Chinese chauvinism. But he thought that Westerners had done a better job of encouraging innovation and individualism.

Chen founded his journal *New Youth* in 1915 as a response to Yuan Shikai's monarchical movement. "All persons," he wrote, "are equal. Each has the right to be independent, but absolutely no right to enslave others nor any obligation to make himself servile." *New Youth* soon achieved a monthly circulation of 16,000, while hundreds of smaller journals were started over the next few years to convey similar messages of social progress and personal liberation. Many students were ready to hear that they themselves, not their fathers, should be choosing their own spouses, and that free marriage was part of any modern social order.

Chen argued that Yuan's monarchical movement rested on the superstitious and backward beliefs of the general population. Confucianism, teaching the morality of social hierarchy and patriarchalism, was incompatible with democracy, for "Confucianism and the Chinese monarchical system possess an inextricable relationship." Chen was an optimist, believing in the progress of civilization. But looking at current conditions, Chen concluded, "although the majority of the Chinese people say they are not opposed to the Republic, their minds are in fact stuffed full of the old thought of the imperial age." And so, "To firmly secure the Republic today, we must totally wash the old thought of anti-republicanism clean away from the minds of the Chinese people."

The institutional basis for the New Culture Movement was twofold, one leg in Peking University and other schools in Beijing and one leg in the Shanghai publishing industry.

In the interstices of warlord China after Yuan's death, a degree of protection was afforded radical critics. Chen became dean at Peking University. Another significant cultural change of the 1910s was a turn toward using the vernacular to replace classical styles of writing. Another Peking University professor, Hu Shi, first made his mark as an advocate of the vernacular—for Hu a matter of clarity in writing and thinking, but for Chen Duxiu equally a matter of overthrowing the old culture.

Not everyone agreed that the correct response to the failure of republican institutions was to turn to cultural reform. Sun Yat-sen organized a new Chinese Revolutionary Party in 1914, attracting some of the old members of the National Alliance to swear personal fealty to him. They were able to establish a government in Guangzhou in 1917, though Sun soon had to retreat to Shanghai. There he further honed his message and bided his time. Sun believed that the only route to change depended on direct political action but that some elements of traditional Confucianism were worth preserving.

The years of warfare across Europe from 1914 to 1918 supported both radical and conservative critiques of Western civilization. While radicals wished to separate out universal ideals from bloody practice, conservatives argued that it was those very ideals—excessive individualism, science pursued at any cost, and outright materialism—that proved the moral bankruptcy of the West. Initially, no Chinese saw a particular reason to support one group of imperialist aggressors over another. However, as French and British citizens went off to be slaughtered in the hundreds of thousands, the Allies realized that Chinese labor could help keep their factories, construction, and transport moving. The Beijing warlord government agreed to send about 150,000 Chinese contract workers to Europe between 1916 and 1918, where a handful of educated Chinese students was on hand to help with translation issues. A number of the workers and students became Communists during their sojourn in Europe. In 1917, pressured by the United States as well as Japan, China declared war on Germany.

The Allied victory in 1918 was thus a Chinese victory too. The New Culture intellectuals were jubilant, seeing in this result nothing less than the victory of good over evil. The president of Peking University, Cai Yuanpei, who had himself studied in Germany, exulted that the Allied victory represented the victory of mutual aid (an anarchist-tinged ideal) over sheer might; transparency over secret plots; democracy over autocracy; and even racial justice over oppression. The Japanese-educated librarian of Peking University, Li Dazhao, wrote: "To put it in a word, democracy is the only power operating in the world today, and the present era is the era of democracy." For men like Chen, Cai, and Li, democracy was not merely a political system but an entire way of life, one that guaranteed that workers, peasants, and women would have an equal chance to develop their characters. Li understood the Bolshevik Revolution in Russia as the logical extension of the Allied victory over Germany. That is, the bourgeois democracy of countries like Britain and the United States had been a significant step forward from an earlier aristocratic social system; in turn, the workers' cooperatives of Russia were now creating an even truer form of democracy that was coming to China.

Utopian longings were a natural response to the continuing disintegration of traditional society. Insofar as Chinese society had held together throughout the Qing dynasty, the means by which it did so were no longer available after the turn of the twentieth century. Instead, a new language of citizenship, equality, and democracy spoke of the political and social incorporation of previously downtrodden groups. Over the course of the "long 1911 Revolution" students, merchants, workers, soldiers, and women all demanded inclusion. The revolution did not immediately build institutions capable of dealing with the challenges facing China—imperialism, agrarian stagnation, poverty, and the like—but it fostered creative approaches and a vibrant if frustrated civil society. Thus limped forward the Republic of China, at least in the minds of its new citizens.

5. *The Rise of Nationalism and Revolutionary Parties, 1919–1937*

JAMES CARTER

ON May 4, 1919, thousands of university students gathered at Tiananmen, the Gate of Heavenly Peace, in Beijing. For 500 years, this gate had served as the entryway to the Forbidden City, home of China's emperors in the Ming and Qing dynasties. The Qing's last emperor still lived behind its walls, but the protesters were not concerned with him. The students wanted to save their nation.

China had joined the Allies in World War I expecting to be repaid by having German colonial holdings—centered around the city of Qingdao—returned to Chinese sovereignty, and US President Woodrow Wilson's (vague) promises of national self-determination reinforced this expectation. While the Allied victory in 1918 seemed to assure this outcome, the peace conference in Versailles dashed Chinese hopes. Bowing to *realpolitik*, Britain, France, and the United States agreed to allow Shandong to remain under Japanese control as it had since the start of the war. Japan's military power—it had defeated Russia in war just fifteen years earlier—gave it political clout, whereas China remained internally divided and militarily weak. Under Japanese pressure, US President Wilson, French President Clemenceau, and the British Prime Minister broke their promises to China and allowed Shandong to remain in Japanese hands.

News of the betrayal reached China on May 1. University students, at the forefront of cultural and political change in China, reacted by organizing demonstrations against Western imperialism, Japanese aggression, and China's weakness in the face of both. Beginning around 1915, students had responded to the failure of the new Republican government to unify and govern China with the New Culture Movement, seeking to renew China's strength by adopting and adapting ideas from the West—especially science and democracy. Rejecting, partly or completely, traditional Chinese values like Confucianism, leaders of this movement embraced the West as a model for modernizing China's society, culture, and politics.

Versailles changed that. By handing over Chinese territory to Japan, the Allies demonstrated that China still could not fully trust the Western imperial powers. China had overthrown its monarchy, established a nominal republic, and sent its citizens to Europe to support the war effort. Many in China expected that these actions would make China an equal member of the family of nations, ending decades of humiliation. Yet after the war had been won the Allied powers again compromised China's sovereignty on the basis of imperial military power (this time Japan's).

Instead of a total embrace of Western ideas, Chinese intellectuals after May 4 took a more nuanced approach, still rejecting traditional Chinese culture (which had, in their view, led China to weakness and domination by foreign powers) but wary of the goodwill of Western imperialists.

The journal *New Youth* exemplified the ideals of the May Fourth and New Culture Movements. *New Youth* was founded in Shanghai in September 1915 by Chen Duxiu, and moved with Chen to Beijing in 1917 when he was recruited to the faculty of Peking University. After 1917, when Lenin's Bolshevik Revolution succeeded in Russia, *New Youth* increasingly advocated Marxism alongside science, democracy, and the usage of the vernacular in place of classical Chinese. *New Youth* also showcased the work of many of China's most prominent and progressive writers—including Lu Xun.

The literature of the May Fourth era is among its most enduring legacies, and Lu Xun (born Zhou Shuren) is its most prominent representative. Three of his short stories illustrate his work's themes and goals: "Diary of a Madman," "Medicine," and "The True Story of Ah Q." "Diary of a Madman," published in *New Youth* in 1918 (before the May Fourth Movement, and so more properly included in the New Culture Movement), takes the form of a "found text," a diary discovered by a young man sent to a village to care for his brother, who has gone mad. With growing paranoia and horror, the diary reveals the brother's discovery that his friends and neighbors, and eventually all Chinese people, are and have been cannibals. The "Madman" discovers the command "eat people" written between the lines of Confucian morality texts. As he explores further, he comes to understand that Chinese society has been devouring its young for millennia, and anyone who discovers and objects to this practice becomes the next meal. Assigning these cannibalistic values to Confucianism, Lu Xun makes a powerful metaphor out of the New Culture Movement's critique of traditional Chinese culture: that it consumes youth, innovation, and individualism, relying instead on ancient texts and customs.

The same themes animate "Medicine," published in *New Youth* in 1919. Just a few pages long, the story focuses on two interrelated deaths: a revolutionary executed by the government, and a young boy sick with tuberculosis. In the opening scene, the sick boy's desperate father tries a traditional remedy: feeding his son a bun soaked in human blood. That blood, of course, flowed from the revolutionary's veins, pierced by the firing squad's bullets. By the story's end, the two boys—one from the Hua family, the other from the Xia family—are buried next to one another, the family names on adjacent tombstones spelling out *huaxia*, a traditional name for China. One killed by reactionary politics and the other by outmoded beliefs, the two boys' deaths represent China's future unless it rejects both.

Lu Xun's best-known story is perhaps the most famous piece of modern Chinese literature: "The True Story of Ah Q," a thinly veiled allegory of the 1911 Revolution and its failures that transcends its immediate context by parodying traditional Chinese culture and politics. Published serially in 1921 and 1922, the story describes the life of a poor villager who claims descent from Confucius himself—or at least from ancient Chinese nobility—but cannot document any of his claims. He mocks others in his village for being low-class, and is routinely beaten up for his insults. Desperate to redeem his reputation, Ah Q takes to slapping himself in the face, declaring this a "great victory" and congratulating himself for delivering the blow. Misogynist, uneducated, and unemployed, Ah Q embodies the worst aspects of Chinese society during this era. Yet he is also a victim. Rejected from participating in the revolution, he finds himself convicted of a crime he did not commit and then executed as an example to others. The assembled crowd of onlookers disdains Ah Q for his crime and his unenlightened nature, and mocks him for failing to sing the opera arias considered customary for a condemned criminal. In the story's memorable final scene, the observers are compared to ravenous wolves who devour Ah Q.

Typical of May Fourth literature, the story of Ah Q depicts Western goods and ideas throughout the story as ambiguous. When the revolution comes to the village, one of its two leaders is a member of the local village elite and the other is an "imitation foreign devil," a young student recently returned from study abroad (apparently in Japan), who gets his name because he dresses in Western clothes and advocates foreign values and ideas. Ah Q deems the revolution too risky and refuses to join, then changes his mind when its success seems imminent, but is barred from joining because of his lack of ideological purity. Lu Xun criticizes both the Chinese people and the revolutionary leaders, as both put ideology and self-interest above the good of their country. He shows reliance on Western ideas to be promising, but dangerous—as China discovered at Versailles. Lu Xun also addresses the interaction of Chinese and Western culture in Ah Q's name, which is written with a Chinese character and a Latin letter: "阿Q." His surname Ah has no real meaning and is usually used either to represent the sound in transliterating foreign words or as a prefix of endearment. It is rarely used as a surname or given name. The "Q" is written, even in the original Chinese text, with the Latin letter "Q." Numerous reasons have been suggested for this choice, such as that it makes Ah Q both anonymous and, thus, very malleable as a character, as well as exotic and strange.

The tension between Chinese and Western models for the intellectuals of the May Fourth Movement is captured in Ding Ling's story "Miss Sophie's Diary." Ding Ling's protagonist, Miss Sophie, encounters nationalism, revolution, and modernization, just as Lu Xun's characters did. Gender, however, also shaped her experience. Lu Xun addressed questions of gender relations and sexuality occasionally: Ah Q attempted to rape a nun who he perceived to have slighted him (and he later begged her to marry him), but these depictions tend to be broad attacks on traditional Chinese culture, including its sexism. Ding Ling takes a much more personal and individual angle on these issues through Miss Sophie, a twenty-something student who is sexually adventurous yet also confused and curious. Readers of *Fiction Monthly*, which published "Miss Sophie's Diary," may have been shocked to read about masturbation, bisexuality, and premarital sex in the story. Among the many challenges Miss Sophie confronts in the story is a choice between two men, a choice that maps closely onto political debates facing China. One of Miss Sophie's suitors, a Chinese man named Wei, is attentive and romantic, with good prospects and eager to fill the role of a conventional husband. Sophie, though, mocks his attention and finds herself drawn to another man, Ling Jishi. Ling is physically attractive, but treats her poorly. He is also from Singapore—a British colony with a largely

Chinese population. The comparison between the weak traditionally minded Wei and the foreign-influenced Ling is a metaphor for the choices facing China: neither was satisfying, and in the end Sophie was doomed either way. Unlike Lu Xun, though, Ding Ling's characters were drawn primarily as human beings, not as metaphors. Sophie's inability to find satisfaction in her personal relationships is partly a commentary on China's dilemma between its traditional culture and Western imperialism, but mainly the inability of the Chinese culture to accommodate a woman who defies conventional social roles. Ding Ling's experience as a woman taking part in the progressive politics of the time was complicated: the revolutionary movement had put women's issues—including access to education, equality before the law, and an end to footbinding—near the top of their political agenda. Yet, women were rarely part of the leadership of revolutionary parties. When conflict arose, "women's issues" were frequently postponed or de-emphasized in favor of concerns associated more closely with class or nation.

The May Fourth and New Culture Movements left powerful legacies of literature, poetry, and intellectual ferment. The style and content of this new literature charted a new course for Chinese culture, and even the language itself changed, as May Fourth writers popularized the use of vernacular language, a movement that had been gaining momentum since the nineteenth century. ("The True Story of Ah Q" was the first story to be widely published that was written entirely in the vernacular.) For the first time in centuries, the written Chinese language corresponded to the way people spoke.

China's urban modernity

Though fictional, Miss Sophie illustrated the mixing and merging of modernity and Western influence with traditional ideas of Chinese culture. Although most of the country (perhaps 95 percent of the population) was rural, coastal metropolises were home to millions of people and were a window into global trends and ideas. It was no surprise that the May Fourth demonstrations occurred in Beijing, the political center of the nation. Ports like Tianjin, Canton, and Xiamen (Amoy) had long histories as hubs for foreign trade. But by the 1920s there was simply no place in China like Shanghai.

Guidebooks to the city were written for foreign tourists, and overflowed with hyperbole. Shanghai was called the "Paris of the East," the "New York of the West," and even "the most cosmopolitan city in the world." The buildings along the Bund—Shanghai's waterfront on the Huangpu River—were the tallest in Asia. Exemplifying the wealth and power of European institutions in semi-colonial China were buildings such as the British Consulate, the Hong Kong and Shanghai Banking Corporation, the Shanghai Club, the Cathay Hotel, and the Customs House. Nanjing Road connected the Bund to the Shanghai Race Club, where horse racing provided a focal point of life in Shanghai for many foreign and local residents.

Shanghai's unique status as a bridge between Chinese and foreign communities fueled its political, cultural, social, and commercial success and importance. In the 1920s, Shanghai's population approached 3 million—about 90 percent of it Chinese—with the city itself behind equally divided between foreign- and Chinese-controlled districts. Foreign concessions such as the International Settlement, dominated by British and American interests, and the French Concession, operated their own governments, police forces, and public works. While not technically colonies, those living in them operated under extraterritoriality. The roaring twenties were just that in Shanghai: with the world at a peak of free trade policies, the Chinese market just upstream from Shanghai offered seemingly limitless opportunities. Hollywood movies, American automobiles, and dozens of dancehalls, bars, and restaurants all tried to capture some of the money flowing through Shanghai. And not all of Shanghai's enterprise was legal. Some estimate that Shanghai was home to more prostitutes per capita than any other city on earth, and the Green Gang crime syndicate effectively governed many parts of the city. Viewed from outside China, Shanghai's reputation of dance clubs, mobsters, hostesses, and the exotic Orient made it a required stop on many tourist agendas. For many foreigners, Shanghai *was* China.

But of course, Shanghai was unlike anywhere else in China, and for Chinese the city's place on the edge of many cultures, nationalities, and jurisdictions had different consequences. Many Chinese took part in the jazz scene and bet on the horse races, but others had more political agendas. Revolutionary movements had found shelter in Shanghai as early as the nineteenth century, when Zou Rong had published his anti-Qing tract *The Revolutionary Army* from Shanghai. With political chaos spreading across China in the 1920s, the protection and stability of the foreign concessions became even more appealing. The protection of foreign jurisdictions combined with the easy access to foreign goods and ideas should make it unsurprising that Shanghai was a center of avant-garde and progressive politics and culture among Chinese intellectuals. Ding Ling wrote "Miss Sophie's Diary" in Shanghai. Lu Xun moved to the city and spent his last years there. For leftist politics, the city was especially important. As China's industrial center it had the largest concentration of workers, and was perhaps China's only city with a Marxist urban proletariat. By the 1930s, there were some 2,500 manufacturing plants in Shanghai, the most numerous of which were textile mills (cotton and silk), but also rice- and flourmills, canneries, and cigarette factories. It was estimated that half of all the cotton spindles operating in China at that time were in Shanghai.

Founding the Communist Party

This concentration of industry made Shanghai a center of labor politics in China, the leaders of which were spurred to action during the May Fourth era. Activists sought a solution that was neither traditionally Chinese nor fully Western. Marxism, which had first arrived in China late in the nineteenth century, seemed to fit the bill. The *Communist Manifesto* had first been translated into Chinese around 1899, and the revolutionary movements that eventually overthrew the Qing dynasty included many strands of Marxism. Anarchism, especially, was powerful in the first decades of the twentieth century. In the years following the 1917 Bolshevik Revolution in Russia, international socialism began to find more adherents in China. This intensified when Russia withdrew from World War I and Lenin proclaimed the anti-imperialist policies of the new Soviet Union.

Clustered around Peking University, early Marxists included the editors of *New Youth,* Li Dazhao and Chen Duxiu, who organized a Marxist study group at Peking University. Mao Zedong, though not prominent at this stage, was also a member of the Peking University group.

The Chinese search for national strengthening coincided with the Soviet desire to export revolution. When the Communist International (the Comintern) set out to develop a Marxist revolution in China, it quickly identified the Peking University group. Using the extraterritorial protection of Shanghai, in July 1921 the Comintern agent Grigorii Voitinksy helped facilitate a meeting in the French Concession that established the Chinese Communist Party (CCP). The meeting was an unusual one: Li Dazhao, generally seen as the founder of the Party, was not present. Chen Duxiu became Party Secretary, working closely with Dutch Comintern agent Henk Sneevliet (known as "Maring"). Among the fifty-three delegates was Mao Zedong, one of two representatives from Hunan.

The Comintern influence on the early CCP was enormous. Comintern agents insisted that the CCP pursue an orthodox Marxist formula for revolution in China. This meant the Party intended to follow Marx's prediction that revolution would be based on the proletariat and also that a "bourgeois" revolution was required to bring national industrial capital to power *before* the socialist revolution could take place. This strategy had several implications for China. First, the base for organizing the revolution was to be the large coastal cities, especially Shanghai, with the most developed industrial sectors. Second, because China had yet to extensively industrialize, revolution there was not imminent. Third, the focus on urban, industrial workers meant that the peasantry (the great majority of China's population) was not to be directly involved in the revolution, at least not yet.

To help bring about the bourgeois revolution that would precede the Communist one, the Comintern endorsed a policy of cooperation with other revolutionary parties. In China this meant the Nationalist Party, or Kuomintang (KMT), which had grown out of Sun Yat-sen's Revolutionary Alliance (*Tongmenghui*), the driving force of the 1911 revolution. The Revolutionary Alliance had brought together numerous anti-Qing groups around the turn of the century. After the revolution, the Alliance merged with several other organizations and was recast as a political party, establishing the Kuomintang in the summer of 1912.

The KMT was soon a victim of its own success. The Party won the great majority of seats in the first republican elections, in 1912, leaving Song Jiaoren (along with Sun, the leading political figure in the Party) in a position to establish a government. The Party's success, though, threatened Yuan Shikai's plans for autocracy, and Yuan had Song assassinated in March of 1913. Shortly thereafter, the KMT was banned. As the Republic crumbled, and Yuan himself died, the KMT and Sun Yat-sen worked to rebuild the Party, once again as a rebel organization rededicated to the ideal of republican revolution.

Disillusioned by the failure of the 1911 Revolution to produce an effective government, Sun tried to learn from the lessons of the past. He remained committed to his "Three Principles of the People"—nationalism, socialism, and democracy—and was keenly aware of the need for a military force to support the Party. Sun had yielded the presidency to Yuan Shikai in 1912 because, in part, Sun's Revolutionary Alliance had no military capability, relying on Yuan and his Beiyang Army to carry out the revolution.

Sun's need for resources and military capability matched well with the Comintern's abilities to provide them. Sun had reservations about the anti-democratic elements of the Soviet Union's centrally planned economy, but he interpreted Lenin's New Economic Policies as a sign of moderation. Sun—then based in Shanghai—met with Comintern agents in 1923, and issued a statement, suggesting that while the conditions for Communism did not presently exist in China, China (and by implication, the KMT) could rely on Russian support. Sun's vaguely worded endorsement of Russian support—and the Russians' vaguely worded endorsement of the KMT—began an ambiguous relationship that would persist for decades.

Befitting this ambiguity, Comintern support came to play a crucial role for both political parties. The Communists were obviously much ideologically closer to the Soviets, but the KMT was the stronger—and much larger—organization. Yet, the KMT badly wanted Comintern support in order to arm itself. Russian aid was only forthcoming, though, if an alliance could be forged between the Communists and the Nationalists. Sun agreed, and the First United Front was established in 1923. The United Front guaranteed that the two parties would work together to combat imperialism and feudalism, and to promote the idea of a unified Chinese state. All members of the Chinese Communist Party (only a few hundred at this time) were automatically made members of the KMT as well.

Embodying the idea of the First United Front was the Whampoa Military Academy, which opened in May 1924.

The academy was located near Sun's new power base in Canton and enrolled both nationalists and communists. The advisers for the academy, and its funding, were primarily Soviet. Political instruction was central to training a Party army along Leninist lines. Yet most of the cadets were not Communists and the academy's first commandant, Chiang Kai-shek, was among the most anti-Communist of the KMT officers. Tension between CCP and KMT cadets at Whampoa was kept at bay largely because of the unifying figure of Sun Yat-sen and due to the practical benefits that Soviet military training and aid could provide. After decades of trying to build an army with revolutionary capabilities, Sun seemed finally to have the pieces in place to do so.

Warlords

The most immediate objective of Sun's Party was to reunify China, which had fragmented after the death of Yuan Shikai. Although a central government remained nominally in charge, disparate groups of local militarists controlled large swathes of China ranging from a few counties to several provinces. Known as warlords, these men dominated Chinese politics and society for more than a decade, from Yuan Shikai's death in 1916 until the late 1920s. An example of one such warlod is Duan Qirui (1865–1936), who was the most powerful man in China after Yuan's death. Duan's power was largely regional, rooted in military power and patronage. Deriving their strength from local military cliques, warlords sought control over Beijing: whoever controlled the capital could claim to rule the entire country. The warlords who dominated this era were a colorful and diverse group. Some were brutal petty dictators, little more than gang leaders on a grand scale. Others were progressive social reformers, bureaucrats, and would-be emperors. Examining some of the most prominent warlords during this era gives some indication of the range of experience across China, and also the motivation for Sun and his Party to reclaim the power of a central government.

Although the personalities of individual warlords are memorable, it is crucial to bear in mind that the roots of warlordism were structural. Yuan Shikai was himself a ruler with power based on military status and the personal loyalty of his troops. When Yuan died and the focus of that loyalty vanished, China's military and political establishment fragmented. In place of a single national army, three dominant factions, or cliques, emerged, each named for the general geography of its power base. The Anhui clique, led by Duan Qirui, was based in central China's Anhui province. The Zhili clique's power was centered on the province now known as Hebei, headed by Feng Guozhang, the vice-president of the Republic under Yuan Shikai, along with Wu Peifu. Finally, the Fengtian clique, taking its name from the old name for Liaoning province, was Zhang Zuolin's personal army, centered in Manchuria. None of these three cliques was able to govern effectively, partly because they were constantly fighting with one another, both politically and militarily. The central government itself divided between these two factions even before Yuan Shikai died. The presidency went to the weak, unpopular Li Yuanhong following Yuan's death, but real power was held by the vice-president, Feng Guozhang, and the Premier, Duan Qirui. Soon, their two factions came to blows, with Wu Peifu (1874–1939) leading the Zhili armies. Within the

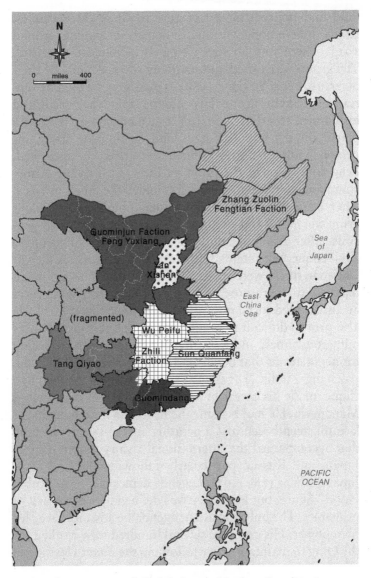

7. How the country was divided (before the Northern Expedition).

fluid and unpredictable structure of these three cliques, China split among various militarists beginning around 1915. There was no such thing as a "typical" warlord. The group was varied and, in many ways, defined by their diversity. Feng Yuxiang (1892–1948) may be seen as representative of the group. His path to power was typical, and his control strictly regional. Yet at moments he became a player on the national stage and, again like many, his personal idiosyncrasies defined the areas he controlled. Feng rose through the ranks of the Qing Beiyang Army, commanded by Yuan Shikai, but joined the rebels in 1911. After being captured and imprisoned, he rejoined Yuan's army's in 1914 and was one of Yuan's most trusted generals. After Yuan's death, Feng rose within the ranks of the Zhili clique, but retained his own independence. A devout Christian (there were rumors that he baptized his troops en masse with a fire hose), he was popular with Westerners and attempted social reforms in areas under his control. He also proved difficult to predict or control, shifting alliances numerous times, and even inviting Sun Yat-sen to Beijing for negotiations that might lead to the unification of China.

Zhang Zuolin (1875–1928), the leader of the Fengtian clique, made his career in northeast China, also known as Manchuria. He had become the head of a local gang in the late nineteenth century, operating in the power vacuum that accompanied the international rivalry among China, Japan, and Russia, particularly following the first Sino-Japanese War (1894–95). Legends depict him as a "Robin Hood" figure, but his career was defined by a clear lack of principles. The only consistent agenda he advanced was his own power. His group of several hundred men worked for the Qing to maintain order following the Boxer Uprising in

1900, and also as mercenaries for the Japanese during the Sino-Russian War (1904–05). When that war ended, Zhang's soldiers were again recognized as part of the Qing army, and were instrumental in keeping the region from seceding following the 1911 Revolution.

Although formally part of the Republic of China, Manchuria acted largely as an independent state in the 1910s and 1920s, and Zhang had himself appointed governor-general of the region. Though this title gave him legitimacy in the Republican hierarchy, his real source of power was his Fengtian Army, which grew to 300,000 strong by the mid-1920s. In a series of wars, he was able to capture Beijing, becoming de facto head of state from 1926 to 1928, and was thus China's internationally recognized ruler. This power, though, was not able to protect him against his Japanese would-be patrons, who arranged for his railroad car to be blown up when they deemed him unlikely to assist their plans for domination in Manchuria.

Numerous other warlords wielded significant local power. Yan Xishan (d. 1960), for example, was a reformer based in Shanxi. Yan outlawed footbinding, prostitution, gambling, and even sleeping late. Another such warlord was Zhang Zongchang (1881–1929), a brutal former bandit leader who kept a harem of women from different countries and made a hobby of splitting the heads of his victims.

Consequences of warlordism

Although the personalities and programs of warlords differed greatly, the consequences of warlordism on rural society (more than 90 percent of China's population) were uniformly dire. The drone of warfare was constant, destroying villages and fields, killing livestock and, of course, people. Boys and men were conscripted into warlord armies, taking them away from their families, but also depriving their village of labor. Desertion was common, yet had mixed consequences. Those who were caught were harshly punished, and even those who succeeded were often drafted again, either into the same army or into rival forces.

The same process of conquest and re-conquest drained peasants' coffers. Desperate for revenue to support social programs, armies, or just greed, warlords heavily taxed many villages, sometimes collecting taxes years in advance. When territory changed hands, the new regime would follow the same procedure, meaning rural families might have paid several years' of taxes to several different warlords. This burden condemned peasants already living on the margins to years of destitution. In a desperate attempt to survive while satisfying the demands of their politicians, peasants often turned away from the traditional food crops they had cultivated in favor of cash crops that would bring higher prices at market. As much as 20 percent of China's arable land was taken up in the production of opium, which could be sold at higher profits but which also reduced the food supply. This conversion of food to cash crops exacerbated the famines that could follow bad weather or military devastation, and the breakdown of central government undermined the relief infrastructure—including a system of granaries that had been a staple of Chinese governance for centuries. Widespread and severe famines were commonplace, including major famines in

1920–21, which left half a million people dead, and another in 1928–30 that killed perhaps 3 million.

Northern Expedition

Since Yuan Shikai's death in 1916, China had been fragmented and weak. In 1917, Sun failed to re-establish the Republic from his base in Canton. This failure, he recognized, was due to his lack of a military force that could regain order. The Whampoa Academy was meant to give the KMT an army that could carry out this plan. In 1922, Sun began planning a "Northern Expedition" that would move the Nationalist Army north to the capital. To facilitate this plan, Sun worked to convince many of the warlords to join the Nationalist cause. It was in 1924, while Sun was in Beijing negotiating with rival warlords to join the Northern Expedition, that he took ill, checking into an American hospital on December 31, 1924. Within ten weeks he was dead of liver cancer.

The loss of a leader challenges any political movement, but Sun's death was particularly damaging for the divided and unstable revolutionary movement. While a nominal truce existed between the Nationalists and Communists, known as the United Front, the agreement understated the differences between the two parties. It also ignored the deep divisions within the Guomindang itself, where Sun's legacy was fiercely contested around two main factions. One camp, led by Wang Jingwei and Sun's widow, Song Qingling, promoted a vision of socialism and state-sponsored capitalism. This left branch of the Guomindang embraced closer cooperation with the Soviet Union and emphasized the third of Sun's Three People's Principles, the People's

Livelihood. The other faction gathered around Chiang Kai-shek and focused on Sun's first two principles— nationalism and democracy—and tolerated the Communists as temporary, yet uneasy, allies. During his lifetime, Sun's stature and connections had obscured these divisions between the two factions; his sudden and unexpected death exposed them quickly and clearly.

Chiang and Wang

The question of succession to Sun Yat-sen revolved around Chiang Kai-shek and Wang Jingwei. Chiang received training at the Qing military academy in Baoding, the Tokyo Military Academy from 1905, and even served in the Imperial Japanese Army 1909–11. He was recruited to the Revolutionary Alliance and following the 1911 Revolution he returned to China to become a founding member of the Guomindang. When the Republic foundered, Chiang, like Sun, fled to exile in the south, working first in Shanghai and then joining Sun in Canton in 1918. It was in 1923 that Chiang established himself firmly in Sun's favor, when he helped Sun to escape assassination by a local warlord in 1923. From that point on, Chiang enjoyed increasingly prestigious appointments, traveling to Moscow in early 1924 to both study Soviet methods and garner greater Soviet support. Following his return from the Soviet Union three months later, he was appointed commandant of the Whampoa Academy.

Three elements in Chiang's biography shaped his political identity. His experience in Japan gave him a strong military training and convinced him of the importance of an effective, centralized military. His time in the Soviet Union proved to him that Soviet-style Communism was unworkable in China. Finally, the instability and chaos of the 1910s and 1920s in China emphasized that a social and political order coordinated by a strong central government was essential if China were to prosper. These three principles—anti-Communism, an effective military, and a strong central government—guided Chiang as he competed for Sun's legacy.

Chiang's rival for Party leadership was Wang Jingwei. Wang's revolutionary credentials were stronger than Chiang's. He had worked actively in the Revolutionary Alliance during the 1910s, and was jailed for plotting the assassination of a Qing prince. Wang was among Sun's closest advisers for the next two decades, holding several positions in the Guomindang's revolutionary government in Canton. Whereas Chiang Kai-shek viewed communism as the greatest threat to China's stability, Wang Jingwei saw Western imperialism as the greater danger. For this reason Wang favored the United Front with the Communists.

The contest over Sun's legacy was especially volatile because his teachings were so ambiguous. The third of Sun's Three Principles of the People (*minsheng*) is most literally translated "people's livelihood." Some have interpreted this as economic well-being or prosperity, while others have seen it as socialism. Most of his actions lent themselves to diverse interpretations: his cooperation with the Comintern, for example, could be seen as a principled endorsement of Communism and an acknowledgment that China's revolution fit into the Marxist revolutionary tradition. It could also have been a practical maneuver intended to gain military and financial support. Likewise, Sun's will was contested: some claimed he had planned to deepen ties with the Soviet Union, while others say he was going to renounce communism. In any case, the uncertainty surrounding the Guomindang did not help Sun's dream of reunifying China under the Party's flag. In the years after Sun's death, Chiang was able to outmaneuver Wang to gain control of the Party, although Wang's left faction of the Guomindang remained important for some time.

As commandant of the Whampoa academy, Chiang emphasized his leadership of the National Revolutionary Army as the vital aspect of the Northern Expedition. Speaking on July 9, 1926, to cadets at the academy, Chiang formally launched his campaign to reunify China. Better trained, organized, and equipped than the armies of the warlords resisting them, the KMT forces moved quickly from their base in Canton, wrestling control from the weakened Zhili faction of most of the territory south of the Yangzi river in just about six months. As the center of the revolution moved north, the KMT established its new capital at Wuhan, a traditional crossroads of China where the 1911 Revolution had first broken out. With Chiang and his troops spending a majority of their time fighting in the field, however, the Wuhan capital became largely a base for Wang Jingwei and his KMT left faction.

Shanghai massacre

Continuing his struggle with Wang Jingwei, Chiang Kai-shek now used his success in the Northern Expedition to rid himself of his Communist rivals within the Nationalist party structure. Shanghai was central to any plan for controlling all of China. The CCP was well positioned to exert influence over the metropolis, an industrial center with

China's most highly developed (some would say only) urban proletariat. In addition, Shanghai was a place where foreign domination often provoked nationalist tensions. This was especially vivid in May of 1925 when Chinese workers in a Japanese-owned cotton mill shot a Japanese foreman during a protest. The perpetrators were held in the Shanghai Municipal Police station (the foreign-run police force for the International Settlement) on Nanjing Road, at the heart of the city's commercial district. When protesters demanded the workers' release, violence broke out and on May 30, 1925, police firing into the crowed killed nine protesters, and injured more than a dozen. The shooting catalyzed anti-imperialist sentiment in China, and in the weeks and months that followed, boycotts and demonstrations against foreign imperialism spread across China, some of which were met with further violence.

While this event, known as the May Thirtieth Incident, led to few practical changes, it undermined the position of foreign powers and began the process of undoing or revising the so-called "unequal treaties" of the nineteenth century. It also reinforced Shanghai's status as a center of both foreign power and anti-imperialist resistance; the center of capitalism in China, but also of resistance to capitalism.

As the Northern Expedition began (with the United Front still in effect), the CCP was tasked with delivering Shanghai to the Nationalists. Workers, mobilized and armed by the CCP, defeated Zhili warlord troops and took control of the city. While the Wuhan government (the KMT Left) initially welcomed the CCP's success, Chiang Kai-shek declared the Communist actions "anti-revolutionary." In early April, the KMT declared martial

law in Shanghai, and on April 12—aided by the connections to the Green Gang—KMT troops entered the city and
disarmed the Communists. Many Communists and suspected Communists were killed on April 12 itself, which
began a period of "White Terror" lasting for several weeks,
during which hundreds were arrested on charges of being
or supporting the Communists. Many of those detained
were ultimately executed. Not long after, the KMT Left
also denounced the Communists, emphatically ending the
first United Front.

The "White Terror"—the April 12 Massacre and the
wave of persecution that accompanied it—brought enormous consequences for both the Nationalists and the Communists. For the KMT, Chiang Kai-shek's victory in
Shanghai led him to establish a new capital in Nanjing.
From there he launched the second half of his Northern
Expedition. Within a year, the major areas of political and
economic power came under Nationalist control. Most
were directly governed by the Nationalists; others continued to be ruled through a coalition with local regional
powerbrokers. This ten-year span from 1927 until the full-
scale Japanese invasion in 1937 became known as the
Nanjing Decade.

Nanjing decade

Now China's pre-eminent leader, Chiang Kai-shek, sought
to remake the country according to the lessons he had
learned during his career by establishing a centralized
state, a modern military, and a sense of social order. The
challenges of this approach were manifold, and results were
mixed. Economically, some parts of China thrived,

especially in the Yangzi Delta—Chiang's powerbase surrounding Nanjing and Shanghai. Many indices showed tremendous progress, such as in the tripling of road infrastructure during the Nanjing Decade. The number of students attending high school grew by ten times, and those attending elementary school grew by five times. Factories, imports, and exports all increased. By some measures, China appeared to be recovering from decades of division and war.

Chiang responded to the decades of weak central government by imposing a top-heavy administrative structure and a strong central government presence. There was little democracy in rural areas, with county administrators being appointed directly by the central government. A large proportion of the national budget was spent on the military, reaching as much as 60 percent in the 1930s. The emphasis on a strong state and powerful military edged toward fascism: he modeled his own "blueshirts" on the Italian blackshirts and German brownshirts of their respective fascist parties, eventually implementing in 1934 the "New Life Movement" that he believed would invigorate the country and enable its survival. Combining Christianity, Confucianism, and Fascism, the New Life Movement sought to enforce social cohesion and national unity by requiring people to care for their neighbors, reject individual rewards, follow government instructions, and practice good manners. In language that echoed Mussolini's, Chiang asserted that the New Life Movement would "Thoroughly militarize the life of the people of the entire nation. It is to make them nourish courage and alertness, a capacity to endure hardship and especially a habit and instinct for unified behavior. It is to make them willing to sacrifice for the nation at all times."

The New Life Movement's attempt to regularize daily habits and manners such as spitting and cursing rang hollow for many Chinese. Indeed, most Chinese were concerned only with earning a living and having enough to eat. For example, a 1929 strike by Beijing rickshaw pullers, the bottom of the city's social order, had ended with thousands of arrests and the executions of several leaders. Nor was such social and economic unrest confined to cities. Despite Chiang Kai-shek's dreams of a strong central government, Nationalist control over the countryside remained weak, and Chiang's ability (and interest) in improving economic conditions in rural areas was marginal at best. Decimated by warlordism and its legacies, peasants were driven to rebellion against the social order by famine and poverty. One such rebellion which took place in Hunan in 1927 was observed with interest by a young CCP operative named Mao Zedong.

Mao Zedong

Born in 1893 to a prosperous peasant family, Mao Zedong received a traditional Confucian education before enrolling in a modern school in the years preceding the 1911 Revolution. He joined the Revolutionary Army, but apparently saw no combat. Although exposed to European, American, and Japanese languages and ideas during his schooling, he did not leave his home province of Hunan until 1918. It was at this time that he went to Beijing and worked for a time in the Peking University library. It was during those years that he met Li Dazhao and Chen Duxiu—the co-founders of the CCP—and it was a 1920 discussion with

Chen that led him to embrace Marxism, becoming in 1921 a founding member of the CCP.

From the beginning, Mao felt that the Chinese peasantry— the great majority of the country's population—would be the key to a successful Communist revolution. This stood in contrast to the official CCP policy under Comintern influence, which advocated revolution led by the urban proletariat. Mao began as early as 1925 experimenting with organizing villages against local landlords. In 1926, his seminal "Analysis of the Classes in Chinese Society" identified the peasants as the "semi-proletariat" that would "provide the revolution with its numbers." Although this failed to persuade the CCP leadership, he was able to continue his observations, including the 1927 visit to Hunan. This visit led to his "Report on an Investigation of the Peasant Movement in Hunan," written just weeks before the commencement of the White Terror. Impassioned, bold, violent, and optimistic, the document asserts that violence was necessary to purge rural China of centuries of oppression. It also argued that the peasants would quickly develop the class-consciousness necessary to enable a full-blown Communist revolution.

Mao was not alone in emphasizing the potential of the peasantry, but he was certainly marginalized. This changed when the White Terror all but wiped out the CCP. With its central strategy in shreds, new approaches to revolution were in order. Mao, along with Zhu De (who would become a pivotal military leader for the CCP), led uprisings in the fall of 1927. Still not approved by the CCP leadership, Mao, Zhu, and others established a series of Communist base areas in the Jinggangshan mountains along the Hunan–Jiangxi border and a provisional soviet in 1930.

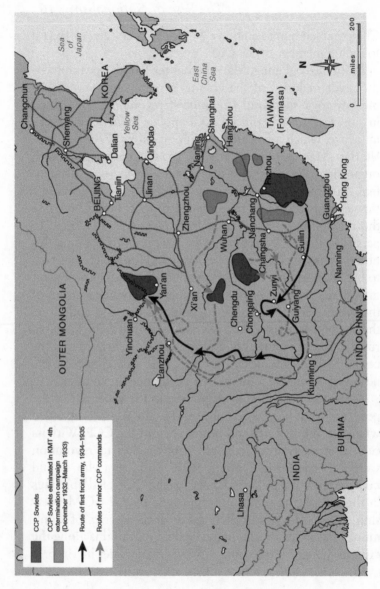

8. Communist base areas and marching routes, 1932–1935.

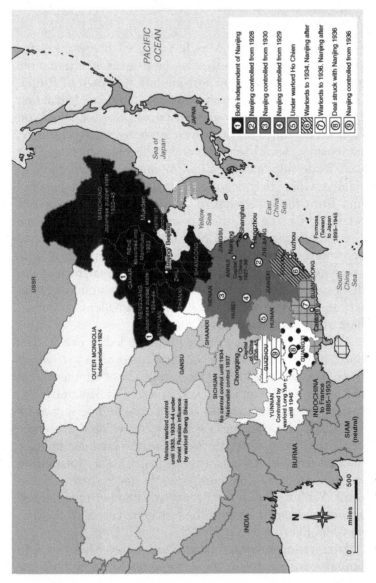

9. China circa the late 1930s.

The Jiangxi Soviet

After the reversals of March 1927, CCP prospects for survival now focused on these base areas in the remote and mountainous region surrounding the town of Ruijin, in Jiangxi province, near the border with Fujian. Led at first by Mao, the Jiangxi Soviet was small, but soon took on many of the functions of a sovereign state, issuing currency, establishing social services, and collecting revenues. The CCP leadership, including its Comintern advisers, came to Jiangxi, where they denounced Mao's tactics and demoted him from the leadership of the Soviet he had helped to establish. Chiang Kai-shek thought he had eliminated the Communist presence in China in 1927, but soon directed enormous resources toward the small Communist base area, starting a series of encirclement campaigns in 1930 designed to exterminate the remaining Communists (similar campaigns were directed against the smaller Communist base areas scattered across China).

Chiang's first three campaigns all ended in defeat. The third of these campaigns ended in September 1931, which by coincidence marked the intensification of another threat to Chiang's government: the Japanese. On September 18, dynamite was detonated close to a railway line owned by Japan's South Manchuria Railway. Accusing the Chinese of attempting to attack the Japanese, the Japanese military flooded troops into northeast China. Chiang, focused on exterminating the Communists, instructed his armies not to resist. Within six months, Manchuria had been proclaimed an independent state with the last Qing emperor, Puyi, as its Chief Executive.

Japanese aggression was not restricted to Manchuria. In January 1932, an anti-Japanese mob killed a Japanese monk in Shanghai, leading to escalating responses that culminated in a Japanese attack on the city, generally considered the world's first large-scale aerial bombardment of civilians. Chinese troops responded, and the battle lasted for a month, with almost all military engagement located within the Chinese parts of Shanghai. Foreigners gathered on rooftops in the International Settlement to watch the fighting, which involved some 150,000 troops. More than 20,000 people were killed, most of them civilians.

This attack in Shanghai occupied Chiang's attention for a time, but despite complaints from many generals, and popular sentiment, Chiang soon redoubled efforts to eliminate the Jiangxi Soviet. A fourth and fifth encirclement campaign took place in 1933. Now mobilizing nearly half a million troops, which was four to five times that of the Red Army, German-advised KMT forces advanced on the CCP stronghold. Although slow, the KMT advance was steady. By the summer of 1934 the Communists had concluded that maintaining a position in Jiangxi was untenable.

The Long March

Facing defeat or surrender, the CCP found a third option. In October 1934, about 100,000 soldiers and support personnel broke through the encircling KMT lines and marched south and west. Nearly half of the Red Army force was lost in the first months of constant fighting. The heavy casualties threatened the CCP's survival, and also called into question the leadership of the Comintern advisers and their allies, especially Otto Braun (1900–74), a German Comintern agent whom Moscow had assigned to work with the

Chinese Communists, and Bo Gu (1907–46), a senior leader within the CCP who had studied in Moscow and was part of an orthodox Marxist faction within the Party known as the 28 Bolsheviks. Disputes over direction, strategy, and tactics were constant, with Mao frequently at odds with the Party Central Committee. At the city of Zunyi, in western Guizhou, the Communist Red Army paused to consider strategy amid these disagreements. After several days of meetings and arguments, the leadership of the army and the Party were reshuffled, with Zhou Enlai emerging as the formal leader, but with Mao poised to take actual leadership. The Soviet-funded Comintern wing of the Party fell out of favor, and from this point forward Mao became the dominant force in the CCP. From Zunyi, the Red Army split into three armies, each seeking a way to link up with other Communist forces scattered across China. A year after their initial breakout, after many thousands of miles, the forces reached Yan'an, in northwest China. While only about 10 percent of the original force that had fled Jiangxi remained, far from the coast, and with Japanese pressure diverting Chiang Kai-shek's attention, the CCP had nevertheless survived and found a place to regroup.

Disentangling the myths from the reality of the Long March is a challenging endeavor. It remains the origin myth of the Communist Party and Mao's leadership, and like all myths its truth is often less important than its meaning. Original accounts that the Red Army marched nearly 10,000 miles have been challenged, though certainly covering 6,000 miles across mountainous terrain is no small feat. Many of the most heroic moments of the Long March have been questioned, and many appear to have been staged or reframed for propaganda value. It seems that Mao and other leaders may have been carried for long stretches of the March. Yet, its significance remains undiminished. Future leaders like Deng Xiaoping, Liu Shaoqi, Zhu Du, and of course Zhou and Mao, took part in the Long March. The myth of the March, as well as the Yan'an years that followed it, provided instant credentials for that generation of leaders as well as an endless source of mythology.

Yan'an spirit

Yan'an was a remote and poor part of a remote and poor province, Shaanxi. But while there, the Communists were able to develop the formula that would ultimately lead them to victory over the KMT. Anti-Japanese sentiment was high across China, and Chiang Kai-shek's refusal to fight the Japanese so that he could focus on attempting to exterminate the CCP was very unpopular. A few months after the CCP's arrival in Yan'an, demonstrations in Beijing (now renamed Beiping to emphasize that the capital—"jing"—had relocated to Nanjing) against the government broke out. Some 6,000 students from Beiping universities clashed with police, demanded an immediate end to the Civil War against the Communists, as well as free speech and other liberal reforms. These December Ninth (1935) demonstrations were the largest of their kind since the May Thirtieth Incident, and embodied the power of anti-Japanese sentiment. Supporting these protests, the CCP was able to identify itself with the patriotic defense of the nation while casting Chiang as weak, perhaps even treasonous.

People now streamed to the Communist base area, including the author Ding Ling who escaped from a KMT prison and went to Yan'an in 1936. Like the Long March, CCP's decade at Yan'an, from the mid-1930s to the mid-1940s, has become part of the fundamental mythology of the Communist Party. This myth celebrates the "Yan'an Way" and the "Yan'an Spirit," that underlay an egalitarian and patriotic community at Yan'an, where the leaders lived, rank and file, in caves alongside the populace, sharing meals, chores, and responsibilities. While later scholarship has questioned this idealized picture, first presented by foreign journalists like the American Edgar Snow, it is certainly true that the Communists during this period successfully identified themselves—not Chiang's Nationalist government—with the cause of Chinese nationalism in the face of Japanese aggression.

The Communists also established a reputation during this period as good neighbors and protectors of rural interests. Unlike warlords, who pillaged the land and abused the people, or the KMT army, which fought other Chinese, the Red Army became known as a friend to peasants, assisting villagers with chores, and defending the nation from Japanese invaders. Movements like December Ninth clearly illustrated the depth of anti-Japanese feeling in China. Yet Chiang remained committed to exterminating the Communists before fighting Japan. "The Japanese are a disease of the skin," Chiang famously said, "but the Communists are a disease of the heart." Determined to destroy the Communist base area in Shaanxi, Chiang flew to Xi'an, the nearest major city to Yan'an, in the fall of 1936.

The general whose troops Chiang intended to lead against the Communists belonged to Zhang Xueliang, the son of Manchurian warlord Zhang Zuolin. Zhang was among the KMT commanders who had been ordered not to fight the Japanese in Manchuria, and had reluctantly surrendered his homeland by withdrawing to Shaanxi. Zhang—whose father the Japanese had assassinated in 1928—remained determined to fight the Japanese armies, and met secretly with Communist leaders such as Zhou Enlai who urged Zhang to join with them against the Japanese. When Chiang arrived in Xi'an, on December 12, Zhang pleaded his case, asking his commander to not attack the Communists, but instead to ally with them against the foreign invaders. When Chiang refused, Zhang Xueliang took a radical and shocking step, kidnapping Chiang Kai-shek and holding him hostage until he agreed to a second United Front to jointly fight Japan.

The kidnapping sparked a crisis that lasted weeks. Zhang Xueliang invited a CCP delegation to Xi'an to discuss what to do. Many in the CCP wanted to execute Chiang for his near-destruction of their party, but eventually it was decided that killing Chiang would damage both the Party and China. Following the arrival of a KMT delegation and intense negotiations, both sides agreed to the Second United Front, allying Communists and Nationalists to resist the Japanese threat. Chiang returned to Nanjing on December 25. Using himself as collateral, Zhang Xueliang flew with Chiang to Nanjing, where he immediately turned himself in for arrest for his role in the kidnapping. Although pardoned, Zhang lived for decades under house arrest.

The year 1937 began, then, with the Communists and Nationalists once again as uneasy allies. Neither side trusted the other, but both maintained the pretense of alliance. For the CCP, the United Front bought them continued time and space to recover from the devastation of the Long March. Chiang worked to solidify his regime, but remained reluctant to confront Japan, which he deemed too strong for China to defeat, even in alliance with the Communists. Yet both sides were not far from being put to the test. In July 1937 Japanese armies began a full-scale invasion of China plunging all of China once again back into war.

6. *The War Years,*
1937–1949

RANA MITTER

The path to war

THE war between China and Japan may have been the single most important event to shape twentieth-century China. The victory of Mao Zedong's Communist Party in 1949 was undoubtedly the most important turning point, but it was the war with Japan that created the circumstances in which the revolution could come to pass. Also crucial was the Chinese civil war that convulsed the country between 1946 and 1949 and allowed the final victory of the Communists. The mere dozen years from 1937 to 1949 saw China go through some of the most profound changes in its era of modern formation.

War broke out in 1937, but the circumstances that caused it were created many decades previously. The early twentieth century saw two major ideological forces in conflict with one another: Chinese nationalism and Japanese imperialism. The Republic established in 1911 was counted a success by few who lived under it or observed it, yet the troubles that defined it ("warlordism from within, imperialism from without") nonetheless helped to create an ever-greater sense, particularly among China's elites, that a more firmly defined nationalist consciousness was essential if China was to become a strong, sovereign state. The establishment of the Nationalist government at Nanjing in 1928 did not bring about that definitive strengthening of the state. However, the government under Chiang Kai-shek did appear to have made some major advances in consolidating its rule, including the regaining of tariff autonomy in 1930.

In contrast, the Japanese state of the early twentieth century seemed solid and well founded to many, benefiting from the modernization of the country that had followed the Meiji Restoration of 1868. However, one part of Japan's modernization was tied to the development of an empire through war; Taiwan became Japanese in 1895 at the end of the first Sino-Japanese War, Japan gained a foothold in Manchuria in 1905 after the Russo-Japanese conflict, and in 1910, Korea was fully annexed and became a Japanese colony. An internationalist note was visible in the policy of the 1920s, but the Great Depression hit Japan hard and turned politics toward greater economic autarky and political control, and away from democracy. As a result, Japanese ambitions on the mainland grew greater, and in 1931, a coup by the locally garrisoned Kwantung Army saw the occupation of Northeast China (Manchuria) and the establishment of the client state of Manchukuo.

Chiang Kai-shek's government did not resist immediately. Chiang knew that China's military capabilities were not strong enough to be able to defeat Japan. However, his government started to plan for a war with Japan that might be under way at some point in the next decade. They established a National Resources Commission, which aimed to make sure that China could maintain a sufficient supply of key metals and fuels in the event of a war. Chiang did not have direct control over large parts of China's armies, and many troops nominally loyal to his government were in fact in the service of rival militarist leaders. Therefore he appointed German military advisers to provide rigorous training for the officers of the Central Army who were eventually expected to be at the forefront of the defense of China in the event of a future war.

Yet Japanese aggression made it harder for Chiang to maintain his policy of open non-resistance to Japan, particularly as he launched powerful campaigns against the Communists in the mid-1930s. The Amo doctrine (1934) made it clear that Japan considered the Asian mainland to be a legitimate area for its own expansion and that it had no intention of ceding to the demands of growing Chinese nationalism. Popular feeling, particularly among Chinese intellectuals and elites, grew against Japan. By the late 1930s, Chiang's government had put out feelers toward a compromise with the Communists on resistance to Japan, although neither side had yet made a formal commitment. Then an event took place that threatened to derail the whole process: on December 12, 1936, Chiang was kidnapped by two warlords, one of his former military allies, the "Young Marshal" of Manchuria, Zhang Xueliang, and Yang Hucheng. At first it seemed that the Communists might weigh in to have Chiang killed, but intervention from Stalin made it clear that this was not on the agenda. If Chiang died, then it was unclear who would take charge in China, but it might be a weak leader who would allow the Japanese to use China as a base for attacking the Soviet Union. After tortuous negotiations, Chiang was released, his reputation if anything raised, and he became now more publicly committed to an alliance with the Communists against the Japanese.

By early 1937, it was clear that war was a distinct possibility, as the Japanese created local alliances with local militarists in north China in an attempt to detach the region from Nanjing's control. Then, on the night of July 7, 1937, there was a minor incident at a bridge at Wanping, near Beiping. Locally garrisoned Japanese troops clashed with Chinese troops, but the incident was soon over and seemed unlikely to balloon further. However, politicians in Tokyo saw it as an opportunity to press for reprisals; in particular, the cession of rights to the crucial railway junctions in and around Beiping. Tensions between the two sides escalated over July and August 1937. On July 11, the Japanese premier Prince Konoye mobilized troops in North China. On July 26 they attacked Beiping and the city fell on July 28, followed by Tianjin on July 30. Realizing that a great conflict was imminent, Chiang legalized the Communist Red Army on August 2.

On August 7, the government held a secret Joint National Defense Meeting, attended by large numbers of China's major leaders. He pointed out that China had no reliable foreign allies, but that further appeasement of Japan would lead to yet more territorial losses, from which it might take decades to recover. He ended the meeting by demanding that those present who supported war with Japan should stand up. Everybody did, including

Chiang's political military rivals such as Wang Jingwei, Liu Xiang of Sichuan province, and Yan Xishan of Shanxi. The decision had been made: China would fight back.

The first phase

Chiang Kai-shek decided that he would have to open up a new front in eastern China. At the center of this decision was the great port city of Shanghai. Shanghai was China's most cosmopolitan and international city, with a large foreign population. It was unlikely that the Chinese could defend their position in Shanghai, but by making a strong defense, they could emphasize how seriously they took the task of resistance.

The battle for Shanghai began on August 13, 1937. On August 14, a horrific incident punctured any complacency left in the local population. Nationalist bombers aimed to hit the *Izumo*, a Japanese warship anchored off Shanghai. Instead, they released their load over Nanjing Road, at the heart of the (neutral) International Settlement area. Over 1,000 people were killed on this "Black Saturday."

Yet if the Japanese thought that they would have an easy time of it, they were mistaken. By early September, some 100,000 Japanese troops had been moved into the area around Shanghai, locked in combat with some 500,000 Chinese forces. The battle continued street by street, causing massive destruction throughout the city. The local British-run newspaper, the *North China Daily News*, reported that "like a nightmare octopus flinging cruel tentacles around its helpless victims, the local hostilities are slowly strangling Shanghai's trade." Finally, in November, the Nationalist troops retreated; they had lost 187,000 men including some 30,000 of the German-trained crack troops who were Chiang's best hope for a revival of the Chinese army.

The Japanese army's failure to make a quick finish in Shanghai served to anger them yet further. This rage manifested itself most terribly in the Chinese capital city of Nanjing in the winter of 1937. The Nationalist government, anticipating the loss of east China, had prepared for the capital to move to Chongqing in southwest China (with the military headquarters at Wuhan until September 1938). However, Tang Shengzhi, the general left in charge of the defense of the city, was left with instructions to defend it to the end. In the end, realizing that he had been left an essentially hopeless task, Tang slipped out of the city. Meanwhile, the civilian population were left to their fate. On December 13, Japanese troops under Prince Asaka entered the capital. A small number of foreigners who had stayed behind in the city hoped to create an International Safety Zone that would protect civilians who stayed inside it. This proved a forlorn hope as the Japanese troops committed horrific acts against the civilian population, murdering and raping them in huge numbers, in an event that would become commemorated as "the Rape of Nanking."

By early 1938, the situation of the Chinese Nationalists was becoming desperate. Then, in April, a morale boost came with the defense of the city of Taierzhuang, in Shandong province. In spring 1938, the Japanese were pushing hard on the city of Xuzhou, a major railhead, but in a fierce battle that lasted from the end of March until April 7 at the small town of Taierzhuang, the Nationalist generals Li Zongren and Tang Enbo carried out a major counter-attack. In the end, some 8,000 Japanese soldiers were killed and the remaining troops were forced to retreat. Chiang urged his generals to step up the attack, but the continuing failings of the Chinese army prevented this once again; China's army was really a conglomeration of interests, not a unified fighting force. Rival militarist leaders controlled huge swathes of China, which were essential to recruitment, food supply, and resource production, and many of the troops on the Nationalist side were responsible to those other leaders. The desire to hoard supplies and not to expend too much of one's own strength meant that Chinese military leaders could offer resistance, as they had done at Taierzhuang, but would often fail to follow up on their initial successes. The Taierzhuang victory was followed by a further Japanese advance, which soon captured Xuzhou.

With the path to central China now lying open to the Japanese, desperation overtook the Chinese leadership. The city of Zhengzhou looked set to fall as the enemy advanced to within 25 miles of the city. Chiang's government turned to a plan that would have been unthinkable at almost all times: to "use water instead of soldiers" (*yi shui dai bing*). In June 1938, they decided to breach the dams on the Yellow River at Huayuankou. This would cause a flood that would inundate much of Henan province, stopping the onward advance of the Japanese army. However, it would have to be done without any warning, meaning that the lives and property of the many millions who lived in the path of the river would be vulnerable. On the night of June 8–9, 1938, thousands of workers were brought to Huayuankou where they dug away at the dyke by hand. By the next morning, the waters had begun to flow, in the words of one officer present, "like 10,000 horses." Some

20,000 square miles of land were covered in water, and in the end some 500,000 locals were either drowned or starved because of the destruction of their land. The Japanese were halted in their advance, however, for the next five months, giving the Nationalists a breathing space for further withdrawal into the interior. The temporary military headquarters at Wuhan (Hankow) finally fell on October 25, 1938.

Stalemate

There then began a period of seeming stalemate. For the capture of Wuhan did not prove to be the next phase of a further Japanese thrust into the interior. Instead, all sides found themselves bogged down in a three-way division: the Japanese in the east, mainly centered on cities and railway lines, the Nationalists in the interior and southwest, and the Communists (of whom more later) in the northwest and parts of central China.

The halting of the Japanese advance in late 1938 meant that the war developed in other ways. From the start of that year, the Nationalist temporary capital at Chongqing was subjected to an increasingly fierce bombing campaign by the Japanese. Over the next three years, there would be repeated raids during the summer months (during the winter, Chongqing was covered by a blanket of fog that made raids much harder to carry out). The air raids were the first major aerial attacks on an Asian city (the only previous major serious attacks anywhere had been in colonial wars and in the Spanish Civil War), and created a whole new ecology of survival. People started to live and work in the same locations, which often had built-in bomb shelters.

When sirens sounded and red balls were hoisted to show an imminent air raid, the population of Chongqing headed for shelters, many of them hewn out of rock. The most memorable raid took place on May 3–4, 1939, when repeated sorties of Japanese bombers caused some 4,000 deaths. In later years, these numbers would be dwarfed by the London Blitz or Tokyo firebombing but at the time they were high tolls indeed, combined with the destruction caused and the feeling of vulnerability to sudden death from the air.

While the Nationalists retreated to China's interior and southwest, their great rivals, the Communists, also tried to develop safe havens of their own. The most prominent was their base at the junction of Shaanxi, Gansu, and Ningxia provinces in northwest China, which they had reached at the end of the Long March of 1934–35. In 1938, Mao wrote his essay "On Protracted War" which argued strongly that China "cannot win quickly." The Communists could consolidate their position, but they were no more able than the Nationalists to strike a decisive blow against the Japanese.

One figure who was increasingly concerned with the turn of the war was Wang Jingwei. Wang was a controversial political figure, with a long history in the Nationalist (Guomindang) party. Originally he had been a close associate of Sun Yat-sen during the years after the 1911 Revolution, but he had lost out to Chiang Kai-shek in the struggle for the Party leadership after Sun's death. By the mid-1930s, Chiang had placed him in elevated but powerless positions within the Party, and in 1937 he had joined the consensus for the war against Japan. But by 1938, he was becoming convinced that the war was a terrible error. He saw the destruction being visited upon Chongqing and other cities in "Free China." He also observed China's lack of formal allies in the face of the vastly superior Japanese forces; and he noted with alarm the United Front between the Nationalists and Communists, regarding the latter as essentially tools of the USSR. He also nursed a strong personal ambition, never having forgiven Chiang for (as he saw it) usurping his position. These different motivations made him vulnerable to approaches from a rival power.

By the middle of 1938, secret negotiations had begun between members of the "Low-Key Club," Chinese officials who wanted to keep open the option of a negotiated peace, and Japanese officials. The Japanese hope was to bring over Chiang Kai-shek to their side, but this proved impossible. Hopes turned instead to Wang Jingwei, who had always been perceived as more sympathetic to Japan (though he had always been staunch in his advocacy of Chinese nationalism during the 1920s and 1930s). In December 1938, Wang responded to the blandishments of the Japanese side. He took a tortuous route, arriving first in Kunming in southwest China, and from there making the journey across the border to Hanoi in French Indochina. Rumors swirled about his intentions. On December 22, Prince Konoye, the Japanese prime minister, gave a press conference at which he declared, in vague terms, that Japan was making a commitment to China to pursue friendship, economic cooperation, and anti-communism. On New Year's Eve, a Hong Kong newspaper published a telegram with Wang Jingwei's declaration that Konoye's statement provided the grounds for negotiation.

Over the next two years, the Japanese made repeated attempts to obtain cooperation from Chiang Kai-shek. Only when it became clear that that cooperation would not be forthcoming did they finally authorize Wang Jingwei to establish his own government (heavily influenced by its Japanese sponsors) in Nanjing, in March 1940. It would survive until the end of the war (unlike Wang, who died in 1944), but it had little real autonomy.

However, another political grouping began to make much greater strides during the same year. In February 1940, Mao released one of his most important speeches, "On New Democracy," which laid out the blueprint for a cross-class alliance to defeat the Japanese and create a new society. Its tone was notably emollient, seeking to downplay ideas of class struggle and emphasize the CCP's desire to unite different groups within Chinese society. Within the base area in Shaanxi-Gansu-Ningxia, with its capital at Yan'an, new experiments in government were tried out by the Communists, including fairer tax burdens and the institution of popular participation in local elections.

The global war

After a series of near-defeats, the Chinese resistance continued through 1940 and into 1941. The start of operation Barbarossa in Europe made it clear that the war at the other end of the Eurasian landmass was expanding, although there was no connection yet between the European war and the Chinese one. For that connection to be made, Chiang was aware, as was Winston Churchill in Britain, that one decisive factor was needed that could promise

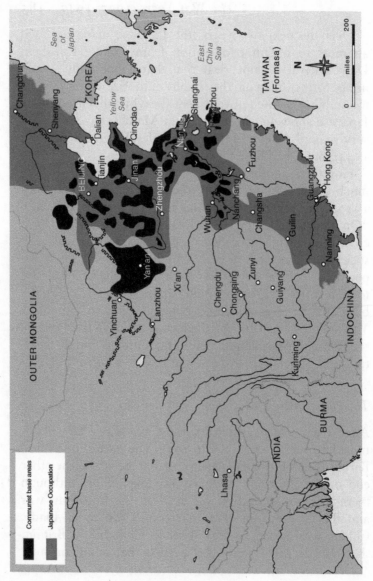

10. China at the end of World War II.

victory rather than just resistance against Japan: the entry of the United States.

At the start of the war, this seemed unlikely. American sympathies were with China rather than Japan, but this was a very long way from a commitment to participation in the conflict. But by 1940, the Roosevelt administration had become increasingly concerned about Japan's aggression in the Pacific. Increasing amounts of financial aid were made to China in 1941, at the same time that Washington and Tokyo engaged in ever-more desperate diplomacy. The United States insisted that Japan must withdraw its forces from China. Japan was equally insistent that it would not do so, and in October, General Tojo took over as prime minister and heightened preparations for war. On December 2, the imperial conference in Tokyo took the decision to attack the United States on December 8.

In the early morning of December 8 (December 7 US time), two waves of Japanese bomber aircraft attacked the vessels of the US Pacific Fleet at Pearl Harbor in Hawaii. Some 2,400 Americans were killed, and 1,100 wounded. Japanese attacks on Malaya, Thailand, and the Philippines quickly followed. President Roosevelt spoke of a "day which will live in infamy" as Chiang Kai-shek made a public declaration of a "common battle." Within three days Hitler had also declared war on the United States, making the conflict truly global.

From Pearl Harbor on, China had formal allies, the United States and the British Empire, in its war against Japan. Yet this alliance would prove a very uneven one, not just because of the mismatch in the resources between the powers involved, but also because of the differing understandings of what the alliance actually meant.

For the United States, the formal alliance with China was a means to "keep China in the war," through the provision of financial assistance but not American combat troops. China was a welcome partner in the war against Japan, and nominally an equal ally. The fact that China was a non-Western nation helped to give credibility to the idea that the war was genuinely a battle for global freedom. Churchill, in contrast, was always much more cynical about the real value of China, his attitude shaped by his strong antipathy to non-European liberation movements. However, China was regarded by the Western allies as a secondary or tertiary concern at best, with the "Europe first" strategy placing more emphasis on the defeat of Nazi Germany before Imperial Japan. There was also a strong sense among the Western commanders that the Americans were coming in to rescue the Chinese, and that the latter were victims rather than actors with any control over their own fate.

This was not how the Chinese government saw the situation. Their perception was that they had been attacked in 1937, and resisted for four and a half years without any significant external assistance. Aid and assistance to the Chinese, they felt, was only their due after their own polity had been brought to the edge of destruction. China had already offered robust opposition to the Japanese well beyond what most observers would have expected. Furthermore, Chiang did not accept that the destiny of China had to be a secondary priority. Indeed, while from a geostrategic point of view it was clearly necessary to prioritize theatres of war, it was also understandable that those who led the less favored theatres might not simply accept their place in the queue. Western leaders could not reasonably expect that Chiang Kai-shek would agree to downplay the fate of China without any concern for his own position.

These mismatched expectations would dog the relationship between China and its Western allies through most of the war. They were expressed most vividly in the relationship between Chiang Kai-shek and the American chief of staff sent to command the Chinese armies, General Joseph W. Stilwell. Stilwell had gone on previous tours of duty in China, and had a high regard for the fighting capacity of Chinese soldiers, but an extremely low opinion of the efficacy of the Chinese generals and officers. The initial relationship between Chiang and Stilwell was fairly warm, but subsequent events would quickly sour the atmosphere between them.

In February 1942, the Japanese attacked Burma. The Allies had not expected this campaign, but the success of the initial assault on Southeast Asia emboldened Japanese military commanders to expand their aim. If Burma was captured, it meant that the Burma Road that supplied Nationalist China would be cut off. At this point, the Allies took rather different views about what their response should be. The British were concerned that Burma should not become a base for an attack on British India; the Chinese were equally concerned that it should not become easier to attack the Nationalist base areas in southwest China. Both sides preferred to maintain an essentially defensive position in Burma, and to give up southern Burma, including the capital, Rangoon, as lost.

Stilwell took a very different view, advocating a bold strategy to push back against the Japanese through the whole of Burma, and trying to recapture Rangoon: "I have a hunch the Japs are weak," he noted in his diary on

March 9, 1942. Chiang was extremely wary about the idea of an aggressive thrust against the Japanese; after all, it was mostly Chinese and British troops who would have to bear the brunt of the attack. But with misgivings, he gave Stilwell his head. Unfortunately, Stilwell's conviction that the Japanese were weak was not borne out by the reality, as they surrounded the city of Toungoo, leading Chiang to advocate retreat. Stilwell refused this order, writing diary entries that blamed the Chinese and the British for refusing to stand firm. After two months of increasingly unsuccessful attempts to retake southern Burma, Stilwell finally decided on May 5 to walk out of the jungle. A fortnight later, he arrived with his party in Imphal, in British India. But while Stilwell's own party escaped alive, their Chinese counterparts were less fortunate: some 25,000 Chinese were killed or injured with some 10,000 British and Indian troops in the same position (versus 4,500 Japanese). Stilwell declared at a press conference that the retreat from Burma had been "as humiliating as hell." But privately, he blamed Chiang Kai-shek for, as he saw it, refusing to support his bold strategy.

Early in 1942, Chiang made a trip that failed in its immediate political effect but the symbolic importance of which was highly significant: he visited India and called on the major independence leaders of the country, Jawaharlal Nehru and Mohandas K. Gandhi. The leaders of the Congress party had been outraged that the Viceroy of India, Lord Linlithgow, had committed India to the war effort without consultation with them, and had withdrawn from participation in government, as well as refusing to endorse the war. Chiang hoped to persuade them to change their minds. The endorsement of India's freedom movement for the Allied war effort would have been a great boost for China, and Chiang in turn was keen to make it clear that he fully supported the independence movement. Churchill was extremely unenthusiastic about the idea of Chiang's visit, and, in particular, tried to prevent him meeting Gandhi. In the end, the results were less transformative than Chiang would have wished. He and Nehru knew and respected each other, but Chiang's arguments cut little ice against Nehru's conviction that non-cooperation with the British imperial government was necessary. A later meeting between Chiang and Gandhi produced even less agreement between the two leaders. Still, this was an important moment; on the soil of British India, the leader of the sovereign Chinese nationalist government was meeting two of the most important advocates of liberation from empire. Chiang publicly declared his support for Indian independence in a radio broadcast, yet another irritation to Churchill. It was clear that the anti-imperialist element of the war could not now be suppressed if it were to have credibility.

The alliance with the Western powers could not, in the short term, address one of the most fundamental problems facing wartime China: its isolation. After Pearl Harbor, Nationalist China could no longer depend on the Burma Road or the border with French Indochina, both of which had been cut off by the Japanese. There was also a limit to the amount of relief that could be flown over the Burma "Hump" from India. The government was forced to maintain large standing armies with limited capacity to feed and pay them. The economic situation was significantly worsened by the government's decision to print money, leading to ever-greater rates of inflation; between 1941 and 1944, prices rose by 10 percent or more per month. In 1941, the government began policies of grain requisitioning to try and keep the armies fed. The policy did reduce inflation because the government was no longer buying so much grain on the open market. However, the burden of the war effort was now being placed even more decisively on the shoulders of the farmers in the countryside.

This burden led to a major tragedy in the central Chinese province of Henan in 1942 where many factors had been coming together. The province was under very loose government control, with large parts occupied by the Japanese. Worse, the rains failed to fall and the crop yield was only some 10 to 20 percent of what it had been in previous years. Yet government officials still demanded that the grain tax must be paid in kind (rather than highly devalued paper currency). Famine began to sweep the province. "During our trip," wrote one government inspector, "starving people were digging up grass roots, taking leaves, and stripping bark from trees." Although food was available in the nearby provinces, the authorities in those provinces refused to allow it to be sent to Henan. In total, some 2–3 million people died from the famine in 1942–43. The government responded in piecemeal and ineffective ways, censoring the *Da gongbao* newspaper for reporting on the famine in February 1943, and doing little to deal with the incompetence and corruption that had caused the disaster.

The horrors of the famine in Henan brought the question of social change into sharp relief. But it was the Communists, not the Nationalists, who had produced the most radical vision of a new China. In their principal Shaan-Gan-Ning base area (with its capital at Yan'an), Mao and the other Communist leaders started to fashion a new social order. The region they controlled was poor and land ownership was very unequal (one estimate suggested that 12 percent of the population owned 46 percent of the land). The Communists began a program of rent and tax reduction that would ease the burdens of a high proportion of the population. In 1940, local politics was reformed by the introduction of the "three-thirds" system, in which an assembly was elected one third from the CCP, one third from other leftist elements, and one third from those who were politically neither right nor left. Between 1937 and 1941, the number of CCP members rose from some 40,000 to 763,447 and the combined Communist New Fourth and Eighth Route Armies rose from 92,000 to 440,000 over the same period.

For the first part of the war, relations between the Nationalists and Communists were workable, if not warm. But the tensions between the two sides became ever greater as both sides, with justification, suspected that the other was trying to maximize its position. By the summer of 1940, the Communist armies dominated much of north and central China, and on October 19, He Yingqin, Chiang's chief of the General Staff, told Zhu De, commander of the Eighth Route Army, that all Communist troops must be north of the Yellow River by the end of January 1941. But at the start of that month, New Fourth Army troops began to move south, not north. Swiftly, Nationalist and Communist troops in the region clashed, ending in a Nationalist victory. However, the military success turned into a public relations nightmare for the Nationalists, convincing many outside observers that Chiang's regime was more concerned with destroying its internal rivals than with fighting the Japanese.

Meanwhile, the increasing isolation of the Communist base area by the Nationalists led to a hardening of policy in Yan'an. In 1942, Mao began one of the most important movements in the process of creating a disciplined party shaped in his image: the Rectification Movement (*zhengfeng*). Rectification marked a turn away from the more pluralist politics of the early war years toward one where CCP control was much more dominant, and Mao's personality came to dominate the Party. Party members and intellectuals who had fled to Yan'an to join the revolution were now told that they had to undergo a process of "thought reform." Mao spoke in ominous terms in February 1942 when he spoke of "ill winds" that needed to be corrected.

In November 1943, two conferences took place which symbolized two different possibilities for postwar China, one in Tokyo and one in Cairo. On November 5–6, leaders from the countries within the Japanese empire gathered in Tokyo as a symbol of the pan-Asian unity that supposedly underpinned the region. Alongside prime minister Tojo appeared a variety of Asian leaders who had made different sorts of agreements with Asia: the Burmese and Indian nationalists Ba Maw and Subhas Chandra Bose had thrown their lot in with Japan with the hope of eventual freedom from Western imperialism for their countries, whereas in contrast Zhang Jinghui of the client state of Manchukuo had little autonomy. In the line-up stood Wang Jingwei, nervous and silent. For China, Wang's presence could not really symbolize an alternative path to Chinese nationalism, as he had once hoped, but rather the hollowness of Japanese promises which a naive Wang had believed.

However, the conference gave added impetus to the idea that there was an alternative discourse of Asian nationalism. This gave extra impetus to the conference held at Cairo on November 22–26, 1943. The three leaders of the Allied powers in Asia—Roosevelt, Churchill, and Chiang—met in the Egyptian capital both to make it clear that the Allies contained a genuinely non-Western element, and to determine the shape of postwar Asia. However, unity proved hard to maintain. One major proposal at the conference was for "Operation Buccaneer," a bold amphibious campaign in which Chinese troops would be involved whose goal would be to seize the Japanese-held Andaman Islands in the Bay of Bengal. Chiang expressed his support for this proposal, which was backed by Roosevelt at the conference, although the British were unenthusiastic. There was also little solid discussion of the shape of a postwar Asia, as Roosevelt played off the British prime minister and the Chinese leader against one another. Still, as Chiang flew back, he was aware that his presence at the conference was a major milestone in China's rise to greater global prominence. But his enthusiasm was short-lived: on December 5 the Western Allies cancelled the plans for Buccaneer, citing the need to maintain their strength for the campaign in Europe.

Yet even while the Nationalist government raised its international profile, the situation at home was deteriorating further. The start of 1944 saw another crisis for the Chinese resistance. The Japanese had made few advances in the previous years, stuck in their existing positions in China while becoming yet more vulnerable to the American assault in the Pacific.

The response of the Japanese high command was operation Ichigo (Number One), devised in January 1944.

Among its aims were the destruction of American air bases in central China, and the opening of a railway connection between central China and French Indochina. However, it had a wider purpose overall: the final defeat of Chinese resistance which stood in the way of Japanese domination over China. If the Japanese could neutralize China, they might just be in a position to bring about a negotiated peace with the United States. The result was the largest campaign ever undertaken by the Japanese army: half a million men were mobilized, and a force of 200 bombers.

In spring, the Japanese army struck against central China. The Nationalist armies responded badly. General Tang Enbo, defending the city of Luoyang, proved an incompetent commander; he had shone at Taierzhuang some six years earlier but had been more interested in padding his payroll than maintaining an army capable of resistance to Japan. In the end, he ended up fleeing the combat zone with just a small group of followers. Following the disaster at Luoyang, the Nationalists lost Changsha, and then Hengyang. By mid-August, it looked likely that central China would all fall to the Japanese.

Meanwhile, other Chinese troops were being brought into action, not in central China but hundreds of miles away in the battlefield that had been so disastrous in 1942: Burma. Ever since the Allies had lost the territory, Stilwell had become almost obsessive in his desire to recapture it. Lord Mountbatten, the head of SEAC (Southeast Asia Command), and American chief of staff General Albert Wedemeyer, felt that it was impractical to commit to Burma. However, Allied attention was concentrated on the upcoming campaign in western Europe, which would start with D-Day. There was little will or energy to prevent

Stilwell following up his idea of reopening the Burma Road. The Americans pressured Chiang to send some 40,000 troops under General Wei Lihuang to Burma, who would be in addition to the roughly 33,000 Chinese "X Force" soldiers based in India.

The Burma campaign of 1944 bore some resemblance to what had happened in 1942. It was a battle with no quarter given, the Japanese up against the combined forces of the Americans, British, and Chinese. Yet there were significant differences. Many of the Chinese troops sent into the campaign had been better fed and trained thanks to their period in India. Stilwell now headed for the town of Myitkyina, and was soon besieged there. The situation was made worse by Stilwell's refusal to allow any relief for Frank Merrill's unit, known as Merrill's Marauders, who had defended the town with great valor but who were exhausted and fever-ridden. Stilwell refused to allow British troops to retake the town, believing that for PR purposes, it was crucial that the Americans should be seen to have dominated. Yet the result was profoundly different. In 1944, the Japanese were on their back foot, and despite the horrendous casualties, the Allies were advancing. By August 3, the Japanese knew they could defend Burma no longer and began their retreat. The road from Ledo in Assam through Burma to China was opened again, and renamed the "Stilwell Road" by Chiang.

But the naming did not mark a reconciliation between the two. Instead, the growing confrontation between them became much worse. By late 1944, China's already perilous condition was becoming critical. Inflation was running at unprecedented rates, conscription to the armies was constant and brutal, and corruption and black marketeering was rife. Chiang and Stilwell had very different views on the significance of this. For Chiang, China's troubles were in large part because the Western allies had failed to support it when the war began and were now immensely grudging in their assistance (less than 1 percent of the total Lend-Lease provisions went to China). In Stilwell's eyes, the problems all stemmed from what he saw as Nationalist incompetence and corruption, along with reluctance to reform either military or political structures, all presided over by "the Peanut," as he called Chiang. Chiang's assessment failed to understand the very real failings in the Nationalist government; Stilwell's assessment had little understanding of the appalling circumstances in which Chiang's government had to operate.

By late 1944, Chiang had been put under a great deal of pressure from Roosevelt and George Marshall (Chief of Staff of the US Army). Stilwell argued to Washington that it was Chiang's reluctance to offer assistance in Burma that had slowed down his campaign there (an argument which failed to acknowledge that Chiang had sent troops to Burma rather than reserve them for use in central China), and that all Chinese troops should be placed under his direct command. Chiang accepted that he would have to place Stilwell in direct command of his armies. But this tentative agreement was then shattered by an action taken on September 19, 1944.

Fearing that Chiang might balk at giving up authority, Roosevelt had a message drafted in his name (Marshall had been responsible for much of the content). It was an uncompromising statement that Chiang must take "drastic action" and give Stilwell command of the armies. Its tone was harsh, rather too much so from one head of state to another. When it arrived, the US ambassador, Patrick Hurley, advised against delivery of the note to Chiang, since its key aim (demanding that Chiang cede command of the armies) had already been achieved. But Stilwell insisted, keen to humiliate Chiang with a note that in the words of his diary, had "a firecracker in every sentence." Chiang read the note in Chinese translation at the meeting, but gave little sign of a reaction until after Stilwell had left. At that point, however, he made his views clear: he could no longer think of working with the American, who would have to be recalled.

Roosevelt and Marshall were extremely unhappy at Chiang's decision that Stilwell must go, arguing to Chiang that they would rather not maintain any American command structure in China at all, but recognized the importance of keeping the Hump route open. They were adamant that Stilwell must stay, but Ambassador Hurley, as he forwarded Chiang's reply, was blunt: Stilwell and Chiang were "incompatible" and Washington would have to choose between them. On October 19, the decision was made: Stilwell was recalled. After a brief ceremony in which both sides mouthed polite words, Stilwell left China for ever on October 24. His legacy would last for decades, however. Stilwell's account of his time in China, aided by allies in the press such as the journalist Theodore White, would paint a picture of Nationalist China as purely a corrupt, incompetent, and brutal state. It was indeed all of those things; but the idea that it had also, somehow, managed to resist Japan's attack when almost all of the rest of Asia had fallen, never emerged in this version of history either.

In the short term, however, Stilwell's departure did relieve pressure as he was replaced by Albert Wedemeyer, a more emollient figure. In addition, the imminent collapse of central China seemed suddenly less likely as the Japanese thrust petered out at the end of 1944. Yet the campaign had cost some 750,000 Nationalist casualties (as opposed to just 23,000 on the Japanese side), wounding the Chinese regime even more seriously.

However, it was not the Japanese but Chiang's former foes turned allies turned enemies once more, the Communists, who now posed a threat. American intelligence rightly feared that the fragile state of the Nationalist government might lead to its collapse, and sought other partners who might be able to continue the war. For many diplomats and military figures, the Chinese Communists seemed possible partners. Yet little was known about them.

So some of the more adventurous of the American foreign policy officers decided to find out more. The young diplomat John S. Service and Colonel David Barrett were tasked with visiting the Communist area of control, in a visit that became known as the "Dixie Mission," an analogy with expeditions behind enemy lines during the American Civil War. On July 22, 1944, the United States Army Observation Group landed on the yellow loess soil at Yan'an, to be greeted by Mao Zedong and Zhu De. Service reported on the Communist area in highly positive terms: "Mao and the other leaders are spoken of with respect," he wrote, "but these men are approachable and subservience toward them is completely lacking." Service noted many other things that provided a contrast between Chongqing and Yan'an: fewer beggars, simpler clothes, and a sense of political purpose that manifested itself in forms such as peasant folk art. Service and his group saw little of the political repression that was also a defining characteristic of Yan'an.

The motivation for the trip was to see whether the CCP might prove a useful alternative partner for the Allies in the final phase of the war in Asia, which would involve using the Chinese mainland as a part of the base for the final assault on Japan. Service was clearly impressed by what he saw, although he was cautious about suggestions from Communist leaders that the United States should make formal gestures such as the opening of a consulate at Yan'an. Certainly the growth in Communist power was impressive: by 1945, the Party had over a million members, along with some 900,000 regular troops, and a similar number ranged in militias. At that point, however, it was not clear how long the war in Asia would last, and therefore both the Americans and the CCP were trying to hold as many options open as possible in the face of a possible Nationalist collapse.

But the situation in China changed significantly in late 1944 and early 1945. First, the Japanese Ichigo assault came to a sudden halt. Southwest China and Chongqing itself, which had looked vulnerable, were no longer under immediate threat. Then in April, President Roosevelt died. His successor, Harry S. Truman, was thrust into the presidency and faced with a barrage of political problems. Meanwhile, Clarence Gauss, the American ambassador to China, had left in late 1944 and was replaced by Patrick J. Hurley. Hurley was much more favorable to Chiang than Gauss had been, but this new warmth had its own dangers: he was inexperienced and unable to see that Chiang needed to find a flexible response to the Communists. He started well, traveling to Yan'an to try and find a workable formula for a compromise between the Nationalists and the Communists, which involved the Communists entering a coalition government while retaining their own forces. However, when Hurley returned to Chongqing, Chiang turned the idea down flat, insisting that the Communists had to give up their armies first. Mao was scornful of the idea and the prospects of Nationalist–Communist collaboration dimmed further. Service felt that it was important to place greater pressure on Chiang, and to point out that the most important thing was to arm anti-Japanese forces. Hurley, in contrast, felt that it was important to shore up Chiang's position in the face of his enemies. However, both American viewpoints missed an important reality: in the end, neither Chinese party was sincere about a coalition government. Both were preparing for a war in which only one party could emerge victorious.

The wretched state of China was relieved in part by a remarkable new international organization, the United Nations Relief and Rehabilitation Administration (UNRRA), the office of which opened in Chongqing in November 1944 under its American director, Benjamin H. Kizer. UNRRA had been set up to deal with the devastation caused by the war in Europe and Asia, and provided much-needed relief in places where the infrastructure of health and hygiene provision had been destroyed. In just one province, Henan, UNRRA calculated that some 70 percent of the population were in dire need, that there were some 130,000 cases of malaria, and over 2 million people in danger of starvation.

Yet still this broken state was supposed to maintain itself for continued warfare that might last another year or more. However, in the end the question of whether the Nationalist government or the Japanese army would fall first was not put to the test. On August 9, Soviet troops started to move into Manchuria. On August 6 and 9, respectively, atomic bombs were dropped on Hiroshima and Nagasaki in Japan. Within days, Japan's government had surrendered.

The Civil War

After eight years of war, the desperate desire of most Chinese was for peace. Hopeful signs appeared when Mao Zedong visited Chongqing for direct talks with Chiang in August of 1945 (accompanied by Patrick Hurley). However, the talks swiftly broke down. Both sides showed that there was little appetite for compromise.

The Communists began to gather in Manchuria, but even in early 1946, they did not make moves into the rest of China. The region was essentially under Soviet occupation, and Stalin made it clear at that point that he would respect the agreement that he had signed with the Nationalist government, which assured Chiang of Soviet support for his government's sovereignty in return for Soviet control of much of Manchuria. Truman made it clear that he would not deploy American troops to fight for the Nationalist government although it received considerable US financial support. He also sent a highly prestigious negotiator, George C. Marshall, to China to try and negotiate a compromise.

Marshall tried hard but the prospects of an agreement faded fast. The CCP refused to give up their autonomy in favor of an ill-defined Nationalist command structure, whereas the Nationalists would not engage with the Communists unless they gave up their arms. In January 1947, Marshall returned to the United States, exhausted and convinced that an agreement was impossible.

Although Chinese society was breaking down, ironically China was, in international terms, more secure than it had been for a century. As a result of its efforts on the Allied side during the war, China had been made one of the five permanent members of the new Security Council of the United Nations. It also had wide standing as the only major sovereign non-Western country with a global role (Japan was now under American occupation and India was not yet independent).

Yet by this time, the whole of China had erupted into civil war, shaped by the breakdown of China's social conditions. The Nationalist government, on return to the capital at Nanjing in 1946, seemed determined to alienate as many sectors of society as possible. Those who had been left behind under Japanese occupation were frequently accused of collaboration with the enemy, in a ploy that allowed many Nationalist supporters to seize money or property that had supposedly been gained in trafficking with the enemy. The fact that the Nationalist government had abandoned the residents of eastern China in the first place was not discussed. Human rights abuses were commonplace, as enemies of the regime were targeted for arrest or assassination. In 1946, for example, the poet Wen Yiduo was gunned down by Nationalist agents after condemning the government's record on freedom for intellectuals. Furthermore, China's financial situation became yet more wretched: inflation grew as the government printed money, and by 1948, sums of millions of Chinese yuan were worthless, with the personal savings of millions of Chinese wiped out. If the Shanghai cost of living index was 100 in May 1947, by July 1948 it had risen to 5,863.

Meanwhile, the military situation became yet more disastrous. Chiang was fatally over-confident, believing that sheer numbers of troops could outweigh the better training of the Communist armies. The Nationalists overstretched themselves by trying to recapture the northeast, only to find themselves pushed back further into north and central China. By May 1948, the major cities of Shenyang (Mukden) and Changchun, although still in Nationalist hands, were surrounded by Communist troops in the countryside. Chiang ignored the suggestions of his American advisers that he should pull back from the region, and found himself throwing more and more troops into an unwinnable battle. By the middle of 1948, the Communists had turned from guerrilla warfare to set-piece battles, and late in the year, in a mighty campaign, took the major eastern railway junction city of Xuzhou (also a target for the Japanese in 1938). By the end of January 1949, Beiping had also fallen to the Communist armies; Nanjing, Hangzhou, Wuhan, and Shanghai all followed in the spring.

Chiang Kai-shek realized that the mainland was lost. He now retreated to Taiwan, the former Japanese colony that had only returned to Chinese rule in 1945. Here he planned to regroup for an eventual recapture of the mainland.

Here he planned to regroup for an eventual recapture of China. In fact, he would never again set foot on the mainland's territory again. Meanwhile, on October 1, 1949, Mao Zedong declared the establishment of the People's Republic of China. A new era for the Chinese people had begun.

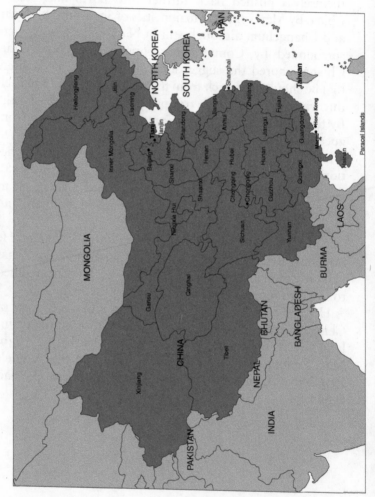

Governance of the People's Republic of China
Administrative districts

7. The Early Years of the People's Republic, 1950–1964

S. A. SMITH

ON September 21, 1949, Mao Zedong proclaimed to the world that "Our nation will never again be an insulted nation. We have stood up.... No Imperialist will ever be allowed again to invade our territory." Despite this bold statement, the situation of the new People's Republic of China (PRC) was deeply unsettled. The economy had been pounded by war, inflation was rocketing, and unemployment was high; society and polity were fragmented, and public order had broken down. Externally, the Communists had defeated the Nationalist army, forcing the Guomindang government to flee to Taiwan, taking the national treasury with it, yet Chiang Kai-shek was bent on regaining the mainland. Internally, the PRC would face significant armed revolt for the next two years, especially in the southwest; and a year after its inception would be drawn into the first "hot" conflict of the Cold War in Korea. Furthermore, although the Chinese Communist Party (CCP) and People's Liberation Army (PLA) had grown rapidly during the Civil War, to reach 4.48m and 3.57m, respectively, the PRC faced a chronic shortage of personnel to run the vast country. With only 720,000 civilian officials at its disposal, the country was effectively under military control up to 1952, four out of its five regions being run by Military Administrative Committees.

Despite endemic insecurity and a crippling lack of resources, the mood of the CCP was positive, one of relentless determination to break with the past and set about building a more just and equal society. The Common Program, passed by the People's Political Consultative Conference on September 29, 1949, was based on Mao Zedong's theory that China was currently in the phase of "new democracy," the country's profound economic, social and cultural backwardness ruling out any imminent transition to socialism. The tasks of the new government were to carry out land reform; confiscate the assets of big capitalist monopolies but protect the "national bourgeoisie" (i.e. patriotic business people); ensure a directing role for the state in banking, trade, and transport; improve the conditions of workers; and allow patriotic parties to participate in government. This is sometimes characterized as a "moderate" program, but it was clear from the start that the Communists would not hesitate to use violence and coercion to carry it out. Streets were cleaned, drains were dug, ruined buildings were demolished. Symbols of the "old society" were removed from public view: opium dens were shut down (although it took much longer to eradicate opium cultivation); gambling was curbed; the secret societies that controlled labor on the docks, in construction, in the rickshaw trade, and in human waste collection were ruthlessly suppressed. Typical of the new government's zeal was the closure on November 21 of 224 brothels in Beijing, along with the arrest of 1,286 prostitutes and 434 owners and procurers.

The principal task of the new government was to improve the lot of the 80 percent who worked in farming and carry out a far-reaching redistribution of land, expropriating landlords and many rich peasants and transferring their assets to poor and landless peasants. Land reform had started as early as 1946 in the "old liberated areas" of the north. There landlordism was less of a problem than in the west and south, since only 10 percent to 15 percent of farmers rented land. Nevertheless it stirred up violent conflict that the CCP stepped in to curb in 1948. In June 1950 the PRC promulgated the Agrarian Reform Law, which extended land reform to the regions that had only recently been taken from the Nationalists. The work teams sent into the villages to carry out the reform often faced a tough challenge. In southeast China, for example, much land belonged to lineages, i.e. families of the same surname who traced their origins to a common ancestor, and poor families belonging to the lineage often balked at the seizure of land from their wealthier kin. In the commercialized region south of the Yangzi River, most peasants worked only part-time in agriculture, landlords owned only a fraction of the land, absentee landlords were common, and smallholders were those most likely to rent out land. The work teams commenced their work by dividing villagers into class categories (landlords, rich peasants, middle peasants, poor peasants, and landless laborers) and then prepared mass meetings to denounce "landlords." In reality, the latter were often those local people considered "evil tyrants" or "bandit chiefs" rather than landlords in the strict socio-economic sense. The most abject members of the village were rehearsed to "speak bitterness," i.e. to narrate the sufferings they had endured in the past in the new language of class exploitation. This theatre of accusation was charged with emotion. In 1947 in Huanghua county in Hebei the work team recorded that among the 5,184 peasants who "spoke bitterness," 4,451 wept bitterly, 12 wept to the point where they fainted, and 195 to the point where they vomited. Women often used the occasion to tell of abuses they had received at the hands of tyrannical menfolk. By summer 1952, the "land to the tiller" movement was complete. About 43 percent of China's cultivated land was redistributed to about 60 percent of the rural population, with about 88 percent of households affected. Poor peasants substantially increased their holdings, but this did not necessarily make their farms more viable; middle peasants fared better, since they started out from a stronger position. Needless to say, there was bitter resentment among those who lost land and property.

The other major campaign through which the CCP projected its power into rural areas was that around the Marriage Law of 1950. This law condemned the traditional family "based on arbitrary and compulsory arrangements and the superiority of man over woman" and affirmed the "equal rights of both sexes," and the "protection of the lawful interests of women and children." In central and south China in 1951, 10,000 women were said to have committed suicide or been murdered in family disputes over marriage and divorce. In the light of this, the campaign focused on abolishing arranged marriages, enforcing a minimum age of marriage, combating female infanticide, and supporting those who wished to escape loveless marriages. Peasants were often frank about their reasons for wanting a divorce: "my husband was too poor so I divorced him. I can find someone better." The divorce rate rose fairly rapidly, although later in the 1950s it became more difficult to obtain a divorce if only one partner wanted it. Freer courtship and marriage became the norm in the cities, but in rural areas families continued to rely on matchmakers. Even as the Marriage Law encouraged "free choice" marriage, it also discouraged those from "good" class backgrounds—poor and middle peasants, workers, cadres, soldiers, and wives of revolutionary martyrs—from marrying those from "bad" class categories, such as former landlords, capitalists, counter-revolutionaries, and "bad elements." In this respect the Marriage Law inserted the authority of the new state into the heart of family and community decision-making.

Land reform and the Marriage Law were just two facets of the vigorous process of state building that got under way, a process that had both institutional and ideological dimensions. The party-state rapidly extended its reach deeper into local society than the Nationalist government had ever achieved. In the cities the neighborhood committees, subdivided into groups responsible for fifteen to forty households, monitored public health, unemployment, marriage and divorce registration, reported visitors, and organized kindergartens and evening classes. The Three Antis campaign from August 1951 to June 1952 targeted corruption, waste, and mismanagement on the part of officials and industrial managers, while the Five Antis campaign of 1952 targeted bribery and tax evasion by businessmen. In the countryside, in addition to peasant associations, new organizations such as the women's federation, the youth league, the people's militia, and trade unions appeared. Every rural household was assigned a class label that not only dealt a blow to traditional identities, based on kinship, patron–client, secret-society, or religious affiliation, but also determined the life chances of the members of the household for almost three decades. That said, in institutional terms state-building was not fully achieved until around 1954 when state and Party organs began to function fully in China's 160 cities, 2,174 counties (or their equivalents), and 280,000 townships. Even then, the functioning of the party-state was compromised by the continuing reliance on officials inherited from the Nationalist regime.

The Korean war saw 2.3m Chinese soldiers fight and up to half a million lose their lives between October 1950 and July 1953. This brutal conflict toughened the government's determination to purge society of internal enemies, whether real or imagined. Loyalties during the war against Japan and the Civil War had been complex and shifting, with spies and double agents active on all fronts, and this made it exceptionally difficult to distinguish friend from foe. In 1950–51, the regime launched an aggressive campaign against counter-revolutionaries that led to 2,620,000 arrests and 712,000 executions. It involved the center handing down quotas for the percentage of the population to be arrested and subjected to mass trials (quotas that were often exceeded by provincial and county Party committees). On May 20, 1951, the mayor of Beijing, Peng Zhen, addressed a crowd of tens of thousands attending the trial of 220 counter-revolutionaries: "What shall we do with this bestial group of vicious despots, bandits, traitors, and special agents?," he asked. "Shoot them!" the audience yelled. As with "speaking bitterness," these trials had a deeply theatrical quality, with the accused assigned roles akin to those of the villains in folk opera, and their crimes rendered according to the conventions of that genre. A trial in Beijing, for example, involved four "despots" who had lorded it over the city's eastern, western, northern, and southern districts. The crimes of Zhang Hui, for instance, included causing a mother to lose her mind and drown herself, after Zhang forcibly conscripted her son; those of Wu Delu included pouring water mixed with millet into the wounds of six captives and then burying them alive. The crowd, hearing the detail of the crimes, was whipped into a frenzy.

The suppression of counter-revolutionaries not only targeted Guomindang special agents and military officials, war criminals, Japanese collaborators, and notorious bandits, but also the heads of redemptive religious societies. Dubbed *huidaomen*, these societies were committed to an ideal of individual salvation, regardless of family or community. Many were strongly millenarian, believing, as White Lotus adherents had during the Qing uprisings alluded to in Chapter 2, that the Maitreya Buddha was about to appear on earth to deliver the faithful from worldly torment. These societies had grown rapidly since the 1920s, especially in the cities and villages of north China, and some of its leaders had collaborated with the Japanese. The CCP's campaign to smash the societies was carefully calibrated. By 1952 in Shanghai, where 768 altars of different societies were suppressed, 3,974 leaders had been punished, of whom 65 had been sentenced to death;

942 imprisoned, and 819 put under surveillance; 10,621 minor leaders had been required to register with the police and 322,400 members required to sign a declaration saying that they had withdrawn from the societies.

Formally, the persecution of the redemptive societies was at odds with the PRC's policy towards religion at this time. In keeping with the theory of "new democracy," the PRC chose not to adopt an "anti-religious" policy of the Soviet type, but instead to subject the five officially recognized religions of Buddhism, Daoism, Islam, Protestantism, and Catholicism to state regulation. These were required to organize national councils approved by the Religious Affairs Bureau and to purge themselves of "feudal" and "imperialist" characteristics. Significantly, the religion of the vast mass of the population—one rooted in local cults, festivals, and ancestor worship—was not recognized as a religion at all, simply dismissed as "feudal superstition" because it lacked the institutionalized structures, trained personnel, and coherent belief system that were assumed to constitute a religion proper. In the early years, the government urged that religion be treated sensitively, not least because it was deeply intertwined with ethnic identity among groups such as Tibetans, Mongolians, and Uighurs. Yet with the onset of the Great Leap Forward, policy became much more repressive. In March 1958, *Red Flag* declared that movements to "smash gods and spirits" were arising spontaneously as a result of the "basic desire of the masses...to raise production and improve livelihood." In many areas local officials ordered the demolition of temples and grave sites in order to extend the land under cultivation or to facilitate irrigation and water-conservancy projects. The result was a decline in the public visibility of religion.

In Anhui province in 1949 there had been 3,158 Buddhist temples, housing 3,933 monks, 2,797 nuns, and 3,500 lay officers; by 1962 there were 700 temples with 560 monks, 889 nuns and fewer than 200 lay officers.

Prior to 1949, the Chinese public had a richer understanding of life in the United States than they did of life in the Soviet Union. In the northeast the population had little love for the Soviets owing to its predatory occupation at the end of World War II. The Sino-Soviet Friendship Treaty of February 1950, however, did much to dispel antipathy and ignorance. In its wake, a large number of Soviet literary and technical works were translated into Chinese; Soviet films were screened and plays performed; exhibitions were staged, and Russian language classes organized. By November 1952, the Sino-Soviet Friendship Association had 38.9 million members—mainly in the cities—making it the largest mass organization in the PRC. Not all Chinese, of course, were enamored of their "elder brother," many finding Soviet propaganda dull and alien. Yet the not insignificant outpouring of grief at Stalin's death in March 1953 is notable. In Shanghai shop assistants spontaneously wore black armbands and lowered the flag to half-mast, though some, including officials, were quizzical. "In the past we were told that the advances in Soviet medicine would guarantee that Stalin would live to be 100 or 150. Why then did he die at 73?" In fact, the death of Stalin eased the rather tense relationship between the PRC and the Soviets. Nikita Khrushchev was more appreciative of the importance of China as a strategic ally in the Cold War and his decision to make China his first port of call in September 1954, following his elevation to

General Secretary of the Soviet Communist Party, was appreciated by the Chinese. Yet though Mao might confess in 1956 that "if I had always followed Stalin's advice I would have been dead," he had always had a deep respect for Stalin, whereas his opinion of Khrushchev was much lower. Mao considered himself to have political and military experience (and putative theoretical acumen) far superior to that of the new Soviet leader, making him the obvious candidate to lead the world Communist movement. It would ultimately prove the undoing of the new friendship.

In mid-1953, the CCP leadership, itching to commence the transition to socialism, announced that the phase of "new democracy" was over. For the next four years, in spheres as diverse as economic policy, state organization, military expansion, law, and education, Soviet models would be followed closely, although not uncritically. The First Five-Year Plan (1953–57), like its Soviet prototype, emphasized central planning and the rapid growth of heavy industry, notably iron- and steel-making, machine building, chemicals and power supply. Industrial output more than doubled, with impressive growth rates of 16 percent to 18 percent per annum. Yet capital formation was relatively slow and there was little agreement about the degree of centralization appropriate to China's regionally diverse and backward economy. Still, there was no blind imitation of the Soviet model. Capitalists, accused in 1952 of widespread bribery and tax evasion, were pressed into joining "public–private mergers," but were notionally compensated for their loss of assets and allowed to continue in a secondary management role. The state took charge of the key industrial and financial sectors, but allowed a "collective" sector of enterprises run by towns and counties—and even some private enterprise—to function. As late as 1964 in Shanghai, for example, there were still nineteen privately owned funeral parlors, nine that were collectively owned and two that were in joint public–private ownership.

In eight years China's manufacturing economy was transformed from one of small workshops and individual artisans to one increasingly dominated by factories, mines, and modern transportation. The urban industrial working class (including construction) grew from about 6 million in 1952 to about 10 million in 1957. The standard of living of these workers improved, certainly when compared with that of peasants. Divisions within the labor force, however, ran deep, with employees in the state sector—about 30 percent of the workforce by 1958—enjoying an "iron rice bowl" of relatively good wages and conditions and impressive job security. Workers in the collective sector, and especially those on temporary contracts, enjoyed fewer welfare benefits and worse conditions. In the state sector workers and employees were organized by work unit (*danwei*), which was responsible for allocating housing and food rations, providing nurseries, schools, and health clinics, administering passports, and approving marriages and divorces. The work unit exercised detailed control over the lives of its members, and this, combined with the fact that relations in the workplace tended to take the form of clientelist networks centered on party-branch officials or security-department chiefs, made collective working-class action difficult. Yet low-level conflict was endemic on the shop floor, not least as a response to the efforts by planners and industrial managers to improve productivity and keep wages low, and this sometimes led to stoppages, as in Guangzhou in 1956 and Shanghai in 1956–57. In the latter case, some 30,000 workers, mainly those excluded from the work-unit system, went on strike.

National figures for female employment show a tenfold increase between 1949 and 1959. Women's prospects for employment were limited by lack of skills, family responsibilities, and patriarchal attitudes. As a result, they found work in low-paid, low-status sectors, such as textiles and food-processing (although banking was something of an exception). Domestic labor remained a female preserve. During the Great Leap Forward there was an attempt to pool housework, childcare, and cooking, but it ran up against the resistance of families who wished to retain control of these basic elements of daily life. The All-China Women's Federation worked hard to improve the health of women and children, and by 1955, more than 90 percent of births in cities and 30 percent of births in the countryside involved modern methods of midwifery. Simple matters such as scrubbing hands and sterilizing instruments helped drastically to reduce infant and maternal mortality. Mao, however, was hostile to population control. His opposition, combined with declining mortality but a high birth rate (women continued to have six children on average), led to rampant population growth. This was but one of the serious problems that the pragmatic leadership, which emerged to clear up the mess of the Great Leap Forward, had to tackle in the early 1960s when the government began tentatively to promote contraception.

Following land reform, state and peasant became locked in a struggle for control of the agricultural surplus. Industrialization depended on the peasantry, since only they could provide the agricultural produce and textiles that the country needed to export if it were to pay for the import of capital goods; and only they could provide the raw materials, such as cotton and oil seed, needed for domestic industry. In addition, only the peasants could feed the rapidly growing urban population, which rose from 58 million in 1949 to nearly 100 million in 1957. In 1953–54, a system of grain procurement was introduced, whereby each district was assigned a quota of agricultural produce to hand over to the state. Simultaneously, the government stepped up efforts to establish mutual-aid teams in the countryside, a move also designed in part to increase state control over the agricultural surplus. Although the share of the agricultural surplus transferred to the state grew substantially, by spring 1955 it was failing to meet its export target (even as a few rural areas were complaining that they were beginning to go hungry). Up to this point, it had been assumed that collectivization of agriculture would be deferred until such time as China's agriculture was mechanized. On July 31, 1955, however, Mao called for the acceleration of cooperativization, albeit on a "gradual and voluntary" basis. His assumption was that since the country could not afford mechanization, labor-intensive methods, such as close planting, extension of double and triple cropping, and collection of natural fertilizers, would bring about the breakthrough in agricultural productivity that was so obviously needed. His speech marked the onset of a "socialist high tide" during which frenetic organizing led to 80 percent of households becoming members of lower-level cooperatives by January 1956. By the end of 1956, 88 percent of households (400 million people) had been pressed into joining "advanced cooperatives," each comprising 200 to 300 households. In these cooperatives, members were paid according to the amount and quality of work they performed, rather than the amount of land and other assets they brought into the cooperative. This hectic process of collectivization was far from voluntary: many peasants resented their loss of control over land and the constraints on their right to sell produce, although there was some support among the young and the poorer layers of rural society. In contrast to collectivization in the Soviet Union in 1928–32, there was no mass violence, thanks to the existence of a disciplined Party apparatus in the country-side. Yet nearly all the forms of resistance that had occurred in the Soviet Union occurred in China too, such as slaughtering livestock, reducing levels of production, withdrawing from cooperatives, and circulating fear-inducing rumors, such as that state grain reserves were about to run out.

The mid-1950s witnessed a drive to eradicate illiteracy though the extension of primary education into rural areas and through a crash campaign targeted at adults. This was prompted by the twin desires to improve the technical skills of the population and to transform political consciousness. However, the literacy drive was dogged by lack of teachers, textbooks, and poor pedagogy. In March 1956, the government announced a new campaign to elim-inate illiteracy within five to seven years. Literacy for peas-ants was defined as mastery of 1,500 characters, plus the ability to comprehend popular books and newspapers, write simple notes, keep basic accounts, and use an abacus. This was less than the minimum 4,000 characters expected of those graduating from senior primary school. A process of simplifying Chinese characters also got under way, with an initial list of 486 characters reduced from an average of sixteen to eight strokes. Over the next three years, nearly 80 million people received some form of literacy training. However, in 1959 it was reported that in Wanrong county in Shanxi more than 12,000 out of 34,000 who had undergone the crash programme had subsequently forgotten the characters they had learned. This spurred experiments in pinyin romanization, the press reporting that 8,750 peasants in Wanrong had read Mao's essay "A Single Spark Can Light a Prairie Fire" in pinyin and "completely emancipated their minds and come to understand how to greet new developments."

The politicization of literacy teaching, together with the mass dissemination of slogans, simple print publications, radio broadcasts, study groups, and speeches, helped to popularize the new language of Communism, mainly in the form of catchphrases and fixed expressions. Spouses were encouraged to call one another *airen* (loved one), rather than "my wife" (*wo taitai*) or "my husband" (*wo xiansheng*). People were encouraged to address one another as "comrade" (*tongzhi*), with the severe exception of the "black" categories of the population. Citizens were exhorted to feel "warm love" (*re ai*) towards the CCP and Chairman Mao. Once the Great Leap Forward was launched, everyday language became militarized as "battles" for production were staged and "battle lines" drawn in the workplace, part of a bid by the authorities to instil the discipline, heroism, and urgency of war into the drive to create Communism. Official language seeped into the oddest places: some Catholics defined the conflict between the officially approved Patriotic Church and the underground church, still loyal to the Vatican, as a "line struggle," echoing Mao's claim of 1959 that "the correct line is formed in struggle with the incorrect line."

Since the PRC did not have the resources to provide primary and secondary education to the entire population, educational policy oscillated between an "expert" pole, which entailed concentrating resources on producing the expertise needed to run a modern economy and administration, and a "red" pole, which deplored academic specialization, lauded the integration of manual labor and academic study, and stressed decentralized, part-time education for the masses. During the First Five-Year Plan, educational policy focused on creating a system of high-quality urban schools designed to feed universities and professional institutes (in 1955 an experiment in short-course middle schools for workers and peasants was abandoned). In early 1957, however, Mao summoned working people "to be simultaneously intellectuals and intellectuals simultaneously to be laborers." This became the watchword of the Great Leap Forward, when emphasis shifted from state-run schools to part-time schools and to schools based on factories, mines, and communes. The syllabus was reoriented towards ideological education and applied knowledge in areas such as agricultural improvement and animal husbandry. Mass cultural, sporting, and scientific activities were also promoted as part of this "technological and cultural revolution." The result was steady improvement in mass education, despite the twists and turns in official policy. Primary schools increased from 346,800 in 1949 to 1,681, 900 in 1965, while the number of secondary schools rose from 5,216 to 80,993.

Mao Zedong was convinced that Communism could only be achieved if there was a spiritual and moral transformation of the masses. He thus ascribed huge significance to ideological and cultural policy, maintaining that it was precisely in the realm of thought that the remnants of "feudalism" and "capitalism" were most recalcitrant. Cultural policy was carefully calibrated. On the one hand, much "feudal" and "capitalist" culture was banned or censored. In Beijing in 1949–50, 2,391 "old society entertainers" were barred from working on the grounds that they "perform and propagate feudal, superstitious and backward ideology." The commercial entertainment industry inherited from the republican era was also suppressed, as dance halls, amusement parks, singsong girls, and pool halls were shut down. On the other, the CCP drew on its long experience in utilizing popular cultural forms such as rice-planting songs or New Year prints to project its message to the unlettered masses. The blind story-tellers of northern Shaanxi, for example, who had traditionally prayed to the gods for good fortune, or diagnosed illness and told fortunes, were retrained to tour villages telling stories about the golden future. A vast range of activities was funded by the government to "raise the cultural level" of the masses: from libraries and reading rooms, to peripatetic film and slide shows, to roving opera performances, to cultural stations in the cities that aimed "to spread literacy, conduct political propaganda, promote recreational activities and popularize scientific knowledge." Again, with the Great Leap Forward, the accent shifted to the masses themselves writing, painting, staging plays, and making music. In Pi county in Jiangsu province peasants produced 105,000 drawings, paintings, and murals in summer 1958 that depicted the Communist future as one of plentiful food, bright, colorful clothing, elegant, Western-style housing, and a splendid Palace of Culture. Nevertheless, many perceived officially sponsored culture as too dry and didactic and continued to practice traditional forms of entertainment, such as local opera. In 1966 the cultural bureau in Jilin bemoaned the fact that in the city's 139 rental bookstalls (50 of which were unlicensed), 70 percent of the books borrowed concerned "emperors and kings, scholars and beauties, feudal morality, feudal superstition, bourgeois ideology, and revisionist ideas."

So far as elite culture was concerned, the PRC did not hesitate to ban or censor artistic and literary production it considered harmful and to promote an aesthetic that stressed an orientation towards the masses and presented the achievements of the CCP and the struggles of heroic individuals to bring about Communism in a positive light. On July 2, 1949, a congress of 753 writers and artists pledged to make their work "a tool to serve workers, peasants, and soldiers," but this was easier said than done. The artist Dong Xiwen was required to repaint his "Founding Ceremony of the Nation" three times, in order to remove Party leaders who had fallen foul of Mao in the meantime. Visual forms of culture, such as posters, cartoons, woodcuts, and serial picture stories, were especially important in getting across the CCP's message to a largely illiterate population. Cartoonists churned out depictions of Chiang Kai-shek as a cunning rat or a running dog, or featured folksy tales of "Aunt Yao," an old lady with bound feet, arresting a Guomindang spy. Yet like all artists, cartoonists found it difficult to reconcile the formal requirements of their art—satire and caricature, qualities guaranteed to discomfit cultural bureaucrats—with the political requirements of the state. It hardly came as a surprise when in 1957 the editorial board of the main cartoon magazine was condemned for producing "poisonous weeds."

A surprisingly high proportion of China's 100,000 "higher intellectuals" had chosen to stay in China in 1949 rather than move to Taiwan or Hong Kong. Many hailed from landlord, bourgeois, or petty-bourgeois backgrounds and, far from being welcomed as patriots, the CCP viewed them with distrust. Yet the new government needed their knowledge and expertise and was ready to pay them accordingly. Teachers, for example, were in such short supply that many with problematic political histories (such as those who had worked for the Japanese or been activists in the Guomindang) were taken on. At the same time, they were pressed to reform their thinking in accordance with Communist principles and values. In 1950–51, tens of thousands underwent "thought reform" at "revolutionary universities" where they were introduced to Marxism-Leninism. This was often a grueling experience, yet even intellectuals who sincerely wished to work for the new government continued to display a certain independence of mind that Party leaders considered suspect. In late 1954 the regime launched a vicious campaign against the left-wing writer Hu Feng, who had had the temerity to complain to the Central Committee about the stultification of intellectual life. By 1956—and typifying the twists and turns in official policy that characterized this period—Mao felt that intellectuals had become too cowed, too reluctant to suggest ways in which the quality of government could be improved. In April 1956, therefore, he proposed to "let a hundred flowers bloom and a hundred schools of thought contend," by encouraging intellectuals to speak their minds. Initially reluctant, they plucked up courage for five weeks in May and June to engage in an unprecedented spate of "blooming and contending." "Who runs the country," some asked, "the Party or the government?" "Which is superior, the Party or the law?" Such criticism far exceeded the bounds anticipated by Mao, confirming his suspicion that the intelligentsia was mired in bourgeois liberalism. On June 8 *People's Daily* announced that a new struggle against "rightists" was about to commence.

Between 1957 and 1958 the anti-rightist campaign was ruthlessly carried out in Party and government agencies, research institutes, and universities. It is reckoned that 1.1 million people were branded "rightists," many picked out to meet centrally determined quotas. They included not only intellectuals but also government and military officials. Subject to fierce attack by colleagues, many were demoted, dismissed, or sent to labor camps in remote areas. Ding Ling, feminist writer and recipient of the Stalin Prize for literature, had in recent times displayed exemplary loyalty to the CCP, yet she was put through twenty-seven "struggle sessions" before being dispatched to work on a chicken farm near the Soviet border. She would not be rehabilitated for twenty-two years. Hu Feng would languish in prison and labor camp for twenty-five years. Yet such was the desire of some to see their country prosper that they maintained faith that the CCP was engaged in a righteous struggle for a better society. In a lightly fictionalized story by Yang Xianhui, a train conductor reflects: "I took part in the war against the Nationalist government and was wounded in the Korean War against the

Americans. After being convicted as a rightist, I still clung to the hope that I could reform myself through hard labor and that the Party would eventually forgive me and embrace me. If I had escaped, it would have meant I had jettisoned all my old ideals."

As the apparatus of rule grew steadily, so did problems of bureaucracy and arbitrary power. In April 1957, the Central Committee announced that leading officials must do stints of manual labor to combat "bureaucratism, factionalism and voluntarism." By 1962, 2 million urbanites had been sent down to the countryside, usually for one month a year, supposedly to learn from the masses. This seems hardly to have dinted the underlying trend and would be a major factor leading Mao to unleash the Cultural Revolution in 1966.

Despite the increased proportion of the agricultural surplus that the state had wrested as a result of rapid collectivization, in September 1957 Chen Yun pointed out starkly that there was a "sharp contradiction" between the limited supply of grain and cloth and the growth in population and urban employment. A debate was under way in the Party leadership at this time concerning the appropriateness of the Soviet model to China, the potential for decentralizing economic decision-making, and the relationship of socialization of agriculture to its technical transformation. In January 1958 Mao cut this short by announcing that a "Great Leap Forward" should commence, intended to be in effect a leap away from the Soviet model. Instead of putting energy into modernizing the forces of production by installing advanced technology and prioritizing heavy industry, Mao resolved that China should rely on the one productive force she had in abundance: namely, her human resources. The "subjective factor," i.e. the consciousness of the masses, Mao argued, could overcome even the most daunting obstacles posed by socio-economic backwardness. So long as values and behavior inherited from the past were renounced and new values of struggle, austerity, and self-sacrifice embraced, then the masses, always, of course, under Party leadership, would achieve a rapid advance to Communism. In winter 1957–58, more than 100 million peasants were mobilized to undertake large-scale irrigation and land reclamation projects and to build and operate "backyard iron furnaces." A campaign against the "four pests" got under way, which saw the population organized to eliminate rats, flies, mosquitoes, and sparrows. Some 220 million people were drafted into the people's militias—30 million of them bearing arms—so peasants marching to the fields bearing red flags and rifles became a common sight.

The attack on book learning and scientific expertise was renewed. Mao opined that many people in history without formal education had intellectual and technological achievements to their credit, citing (with varying degrees of accuracy) Confucius, Jesus, Sun Yat-sen, Marx, and Benjamin Franklin as examples. On the positive side, school students, workers, and peasants were encouraged to become red *and* expert, not least by getting involved in scientific experimentation. On the negative side, many Party leaders proved breathtakingly ignorant. Kang Sheng promised that "if by National Day next year (1959), Shanghai's schools are able to launch a third-grade rocket to an altitude of 186 miles, they should get three marks... A third-grade rocket with a satellite should get five marks. This is very easy." A book entitled "They Are Creating

Miracles" described how children at a primary school had "developed ten more new crops on its experimental plot." "It's a story that...involves no fairy-tale magicians, no white-bearded wizards of never-never land. The heroes of our story are Young Pioneers studying in an ordinary primary school."

Mao convinced himself that massive communes responsible for production, consumption, residence, social services, and local modernization were the solution to China's backwardness. The Beidaihe resolution of August 1958 extolled these as a combination of the Communist principle of "each according to his needs" and the socialist principle of "each according to his work" and predicted that "ownership by the whole people" would be realized within a few years. In the most "advanced" province of Henan, the drive to create communes was declared completed by the end of August: 38,473 advanced cooperatives, comprising an average of 260 households, had been converted into 1,378 people's communes, each with over 7,200 households. An extraordinary utopianism gripped society. In the words of one Western observer: "There were communal mess halls, communal kitchens, communal labor, communal indoctrination, and hortatory meetings—a form of communal living totally different from the family and village way of life." In Henan, Hebei, and Shandong provinces model communes provided their members with free food, clothing, medical care, education, and housing.

Commune "workers" (as peasants were now called) received work points for all the tasks they performed for the collective. These points were calculated according to the size and value of the year's harvest, minus the state-levied grain taxes, and could be exchanged for grain and cash.

Work was assigned by team leaders and workers had little or no say in the decisions they took. Though the press hailed all this as a sign that Communism was just around the corner, many—probably most—peasants were less than enraptured. Li Anyuan, a middle peasant from northern Sichuan, recalled: "When we had our land we could harvest between 500 and 2,000 kilograms of rice a year. During collectivization, all our food was taken away by the canteen—that was the policy. We were not even allowed to cook at home. The cadres sent people to destroy our stove and took away our wok." In reality what was hailed by the media as a bold experiment in collective living was more like barracks-style regimentation.

It is now indisputable—and has become the clinching piece of evidence in the case against Mao Zedong—that by late 1958 the leadership knew that famine was spreading in certain regions. Indeed in spring 1959 Mao seems to have been minded to curb excesses in the implementation of the Leap. Yet when he heard Marshal Peng Dehuai criticize "petty-bourgeois fanaticism" at the Lushan plenum in July 1959, he dug in his heels and ordered a "second leap" to go ahead. The result was cataclysmic: the worst famine in human history, judged in terms of absolute numbers. The estimate that 30 million peasants starved to death does not seem wide off the mark. This was, in effect, a "man-made" famine, brought about by the quixotic aspirations of the central leadership to create Communism as quickly as possible and by draconian procurement of grain by local officials keen to prove to that they were "overcoming reactionary conservatism." Compounding factors were the diversion of labor power and other resources away from farming—the agricultural labor force was reduced by 38 million between 1957 and 1958—together with the waste of grain resulting from communal eating and poor storage. In early 1959, several provincial governments inveighed against supposed under-reporting of the grain harvest and set cadres to hunt for "hidden grain" in peasant houses. Starving peasants staggered into the fields to eat unripe grain before the state could get its hands on it, and were beaten for their audacity, occasionally to death. The rate of "unnatural deaths" (that is, death through starvation plus direct killing) was appallingly high in the provinces of Henan, Anhui, Gansu, Sichuan, and Guizhou, lower in others, such as Zhejiang and Shanxi, this variation reflecting the zeal of provincial Party leaders in squeezing grain from starving peasants. One confidential CCP report noted: "For a long time, the masses have lost interest in collective production. They have lost faith in the future. They say they would rather be dogs somewhere else than people here."

It fell to a new pragmatic leadership under Liu Shaoqi and Deng Xiaoping to cope with the disaster between 1961 and 1964, Mao withdrawing from routine policy-making. Although the official talk had been of "walking on two legs," i.e. of balanced development of agriculture and industry, investment in heavy industry had run at a level that would have made Soviet planners blanch. Between 1956 and 1958 the percentage of state capital investment in heavy industry had risen from 38 percent to 56 percent. The Leap then led to financial chaos, as controls on capital construction and the ordering of supplies disappeared; as the abolition of material incentives caused labor productivity to plummet; as labor costs spiraled as a result of a doubling in the size of the workforce; and as massive waste resulted from campaigns such as that to make "backyard steel" (steel produced using small blast furnaces constructed in the backyards of communes). The new leadership imposed massive financial cutbacks and scrapped prestige construction projects, once again illustrating the Maoist pattern of breaks and leaps followed by troughs and retrenchment. It was agriculture, however, that cried out for a change of policy. The government thus scaled down the size of communes and devolved decision-making to the brigade and later to the production team. By summer 1962, 30 percent of households were farming independently, on the basis of contracts with the production team. Private plots were restored and farmers were allowed to sell produce in rural markets. Similarly, small industrial enterprises were made responsible for their own profitability. Mao seethed at these measures, warning in August 1962 that China faced the "danger of capitalism and revisionism," and urging the country the following month "never to forget class struggle."

The consequence was a new national campaign to uphold ideological rectitude, known as the Socialist Education Movement. This was motivated by a desire to pin the blame for the Great Leap disaster on local Party officials. In rural areas, where the movement was known as the Four Cleanups, 1.5 million to 1.6 million cadres descended on the villages to ferret out bribery, embezzlement, illegal trading, gambling, and general back-sliding by grassroots cadres. In the course of struggle meetings, peasants sometimes took vengeance on those they held to be responsible for their suffering. In Hubei some 2,000 officials were murdered. Following the issuance of the Ten Points in May 1963, the movement was stepped up: Party leaders warned that landlords and rich peasants were "trying to stage a comeback" and "carry out class revenge." In Guizhou the first secretary of the provincial Party committee, Zhou Lin, who as late as December 1960 had described the famine as "an expression of the most acute class struggle in the village," now found himself accused of spreading capitalism. In Qinglong county in that province the work teams uncovered 164 households of "newly emerging landlords or rich peasants"; 129 "black category" households; and 212 "newly discovered households of secret counter-revolutionaries or backbone elements of reactionary political parties." Out of 1,875 CCP members in the county 430 were subject to disciplinary action. In 1964 Zhou Lin was dismissed and the following year the entire leadership of Guizhou province was removed.

The work teams were shocked at the extent to which village life had slipped the anchor of Party control. Everywhere, peasants engaged in free trade, gambling, and "extravagant" weddings and funerals. Occasionally, there were more political, if desperate, attempts to escape the status quo. Between 1960 and 1965 there were 195 "attempts to restore the old order" in Jiangsu province and 184 in Liaoning province, many involving would-be emperors announcing the inauguration of a new dynasty. The work teams expressed particular disapproval of the rampant "feudal superstition" that was everywhere visible, evinced in everything from temple rebuilding, spirit mediumship, pilgrimages in search of holy water, to the circulation of disturbing supernatural rumors. Millions were convinced that the famine had come about because they were no longer free to practice the rituals designed to harmonize relations between the spirit and human worlds.

In Pei County in Jiangsu, peasants declared: "In recent years, people have lost their good conscience and are not offering incense. Consequently, we haven't had good harvests." They vowed to pray to the gods to "wipe out disaster and bestow happiness." For their part, the work teams vowed to "uproot superstition utterly, to bring materialist education to the masses, and to propagate scientific atheism." In 1965 in Kaifeng alley in Zhabei district of Shanghai the neighborhood committee tore down red-paper strips bearing good-luck sayings and replaced them with strips bearing quotations from Mao. It pressured 180 households to throw out their ancestral tablets and images of Guanyin, Guandi, and other gods and replace them with portraits of Mao.

A monumental cult of Mao had been burgeoning since the early 1960s when Minister of Defense Lin Biao exhorted PLA soldiers "to arm our minds with Mao Zedong Thought, to defend the purity of Marxism-Leninism, and combat every form of ideological trend of modern revisionism." Soldiers were organized into study groups to read Chairman Mao's essays, and out of this experience a book of quotations was published in 1964 that would have a global impact as the Little Red Book. The potency of Mao's ideas was propagated through campaigns "to learn from Dazhai" (a brigade in eastern Shanxi) in agriculture, and to "learn from Daqing" (a giant oilfield in Heilongjiang) in industry, the success of these two model sites being ascribed to assiduous study of Mao Zedong Thought. Educated youngsters were sent into the villages as Mao Zedong Thought counselors to teach the masses the "three constantly read articles," which dealt, respectively, with serving the people, Communist internationalism, and perseverance in the face of hardship. In Chen village in Guangdong one counselor recalled: "We had every party member, every Communist Youth League member, and every counselor memorize the entire articles. After that, all the peasants were set to memorize the articles, but their level of literacy was too low." Nevertheless study sessions and struggle meetings do appear to have instilled rudimentary elements of Maoist ideology into the peasantry. "Hey, you're selfish!," one might say to another: "Chairman Mao tells us to work selflessly for the collective." At a deeper level, the ceaseless blitz of propaganda reinforced in millions of people a sense of Mao as an emperor, the symbolic father of the nation, his every utterance a sacred edict.

The years between 1949 and 1964 witnessed the most ambitious attempt in history to smash an existing social order and to replace it with a radically improved society, in this instance one based on collectivism, equality, and ideological uniformity. Against the odds, the CCP rapidly built a powerful state, using violence, mass campaigns, and relentless propaganda, and extended its extractive power and ideological influence deep into the population. In many respects, the PRC was a quintessentially totalitarian state in that the population, especially in the countryside, was subjected to traumatic social engineering, with little thought to the human cost, and to a remorseless campaign to rework its beliefs and values in line with those of the Great Helmsman. Yet beneath the totalitarian carapace, the population displayed a qualified independence of mind and action, proving restive and truculent by turns, which was partly a reflection of the limits of state power and partly a reflection of the resilience of traditional culture.

These years between 1949 and 1964 also saw China fall in and out of love with the Soviet Union. Up to 1958, the Sino-Soviet alliance was purposeful and dynamic, although never free of tension. It was Mao's unwillingness to play "younger brother" to Khrushchev plus his determination to institute rapid and far-reaching economic and social transformation with no heed for "objective" circumstances that were the fundamental causes of the rift that opened up between the two largest Communist states between 1960 and 1963. Following the withdrawal of Soviet experts from China in 1960, Mao began to reflect on the evolution of the Soviet regime, coming to the view that it had turned into a state-capitalist society in which a privileged stratum of bureaucrats had "converted the function of serving the masses into the privilege of dominating them." Seeing the revival of the market, the restoration of material incentives in industry, the re-emergence of a two-track system in education, or the resurgence of "feudal superstition," Mao was haunted by the fear that capitalist restoration would occur in China too.

The Great Leap not only initiated the break with the Soviet Union, it proved to be a watershed in the evolution of the CCP. Up to 1958, the Party leadership was relatively united, but the Great Leap divided it permanently around the appropriate strategy for taking China out of backwardness. The Great Leap, too, irrevocably undermined the prestige of the Party at the grass roots, so that it never regained the trust it had enjoyed in the early 1950s. Ironically, however, one consequence of the Leap was that it opened the way for the apotheosis of the man who was most responsible for its terrible human and material cost. Yet if Mao achieved godlike status in the first half of the 1960s, the adulation of millions was clearly insufficient to quell his fear that he was losing control over the course of the revolution.

8. *The Cultural Revolution Era, 1964–1976*

RICHARD CURT KRAUS

THE Cultural Revolution era of 1964–76 marks the high tide of radical politics in China. The great question of the time was how to consolidate, sustain, and extend China's revolution. For some Party leaders, this meant developing orderly routines of economic development and governance. For others, including Chairman Mao Zedong, it meant experimenting with new forms of political practice in order to avoid the ossification of the revolution into rule by a cautious Party elite. More concretely, it was a period of considerable chaos and change in daily lives, in the constitution of the political elite, and in China's place in the world. Three periods emerge, according to political climate. First was a "prelude" to the Cultural Revolution in 1964–66, when intra-elite tensions were high, despite declarations of political unity. Second was a 1966–68 radical phase, two years of mass mobilizing politics that often stands in our memory for the whole era. Third was the late Maoism of 1968 until the Chairman's death in 1976, a time of demobilizing the mass movement, palace intrigues, popular anxiety, and the seeds of subsequent reforms.

The "Cultural Revolution" overwhelmed the arts world, but it was not primarily an aesthetic movement. It was a political and social struggle in which culture was a visible target.

Prelude to the Cultural Revolution, 1964–1966

The "Great Proletarian Cultural Revolution" was Maoist China's most sustained and disruptive political campaign. Its unpredictable twists and turns touched everyone. The Cultural Revolution is often characterized as the brainchild of an aging Mao Zedong, frustrated by resistance to his increasingly radical policies. Extreme versions of Mao-centered interpretations portray the Chairman as a political monster, inflicting the Cultural Revolution upon an innocent society. Some analysts present the movement as the whim of Chairman Mao, a personal defect of this dominant figure. While it is difficult to imagine a Cultural Revolution without Mao, the movement reflected real tensions within Chinese society.

The pre-Cultural Revolution period of political stand-off was full of radical rhetoric but quiet resistance to Mao from many of the senior leaders of the Communist Party, especially President Liu Shaoqi and Party Secretary General Deng Xiaoping. Many running the day-to-day operations of the Chinese state were skeptical about Mao's political enthusiasms, recalling the damage of the Great Leap Forward (1958–60). In the wake of that disaster, Mao had ceded considerable power to more conservative colleagues. He retained his position as Party Chairman, but the daily running of China was in the hands of President Liu Shaoqi and the Party Secretary General Deng Xiaoping. Liu and Deng pressed for reforms such as private farming initiatives to supplement communal agriculture and a less restrictive cultural policy.

Mao believed that the Party was forgetting its revolutionary roots, that China's revolution was incomplete, and that the apparently overthrown landlord and capitalist classes retained impressive ideological influence. Mao (and his followers) argued that even after the socialization of most private property, class remained etched in political consciousness. The rewards of high wage differentials, foreign models, and an urban-centered development were among the bourgeoisie's "sugar-coated bullets." Only a powerful ideological campaign could protect China's revolutionary heritage. Mao's ideal Party consisted of workers, peasants, and soldiers, in contrast to the Liu-Deng concept of a Party that reached out to intellectuals, technical experts, religious leaders, overseas Chinese, and former capitalists.

Mao's approach was strikingly non-material for a life-long Marxist. But it represented his effort to come to grips with the new dynamics of socialist China, in which formal property ownership by capitalists and landlords was an issue of the past. It served to justify a massive purge of his enemies. "Capitalist roader" was a favorite Maoist epithet that could destroy any veteran Communist who strayed from the Maoist path.

Eager to regain control, Mao began a "leftist initiative," scolding others in 1962 for neglecting the main point of the revolution and exhorting them to "never forget class struggle." It was, he went on, something which Communists should talk about "every year, every month, every day, at conferences, at Party congresses, at plenary sessions, and at each and every meeting."

The upshot was a political stand-off. All leaders maintained a façade of unity, while factional tensions simmered. All honored Mao, contributing to the growth of the Mao cult which came to dominate political life. However, Mao complained later that Deng Xiaoping treated him like the corpse at a funeral, respecting his image while ignoring his opinions. Mao's frustrations reflected sometimes vague longings within the Party for faster change, for more jobs amidst a baby boom, and for upholding the stern values of the revolution. As conservative leaders sought to sidetrack Mao's radical impulses, the Chairman turned to four critical allies.

First, the People's Liberation Army became the left's model institution. Mao had purged the moderate Defense Minister amidst the controversy which followed the collapse of the Great Leap Forward, replacing him with Marshal Lin Biao, a hero of the revolution who had been politically inactive. Lin expanded the army's political clout by championing radical initiatives. Reflecting Maoist suspicion of high-status experts in all realms of society, Lin abolished military titles and insignia, thereby slowing the professionalization of the officer corps as he summoned up memories of the more egalitarian red army of China's revolution. Mao's "Little Red Book" (*Quotations from the Works of Mao Zedong*), later made famous by the

Red Guards of the Cultural Revolution, was initially prepared by the army to spread revolutionary values among soldiers through political study sessions. Army political campaigns, such as the drive to emulate Lei Feng, a model soldier, spread to civilian life. Technical accomplishments, such as China's 1964 nuclear bomb test, reinforced the army's growing prestige.

A second favored group was poor peasants, the rural laborers who received the most revolutionary class designations in the great land reform. Mao pressed them to defend the revolution and their own improved social status, organizing them into "poor and lower middle peasant associations" to control politics in rural communities. The Dazhai production brigade, in Shaanxi province, became a national model for implementing Maoist politics, with a sternly puritanical regimen of land reclamation and political study sessions. The close connection between the peasantry and the army, which was drawn from peasant recruits, meant that the Ministry of Defense acted as the political patron of what it regarded as the broad interests of China's countryside.

A third source of Maoist influence was a group of civilian junior officials, often too young to have played important roles in the revolution, but eager to prove themselves politically. Bureaucratic promotions were often slow, as the revolution had staffed state and Party offices with relatively young people. Some of these younger leftists concentrated around the controversial figure of Mao's wife, Jiang Qing. Other Party leaders disapproved of Mao's 1938 marriage to this Shanghai actress. They demanded that Jiang Qing stay out of politics, and she worked unobtrusively in cultural organizations in the 1950s. But as Mao's anger toward his colleagues grew in the 1960s, his resentful wife became an energetic political ally. She collaborated with Lin Biao to organize a February 1966 conference on arts work in the People's Liberation Army, declaring her new public role as Lin showed off his loyal leftist army.

The fourth group which Mao cultivated was urban youth. The most prominent program before 1966 did not seem like much of an inducement: a large-scale program to resettle urban young people to rural areas. But many volunteered to steel themselves in revolution by learning from the poor and middle-peasants. Others avoided the "down to the villages" campaign as best they could, although growing activism and radical politics among urban students affected almost all of them. When the political deadlock among adult political factions reached a crisis, Mao summoned the students into the political arena as a new force, the Red Guards.

Radical Cultural Revolution, 1966–1968

In the stand-off leading up to the Cultural Revolution, Mao's rivals controlled Beijing and its national media. Mao's initial political base was Shanghai, where writers associated with Jiang Qing were protected by local politicos who threw their support behind Mao. Debates were heated, yet opaque. Encouraged by Mao, critic Yao Wenyuan attacked a 1961 drama, *Hai Rui Dismissed from Office*. Despite its Ming dynasty setting, the play was read as a critical allegory of Mao's purge of Defense Minister Peng Dehuai for resisting the Great Leap Forward. Its author was deputy mayor of Beijing, and this drama review signaled to the nation that Beijing's mayor Peng Zhen could not protect his own entourage, and was thus next to be purged himself. Sowing chaos in the capital, Maoists were better able then to attack their major targets, President Liu Shaoqi and Secretary General Deng Xiaoping.

The Red Guards became the shock troops for the Cultural Revolution, which the Party Central Committee declared on May 16, 1966. Most Red Guards were urban high school students. A 16-year-old Red Guard would have been born in 1950, and personally unfamiliar with the revolution. Red Guards were not organized by the state but sprang up spontaneously, drawn into politics by controversies within their schools, and by the excitement of breaking down established routines.

Peace and economic growth had led to a large demographic increase in the numbers of young Chinese. Schools expanded, fueling ambitions for good, non-agricultural jobs. But new graduates faced limited opportunities because the 1949 revolution installed a cohort of relatively young leaders, many still on the job. Thus the political ideals of the young were joined by anxieties about their personal futures; Maoist politicians channelled this explosive combination.

Mao Zedong, although 72, reached out to China's youth through a highly publicized swim in the Yangzi River. Millions of young people responded with a sudden fad for swimming. Well-staged mass rallies of Red Guards in Tiananmen Square continued the momentum. Mao wore the Red Guard armband and wrote his own "big character poster," showing his respect for the tens of thousands of revolutionary declarations that young rebels pasted on public walls.

These big character posters ranged from high-blown polemics to revelations of apparently scandalous political behavior by officials under attack. Posters were supplemented by Red Guard newspapers and magazines. Maoist officials often leaked documents to Red Guards in order to damage their adversaries through new media, beyond the control of conservative bureaucrats. This information was generally accurate, although often taken out of context and given the most damaging interpretation.

The Red Guards combined political zeal with teen rebellion, breaking social barriers as they looked for ways to promote revolution. Maoists ordered China's railroads to provide free transportation to Red Guards in the autumn of 1966, in order to encourage the "exchange of revolutionary experiences." Whatever the political motives of adult Maoist politicians, this "revolutionary tourism" allowed young people their first opportunity to travel.

Some of the early Cultural Revolution's shocking violence flowed from the fact that no one dared oppose the gangs of students, for fear of being labeled a counter-revolutionary. August and September 1966 saw a Red Guard rampage. In Beijing, Red Guard teams searched over 100,000 homes looking for "reactionary materials," which might include old phonograph records, Confucian books, or private collections of art. They treated intellectuals roughly. Some Red Guards beat people with belt buckles and tortured them with boiling water. Nearly 2,000 died in Beijing, including some high officials. Red Guard humiliations induced suicides, including that of the famous novelist Lao She.

It is important to recognize internal diversity among the millions of Red Guards. The majority did not beat up anyone, and many spoke out against violence. Some Red Guards even staged mock raids on private art collections, with the connivance of the owners and museums, in order to remove fragile art treasures from harm's way. Although all claimed to be "revolutionaries," some were children of officials under Maoist attack, and organized themselves to protect their elite families. One notorious Beijing Red Guard unit, the "United Action Headquarters," promoted a "bloodline" theory. Children of workers, poor peasants, and revolutionary cadres were hailed as natural revolutionaries, while children of capitalists and landlords could never overcome the stigma of their social origin. The bloodline theory avoided Mao's single-minded concentration on "capitalist roaders" within the Party by deflecting attention to the revolution's long-defeated class enemies.

The United Action Committee was soon suppressed, but it remained easy to scapegoat the vulnerable. Many were forced to "draw a clear line" to separate family members of bad class background or with complicated political histories. Members of the "five black categories" (landlords, rich peasants, counterrevolutionaries, "bad elements," and rightists) were avoided even more than before, even when they were not actually abused.

The heyday of the Red Guards was relatively brief. Most violence against teachers and officials occurred in August 1966. Most raids on privileged households and destruction of books and art came early in the Cultural Revolution. After using the Red Guards to disorient his rivals and shake up the country, Mao found them an awkward political tool. While Maoist leaders tried to stop the public assaults, Red Guards increasingly turned to internal conflict. Factions armed themselves with homemade weapons, later seizing Russian arms from trains on their way to Vietnam. Pitched street battles and intra-Red Guard violence tested the patience of a shaken political establishment.

The established Party organization was a shamble. An ad hoc "Cultural Revolution Group" of five Maoists supplanted normal central Party organs. They initially had a hard time extending their authority beyond Beijing. The new leadership appealed increasingly to workers and the army to restore order. The "Shanghai Commune" of January 1967 stressed proletarian power as it strengthened the political base for three radical politicians: the propaganda official Zhang Chunqiao, the literary critic Yao Wenyuan, and the factory security man Wang Hongwen, all of whom were later linked with Jiang Qing as the Gang of Four.

An alternative and longer-lasting model was the "Revolutionary Committee," based upon a "triple alliance" of new mass organizations, army representatives, and veteran officials who had declared loyalty to the Cultural Revolution. The army worked patiently to create new Maoist local governments by forcing agreements among radical rebel groups and acceptable veteran cadres. But continuing social disorder drew the army more deeply into regional administration, despite its efforts to stand above local political disputes. Conflict in the city of Wuhan during the summer of 1967 resembled civil war. A Beijing leader sent to broker a settlement was kidnapped; he had to be rescued by troops sent by air. This steeled the army's resolve to be tough. By mid-1968, most provinces established Revolutionary Committees. By that time, the Red Guards were relocated to the countryside, "to learn from the poor and lower middle peasants."

Late Maoism, 1968–1976

The final stage of the Cultural Revolution was longer and quite different in political quality from its frantic, exuberant, and chaotic opening period. Mao sought to replace mass mobilization and street politics, to restore public order, and to devise a formula for continuing revolutionary ideals with less disruptive methods. Maoist suppression of spontaneous mass organizations was more violent than Red Guard brutality. In 1967–68, the Cultural Revolution Group, hoping to re-establish order, investigated an alleged, but imaginary "May 16 Conspiracy," resulting in the arrest of leading radical figures. Millions were scrutinized and tens of thousands executed. A related campaign to "purify class ranks" between 1967 and 1969 killed even more. Maoists examined personal dossiers for problems such as relatives in Taiwan, or formerly capitalist in-laws. Newly promoted local and provincial leaders were insecure in their positions, which perhaps exacerbated the viciousness of these campaigns. The new Revolutionary Committees consolidated their power by demobilizing mass politics, beginning with organizations that resisted their legitimacy. Much violence took place in suburban or rural counties, where it was less visible than the early Red Guard violence in the cities.

The 1969 Ninth Congress of the Communist Party signaled the return to a kind of political normality. With the purge of conservative leaders, loyal Maoists gained high Party positions. Most members of the old Central Committee were not included in the new one. Twenty-five of twenty-nine provincial Party first secretaries lost their jobs. The victors included Jiang Qing and her radical civilian allies from the Cultural Revolution Group, and leaders of the People's Liberation Army, especially the Minister of Defense, Lin Biao. Lin became Party Vice-Chairman and, as Mao's "closest comrade in arms," was treated as his presumptive heir.

The leftist rhetoric remained, but Maoists became less concerned with seizing power than in consolidating their victories. The Party railed against factionalism and claimed to be united. But obvious divisions split the civilian radicals, pragmatic officials under the leadership of Prime Minster Zhou Enlai, and military officers. All competed for the ear of Mao Zedong, who tried to balance the rival voices.

Mao apparently wanted to limit the army's political power. Lin Biao (or more likely his son, Lin Liguo) organized an inept assassination plot and coup. When the plot failed, Lin Biao was put on a plane that fled China, crashing in Mongolia on September 13, 1971. Mao and the Cultural Revolution Group were stunned, and worried that the incident would break the confidence of millions of Chinese in the Cultural Revolution. The unprecedented cancellation of the October 1 (1971) National Day parade and celebration demonstrated Beijing's disarray. It would take a year for citizens outside the political elite to learn of the scandal through carefully organized and secret Party briefings. Party leaders prepared a dossier that attempted to explain how Lin, Mao's closest comrade, could become a traitor. They had no more success than the Warren Commission in the United States, which tried to explain the assassination of John F. Kennedy. As Mao feared, former enthusiasts for the Cultural Revolution dated their political disenchantment from the Lin Biao affair. The scandal unsettled most citizens, who retreated from the more extravagant forms of political involvement.

Mao purged Lin Biao's top aides, thereby strengthening two competing civilian groups. The activists group, associated with Mao through his wife Jiang Qing, consolidated much of their power. One of their leaders, Wang Hongwen, became vice-chair of the Party, nominally second to Mao. But Mao also elevated a group of more moderate career officials, led by Premier Zhou Enlai. At the tenth Communist Party Congress in 1973, many former Cultural Revolution targets rejoined the Central Committee. Even Deng Xiaoping, recently denounced as "the number two person in authority taking the capitalist road," was called back to the capital to serve as Vice-premier, assuming a leading role in economic policy. Former President Liu Shaoqi, expelled from the Party, had died under squalid conditions in 1969. But Mao had protected Deng's Party membership and dispatched him to internal exile in Guangxi province, where he worked in a machine tool factory. By 1975 Deng was reinstated to the inner circle of power, the Political Bureau's Standing Committee, probably as a possible replacement for Premier Zhou Enlai, who would soon die of cancer.

In the shadowy realm of elite politics, Mao's own deteriorating health meant that he presided rather distantly amidst factional infighting. Elite rivalries played out through public political campaigns, made deliberately obscure as they targeted surrogate issues that represented conflicts among top leaders. A lengthy but puzzling "Campaign to Criticize Lin Biao and Confucius" indicated continuing uncertainty at the top of the Party. Zhou Enlai's appeal for the "Four Modernizations" of agriculture, industry, science and technology, and national defense was more concrete, tapping the economic practicality of Deng Xiaoping and other rehabilitated old cadres.

By 1976, Mao's Parkinson's and heart disease disabled the one leader who could balance increasingly anxious factions. After Zhou Enlai died in January 1976, radicals seized upon April demonstrations in his memory in Beijing's Tiananmen Square to persuade Mao to purge Deng Xiaoping a second time. Minister of Public Security Hua Guofeng, who had risen with the Cultural Revolution, became new acting premier and first Party Vice-Chairman. Mao was too weak to receive foreign visitors; his voice and his handwriting had become very difficult to understand, rendering his comments ever more oracular. When a devastating earthquake killed a quarter of a million people in the north China city of Tangshan in July, people commented privately about the loss of the traditional "mandate of heaven."

Mao's death on September 9, 1976 triggered a confrontation between rival factions. The leading civilian radicals were arrested in a coup organized by the heads of the army and Mao's bodyguard. The coup leaders had a majority in the Politburo, but feared that a majority of the Central Committee might support Jiang Qing and her allies. Hua Guofeng became Party Chairman. The losers were identified as a "Gang of Four": Mao's widow Jiang Qing, the literary official Yao Wenyuan, the Shanghai boss and deputy premier Zhang Chunqiao, and the Party Vice-Chairman Wang Hongwen. Although they were at first charged with undermining the Cultural Revolution, it soon became clear that the new leadership would ultimately disavow Mao's final mass movement. Few were unhappy to see the imperious Jiang Qing removed. The Gang of Four, along with Lin Biao's generals, became the public scapegoats for the Cultural Revolution.

Impacts of the Cultural Revolution

The political impact was clear at the level of elite politics, where the Communist Party establishment was left reeling, forced to share its power with radical outsiders. Yet these revolutionary impulses were halted and the old order was re-imposed beginning in 1968, albeit with striking changes in personnel. Even those targeted by the Cultural Revolution were rehabilitated within a few years of Mao's death, if they were still alive.

Less obvious, but profound in its consequences, was the systematic victimization of a political minority. Both radicals and conservatives shared a contempt for the "five black elements." They treated millions of people with suspicion, rendering them vulnerable to sudden injustice as political scapegoats.

The disruption of political institutions raised the importance of personal networks, as citizens sought security against unpredictable political campaigns. Networks based upon kinship, shared native place, education, or work experience became places of refuge, despite Maoism's universalistic rhetoric and critique of personal connections. After the suppression of the Red Guards, a new cynicism encouraged gifts and bribes to secure a "back door" advantage for better housing, residence transfer, or specialized medical care. Even at the center, Mao Zedong relied upon Jiang Qing because of her personal loyalty in a duplicitous world. According to Jiang Qing, "Everything I did,

Chairman Mao told me to do. I was his dog. What he said to bite, I bit."

In culture, Jiang Qing, the former movie actress, assumed a central role in the arts, overseeing production of a series of model stage works. Mostly Beijing operas, ballets, and their film versions, these works were created and staged with China's top arts professionals. The stories they told were revolutionary, sometimes adapted from older works, such as the ballet "White-Haired Girl." These works continued a much longer tradition of adapting "modern"(Westernized) techniques to music and theatre. Artists feared making political errors, which slowed production of new work. In less favored cultural genres, such as painting or writing, many artists were jailed or exiled to rural areas, their voices perforce silent. For some, the Cultural Revolution provided an underground, private literary life, with access to ostensibly forbidden books and opportunities to practice calligraphy or perform. Much depended upon personal connections and happenstance. The massive transfer of Red Guards to the countryside altered local cultural conditions, and the experience had a lifelong impact on many of the urban youth, even after they returned home after the Cultural Revolution.

The economic impact of the Cultural Revolution was not so disastrous as many imagine. The Cultural Revolution initially halted economic growth in 1966. Some resisted the political disruptions, urging that young rebels get back to work, "making revolution by promoting production." The 1968 restoration of Party authority and the dispersal of the Red Guards led to two years of extraordinary growth; by Mao's death, China had a decade of moderate economic expansion. China's gross domestic product increased nearly 6 percent annually. This is a slightly slower rate than during the earlier years of the People's Republic, but is by no means an economic disaster. China grew somewhat less rapidly than Indonesia, but twice as fast as India during the same period. All three poor and heavily populated Asian nations grew more slowly than Taiwan, South Korea, Singapore, and Hong Kong, smaller states whose export-driven economies grew by 8–9 percent.

The Maoist political economy substituted China's abundant labor for scarce capital. In the absence of sharp material incentives, it relied upon political campaigns to mobilize labor. Campaigns were effective for some purposes, but ill suited and inefficient for many. China's economic growth was rested upon individual austerity and Spartan consumption, which freed funds for greater public investment. These investments were often inefficiently allocated. One large and secret investment program called the "Third Front" built factories and infrastructure in China's interior. These plants, often military, were further removed from the range of US bombers and missiles based in Taiwan. Despite this investment, which often benefited old revolutionary areas, large regional gaps persisted. The service sector languished, tarnished as bourgeois (there was only one restaurant for 8,000 citizens). Ration coupons regulated the purchase of cotton, grain, meat, cooking oil, and other essential goods.

The Cultural Revolution also pursued longer-term policies to improve China's human capital. Improved nutrition, lower infant mortality, and control of infectious disease helped increase life expectancy, which increased from only 35 in 1949, to 65 by 1980. Nearly two million peasants trained as "barefoot doctors" in an ambitious paramedic network. The barefoot doctors were neither sophisticated nor well equipped, but they were accessible and their services nearly free, as they worked alongside fellow-villagers. They were the best-known aspect of a vast increase in rural medical care. By the end of the Cultural Revolution, two-thirds of China's hospital beds were located in the countryside.

Education was another success in many realms. Most impressive was the growth in literacy, reflecting a fifteenfold increase in rural junior middle schools between 1965 and 1976. Ninety percent of Chinese between the ages of 15 and 19 were literate in 1982. Adult literacy also increased markedly. Schools put work into the school curriculum (such as student gardens) in an effort to make the classrooms relevant to students' lives, thereby rejecting the Confucian educational goal of producing a sophisticated elite.

Against these achievements, high schools were closed during the height of Red Guard activism, although primary schools remained open. In fact, high schools resumed by 1967, as Maoists were desperate to get the Red Guards off the streets. However, universities stopped admitting new students until 1970. Maoists suspected that universities formed a base for conservative elites, which the radicals addressed by recruiting "worker-peasant-soldier" students, a kind of affirmative action scheme. The Cultural Revolution expanded the educational opportunities for people at the bottom, but severely constricted elite access to universities.

China's place in the world

As a self-consciously revolutionary voice in world affairs, China played the role of bad boy in international politics.

Isolated by US, then Soviet pressure, China ended the period with a new and friendlier relationship to the Western powers and Japan.

The United States had not yet come to terms with China's revolution, and in fact continued to recognize the Chiang Kai-shek government in Taiwan as the "Republic of China," pretending that it controlled the mainland. US backing for Chiang Kai-shek kept the People's Republic of China out of the United Nations, and generally isolated in international affairs. The United States gained military bases in Taiwan, to the great frustration of Beijing. US troops were thus closer than the bases in Japan, which followed its US patron in hostility toward Beijing. The United States also based troops in Korea after the armistice ending its war with China.

Poor relations with the West and Japan were perhaps an expected heritage of the revolution. The People's Republic of China had formal relations with Britain, although (or perhaps because) London remained master of its colony in Hong Kong. France broke ranks with the United States to recognize Beijing in 1964, as China looked to reduce its isolation, which appeared more worrisome in light of deteriorating ties with the Soviet bloc. After the 1949 revolution, China looked to the Soviet Union to be its "elder brother in socialism." Thousands of Soviet experts provided advice on Chinese economic projects, and even more Chinese studied Russian. Stalin's death in 1953 made Chinese leaders feel less like younger brothers, and disagreements over development strategy festered. By the early 1960s, China's Communist Party published a series of polemics against Moscow. Titles such as "On Khrushchev's Phoney Communism," drafted by Mao, asserted

Chinese leadership in a world revolutionary movement that Moscow had abandoned. When Cultural Revolutionaries denounced Liu Shaoqi as "China's Khrushchev," he was seen as ignoring class struggle. By 1969 bad feeling spilled over into a pitched battle for control over an island at the Ussuri River border, part of what Beijing and Moscow had formerly celebrated as the world's longest peaceful border.

It is remarkable to achieve the simultaneous enmity of both Washington and Moscow. This strategic disadvantage left China surrounded in a hostile world, with armed enemies on all sides. China possessed one military protection, the nuclear bomb which it tested in 1964. Even with primitive delivery systems, China's bomb caused its rivals to hesitate. The United States and the Soviet Union discussed, but never implemented a joint strike on Chinese nuclear facilities. China railed against Soviet–American steps toward nuclear arms reduction, which it regarded as protecting the international status quo. Although Beijing hailed its bomb as a Maoist victory against imperialism and revisionism, in practice its military posture was defensive, relying upon a massive infantry to discourage foreign meddling.

China repeatedly appealed to third world unity against the super-powers, but did not find much success. The 1950s heritage of anti-colonialist politics which China endorsed at the 1955 Bandung Conference failed to prevent India and China from fighting a brief, but fierce border war in 1962. China looked to Indonesia as a partner, but the 1965 coup, which overthrew the Indonesian leader Sukarno, resulted in the massacre of hundreds of thousands of Indonesian leftists and overseas Chinese, and the installation of a US client regime.

On its own doorstep, China could not prevent the American military intervention in Vietnam. While China aided its neighbor, it never matched the greater material assistance offered by the Soviet Union. Soviet weapons were in fact sometimes pilfered by Red Guards from trains in transit from Russia to Vietnam. Chinese support for revolutionary and anti-colonial movements was strong on rhetoric, but weak in material terms. China expected other rebels to practice the self-reliance that the Communists had learned in their own revolution. The rhetorical exuberance was accompanied by organizational maneuvers, and China encouraged Communist parties around the world to split, typically leaving the major established Party allied to Moscow, with a smaller and weaker "Communist Party (Marxist-Leninist)" which followed Beijing's more radical language.

China was diplomatically isolated during the 1966–68 radical phase of the Cultural Revolution. Foreign diplomats in Beijing were subjected to ill-treatment. A mob burned down the office of the British *chargé d'affaires*. Premier Zhou Enlai raged at those who failed to control the demonstrators, but the episode demonstrated the breakdown of central control. Unable to maintain the fiction of normal diplomatic relations, Beijing recalled all ambassadors except the ambassador to Egypt.

By 1969 and the end of the radical phase of the Cultural Revolution, China's ambitions to break free of encirclement had obviously failed. American bombers flew across China (especially Hainan Island) with impunity to drop bombs on China's ally, Vietnam. Although US arms drops to rebels in Tibet apparently ended in 1965, the Central Intelligence Agency continued to pay the Dalai Lama an annual retainer in order to annoy China. China's 1969 battle with Soviet troops on the Ussuri River pushed Mao toward reconsidering his nation's global position. Beijing could identify only a few friendly governments beyond Vietnam, North Korea, Pakistan, Algeria, and Albania. China had sought to win over the affection of the "peoples" of the world rather than their governments, but this failed to make hostile governments change their policies.

In a bold shift, Mao imagined that rapprochement with the United States would divide the two superpowers from pursuing an anti-Chinese common front. China offered the United States a reconciliation, which would smooth its pending military defeat in Vietnam. Beijing invited the American journalist Edgar Snow to stand beside Mao at the 1970 national day parade on October 1. In 1937 Snow had written the best-selling *Red Star over China*, which introduced the Chinese Communist movement to the world. Red-baited in the United States and driven into exile in Switzerland, Snow welcomed the visit as a personal vindication, never imagining that Mao believed he was a CIA agent all along. Other "people-to-people" diplomacy, including the visit of an American ping pong team, prepared the way for Henry Kissinger's secret trip as National Security Advisor in July 1971. Kissinger, who travelled via Pakistan and avoided the press by feigning illness, negotiated Richard Nixon's visit to Beijing for February 1972.

The United Nations awarded Beijing China's seat in October 1971, signaling Mao's strategic realignment. Third world nations had embarrassed the United States by an annual campaign to expel Chiang Kai-shek's representatives, but had failed to win enough votes before the signals that Sino-American relations were shifting.

The secrecy and suddenness of this realignment led to bumpy transitions. Japanese politicians, loyal supporters of US anticommunism in East Asia, were humiliated when the United States abandoned its old policy without consulting them. The US puppet government in South Vietnam real-ized that its end was in sight. An even greater sense of betrayal and panic emerged in Taiwan, when American pretensions to support Guomindang claims to the mainland collapsed. Perhaps only a zealous anti-Communist like Richard Nixon could have overseen the rapprochement without political risk, but even he had to deal with out-raged or at best highly doubtful conservative supporters. CIA counter-intelligence chief James Jesus Angleton believed that the Sino-Soviet split was only a trick by Mos-cow to encourage the West to let down its guard. Forces invested in the Cold War status quo dragged their heels on both sides, including Chinese Minister of Defense Lin Biao. Serious resistance from the Chinese military ended with Lin's violent death.

China's deal with the United States was ambiguous, but helpful to both sides. Both nations backed away from their allies in the Vietnam War and combined to oppose the Soviet Union. The United States removed both its troops and diplomatic recognition from Taiwan in 1979. China probably imagined this would lead to political unification with Taiwan. But removal of US military bases from Taiwan enabled China to redirect its own investment toward coastal regions and wind down the costly Third Front program in the interior. In an unplanned outcome, the end of US military backing for the Guomindang martial law government opened the way for Taiwan's democratization, moving the island even further from unification.

The *realpolitik* of reconciliation with the United States shows how pragmatic Chinese foreign policy had become in practice, despite often flamboyant anti-imperialist rhetoric. Underscoring this unsentimental long view of national interest was China's 1974 seizure of the Xisha islands from South Vietnam, taking advantage of the weakness of the US puppet government, and ignoring the claims of its ostensible North Vietnamese allies.

The fall of Maoism

The calculating realism of China's foreign relations reminds us of the limits to the idealism of the most ardent Cultural Revolutionaries. The earliest academic analyses of radical Maoism depended upon documentary sources which tilted toward beliefs and ardor; later accounts by participants shifted the perspective to stress the importance of more pragmatic, often self-serving, actions.

The relationship between the 1964–76 era and the newly powerful China of the contemporary global economy is not simple. A conventional narrative dismisses the Cultural Revolution as a decade of xenophobic chaos and economic ruin, one only put right when a shrewd Deng Xiaoping recognized reality and reintegrated China with the world economy. This is too simple.

The rapid economic growth of the Deng Xiaoping era depended upon the physical infrastructure and human resources created by Mao Zedong's regime. Mao's radical politics were obviously a desperate effort to sustain China's revolution beyond the lifespan of the revolutionary generation, producing a political turbulence of the kind that has followed other great revolutions. Less obvious were the contributions of modernization, ending illiteracy, combating chronic disease, and setting the foundations for industrialization. For all of Maoist China's obvious short-comings, the subsequent economic boom built upon its achievements. It may be tempting to view the Cultural Revolution as a lost decade for China's development, but China enjoyed much greater international opportunities after the Cultural Revolution than before. The world economy did not need China's huge labor pool in the 1960s. But when China turned outward after the Cultural Revolution, a rapidly expanding global economy used offshore production in China to discipline workers back home with threats of job loss, as wages stagnated and labor unions weakened.

This is not to say that Mao consciously placed China on the course it has pursued since his death. Mao worried about capitalist "representatives" who had "sneaked" into positions of power, as he explained in the May 16, 1966 "Notification" that opened the Cultural Revolution: "Once conditions are ripe, they will seize political power and turn the dictatorship of the proletariat into a dictatorship of the bourgeoisie. Some of them we have already seen through; others we have not. Some are still trusted by us and are being trained as our successors, persons like Khrushchev for example, who are still nest-ling beside us."

But Mao had mellowed by 1973, recalling Deng Xiaoping from disgrace and making him a top economic administra-tor. A further continuity between the late Mao era and the present is the state-directed character of economic policy, however more liberal it has become. China's revolution, including the Cultural Revolution, formed a long-term movement to strengthen China to compete in the broader world. Hiring out its cheap labor supply to global capitalism was a politically crafted strategy, much like earlier Maoist efforts to harness these same workers through political campaigns.

The Cultural Revolution era remains unsettling in Chinese memory. It has been the subject of thousands of stories, films, memoirs, and articles, so it is untrue that is a forbidden topic. It is more accurate to say that most Chinese treat the Cultural Revolution with caution, and that the Party remains quite sensitive to what is said. In part this is because many of China's senior leaders were themselves Red Guards, and are both anxious about their reputations and mindful of the costs of political disorder. Caution is also increased because of the heritage of the June 4, 1989 massacre, which has made the Party even more determined to discourage the memory of political activism.

Despite the restrained discussion, Chinese representations of the Cultural Revolution era can be highly divergent. Among the most successful artistic representations the differences are noteworthy. Jiang Yang's memoir *A Cadre School Life: Six Chapters* employs lapidary prose to record the everyday life and struggle of a family of prominent intellectuals forced to resettle in an impoverished countryside. In contrast, Jiang Wen's 1994 film *In the Heat of the Sun* looks at the period through the eyes of a young teen, unfettered by adult controls, who enjoys exuberant self-discovery amidst the chaos. There is no consensus, but a range of voices, just as there was an array of personal experiences. As the era becomes more distant, images of the Cultural Revolution are now just as likely to be provided by pop culture phenomena such as Cultural Revolution themed restaurants as by family memories that perhaps are not often shared.

9. *Reform and Rebuilding, 1976–1988*

TIMOTHY CHEEK

THE initial phases of the post-Mao reform period in China began with a coup in October 1976 and ended with military repression in June 1989. It also started with the CCP leadership promising a "liberation of thought" and closed with demands for more political voice from a broader public. Throughout these dozen years China opened more and more to the world beyond the Communist bloc, society relaxed, and the economy grew. The reforms and the various reactions to them that shaped this history grew out of the experience and challenges of the Mao period—the economic disaster of the Great Leap Forward (1958–60) and the social dislocations of the Cultural Revolution decade (1966–76). The reforms were intended to correct the errors of Mao's final years, rebuild the Communist Party, and improve life for all Chinese. The results were mixed: the Party survived, China's economy grew, but new social forces were released leading to the great confrontation and crisis of Tiananmen in 1989, the main subject of the next chapter.

The reform was engineered by the CCP leadership but shaped by responses from among both Party factions and social groups. Three phases of reform and response define the political history of this period: succession politics (1975–78), reform efforts (1980–86), and political stalemate (1986–88). This history of reform–reaction–readjustment profoundly changed the lives of Party members, intellectuals, economic elites, rural society, and popular culture. While reform came to an impasse by early 1989, by the end of the first long decade of reform the essential features of the model of economic openness and authoritarian rule that has overseen China's tremendous economic growth into the third decade of the twenty-first century were laid down. The economic plan endorsed by the CCP in 1987 set the model of authoritarian state capitalism, a system that mixes market economy elements with tight political control and only the partial privatization of State Owned Enterprises (SOEs). The political will to follow through took the struggles of the next decade to resolve, and the social consequences—particularly in official corruption and a staggering gap between rich and poor—remain unresolved.

Politics: succession, reform, and stalemate

China's economic reforms began after the failures of the Great Leap in the early 1960s, but were cut short by the Cultural Revolution. They were revived in 1972, following the rapprochement with the United States, but again sidelined by central political struggles, as various political

groups within the CCP positioned themselves for the anticipated succession crisis—who would take over from Mao?
At the Fourth National People's Congress in 1975 it seemed
the bureaucratic "moderates" would prevail under the ailing Premier Zhou Enlai. Deng Xiaoping was brought back
from disgrace to manage the economy. But Zhou died in
January 1976 and the "radicals" around Mao's wife, Jiang
Qing, took the initiative and pressed for a return to radical
Cultural Revolution policies of "all-round dictatorship of
the proletariat." When Mao died in September those political struggles were quickly resolved in the arrest and purge
of Madame Mao and her colleagues, now dubbed "The
Gang of Four."

The three major forces within the Party—the radicals,
the bureaucratic survivors, and the old leadership (soon to
be officially rehabilitated)—cobbled together a succession
plan. Mao was buried with great pomp and ceremony and
a huge mausoleum built for him in Tiananmen Square. The
slogans and images of the Cultural Revolution would be
continued under a new Chairman, the distinctly uncharis-
matic Hua Guofeng, but the substantive policies of the
radical decades would be reversed, the technocratic policies
of the 1963 Four Modernizations (in Industry, Agriculture,
National Defense, and Science & Technology) revived, and
the purged Party leaders and cadres rehabilitated and
reinstated. However, beyond a firm commitment to avoid
any more of the chaos of the previous decades and to
restore some predictability to political life there was no
consensus among this collective leadership on what reform
would look like.

The succession was resolved in December 1978 when
a major Party conclave endorsed Deng Xiaoping as

Vice-Chairman and put into leadership positions rehabilitated colleagues supportive of him. Deng undertook several key political reforms. His first and fundamental act was to restore Leninist administrative order and put an end to charismatic leadership—that is, rule by Party committee. Deng refused to take up Mao's mantle as "Chairman." Since Deng Xiaoping held acknowledged revolutionary credentials among his colleagues, he could and did use his revolutionary charisma to blunt the public charisma of the Party Chairman, thereby sidelining Hua Guofeng. This required the Party apparatus to return to its earlier Leninist norms of collective leadership under the General Secretary of the Central Committee of the CCP, now the highest post in China. The first new General Secretary was Hu Yaobang, appointed at the same Twelfth Congress of the CCP in 1982 that abolished the position of Chairman. The reform era CCP is not a democratic party, but it is an organized one with bureaucratic hierarchy and lines of authority. This has produced the coherent and resilient government that has overseen China's reforms for nearly four decades.

Deng Xiaoping's second attack on charismatic leadership was a careful de-Maoification, enshrined in the June 1981 "Historical Resolution" passed by the Central Committee. Its main purpose was to lay the Cultural Revolution to rest and to account for Mao's failings without undermining his role as the legitimization of the CCP. To discredit Mao utterly would be to make the mistake of Khrushchev who undermined the CPSU in the Soviet Union with his accurate denunciations of Stalin. The resolution lays down a narrative, a way to think about China's revolutionary history that begins with a litany of achievements of Party rule up to 1966—going lightly over the disasters of the Great Leap—and admitting the responsibility of Mao and the collective leadership for the errors of the Cultural Revolution. Collective leadership and Party organization are the theme of the Historical Resolution—claiming the organizational side of Maoism and laying aside the charismatic parts.

Putting Mao in his historical place did not mean the end of ideology. This key document for reform of China is all about ideology; the issue was simply *which* sort of ideology the CCP should follow. "Many outstanding leaders of our Party made important contributions to the formation and development of Mao Zedong Thought," the Historical Resolution declares, "and they are synthesized in the scientific works of Comrade Mao Zedong... " The collective nature of this body of political wisdom is emphasized in order to justify not only the relevance of Mao Zedong Thought but also to certify the surviving leaders: they were contributors to this ideology and thus are the legitimate leaders of China. The prophet is gone, but the Church remains.

Reform as experimentation

Deng Xiaoping's reforms did not go smoothly. In addition to the internal contradictions between social and economic relaxation while maintaining political control, the Four Modernizations program was bedeviled by residual political resistance among the leadership and rank and file who either felt the de facto capitalist nature of the reforms was a repudiation of socialism and Mao's ideals or, regardless of ideological niceties, saw their privileges threatened. These people coalesced around the senior figure, Chen Yun, the only Party leader of rank, experience, and prestige to challenge Deng Xiaoping's position—even though the two leaders were not necessarily competitors politically. Throughout the 1980s these two "political parties" within the CCP contested. Deng Xiaoping, however, was a wily politician, second only to Mao in his ability to manipulate the Chinese political system. Putting in his protégé, Hu Yaobang, as the General Secretary left Deng as the king maker and arbiter as the forces around the Party reformers and Party traditionalists debated goals, put forward policies, and tried to subvert each other's programs. After many ups and downs, social changes in China gave market-oriented reforms the edge despite the political stalemate in the late 1980s and the turmoil of Tiananmen.

The Third Plenum in 1978 set Deng Xiaoping's reform goals. First, it made economic modernization the central goal of Party work. Second, it began to address the wounds of the Cultural Revolution by reversing verdicts on Party cadres who had been purged by Mao. Third, the plenum approved experimentation with market forces, beginning the breaking open of the Planned Economy. The slogan from that time was "practice"—and would produce the key slogan of the 1980s, "practice is the sole criterion of truth." These policies were implemented over the next few years in a series of administrative changes designed to "open" China to the world market and to extricate the CCP from daily management of farming, factories, and business.

The heart of this first wave of reforms was decollectivization, in which the communes established in the late 1950s were broken up. This was formalized in the 1983

Responsibility System. Land was not returned to the individual farmer, but to the natural village, which, in turn, leased individual family farming plots for at first fifteen years (and by the 1990s up to fifty years). In the cities, reform in the State Owned Enterprises was much slower, but management authority was given to enterprise managers, along with some freedom to keep profits above the State Plan and some responsibility to cover their unit's own debts. Party leaders could not agree on whether to adjust the centrally planned economy or give over to a market system. Piecemeal policies pushed first for more enterprise reform and then retrenched to more central planning. There was considerable confusion.

In addition to rural and industrial reform, the Party began to experiment with administrative reform. In the countryside, it replaced the administrative role of the 55,000 People's Communes with 96,000 rural townships, making this lowest level of formal administration more effective by having to care for a smaller population. Administrative reform also included the promise of more citizenship participation by allowing some a small degree of democracy. But what this meant was not entirely clear at first. For example, there were local elections in municipal districts within Beijing in the early 1980s, but the Party subsequently got nervous and reverted to administrative appointment of local leaders.

Reactions to reform

The issue of democracy became one of the first challenges to the leadership arising from the unanticipated consequences of reform. Mao Zedong, after all, had declared the Cultural Revolution to be a form of "big democracy" for the revolutionary masses. In the 1980s, the challenges to Party policies started at the top, among China's prestigious intellectuals inside the Party and its major universities. Hot debates on the reform of socialism, advocating socialist humanism and Party reform, as well as exposing in detail the errors of the Great Leap and Cultural Revolution, scandalized the political public in China's cities. The Party traditionalists feared that too much criticism would bring a chaos similar to that of the Cultural Revolution. The result was a political seesaw of thaw and repression.

In 1978 Democracy Wall in Beijing caught worldwide attention. Could China be going democratic already? For some heady weeks in December 1978, Beijing residents could stroll down to the Xidan district and read astonishing posters that talked about the (until recently) unmentionable: the abuses of the Cultural Revolution. These were the same "big character posters" that Red Guards had used in the Cultural Revolution to denounce "capitalist roaders" and "Soviet revisionists" inside the Party, but now this form of Maoist democracy was turned on the abuses and suffering of the Cultural Revolution and pointedly called upon the CCP to make amends. "Democracy," declared a wall-poster by Wei Jingsheng, an electrician at the Beijing Zoo, "is the *fifth* modernization!" China seemed, in the words of one journalist, Roger Garside, to be "coming alive."

During his visit to the United States in 1979 to celebrate the recognition of China by the world's dominant economy and power, Deng Xiaoping let the press wonder about Democracy Wall. Domestically, the revelations of abuses of power by the radical leadership also served to discredit remaining leaders in the CCP who were closely associated with the Cultural Revolution and who were standing in the way of Deng's reforms. However, in spring 1979, Democracy Wall was unceremoniously moved to a small park in western Beijing and those who wished to put up posters had to register their name and address with the authorities. By fall, the leaders of Democracy Wall (most notably Wei Jingsheng) were arrested, tried, and jailed. Public advocacy of political democracy of the liberal or parliamentary sort came to an end then, as Deng Xiaoping laid down the Four Cardinal Principles in March 1979 (which insisted that all public acts should uphold socialism and support Party leadership). It became clear from this example that Deng Xiaoping's tolerance of political free speech was tactical rather than substantive. It also became clear that the Party could and would shut down inconvenient public speech or assembly by force.

Intellectual agitation for change moved to the safer channels of the Party press, think tanks, and universities. These establishment channels frightened the Party much less. Indeed, various leaders hurried to gather together their own think tanks and professors to "research" their policy preferences. In the early 1980s reform intellectuals backed by one or another Party leader pushed for a latitudinarian interpretation of Maoism that focused on the need to protect individual and collective rights against the abuses of those in power. These debates were the public face of inner-Party divisions over the nature and directions of reform: was the planned economy to remain? Were markets to take over? What would be the role of the CCP? Of Maoism?

These debates were also national in character. The public sphere of reform China is a "directed public sphere."

Press and public discussion is managed by the CCP's propaganda department. In the 1980s Party control was still total—press, radio, and very soon TV, were centrally controlled and heavily censored. The major newspapers were limited—*People's Daily*, *Guangming Daily*, and *Liberation Daily*—but they were available more or less for free everywhere. As the central leadership experimented and argued over reform, these tools of propaganda became avenues for public discussion that were much livelier and more varied than had been the case under Mao. In short, when an intellectual or policy adviser, such as Liu Binyan or Wang Ruoshui (whom we will meet, below), could get an article into the *People's Daily*, it was read by not only intellectuals and professionals across China, but also workers, farmers, and cadres in the villages. This was not a free public sphere, but it was a coherent national public space. While the proposals and suggestions that survived the censor's pen were incremental rather than revolutionary, they reached the broadest possible audience and built a public presumption that reform was good, necessary, and required being open to taking chances.

Meanwhile, by 1985 the economy was in trouble. The flurry of economic energy released by rural decollectivization slowed by 1984 and the government's abolition of mandatory grain purchases in 1985 depressed agricultural prices. Farmers began to be squeezed by the classic scissors effect—rising costs for inputs (fertilizer and pesticides) and falling price for produce. Farmers began to look to sideline industries for more cash, to move away from grain to specialized crops, and to migration to the towns and cities for urban employment. Importantly, farmers experienced these changes as a promise broken and they complained.

In the cities, the transition to a more market-oriented economy was painful, as well. The incentive system for enterprises, involving relaxation of the planned economy and price controls, led to overheating of the economy and a surge of inflation by 1985. The response of the CCP leadership, under Premier Zhao Ziyang, was put forth in April 1986 as the Seventh Five-Year Plan. Rated by scholars as one of the most realistic and sound plans ever promulgated in China, Zhao proposed further extension of market mechanisms, in essence a gradual "growing out of the plan," as economist Barry Naughton has described it, under the slogan "socialist commodity market."

Stalemate

Politics, however, intervened. The trouble was not on the streets or in the salons, it was in the halls of power and stemmed from the incomplete de-Maoification of Deng Xiaoping's reforms. There were strong forces inside the CCP and the military that were not happy with such reform plans. Three major groups opposed reform. First, the leaders and officials who ran the planned economy. They found their advocate in the senior leader Chen Yun. He supported a role for the market, but only in support of the Plan. This group worried about lower grain production, the growing gap between the developing coastal regions and the interior provinces, and the explosion of corruption which they saw as a result of more liberalized policies and contact with the West. To this group, reform was leading to chaos. Second, orthodox Party leaders such as Peng Zhen worried about the consequences of reform for the social fabric of China. This group took seriously the moral claims of Maoism and saw in the vibrant but uncontrolled changes of the early 1980s the "corrosive influence of decadent bourgeois ideology and remnant feudal ideas." While no supporters of radical Maoism, these members of the Party's ideological organizations still believed in "socialist spiritual civilization" and saw the need for the Party to educate the public and protect the weak from the ravages of bourgeois markets. Of course, they felt that they themselves were best suited to undertake this task as teachers of society. Third, senior military leaders also held to a similar socially conservative version of Maoism. They didn't like the "disorder" of the newly freed social life and even less did they like recent cuts in their budgets.

Resistance inside the Party to reform coalesced around a leadership fight against Deng's current successor, General Secretary Hu Yaobang. Demonstrations by students in December 1986, which Hu failed to suppress with sufficient vigour, frightened the Party elite and provided the opportunity to dismiss Hu Yaobang in January 1987 and to slow down reform. This success for the Party traditionalists also saw the public "Anti-Bourgeois Liberalization" campaign that, amongst other things, expelled reformist editor Wang Ruoshui. This 1987 retrenchment against market and political reform succeeded in having Hu Yaobang criticized and purged. However, unlike the practice of earlier years, Hu was not demonized, humiliated, and imprisoned (or killed). In fact, he maintained his Party membership and comfortable living situation, but he was politically neutralized. In his stead, Deng Xiaoping moved the Premier, Zhao Ziyang, to become the new Party leader

(General Secretary). The tensions between Party traditionalists and Party reformers did not lessen; they increased. While Zhao Ziyang was a reformer, his successor as Premier (at the top of the National People's Congress and state government structure) was a Party conservative, Li Peng. Deng Xiaoping was playing his balancing act.

Yet reform was not to be stopped. As far as political leadership was concerned, this was because Deng Xiaoping remained committed to the basic line of reform: market liberalization, opening to the world, continued Party rule, and no charismatic rubbish. Thus, the Thirteenth Party Congress in October 1987 recommitted to reform under the slogan, "initial stage of socialism." This odd slogan explained the capitalist market reforms of the CCP in terms of orthodox Marxist-Leninist theory—China had to pass through an actual and developed capitalist mode of production before "fully" coming to socialism. This way of looking at reform policy may seem tortured to outsiders, but it made sense to insiders, as it allowed both economic and administrative reform while maintaining the commitment to the Party's ordering of society.

The compromise did not hold, mostly because the social consequences of reform sharpened. On the one hand, Party traditionalists were increasingly worried that the Party was losing control of changes in society, on the other hand, new social groups were emerging that pressed for more change.

Society: the costs of "coming alive"

Socially, the two greatest unintended consequences for reform were inflation and official corruption. No one really knew exactly how to shift from a planned economy, where prices for inputs or products are set by economists working for the central state, to an economy where those prices are determined by market exchanges. The government experimented with a two-track price system for industrial enterprises. Basic production operated under the state plan at set prices. Once the quota set by the plan had been met, extra production could be sold at higher market prices and the extra profits could be kept by the enterprise. In one sense, this legitimized the "grey market" for resources that had existed under the plan for years, but the opportunity to exploit the price difference between, say, iron at the plan rate and iron at market rates, was too much for many factory managers or local officials to resist. Profiteering was common and obvious to ordinary Chinese who resented it. Resentment turned to outrage in the face of inflation that cut into the daily lives of urban residents who still lived on fixed work unit incomes. In fact, 1989 saw the worst inflation and the most visible official corruption in China since the founding of the PRC.

The social experience of reform in the 1980s was profound and varied. Life in the Party and for cadres changed, a new business community emerged (albeit in close collaboration with local Party leaders), intellectuals struggled to find their role in public life, while youth developed a new popular culture, and rural life prospered but still struggled.

Party life

Reform saw the power and position of Party cadres change. Under Mao they had been the all-powerful agents of the total state with not only police powers to back up their decisions but daily control over the housing, ration coupons, employment, and health care of those under their charge. Reform in the 1980s both decentralized administrative power from the center to provincial and local authorities and also put much of the everyday necessities of life onto "the market." Increasingly workers or university graduates could find work independently of the allocation system controlled by local Party leaders. Farming choices and revenues devolved to the peasant household, ration coupons were phased out. To be sure, Party approval for important decisions remained, not least in the required permission to move one's personnel file from one work unit to another or to approve registration in a new city. However, by the late 1980s being a Party cadre had changed from local lord to local fixer. In this context it was their cultural capital—knowledge of how the system worked, privileged access to forthcoming Party decisions and initiatives, and a fearsome network of connections—that propelled local Party cadres into a new formulation of elites in local China: the Party–business alliance. Working with local business interests (often made of retired or even sitting Party officials), Party cadres could "deliver the goods" (Deng Xiaoping's call to develop local economies) and also do well for themselves. This required, however, a continuing display of loyalty to the Party and Party norms, slogans, and campaigns. If at the central level, the "King is Dead, Long Live the King!" version of Maoism saw a return to collective leadership, at the local level Party administration under the name of continuing socialism— albeit designated a "primary stage of socialism"—created a new political economy of Party–business collaboration that has continued to today. Some call this crony capitalism but the local Chinese version of this Party–business alliance is far more widespread (numbers of people and range of areas involved) and economically generative than simple favours for friends of the national elite. It is both corrupt and, so far, effective.

The CCP began its transformation to a modern authoritarian regime in the 1980s. The excesses of charismatic leadership were curtailed, though the commitment to guiding ideology and "the thought" of the current top leader remained. Nationally, the balance of power between central and regional authorities was adjusted, beginning with decentralization in 1984 (and counter-balanced by fiscal recentralization in 1998). Locally, the same devolution of authority put more discretion in the hands of township Party secretaries. The trade-off at all levels was clear: the local leader gets more leeway but is also now personally responsible for the results. China went from one dictator to 10,000 who had to live cheek by jowl with those over whom they ruled. Socially, the Party in the 1980s began its retreat from the full-fledged Propaganda State of the Mao period. More like Taiwan under Chiang Kai-shek in the 1960s, Chinese were offered much more personal latitude and increasing market or consumer freedom. In exchange they needed only to profess loyalty to the current leadership and stay out of political trouble. No more thought reform, no more "struggle campaigns." It was not freedom in the sense of a legally protected civil society, but most Chinese experienced this political relaxation as a "second liberation."

Business and commerce

China under Mao had been a planned economy with all economic actors owned either by local collectives or by the state. Deng Xiaoping's reforms returned a measure of private business in China by allowing small businesses and permitting foreign businesses to invest in China. The Joint Venture law of 1979 began the process of bringing in capital and know-how from Western and Asian firms by allowing co-investment in a Chinese business. Domestically, the surplus labor power of rural China was engaged in Township Village Enterprises (TVEs). The old workshops, mills, and handicraft sheds of the communes were converted into semi-commercial enterprises that sold their agricultural equipment, soya sauce, or fertilizer on the market. Approved in 1984, TVEs grew from 1.3 million to 6 million that year and reached some 23 million by the end of the "Golden Decade" of TVEs in 1996. In all, TVEs provided 135 million jobs and produced one third of China's industrial output in the early 1990s.

The stars of Deng's reforms were the Special Economic Zones. These were export processing zones that enticed foreign investment with promises of low wages, little red tape, and tax incentives. They were modeled on Taiwan's successful export processing zone in Kaohsiung that had opened in 1966 and spurred the island's spectacular economic development. The first four SEZs were established in China in 1980 with Shenzhen, a sleepy village on the border of Hong Kong as the test case (the other three were: Zhuhai, Shantou, and Xiamen—all in Guangdong or neighboring Fujian province). In 1984 preferential terms for foreign investment were extended to a further fourteen cities—up and down the coast from Manchuria in the north to Hainan Island in the south. By 1988 trade and exports were booming. China's foreign trade soared from US$21 billion in 1978 to US$166 billion in 1992. The SEZs became the home of over 5,000 companies authorized to conduct foreign trade—in 1978 under the planned economy there had been exactly 12 authorized trading firms.

These new, globally engaged firms began to change the face of Chinese society. Private business had been banned in Mao's China as capitalist exploitation. But Deng Xiaoping had declared, "To Get Rich is Glorious!" Now business people were "entrepreneurs" contributing to "socialism with Chinese characteristics." And they were not alone. Domestically, plucky farmers and workers set up their own small businesses as street vendors, petty traders, and curb-side repair services. Known as *getihu*, these small-scale independent business operators quickly filled the consumer and service needs of urban populations tired of the limited offerings, long lines, and poor service of state-run retail outlets. At the same time the *getihu* were viewed with suspicion by local Party officials who resented the devolution of market access to these parvenus. Customers also viewed them with ambivalence, fearing these hucksters were somehow cheating them. The fabulous rise in wealth of some clever *getihu* would engender the resentment of Beijing students in the late 1980s who blamed the Party for allowing such "cheaters" to prosper.

Intellectuals and popular culture

The 1980s saw the final efforts of China's establishment intellectuals to act out their role as servants to the state and teachers of the people. A range of talented, thoughtful, and daring intellectuals committed to their service as Party members spoke up forthrightly to address the errors of the past and the challenges of the present. Their reception was decidedly mixed and by decade's end they had been silenced. With the waning of their establishment role, intellectuals turned to the emerging cultural realm that was growing in the newly allowed sphere of commercial media. A "culture craze" in the 1980s shook intellectual and Party circles alike. Whether speaking for the Party or from society, 1980s intellectuals maintained their role as teachers of the people in search of a "total" answer to China's problems—the same form of ideology they had learned under Mao, but with changing content.

Liu Binyan (1925–2005) was a Party journalist for whom the experience of the Cultural Revolution demanded that he push Party reform further than simply as a return to the status quo of the early 1960s. Liu reflects the success of Mao's efforts to get intellectuals back into touch with the common people. "Fate brought us into intimate contact with the lowest levels of the laboring masses; our joys and worries became for a time the same as their own. Our hopes were no different from theirs." And yet, Liu assumes an elite role: "This experience allowed us to see, to hear, and to feel for ourselves things that others have been unable to see, hear, or feel." Liu was confident that if writers had been allowed to speak the truth of their experiences "they would have helped the Party to see its mistakes while there was still time to make changes." It was a call to let intellectuals and professionals do their work without political blinders.

Wang Ruoshui (1926–2002), a theorist working in the *People's Daily*, set out to provide the ideological platform for the reforms by promising to create "Marxian humanism." The key term in Wang's reformist Marxist analysis was "alienation." In Marxist theory this is the "alienation" of labor that workers experience under capitalism—commonly referred to as "exploitation"—that drives their struggle for socialist revolution. Under Stalin and Mao, the Communists declared that this alienation was a thing of the past under the glorious rule of the Party. Wang spoke for a generation of Party intellectuals who survived the Cultural Revolution and they disagreed. In a piece translated by the Sinologist David Kelly, he wrote:

In the past, we did many stupid things in economic construction due to our lack of experience.... And in the end we ate our own bitter fruit; this is alienation in the economic realm.... [T]he people's servants sometimes made indiscriminate use of the power conferred on them by the people, and turned into their masters; this is alienation in the political realm. As for alienation in the intellectual realm, the classic example is the personality cult...

Wang's critique of the "personality cult" pointed to Mao, of course. Wang saw the personality cult as the willing transfer to the leader of powers and dignities that rightfully belonged to "the people." Wang Ruoshui was no dissident. He was part of what has been called the "counter-elite" in Eastern Europe in the 1980s, in-house critics within Communist Parties. Indeed, Wang Ruoshui and his colleagues were aware of developments in Eastern Europe and cited their writings. We often think of Communism as monolithic, but this was not.

Fang Lizhi (1926–2012) went further. By the 1980s Fang was an internationally respected astrophysicist and a vice-president of China's prestigious Science and Technology University. His experiences as a victim of both the anti-rightist campaign in the late 1950s and in the Cultural Revolution radicalized him: he had had it with Party ideology; he trusted in science. In 1986 Fang spoke to demonstrating students in Shanghai on democracy and the role of students and intellectuals. "If you want to understand democracy," Fang advised, "look at how people understand it in developed countries." According to Fang, the root of democracy resided in "the rights of each individual." Fang implored the students to stand up for themselves and for the good of China: "the most crucial thing of all is to have a democratic mentality and a democratic spirit." He wanted the students to apply the scientific attitude to politics. Fang Lizhi, who had recently travelled to Europe, held up European universities as bastions of intellectual freedom protected both from government meddling and pressures from big business. "The intellectual realm must be independent and have its own values," Fang declared. This was a frontal attack on the establishment intellectual role. Fang concluded, "We must refuse to cater to power. Only when we do this will Chinese intellectuals be transformed into genuine intellectuals." Although supported by the reformist leadership under Hu Yaobang, in the end all three reformist Party intellectuals were purged in 1987 in the "Anti-Spiritual Pollution Campaign."

Meanwhile, intellectual effort moved to the emerging public sphere of commercial publishing and TV. The newest generation of youth in high schools and universities and the emerging popular culture, now somewhat freed from total direction by the Party, created a "culture craze" in the mid-1980s that sought to explore and discuss the cultural roots of China's problems and to promote a "New Enlightenment" movement. While popular in the sense of being non-governmental, these groups of students and intellectuals were largely speaking to each other, and to Party sponsors behind the scenes. The new mood reached the mass media in part through the book series published by these groups, which turned out to sell quite well, and also through TV and film, most notably the controversial 1986 TV series, *River Elegy* and new films like Chen Kaige's *Yellow Earth* in 1984 and Zhang Yimou's *Red Sorghum* in 1987. These films drew from the emerging mood of critical fiction (Zhang Yimou's film was based on Mao Yan's 1986 novel of the same name). Writers such as Su Tong (b. 1963), Yu Hua (b. 1960), and Mo Yan (b. 1955) probed the psychology of their generation's experiences through the Cultural Revolution. Together they re-tell the story of China's revolution in dark and complicated terms, focusing on individuals, families, and ironic twists of fate rather than the drama of class struggle and the "shining road" of Socialism.

Su Tong's and Yu Hua's short stories offered a voice for the children who grew up when the Cultural Revolution came to their town. Their stories will remind English readers more of *Lord of the Flies* than *Tom Sawyer* or *Catcher in the Rye*. Su Tong's 1990 novel that became the film *Raise High the Red Lantern* (1991) takes the critique of Chinese culture to gender politics in the story of four concubines in an unnamed time that focuses on culture and gender oppression rather than national politics. Meanwhile, Wang Shuo (b. 1958), most famous for *Playing for Thrills* (1989), scandalized the reading public with irreverent and pugnacious stories of working-class life, introducing "hooligan literature." These were the backdrop of youth and popular culture when a series of events would catapult a million students into Tiananmen Square in defiance of the Party in spring 1989.

The most widely viewed example of the 1980s culture craze was the TV program *River Elegy*. It condemned China's traditional civilization, as symbolized by the Yellow River, the Great Wall, and the dragon, for stifling China's creativity. The series had vivid imagery that conveyed the sense that China, like the Yellow River, once at the forefront of civilization, had dried up because of its emphasis on stability, isolation, and conservatism. By contrast, it showed flowing blue seas as symbolizing the exploring, open culture of the West and Japan. The series also used documentary footage from the Great Leap Forward and the Cultural Revolution. The juxtaposition of images and statements created a subtext equating Maoist-Stalinist orthodoxy with state Confucianism and traditional culture—and both were portrayed as disasters. The solution to China's problems, it suggested, was to abandon this "yellow earth" and embrace the "blue world" of the sea, commerce, and contact with the outside world. According to China Central Television (CCTV) statistics, over 200 million people saw the series.

Television was not the only new resource open to intellectuals in the late 1980s. The beginnings of independent organizations emerged, weakening the establishment intellectual model. A notable example is Chen Ziming (b. 1950) who had participated in the 1976 Tiananmen marches known as the April 5th movement. He published in the "Beijing Spring" of 1979 but went to university to study chemistry, training at the Biophysics Institute of the Chinese Academy of Sciences. Throughout, Chen stayed politically engaged and he tried to interest his university and political leaders in reform. He was rebuffed, and for his pains was punished by not receiving a good job placement. Chen subsequently became one of the first dis-established intellectuals, an accidental intellectual entrepreneur. In 1985 Chen and his wife, Wang Zhihong, set up two private correspondence schools that taught business skills to administrators. It was successful and lucrative. In the fall of 1986, they established the Social and Economic Research Institute, the first non-official political think tank in Beijing. In 1988, Chen and Wang bought a trade magazine, *Economic Weekly*, which nonetheless came with official registration—giving them a legal outlet for publishing. Chen proceeded to turn this pedestrian trade magazine into a forum on a broad range of social and political topics. While the magazine was non-establishment, it still published establishment intellectuals working for reformist think tanks and aimed at Party reformers. Nonetheless, Chen's and Wang's independent think tank and magazine were a first for Chinese intellectuals since the demise of liberal organizations and the nationalization of their periodicals in the early 1950s.

Rural communities

China's reforms began by addressing the glaring gap between urban and rural development. The effort in the 1980s began well, ran into trouble by mid-decade, and entered the 1990s by privileging some areas (near cities and the coast) over others. From the start more wealth was generated under the reforms but at the cost of producing huge gaps between regions—with coastal areas booming and hinterland regions declining. Broadly speaking, per capita income between the early 1980s and early 1990s grew twice as fast for urban residents as for rural, and the average income for urban Shanghai was about eight times greater than that for rural Gansu. Deng Xiaoping's reforms in the countryside began with the decollectivization of farmland, the household responsibility system. By 1982 these were under the supervision of the revived townships. By 1984 cropping contracts to individual farm families were guaranteed for fifteen years. This allowed farming families to make their own farming choices and to engage in sideline production. Private markets were once again tolerated. At the same time, the state subsidized agriculture by spending over 1 billion Yuan (US$125 million) to keep the price of grain up for farmers but down for urban consumers.

While the promise of markets brought welcome opportunity to rural families, it was the state subsidies and broader market forces that determined the slide back into poverty for much of rural China. By 1984 the state could no longer afford the subsidies for grain and so ended mandatory purchases. The price of rice fell, along with other staples, and rural communities that had seen a burst of wealth—and new construction—in recent years then came upon hard times. New production quotas for grain were introduced at low prices (that the state could afford). The net result was that many farmers quit farming, or limited it to subsistence, and stalked off the land to the cities to try their luck. In the late 1980s this was only a trickle but since the 1990s this migrant labor, now a "floating population" of 200 million, has defined both urban life and the rural communities to which it sends remittances. At the same time, rural industrialization in the TVEs mitigated these pressures somewhat.

China's reforms began with essentially the neo-liberal promise that privatization and an open market would bring prosperity to rural China. As has been the case elsewhere, the market alone has not been able to deliver such economic dynamism with equity. Realities of institutional heritage (the tangle of land claims from Mao's communes), price supports (and their removal), and gendered access to work in the cities had far more impact on most rural Chinese than the small number of market-gardeners in the suburbs of big cities who made small fortunes. The rural experience of reform has been that the market has helped, but the market alone is not enough, and the market alone can be disastrous for many.

One of the major social policies of the reform era was the one child policy. First articulated in 1979 and implemented harshly in the early 1980s this policy set out to forestall what scientists in China saw as a looming demographic disaster of over-population. Mao had famously declared that the more people there were in China, the better. In the post-Mao turn to science and evidence-based policy, the Party turned to the only active scientists still in their labs at the end of the Cultural Revolution: military scientists and, literally, rocket scientists working under the policy entrepreneur, Song Jiang. Using computers, cybernetics, and advanced statistical analysis—but not consulting varying conditions in rural China—these scientists advised stringent limits on births. It got results: birth per woman fell from 2.9 in 1979 to 1.7 in 2004. During the 1980s there became an ongoing tension between the realities of rural life (in which farming families need sons to continue the family line and, due to the prevalence of patrilocal marriage, both work the land and provide for care for elders in old age) and Party officials. Some rural families were reduced to "washing the baby": drowning an infant daughter in hopes of being able to have a boy. Famously, or rather infamously, in some areas there were forced abortions and sterilizations (of women, not men). The long-term consequences would be seen in the twenty-first century with a distorted male-female ratio of 115:100 and a resultant lack of marriage partners for men.

Legacies of the 1980s

The reforms of the 1980s began as a revival of earlier adjustments, the Four Modernizations program first announced in 1963 and revived in 1977. The effects of the Cultural Revolution and the changed international environment of the 1980s transformed those reforms fundamentally. The Party of 1980 was not the Party of 1963. There was no more Mao, faith in the Party was greatly diminished both inside and outside the CCP, everyone was ready for a change and more freedom from political pressure, and localities had learned it was possible to lie to the center and get away with it and that, fundamentally, they were on their own. In a way, everyone had learned "self-reliance" from Mao but it was a reliance that taught people to manipulate the Party and, in years ahead, the market and the law. This was the birth of China's political secularization, the "disenchantment" with the old order that the German sociologist Max Weber, writing in the early years of the twentieth century, saw as the prerequisite for modernization in Europe. The late 1980s began the search for another order, something to believe in.

The reforms of the 1980s delivered the makings of a workable economic model and authoritarian state with land reform and partial privatization of SOEs but had not yet settled on a stable political solution to the stalemate of Mao's last years. Thus, the 1980s saw the end of the Propaganda State and its ruinous political campaigns. However, it did not see the end of the Party, of ideology, or of a directed public sphere (albeit this last was now more nimbly managed). Most ominously, the Party had not found a way to achieve leadership unity on how to proceed with reform. Those committed to further market reform and political decentralization could not convince nor could they outmanoeuver those committed to a planned economy and Party rule. This leadership struggle contributed to the Party's inability to respond effectively to public demonstration in Beijing in 1989.

Intellectuals began the reforms as reinstated establishment intellectuals: servants to the state and teachers to the people. Daring journalists like Liu Binyan sought to "be a voice for the people." Theorists like Wang Ruoshui sought to recast the guiding ideology in terms of "Marxian humanism." But others had already begun the transition from establishment intellectuals to something else—roles that would only emerge in the 1990s. Those who moved on were, in fact, shoved by the Party: expelled or sidelined. Fang Lizhi was first demoted, then expelled from the Party for putting science and democracy over ideology and the Party. Chen Ziming only became an intellectual entrepreneur when his normal employment (through the state allocation system) was denied as punishment for his unorthodox ways. In the late 1980s to be ostracized from the establishment limited an intellectual's public role (as almost all media was still firmly in the hands of the propaganda authorities).

The life of China and the life of ordinary Chinese in the 1980s began their engagement with the broader family of nations and the international commercial market beyond the limited, and ailing, socialist camp of the Soviet Union and Eastern Europe. This was China's entry to the current round of globalization. The PRC had taken up the China seat in the UN in 1971, but normalization of relations with the United States in 1979 opened a new era of acceptance and engagement in international organizations. The relative lessening of censorship and slowly increasing flow of foreign students and business people into China and Chinese students overseas to study opened cultural doors for urban Chinese. It began first with those in privileged positions but soon expanded to enterprising Chinese able to surf the tides of new connections with foreign countries, including re-established links with overseas Chinese communities. This contributed to a vibrant youth and popular culture in China's urban areas rooted in the independence and bitter experience of *zhiqing* (educated youth), the sent-down youth of the Cultural Revolution. Such a culture was nurtured by the mesmerizing allure of new books, ideas, images, and desirable objects—from fashions to refrigerators—that appeared to come from the outside world. In the 1980s America was El Dorado, the perfect place: perceived as a rich and democratic utopia, where people were (unlike the typical Chinese person's school or work unit) free to be themselves. It was an infatuation that, as we will see in Chapter 10, saw its peak in Tiananmen in 1989, followed by the inevitable disillusionment in the 1990s, as America turned out to be full of depressingly familiar imperfect people and sometimes took actions abroad that threatened Chinese sovereignty and even at times Chinese lives.

10. *Tiananmen and its Aftermath, 1989–1999*

JEFFREY N. WASSERSTROM AND KATE MERKEL-HESS

THE dramatic events of the final years of the twentieth century, both within and beyond China's borders, left deep marks on Chinese politics and profoundly altered the country's place in the global order. When 1989 began, the Soviet Union was still intact. Communist parties were in control of more than a dozen other nations, including many that were allied with Moscow and located in Eastern and Central Europe. By the mid-1990s, however, after events such as Solidarity's rise, the Velvet Revolution, and the Soviet Union's implosion, China's Communist Party was left as one of the only Marxist-Leninist organizations still in control and the only one helming a major world power. This global shift came in the wake of widespread unrest in China in 1989: protests rocked Tibet in the far west in March and then demonstrations focusing on corruption and political reform brought crowds ranging from tens of thousands to a million into the streets of scores of cities between mid-April and early June. Its near death experience and the demise of many kindred organizations around the world encouraged the CCP to retrench. In almost every aspect of Chinese life, conservative tendencies dominated in the immediate wake of the protests, during which martial law had been imposed in Tibet and then later, much more surprisingly, in China's capital, and Zhao Ziyang had been placed under house arrest for being too ready to consider compromising with the demonstrators. Replacing Zhao as Deng's heir apparent was Jiang Zemin (1926–), a less liberally minded figure who had served as Shanghai's mayor and as Party Secretary of that metropolis. China at the close of the twentieth century was a rare outlier in the Communist bloc's widespread shift from Leninist one-party rule and tight control of daily life, joined only in its apparent failure to change by a handful of other, much smaller countries. But any sense of the 1990s as simply a time of stasis was illusory.

In important ways, the country was transformed, and not just in minor ways, during each part of the decade that followed the 1989 upheavals so often associated in the West with the term "Tiananmen" (in honor of the Beijing site of the biggest rallies) and in Chinese with the term *liusi* (literally 6/4, standing for the date in June when hundreds of protesters and bystanders were killed in the capital). Economically, Deng recommitted himself in 1992 to continuing with his experiments in combining market forces and state control. In a series of speeches that year, described as part of his "Southern Tour" since he made the most important ones in the Pearl River Delta region, he also doubled down on promises he made early in the Reform era to work to open China to the outside world. His key allies in these moves included Jiang, who would break precedent by remaining Deng's successor throughout the rest of that Long March veteran's lifetime. Jiang joined with his aged patron on these calls and also worked with him in allowing personal freedoms to expand in many realms; the state pulled back from trying to micromanage such things as the jobs assigned to college graduates and even the people those students could date and music they could listen to.

The country's very borders even shifted during the post-1989 decade. On July 1, 1997, a date eagerly anticipated by Deng, though he died just before it arrived, Hong Kong changed from being a British Crown Colony to a Special Administrative Region (SAR) of the PRC. The pomp and circumstance associated with this handover of power, in which Prince Charles took part as Britain's representative, was watched by television viewers around the world. The date's arrival was a cause for considerable anxiety in Hong Kong itself, in spite of Beijing's claim that under a policy called "One Country, Two Systems," the territory would be allowed to be governed in a distinctive way for half-a-century, its residents able to enjoy greater freedom of speech and of the press and more democracy than those in mainland cities. The handover was celebrated, though, by crowds in Beijing who gathered during the months leading up to July 1 to see the time until it arrived ticked off on a giant countdown clock that the government had erected in Tiananmen Square. Two years later, in December 1999, Macau, a former Portuguese colony, was also incorporated into the PRC as an SAR, albeit with somewhat less attention. That Pearl River Delta city then began its curious transition, despite now being within a

Communist Party-run country, into a city associated more than anything else with gambling, which soon earned it the nickname of "Las Vegas of the East," in honor of the Nevada city whose take from casinos it would first rival and then, early in the twenty-first century, surpass.

The 1990s also saw important transitions that were unrelated to official policies. One of these was a search for something to believe in among those who felt a spiritual or emotional void. Disenchantment with the state, frustration with the way protest surges were crushed, and other factors led to rising interest in Christianity, a religion to which a number of former 1989 activists converted, and homegrown syncretic sects, including Falun Gong, which was led by Li Hongzhi, a charismatic figure who some followers believed could accomplish miracles.

The period lasting from 1989 to 1999 was, as this brief survey suggests, an eventful decade, and there is much more worth knowing about it beyond the fact that dramatic protests and brutal acts of repression took place in its opening year. To understand what did and did not change, though, it is crucial above all to make sense of the drama of 1989. This is not just because the Chinese events of that year are fascinating and consequential for their own sake. It is also because examining them is a crucial first step in explaining the domestic policies and cultural shifts of the final years of the last century—as well as the things that were not altered in the 1990s, such as the government's limitation on the creation of any form of formal opposition group that could threaten its monopoly on power.

The wave of protests and the violent methods that ended them—which included not just the killings in Beijing very late at night on June 3 and early on June 4 but also a second massacre in Chengdu soon after the Beijing one, as well as mass arrests of protesters across the country—laid the groundwork for a government–society détente on big questions about how political and economic reform should be linked. These questions, which had been raised by the 1989 demonstrations, and before that by the 1986–7 protests and the speeches and writings by figures such as Fang Lizhi, as the previous chapter shows, were taken off the table, as Deng and those who shared power with him until 1997 and then succeeded him made the following case to the Chinese people: We will foster policies that help more of you share in the spoils of economic development, if you will desist from pushing for further political rights. This "deal," widely understood if never articulated in such bald terms, meant immense government investments in the economy, kick starting it after the stalls of the late 1980s. Foreign investment was courted, including from Taiwan, and Deng pushed for China to gain entrance in the World Trade Organization (this was granted in 2001). Beijing launched large-scale infrastructural projects, from the rapid transformation of sleepy Shenzhen into a major metropolis to the remaking of the Shanghai skyline. This started to give Pudong (East Shanghai) its current futuristic feel and was seen by some as a sign of the increased influence in Beijing of Jiang and other figures with ties to that city, such as Zhu Rongji (1928–), another former Shanghai mayor elevated to a top central post after the 1989 protests.

These policies laid the basis for the incredible economic boom of the early twenty-first century. Not surprisingly, this growth had ugly downsides: pollution, the depopulation of the countryside, a staggering gap between rich and poor, and a state that staked its legitimacy on maintaining high levels of economic growth rather than being responsive to the people. By the end of the 1990s, the problems associated with rapid development and continuing if shifting forms of authoritarian rule were clear, if not as widespread in scope and as impossible to ignore as they are today. Yet growth also meant many more opportunities for many more people, not just economically but also culturally. Foreign TV and movies were widely viewed, growing numbers of Chinese had access to the young Internet, restrictions were eased on topics for discussion that did not directly link up with calls for change within China, and increasing numbers of Chinese had the chance to study or travel abroad.

Even as China was opening up, the legacies of the government's concerns over the protests shaped political culture. Most notably, the state encouraged a resurgence of patriotic education in China's schools that fueled a renewed nationalism that emphasized moments in the past when Western countries and Japan had infringed on Chinese sovereignty or harmed Chinese people. This nationalism focused on moments of "national humiliation," an increasingly common term in historical works of the time, though one whose lineage goes back many decades, and was bolstered by the international reaction to the 1989 protests. The response to the June 4th Massacre included many harshly worded editorials and opinion pieces in major world newspapers, some strong condemnation by world leaders, and seven countries joining together to impose economic sanctions on Beijing. This last action inspired a revealing comment by Deng. In April 1990, during a visit to Thailand, while speaking to Dhanin Chearavanont, a Thai businessman of partially Chinese descent, Deng said, in a statement that would appear in his selected works under the title "We

Are Working to Revitalize the Chinese Nation," that as a "Chinese" person who knew his country's history, when he heard of many nations banding together against his country, "my immediate association was to 1900, when the allied forces of eight powers invaded China."

The period's resurgent nationalism, expressed in many forms—including a 1996 book, *China Can Say No*, that was briefly banned for staking out too extreme a line, but sold well and inspired a series of knock-offs with similar titles that played on the country's ability to stand up assertively to countries that had previously pushed it around—sat alongside a dramatic growth by the end of the decade in the number of foreigners living in China. It also coexisted with an expanding sense of China's place in the global community. This sensitive and nascent consciousness of China's power led to occasional outbursts over real or perceived international slights, which the authorities either sought to tamp down or at least steer into more manageable channels, due to fears that protesting crowds expressing anger at foreign actions might bring up domestic issues as well. The decade ended with examples of both sorts of responses. In 1998, when anti-Chinese riots took place in Indonesia, angry editorials ran in the state-run media, but students who sought to take to the streets to express their outrage were kept from doing so. In 1999, by contrast, when during NATO actions in Yugoslavia the United States dropped five bombs on the Chinese embassy in Belgrade, killing three Chinese, the result was different. The United States insisted that the bombing had been an accident, the result of using out-of-date maps. The perception in China—one that steadfastly remains today—was that the Chinese embassy had been intentionally targeted. Passionate protests erupted in several Chinese cities, as well as among students studying abroad in some communities outside of China.

The most dramatic moment came when angry crowds gathered outside the US and British embassies in Beijing and several consulates in other cities. It was an inauspicious end to the decade, but reflected the growing pains of a China re-emerging after the isolation and fear that followed the events of 1989. It also revealed how divergent ideas about China's past can be. When the American ambassador was pinned inside his Beijing residence, *USA Today* likened the actions by angry youths armed with paint balls to those of the Boxers, asking why China had learned so little in the last century. One Chinese magazine, however, saw a different parallel to 1900, more in step with the comments by Deng quoted above: Western powers were still often meddling in the affairs of other countries and Chinese lives were sometimes lost due to this. Another contrast relating to history was that the Western press often emphasized how different the 1999 protests were from those of 1989, during which some demonstrators had quoted Americans ranging from Patrick Henry to Martin Luther King, Jr, with approval; Chinese commentators, by contrast, tended to avoid all mention of things that had happened a decade previously and tried to place the demonstrators in a lineage of patriotic youth exemplified above all by the May Fourth Movement of 1919.

The 1989 protests

The events of 1989 deserve detailed attention for many reasons, including because they are a relatively rare case of a major watershed moment in Chinese history about which many general readers in the West have a good deal of knowledge. Or, rather, think they do. In fact, what many know is a version of events that misleadingly reduces a complex social movement to a simple drama: students stood off against soldiers in Beijing in order to champion democratizing reforms; the international media watched helplessly on June 4 as massive numbers of people were slaughtered in Tiananmen Square; and an iconic photograph of a student standing in front of a tank captured the bravery as well as ultimate failure of those who fought for change. This narrative gets some key details wrong: for example, it is likely that very few people, perhaps none at all, died right in Tiananmen Square itself in early June. The main killing fields were on nearby streets, where hundreds died, rather than on the vast plaza itself, and automatic weapon fire rather than tanks claimed the most victims. Moreover, the young man who stood before the tanks was almost certainly a worker rather than a student. In addition, the conventional version of the story is often accompanied by not quite accurate bits of information. Democracy was not, for example, the central demand of the protestors. Instead, they were motivated by anger over growing corruption, by the increasing economic volatility that resulted from the 1980s economic reforms, and by the government's insistence that the protestors were ruffians and troublemakers rather than concerned citizens. In general, this simplified Western narrative diminishes the complexity of the protest, while admittedly remaining much closer to the truth than the "Big Lie" promoted by the Chinese government, which wrongly insists that there were no innocent victims of a massacre (just some "thugs" and "counter-revolutionary" rioters restrained by soldiers who showed great reserve).

Placing 1989's events into a more complex framework than either the standard Western or "Big Lie" narratives allow is critical for making sense of what would follow. For throughout the 1990s, many actions that the government took were designed in part to minimize the likelihood of a recurrence of the protests that rocked China's cities in 1989, and also to help guard against a Chinese variant of the even more obviously consequential struggles that swept through Eastern and Central Europe between that year, when Communist Party rule ended peacefully in places such as Poland and with violence in Romania, and 1991, when the Soviet Union imploded. The upheaval of 1989, even though it was crushed before effecting any institutional political change, has had lasting repercussions, affecting everything from the kinds of public relations and propaganda campaigns the government has launched to the calculus used to determine which kinds of dissenting opinions and actions are treated lightly and which responded to with brutal measures.

One crucial point about the Tiananmen Uprising that is often overlooked in the West is that it did not come out of nowhere. It was a sequel of sorts to the earlier wave of campus protests discussed in Chapter 9 and was rooted in a complex mix of frustrations and desires that had been building up for years. The youths involved in the 1989 protests, like those who had marched in 1986–7, wanted more personal freedom and were frustrated with various aspects of university life, from compulsory calisthenics to the low quality of cafeteria food. They also wanted campus leaders to be chosen via open elections rather than being handpicked by the Party, a desire evinced as far back as 1980, during a still earlier wave of protests that some who were professors in 1989 had participated in during their own student days.

There were some scattered protests in 1988, which kept alive the new patterns of action of 1986–7. In addition, in 1988 and early 1989, reform-minded students and professors on various campuses banded together to hold small-scale gatherings focused on discussing progressive ideas, sometimes known as "salons." But the resurgence of a true movement did not come until mid-April of 1989. There were plans in the works for a demonstration on May 4 of that year, when the seventieth anniversary of China's greatest student movement arrived, but a fluke event jump-started the struggle ahead of time. This was the April 15, 1989, death of Hu Yaobang, who had become a hero to the students when he was criticized and demoted for taking a soft line on the 1986–7 protests. Hu's death opened a window of opportunity for the students, since when he died he was still an official, just not one with a top position, so the state could hardly prevent people from gathering to mourn his passing. The students turned the occasion into an act of protest when, alongside expressions of sadness, they began saying things like what a shame it was when good men died, while bad ones lived on and stayed in control.

It was in Beijing that students first began to memorialize Hu. Students from Peking University organized students from campuses around the capital to hold a demonstration on April 17—a demonstration that grew into successive days of protest marches and then into the famous student hunger strike. While students should remain at the center of any account of 1989, in fact educated youths were quickly encompassed by a much broader group of supportive citizens drawn from workers' unions across Beijing. Workers and other Beijing residents marched with the students, provided the necessary medical, logistical, and sanitary support for the crowds in Tiananmen Square, and kept military forces at bay, blocking roads when convoys eventually attempted to enter the city.

We know the most about the Beijing protests because they were the largest and, most importantly, because the international media, in town to cover talks between Deng and Mikhail Gorbachev, was on hand to beam images to the world of the events that took place in China's capital. But demonstrations took place in cities around the country, from Guangzhou in the south to Shenyang in the northeast and Chengdu in the west, and, as the weeks of protest went by, demonstrators from the provinces trickled into Beijing, reinforcing the lagging crowds of hunger strikers and their supporters. Given the cross-class make-up of the crowds at the biggest marches, the majority of the hundreds of people killed in early June were not educated youths. Some students died, to be sure. Yet the majority of those slain, both in Beijing and in Chengdu, were laboring men and women and other ordinary city-dwellers.

Another important step toward clarifying the story of what occurred in 1989 involves looking closely at the messages protestors carried into the streets. In popular Western accounts of the movement, it is sometimes simply said that protesting students called for "democracy," pure and simple, and many foreign observers at the time speculated that a "revolution" was under way in China. In reality there was much more emphasis on the streets on the evils of corruption in general and the selfishness and nepotistic tendencies of particular leaders in particular than on a desire for elections. Anger over government malfeasance and an economy where the fruits of development were not being shared fairly was the driving force behind the protests, and protestors wanted change on these matters and framed their struggle as one to save the nation, a time-honored theme in student-led struggles from early in the twentieth century. Student leaders, some of them privileged children of high-ranking Party members, did not want to overthrow the government and reiterated this in their publications, as they knew they had to in order to maintain the movement's legitimacy and to minimize the chances of harsh reprisals, a reaction that this strategy did not avert but may well have delayed.

Students and intellectuals, while stopping well short of calling for revolution, did express support for Hu Yaobang's calls for "democratization and reform of the political system" and demanded a political system that would live up to international ideals as well as the rights enshrined in the Chinese constitution. In the words of one handbill from professors at Beijing Normal University, "the citizens' basic civil rights ... must be protected. ... Efforts opposing political democratization under the pretext of 'not being suitable to China's conditions' enjoy no popular support and are extremely harmful." But document after document from 1989 reinforced that protestors were calling on the government to change, not demanding its removal, making it in some ways much more like the Prague Spring of 1968, which ended with tanks being sent from Moscow to quell unrest, than Prague 1989, which culminated in the Velvet Revolution that brought former dissident Vaclav Havel to power.

By mid-May 1989, the protests had garnered a broad base of support not just from other students, but also workers, journalists, and members of the military. People of all backgrounds marched in the streets. That support peaked after students staged a hunger strike, an act that had special potency since lavish banquets had become a symbol of the selfish behavior of officials. Tapping into a long-standing Chinese tradition of educated youths laying their bodies on the line to protect the nation, the hunger strikers were seen by many as having proved that they were far more deeply committed to the good of the country than were Deng Xiaoping and other Party oligarchs.

The mid-May swing of popular sentiment to the students was obvious in a shocking shift in domestic press coverage. Usually tightly controlled by the government and generally hewing to a government line, journalists were broadly supportive of the student movement, marching with their work units throughout April and May 1989. During three days of so-called "press freedom" from May 17 to May 19 negative coverage of the government surged. This coverage signaled to society that the government's controls were briefly loosened. And it was during this period, we now know, that serious discussions were taking place among the upper tiers of CCP leadership as they tried to figure out how to proceed. The government's delicate position was reinforced by an awkward meeting on May 18 between the imperious Premier Li Peng (1928–) and the leaders of the fasting students in the Great Hall of the People, a meeting broadcast on national television. The student representatives included several of the main faces of the student movement, including the bookish history major from Peking University, Wang Dan, who had been active in democracy "salons" early in the year, and the charismatic and outspoken Wu'er Kaixi, who attended the meeting in pajamas (he claimed to have come directly from being treated at the hospital) and interrupted Li's initial statement to harangue the Premier.

This mid-May moment of openness and failed dialogue was a critical turning point for the movement, and part of what made it nationally resonant. Broad support for the students among workers, the Party's traditional power-base, was key in further mainstreaming student demands, and also marked a challenge to government rule. Workers were particularly numerous in marches, drawn to the cause in part by the fact that, though students made democracy one of their watchwords, they spent as much energy attacking the leadership for growing corrupt and failing to spread the fruits of economic development broadly enough. This was a message that echoed powerfully throughout Chinese society at a time when inflation was rampant and it often seemed that the only people growing rich were the children of top leaders and those with high-level official connections. It was very probably this broad cross-class coalition taking up the students' demands that made those within the Party leadership realize that this protest was unlike that of 1986/87, though an appropriate response seemed yet unclear.

On the morning of May 20, martial law was declared in Beijing. The previous evening, in advance of the declaration, troops from the People's Liberation Army (PLA) attempted to enter the outskirts of the city, with plans to march toward the demonstrations at the city center. Ordinary Beijingers flooded the streets, surrounding the transport vehicles and blocking their advance. They kept the troops stuck in place, bringing them food and drink and lecturing them about citizens' rights and the meaning of the demonstrations, for the next four days. Finally, on May 23, the troops were withdrawn, to firecrackers and jubilant celebrations. Also on the evening of May 19, Zhao Ziyang visited Tiananmen, pleading with the students to end their hunger strike (which they did). He began his address to them, "Students, we came too late." His words foreshadowed the violence to come.

After withdrawing the troops, the government planned its next move. On June 3, the troops were ordered back in. Having learned a lesson from the failed advance, their superiors ordered some of them to dress in civilian clothes and go clandestinely, on foot, bus, or subway, to the center of the city. They were followed, later in the evening, by tanks and troops armed with AK-47s and other combat weaponry who wended their way toward Tiananmen along the main thoroughfares of the city. The mood of the city had changed. Beijingers attempted to block the path of advance, dragging roadblocks and even buses into major thoroughfares. Some soldiers were dragged from their buses and beaten or burned to death inside armored vehicles and tanks that were torched. In the months and years to come, the Chinese government would focus on these attacks, using them to bolster a narrative of an out-of-control group of hooligans, but indisputably, the majority of those who died were civilians. Troops raked protesting crowds and the buildings behind them with gunfire. Some people died standing peaceably on the sidewalks; some people died in their own kitchens. Hospitals throughout Beijing were overwhelmed with the dead and wounded.

By the morning of June 4, however, Tiananmen Square was empty. The small core of protestors who had remained there had voted, on the evening of June 3, to depart peacefully from the square. It remains a matter of debate, even among those harshly critical of the government, whether any protesters were killed in the square itself in early June. But the last protestors to leave were quickly, once again, government quarry. Public arrests and trials followed. Some went into hiding, sometimes for months, and eventually escaped from China. This was the case, for example, with Wu'er Kaixi, who as a Uighur was the only protest leader not of the Han ethnicity, and Chai Ling, the best known female activist. Others, such as Wang Dan and leading labor organizer Han Dongfang, spent years in jail.

The Chinese government, meanwhile, began to spin an alternate story of the protests, insisting that there was no massacre at all—a view of the events of 1989 that has been labeled, quite appropriately, the "Big Lie." The government maintains that the event was simply an effort by soldiers—who showed great restraint when dealing with crowds and sometimes lost their lives in the process—to put an end to a "counter-revolutionary riot" that had disrupted life in China's capital, threatened the stability of the nation, and if left unchecked could have sent the country spiraling back into the kind of disorder that had characterized the Cultural Revolution era. This papers over the reality of the protests. The "Big Lie" narrative proved useful, however, as the government reshaped the story of the protests and attempted to put in place an architecture that would prevent another 1989 from ever happening again.

The domestic legacies of 1989

Economic prosperity and slow political reform were the government's peace offering to angry and discontented Chinese in the years following 1989. In the wake of the crackdown, the government insisted that a strong state was critical for China. Consider, for example, how well events of the 1990s fit in with the regime's assertion that China's national interest was best served by a strong state and its emphasis on stability as something to be valued. For Beijing propagandists trying to argue for this point of view, the Yugoslavian descent into chaos was a godsend. The collapse of order in that part of Southeastern Europe allowed the CCP to suggest, if never in overt terms, that no matter how dissatisfied someone might be to live in a *Communist* land, there was a less appealing alternative out there: living in a *post-Communist* one like the unstable and war-torn region that Tito had once governed. Furthermore, after NATO forces intervened to protect Kosovo from Slobodan Milosevic's brand of authoritarian ethnic nationalism, the CCP was able to claim that a post-Communist era involved not just economic collapse and widespread violence, but a loss of independence—an especially sore point in a nation that had long suffered from imperialist encroachments.

The year 1989 presented a major challenge to the CCP that many thought it only barely managed to withstand. The Party survived, but only, as we have seen, after Deng Xiaoping and the other oligarchs of his generation took a series of drastic steps. They ordered the June 4th Massacre; they carried out a campaign of mass arrests; and they demoted Zhao Ziyang and placed him under house arrest. The other key event of 1989 was the rise to power of Jiang

Zemin, the Shanghai leader who proved his skills to the oligarchs by taking a firm stand against the protests and restoring order in his city with a limited use of force.

The government worked hard throughout the 1990s to address the two primary drivers of the 1989 protests, if sometimes in a limited way and with occasional backsliding. First, the government recognized that economic conditions exacerbated popular unrest, and implemented an ambitious project of economic growth. Second, the government slowly took steps toward increased local self-governance. The efforts stopped far short of popular rule and they are not rights universally enjoyed in China. Some analysts felt these efforts were just window dressing. While there was optimism that these localized changes might have broader implications for civil rights in China, such hopes faded in the 2010s as the government turned to increasingly authoritarian means of imposing local order. Even so, it is important to acknowledge the power of the 1989 protestors' demands, resonating through the decades as the government formulates policies to maintain its control.

The government investment in economic growth in the 1990s was an acknowledgment that economic instability had been the underlying driver for the broad-based coalition that mobilized in 1989. The late 1980s marked the end of a decade of economic reform, but for many people—and particularly for young people—the greatest impact of the reforms had been greater insecurity, as the government closed government-run businesses, phased out guaranteed jobs for college graduates, and began to curtail the basic social security and social services that had sustained families during the Mao years. By 1989, some of the inequities of China's marketization were also increasingly apparent. For instance, although many cities had adopted new regulations in the mid-1980s to expand migrant legal status in the cities, nevertheless migrant access to social services remained limited. And while in the late 1980s growing urban–rural divides had in fact been reversed and many rural residents were doing better economically than poor urban dwellers, all the same a yawning gap opened between rural and urban access to social services like education and healthcare. Moreover, as sociologist Deborah Davis wrote in 1989, "the Chinese education system was more fragmented, less egalitarian and more stratified than it had been since the late 1950s." For Chinese of all backgrounds, the late 1980s were thus a moment of increasing insecurity as the economic system and social safety nets were renegotiated and reshaped.

During this period of late 1980s upheaval, while many Chinese had yet to feel the impacts of the economic changes happening in major coastal cities and the handful of special economic zones, they were getting increasing glimpses of the world beyond China and coming face-to-face with the material and cultural discrepancies between China and more developed countries. Student leader Wu'er Kaixi reflected later that students wanted Nike shoes—and that this desire to participate in the increasingly global material youth culture was a strong motivator for students. And, in fact, the student movement itself became a consolidator of a new Chinese youth culture, highlighting for youth across the country, for instance, the music of singer Cui Jian, whose ballad "Nothing to my Name" became the unofficial theme song of the movement.

The government met these tensions head-on with an unofficial "deal": economic growth, increasing cultural openness, but continued limitations on speech. The economic reforms that Deng Xiaoping committed to in 1992 sought to create a "socialist market economy." Throughout the 1990s the government built a new financial structure to undergird the growing economy, which had recovered quickly from the brief dip it had suffered in the wake of 1989. Stock markets were established in Shanghai and Shenzhen in 1990, the number of shareholding companies was increased, price controls were reduced, and a new tax system was implemented. The government significantly downsized the state enterprise sector in the late 1990s, with an eye to efficiency and profitability. The result of these shifts was a massive increase in state budgetary revenues. Though most of the effects of the cash that this has sloshed into government coffers have been felt since the turn of the millennium, even in the late 1990s there was a growing amount of money available to local official bodies to reinvest in development projects. Above all, the new economy reflected the same approach that government elites took in the political realm (discussed in greater detail below), one strongly informed by the experiences of 1989: that greater centralization was a good thing. However, they did so now with a sharp eye to the way that economic instability could lead to political instability. Above all, economic growth was seen as a way to ensure political stability and the replication and continued control of the CCP.

Many people profited from the new money circulating in the Chinese economy, taking advantage of new investments and new opportunities. A middle class began to emerge in China's cities, demanding new educational opportunities for their children, more secure property rights, and other changes. The children who were making their way toward high school and college in the 1990s—those growing up as part of the so-called "post-1980s generation" (*balinghou*)—had no memory of a pre-economic reform China, were almost entirely (at least in urban areas) only children, and were widely observed to be politically and spiritually disconnected, focused entirely on performative success. In contrast, their parents' generation—the once sent-down youth who had sustained the Cultural Revolution—experienced nostalgia for the nicer aspects of the tumultuous period of their youth. A few "Cultural Revolution"-themed restaurants were even opened, to the horror of those who remembered the period as one of widespread and indiscriminate violence and a paranoid search for internal "enemies."

Yet the economic growth left out a lot of people. In particular, the government found one of the 1989 protestors' main objections—official corruption—a more intractable problem than economic growth or cultural openness, and one that contributed to both real and perceived inequalities. As increasing amounts of money poured into the Chinese economy, Beijing found it harder and harder to monitor local level corruption. In the new millennium, majorities of Chinese would, when polled, consistently identify official corruption as one of the biggest problems facing China. Those issues were rooted in the corruption of the 1990s, when Internet muckraking was not yet available to make corruption widely known.

The reading public was shocked in 2003 when a husband-and-wife team of investigative journalists named Chen Guidi and Wu Chuntao published an exposé of local-level official corruption in rural Anhui, one of the poorest provinces in the country. The reported incidents took place in the 1990s and laid bare the brutality and pettiness of village- and county-level corruption as directed at its poorest and least connected citizens, where local officials piled on taxes and surcharges and anyone who dared to protest was set upon by hired thugs. *Will the Boat Sink the Water* (in Chinese, titled simply *Zhongguo nongmin diaocha* or *An Investigation of the Chinese Peasant*) was banned but circulated widely, stunning an urban reading audience with the incredible disparities between their growing wealth and opportunity and the profound limitations faced by rural Chinese. When one of the authors of this chapter taught the book in class in the United States a few years ago, several middle class students who hailed from metropolises in Anhui province were moved to tears during class discussions—their reaction, like so many Chinese at the time of the study's publication, a mix of horror and humiliation at the growing inequality built into the system.

All of the elements of inequality just described would worsen in the new century, but no problem of wealth and growth would be quite as apparent as environmental pollution. For foreigners, Chinese pollution has mainly been a concern of the post-2000 period, but the roots of those problems were laid in the unregulated growth of the 1990s. When President Bill Clinton visited China in 1998, one *Philadelphia Inquirer* article opined that his trip would reinforce the idea that "China's environmental problems are so enormous that they are not only degrading the quality of life in China, but are threatening the rest of the world."

At the time, air pollution in China's cities was beginning to garner attention (the terrible air quality in China's cities has drawn even wider attention more recently, with discussion in 2013 and 2014 of Beijing's "airpocalypse").

Reports were beginning to filter out of the incredible pollution in the waterways, with stories of "dead" rivers, and increases in cancers, and acid-rain falling across China. Though there was small-scale organizing around environmental issues in the 1990s, most Chinese saw the pollution as an unfortunate but necessary component of economic development and industrialization. There would be an upsurge in protests relating to polluted air and water in the coming decades, but in the 1990s, it was different sorts of issues that triggered the most significant forms of collective action.

Protest and control since 1989

More social and cultural freedoms and greater economic security did not mean that the Chinese people did not question the country's direction or policies. Different groups registered discontent in different ways, from ethnic uprisings in the West to a growing number of small-scale protests against local policies. Chinese citizens continued, albeit with great caution, to test the speech limits the government imposed. The government, meanwhile, polished methods of dealing with discontent and protest with the goal of never facing another broad-based social challenge like 1989 again. These efforts would be increasingly important by the end of the decade, as Internet access exploded in China and the government had to think increasingly creatively to keep the lid on speech and political organizing. For most of the 1990s, however, they were dealing with a media environment much like what they had faced in 1989.

China's image abroad in the 1990s was often that of a thuggish state readily willing to take harsh measures to silence those who disagreed with it—an image for which a key reference remained June 4th but that was reinforced powerfully by several later events, especially the campaign against Falun Gong that began in 1999 and periodic crackdowns in Tibet and Xinjiang. The pattern that began to take shape in the 1990s has never, however, been one of unrelenting and uninterrupted stifling of all forms of dissent, nor complete repression of protest. It has rather been something more multifaceted. Periods of relative loosening and tightening of control have tended to follow one another, with the authorities using harsh measures to suppress some kinds of unrest, especially when protests involve sophisticated levels of organization (the case with Falun Gong) or border regions (the case with Tibet and Xinjiang)—albeit, they have gone to extraordinary lengths to limit awareness of these actions. On the other hand, the authorities have taken a less draconian stance toward others sorts of resistance, including strikes at individual plants and factories. The central government has even at times punished local officials who have been criticized by protesters. So the mix of factors that determines how exactly the government responds to a particular protest is far from straightforward. And in the post-1989 period, the state's toolbox of suppression techniques has broadened considerably, particularly its deployment of soft power methods that prevent the necessity of force.

The calculus that tips the official response toward or away from outright repression is complex. Equally complicated is the decision about whether there will be a complete, or merely partial effort to block information about what has occurred. Memories of the cross-class coalition of 1989 are obviously critical here. Because of what happened during the Tiananmen Uprising and an awareness of the importance of cross-class protests in places like Poland in the 1980s, movements involving members of more than one occupational or economic group are seen as particularly dangerous. While the spread of protests from city to city in 1989 was clearly worrying, it appears that the leadership felt particularly threatened—and the tone of government rhetoric toward and official tolerance of the protests correspondingly changed in response—as the make-up of the crowds shifted in mid-May 1989 from primarily students and other intellectuals to a broader coalition of workers, urban residents, and young activists. Not only did this mark 1989's events as distinct from the protests of 1986/87 but it signaled to the Party the social spread of the students' circumscribed demands to a wider expression of dissatisfaction with the Party's leadership on economic and social matters.

Another key factor is how geographically dispersed dissenters are: tightly localized events—ranging from small-scale tax strikes to neighborhood discussions of new chemical plants—tend to be treated more leniently. A third factor that influences the severity of the regime's response, both toward protesters and the ability of domestic and foreign journalists to cover events, is how well organized the participants in an outburst seem to be. The less evident careful coordination is, the more likely the response will be to mollify crowds, rather than strike terror into them—and the more likely that reporters will be able to cover the event.

Two additional things are worth noting here. First, geography helps determine whether a hard or soft line will be taken. Force tends to be used much more swiftly when unrest occurs in frontier zones, where large percentages of the population do not belong to the majority "Han" group, and where economic grievances and anger associated with ethnic and religious divides make for a particularly volatile combination. Recent protests in these regions, such as the Tibetan uprisings in February and March 2008 as well as on-going self-immolations and corresponding protests since 2009 and the Urumqi riots of July 2009, drew swift, harsh responses.

Second, the regime's relatively lenient treatment of some protests could be interpreted as a sign of self-confidence. Political scientist Kevin O'Brien has made a persuasive case that it is a mistake to treat reports that many protests occur as indicators of weakness. It may in fact be a sign of regime strength that the government is ready, not just to admit that protests are occurring, but sometimes even to allow people to let off steam without responding harshly.

One of the regime's campaigns of repression that has most baffled foreign observers is the quick moves it took to crush the Falun Gong sect in April 1999, and the resoluteness of its policy toward the group ever since. When the crackdown began, the group in question had never engaged in a violent protest, and seemed—to outsiders at least—to be simply a spiritual movement. Led by a man named Li Hongzhi, whose admittedly unusual ideas include claims to powers that many Westerners would consider akin to magical and a version of "scientific facts" many would dub superstitions, it nonetheless did not have a political agenda. A self-described "Buddhist" sect adopted by adherents seeking inner peace and spiritual enlightenment, Falun Gong prescribes physical and breathing exercises, techniques typical of the traditional Chinese art of *qigong*, which is meant to help the practitioner cultivate morality and virtue by "aligning" body, breath, and mind. This might all sound relatively harmless. But it is easy to understand why the Chinese government might view Falun Gong as a threat if we use the rubric outlined above. Its adherents come from all walks of life (even some CCP officials had joined it); they are spread out throughout the country (cells formed in many cities); and they have shown a definite capability for coordinated action (evidenced by 10,000 protesters appearing, seemingly out of nowhere, to hold the 1999 sit-in demanding an end to official criticism of the group).

Other reasons have also been suggested for the ruthless campaign against Falun Gong. For example, a leading scholar of the subject, historian David Ownby, stresses the ideological challenge that Falun Gong posed to the CCP even before it began to present the Party as an evil organization (something that took place after the crackdown against its members began). Ownby convincingly argues that the CCP was threatened by Li Hongzhi's novel fusion of Chinese traditions and modern "science," for the Party claims a monopoly on bringing together what it means to be both Chinese and modern, via the "scientific" socialism of Marx.

The CCP response to Falun Gong needs to be seen as a special case for other reasons as well. For example, during imperial times, Chinese regimes were sometimes weakened or overthrown by millenarian religious movements, including some that began as quiescent self-help sects. And the Party is especially concerned about protests that have ties with charismatic figures, a term that fits Li Hongzhi well.

That said, the CCP response still illustrates the general pattern described above of struggles being treated as most serious when they are multi-class, multi-locale, and well organized. And as we have already seen, this corresponds very much to the Party's reaction to the situation in Beijing in 1989, where events in multiple locales and, particularly, that included a broad range of participants, ultimately provided the catalyst for the government's violent response.

Falun Gong is important as the most widespread and major case of government suppression of a movement since the 1989 crackdown. It illustrates the lessons learned by the government from the Tiananmen struggle. Since the suppression of Falun Gong, however, the government's most commonly used tactics have shifted once again, mutating in response to changing technologies and their impact on the ease of communication and organization. David Bandurski of *China Media Project*, for instance, has identified in recent years a shift in Chinese government communication policies towards shaping rather than just responding to (or attempting to suppress) media narratives. Bandurski refers to this shift as "Control 2.0," a kind of Big Brother public relations campaign that seeks to channel and direct public opinion through the media. While "Control 2.0" plays out in the media, a gentler obstructionist secret police force works to obfuscate coverage of 1989 by foreign media. For instance, reporters wishing to use Tiananmen Square as the backdrop for their reports on 1989's twentieth anniversary in 2009 found their cameras blocked at every turn not by heavy-handed thugs but by the slapstick version of the secret police: strolling undercover police who, on a bright sunny day, purposefully wandered in front of cameras with umbrellas, effectively blocking the shots (though not the audio). The goal seemed to be not to prevent reporting on the event completely but simply to annoy, an indication of a state so confident in its message that it no longer needed to suppress the story of 1989 (at least for a foreign audience) but instead could simply mock its efforts at reportage.

Detailed discussion of events of the 2010s appear in a later chapter, but it is worth mentioning here how they fit in with the pattern just described. Overall, events of that decade would offer many reminders that the government remains wary of the same set of factors that has concerned it since the time of Tiananmen. Cross-class coalitions, such as those that manifested themselves in Hong Kong's 2014 and 2019 movements to protect the city's rights from premature encroachment by Beijing, as well as harsh repressive moves in Tibet and Xinjiang justified in part by a sense of grievances against the center that could unite broad segments of the population over a large area, continued to cause official consternation. This was accompanied by repeated and sustained police and state actions, from extensive tear gassing of protesting crowds and large-scale arrests in Hong Kong to the extrajudicial incarcerations of over a million Uyghurs and some members of other ethnic groups in detention camps in Xinjiang. While these human rights abuses drew international condemnation, they were often broadly popular in China. When coupled with actions in the core—such as a 2016 crackdown on foreign-affiliated NGOs (often undertaking human rights work) and efforts to undermine feminist activism in that same year—by the end of that third decade after Tiananmen, it is fair to say that the space for citizen participation had been severely curtailed across the nation.

It is not only the government that has learned to navigate the management of dissent in the post-1989 period more smoothly; active citizens, too, have a carefully honed sense of which activities will draw official attention and which will not. The result in recent years has been a continued tension between, on the one hand, a measured growth of citizen activism and speech that falls largely within limitations set by the government, and, on the other hand, the government's moves to prevent the open discussion of certain topics and events. Informed Chinese citizens are well aware that 1989 remains one of those topics and this explains why calls for truth-finding and reconciliation remain marginal. Chinese citizens have for the time being largely refrained from open discussion of 1989 and other similar events in favor of wider economic and intellectual horizons and a very slow expansion of rights for the majority of people.

China and the world

The iconic images from Tiananmen, for instance of the Goddess of Democracy statue, which resembled the Statue of Liberty, or of the Beijing citizen standing in front of a line of tanks, inspired action and response worldwide. In Eastern Europe, the man in front of a line of tanks became a symbol of government resistance for protestors calling for the end of Communist governance there, and replicas of the Goddess of Democracy began to be used in gatherings of remembrance of the June 4th Massacre held everywhere, from Canadian Chinatowns to Hong Kong. The international response to the movement—as well as the international context of growing attacks on Communism's strongholds—may well have shaped the Chinese government's violent response, even if the international inspirations for the movement are often overemphasized, both by Westerners ready to see the struggle through the prism of their own ideals and by Beijing propagandists eager to portray the protests as the work of foreign conspirators and unpatriotic or simply naive domestic actors.

Ironically, though, the decade that followed 1989 marked China's most ambitious period of international engagement up to that time. China became the world's factory, and thus economic ties became a crucial part of its global reach. China also worked steadily to deepen its diplomatic ties and join international governing bodies like the WTO, as well as play increasingly robust roles in projects linked to the United Nations, whose Fourth World Conference on Women was held in Beijing in 1995. That same year saw a brief flare-up of Cold War era tensions and sabre rattling between Beijing and Taipei, but this did not stop the period as a whole from seeing a rise in the flow of money and people between Taiwan and the mainland. Just a few years beyond the period examined in this chapter, China would start to experiment with its newfound global power, as in Beijing's belligerent response to the mid-air collision between a US Navy plane and a PLA Navy jet over Hainan Island in the South China Sea, and the subsequent week-long detention of the US crew members in April 2001.

China's economic and political might has made the world more cautious of condemning it than was true in 1989, and in that regard the efforts of the 1990s have proved successful. Such efforts—a "China that can say no," in the parlance of the time—are widely supported by the Chinese people. In this regard, there has been less change since 1989 than we might suppose. The 1989 protests were perceived as friendly to international ideals. Back then, protesters embraced the visiting Russian reformer Mikhail Gorbachev and prepared welcoming signs for him. They repeatedly sang the *Internationale*, and not only erected the Goddess of Democracy statue in Beijing but in Shanghai carried a model of the Statue of Liberty. Yet the crowds in Tiananmen were not always welcoming to foreign reporters attempting to convey information about the protests to overseas audiences. As Philip J. Cunningham relates in his memoir of the protests, *Tiananmen Moon*, in the highly charged atmosphere of the Square anti-government sentiment could quickly turn to anti-foreign rhetoric, old grievances overlapping with the new. While the protestors of 1989 were eager to draw global attention to their cause, to get the Party leadership to respond to their calls for greater transparency and greater rights for the Chinese people, at no time did they call for international intervention on their behalf. The students perceived of themselves as acting on behalf of the nation—a belief reinforced by their adoption of Hou Dejian's famous patriotic song "Heirs of the Dragon" as one of the theme songs of the movement. Even so, in the end, having misread cues from protestors for months— arguably causing the protests to quickly balloon in size and scope as popular sympathy turned to the students— the government once again misread the protests as a referendum on their control over China (rather than, say, seeing it as a referendum on their *style* of governance and their recent policies). The role of the international community in this relationship was critical, at least symbolically. For the Party, the protests that curtailed Gorbachev's visit were an international humiliation, and an attack in front of the international community on their legitimacy. Protestors, on the other hand, saw themselves as patriotic voices, speaking out in the hope of strengthening their nation. This mismatch in perspective may help to explain the government's violent response as well as its unexpected nature among Beijing's population.

Those lessons, like others examined in this chapter, have since been incorporated into Beijing's political repertoire. In particular, the government took different approaches to two ideas that were prevalent in 1989: nationalism and the need for a more transparent and democratic political system. Throughout the 1990s the government cultivated a sense of nationalism among the population while discouraging the notion that the Chinese should aspire to universal ideals like human rights or democracy. In fact, the CCP actively challenged the notion that these universal ideals are indeed "universal," and instead accused the West of attempting to impose its values on China, another ideological conflict with a long history.

Further events in the months and years that followed the protests seemed to confirm for many in China that the promise of those supposedly universal ideals was fleeting and potentially destabilizing. For instance, as we have seen, the collapse of order in Southeastern Europe in the 1990s allowed the CCP to imply that, no matter how dissatisfied someone might be to live in a Communist state, the *alternative* might be worse. The CCP was moreover able to claim that a post-Communist era involved not just economic collapse and widespread violence, but a loss of independence—an especially sore point in a nation that had historically suffered from imperialist encroachments which had themselves long fueled nationalist sentiments. Ironically, then, although many foreign accounts of China in the 1990s stressed the anomaly of the Communist Party staying in power there while similar organizations lost control elsewhere, the economic troubles, instability, and declining geopolitical clout of many former Communist states around the world were actually in some ways a boon to Deng and his allies, who were able to use this turn of events as evidence that another 1989-style protest would be devastating, a belief still widely held in China today.

11. *China Rising,*
2000–2010

WILLIAM A. CALLAHAN

ON August 8, 2008 the world's gaze focused on China for the opening ceremony of the Summer Olympic Games. Just before 8:08 p.m. the ceremony began with 2,008 drummers banging 2,008 drums, while chanting a line from the Confucian *Analects*: "It is glorious to receive friends from afar." Fireworks lit up the skies of China's capital, tracing gigantic footsteps along the sacred north–south axis from the ancient Forbidden City to the futuristic Olympic stadium. Fifty-six children, who represented China's fifty-six official ethnic groups (though many if not all turned out to be members of the major Han ethnicity dressed in the clothing associated with minority groups), then accompanied the national flag and an honor guard of the People's Liberation Army across the stadium floor. As they did this, a darling little girl sang the "Ode to the Motherland"—or, rather, appeared to do so, as it later emerged that the voice of another, supposedly less photogenic girl with better musical skills, was dubbed in. As soldiers raised the flag, the hometown crowd sang China's national anthem "March of the Volunteers."

After more spectacular fireworks, a seventy-five minute show narrated the glories of China's much vaunted "5,000 years of civilization," presenting achievements ranging from classical calligraphy to Beijing Opera to China's four great inventions: paper, printing, gunpowder, and the magnetic compass. The Tang dynasty (618–907), which many Chinese see as the apex of their civilization, was celebrated with hundreds of women dancing in elaborate costumes. This cosmopolitan empire was open to the world, spreading both silk and Chinese values across the globe. The message was clear: open doors lead to prosperity, and the inner harmony of Confucian values leads to the external peace of mutually beneficial foreign relations; now that China is once again open and harmonious, nothing can stop its "peaceful rise."

While Chinese athletes won the gold medal tally, the main Olympic victory went to China's party-state, which took credit for a successful Olympic Games that impressed audiences around the world. As a young woman in Beijing explained to the *New York Times*, "For a lot of foreigners, the only image of China comes from old movies that make us look poor and pathetic. Now look at us. We showed the world we can build new subways and beautiful modern buildings. The Olympics will redefine the way people see us."

The confidence, pride, and optimism showcased in the Beijing Games was indicative of China's national mood in the first decade of the twenty-first century. While in the West this period was a time of decline, depression, and pessimism due to the 9/11 attacks, the Iraq War, and the Global Financial Crisis, many Chinese people were optimistic that the future was theirs: the twenty-first century, they believed, would be the "Chinese Century." Not all residents of the PRC shared this sense of hopefulness, of course, and pessimism could be found among not just many non-Han residents of frontier areas but also those left behind by economic tides in some rural areas and cities in China's rustbelt. Still, a great many people felt they were living in much better times than those of their parents or grandparents.

This general if not universal optimism was a huge change from China's experience in the previous decade. As the last chapter showed, that had been bookended by domestic protest and then harsh repression in 1989 and the NATO bombing of the PRC's embassy in Belgrade in 1999. The 1990s were characterized by diplomatic isolation after 1989, which contributed to the popular hyper-nationalism of 1999. By contrast, many in China experienced a millennial optimism in the 2000s, due above all to economic trends. By the end of the decade, China boasted the second largest economy in the world, with 300 million of its people recently risen out of poverty. It was en route to being home to the world's largest middle class and had multinational corporations with global reach.

China thus shifted from being an outsider to being a key insider in the international community not only economically, but also politically and culturally. China's new engagement with the world could be seen in July 2001 in the reaction of crowds in Beijing when they heard that the PRC had won the right to host the 2008 Olympics: they spontaneously started singing "La Marseillaise," which is both a French national song and an anthem of internationalism.

By the end of the decade, however, the mood had shifted again—but to a newly confident nationalism rather than back to the wounded nationalism of the 1990s. While Beijing converged with the West in terms of technical and social norms, there was a hunger for indigenous Chinese political and cultural models that were different from those that originated in Europe and America. After the Olympics, a Chinese think-tank scholar declared in the *China Daily*, an official English-language newspaper, that

The Games proved not only the existence of the China model, but also its success.... At the opening and closing ceremonies of the Beijing Olympics, athletes, volunteers, the audience and even local residents all sent one clear message that the Chinese people act according to their own mode of conduct and will not succumb to any allegedly superior Western values.

That the Global Financial Crisis started in New York less than one month after the Olympics confirmed for many that China could be successful on its own terms, especially in comparison with the United States.

Hence by the end of the 2000s, the idea of a distinct "China model" of economics, politics, and culture was popular. This nativist sensibility was manifest in the celebration of the sixtieth anniversary of the founding of the PRC in 2009: while the Olympics showed the world that China had soft power, the National Day military parade reminded everyone that China also had hard power. A more assertive foreign policy emerged that renewed long-dormant territorial disputes with Japan, the Philippines, Vietnam, and India. China thus shifted from "joining the world" in the early 2000s to demanding that the world pay attention by 2010.

Most analyses of economic, political and social change in China understand it in terms of the grand teleological narratives of modernization and progress. This chapter, however, understands this decade's quiet revolution in terms of a series of shifts, illustrating how China's social space is elastic, both continually opening and closing. It looks at how China (and specific Chinese groups) have experienced a complex and sometimes contradictory process of moving from the margin to the mainstream, moving from the mainstream to the margin, as well as moving from the mainstream to the center. It also examines Chinese nationalism in terms of moving from wounded nationalism in the 1990s, to internationalism in the mid-2000s, to confident nationalism after 2008.

Economy and society

It is hard to overstate the impact of China winning the right to host the 2008 Olympics in 2001. To many, it fulfilled what they called China's "century-long dream" to host the Games. More importantly, it signalled that China was finally accepted as part of the world community. To understand this feeling, we have to go back to 1993, when Beijing lost the competition to host the 2000 Olympics to Sydney. There were many reasons why Sydney won; but in China, people blamed the West for blocking China's bid as a punishment for the June 4th massacre. This rejection was used by the party-state to rally Chinese public opinion against the West, and was an important source of the virulent nationalism that mushroomed in the mid-to-late 1990s. The International Olympic Committee's award of the 2008 Olympics to Beijing thus was seen as redemption of not just the party-state, but of China and internationalism more generally.

This Olympic victory was part of a trend, where China progressively joined international organizations and even created its own regional organizations. In 2001, China entered the World Trade Organization and banded with its Central Asian neighbors to form the Shanghai Cooperation Organization. By 2003, China had become part of nearly all of the major international and regional organizations, prompting Harvard political scientist Alastair Iain Johnston to declare that the PRC was a "status quo power," rather than a revisionist or revolutionary one. This was all part of China's new "going global strategy" to gain both hard and soft power through diplomacy, international commerce, and global cultural promotion. The PRC thus became the factory of the world: the country's plants made roughly 90 percent of the world's personal computers and mobile phones, 80 percent of its air conditioners, 70 percent of its solar panels, and 65 percent of its shoes.

China also gained international status by hosting global mega-events; in addition to the 2008 Olympics, in 2002 the PRC won the right to host the 2010 World Expo in Shanghai. In hosting first an Olympics and then an Expo—a genre of event that remains symbolically significant in countries that did not have a chance to hold a World's Fair in the late 1800s and early 1900s, when those events were even more important than the Summer Games— China repeated a two-step of lavish spectacles that Japan had carried out during its own rise to economic centrality after World War II. These were repeatedly trumpeted in the press as China's "coming out party" on the world stage.

But the Olympics and the Expo were not simply cultural events. Like in other countries, political leaders used these splashy undertakings to change Beijing and Shanghai, rebooting their status as modern metropolises, and in doing so to move forward the process of modernizing China as a whole and making it seem again a central site of "civilized" modes of life.

To support this rapid industrialization and urbanization, China engaged in massive infrastructure projects in the 2000s. Beijing's new airport terminal, built for the 2008 Olympics, made it one of the largest airports in the world. This was not a one-off, but part of a massive airport building scheme that resulted in the growth from 121 civilian airports in 2000 to 175 in 2010—including Shanghai's Pudong International airport—not to mention the expansion and relocation of 100 existing airports, such as Guangdong's Baiyun International Airport. China's expressway and high-speed train networks likewise expanded dramatically starting in the 2000s. The total expressway length more than quintupled from 12,000 km in 2000 to 65,000 km in 2010. China introduced high-speed rail travel in 2007, and now has the largest high-speed rail network in the world.

Major cities also developed their infrastructure: Beijing's development can be traced by the progressive construction of ring roads: the fourth ring road was completed in 2001; the fifth in 2003; and the sixth in 2010. The fifth ring road was particularly symbolic as it enclosed the Summer Palace, which used to be on the far outskirts of the capital. The most important infrastructural enhancement, however, took place underground: as part of the modernization of Beijing for the Olympics, starting in 2002 the subway network expanded from two lines (built during the Cultural Revolution and soon after) to seven lines by 2010. Shanghai's metro expansion, as part of the Shanghai Expo 2010 spirit, is even more dramatic: the first line opened in 1993, the second in 1999, and by 2010 it had eleven lines.

The Internet also exploded in the 2000s, going from having 820,000 users in 1998 to 253 million in 2008. More importantly, starting in 2000 users could register anonymously, while the party-state's "Great Firewall" that controls the Internet also went online. The number of college graduates surged from one million in 1998 to 7.5 million in 2012. There was an explosion in research-and-development investment: in 1993, China accounted for just 2.2 percent of the world's R&D spending; by 2009, the figure was 12.8 percent, which was well ahead of most European countries.

It is easy to be overwhelmed by the scale of these statistics, and experiencing China's rapid growth in the 2000s also impressed many people at the personal level. As Indian novelist Amitav Ghosh described his first trip to China in 2006:

My first impression, like everybody who goes to China, especially every Indian who goes to China, was one of astonishment. I went there from New York. . . . We think of New York as the sort of big city, the big tall city. And you suddenly arrive [in Guangdong] and you realize that this place can accommodate a hundred New Yorks. For about 50 miles you drive through skyscraper after skyscraper, these amazing freeways and motorways. So it was just a sense of astonishment, that even though one had read so much already about all that's happened in China in terms of infrastructure, the actual reality of it doesn't strike you until you've actually seen it close up.

Although China's rapid growth comes from an export-oriented economic model, one of the other developments of the 2000s was the appearance of a new social phenomenon: the Chinese middle class, which by the end of the decade was the largest middle class in the world. The expanding secondary and higher education sector facilitated much social mobility, and subsequently the rise of a consumer culture. People were no longer just concerned with the material issues of food and housing, but also the symbolic experience of purchasing a lifestyle. In 1999, for example, Starbucks opened its first coffee shop in Beijing (there would be more than 400 in the country a decade later). Since China is a tea-drinking nation, Starbucks' commercial success was made possible by the expanding middle class that could afford to pay $4 for a latte. In 2009 China became the world's largest car market, with private car ownership quadrupling since 2000. At the same time, urban individuals and families began to purchase private property, in the form of houses and apartments, not just for habitation but as an investment.

To get a sense of the new consumer lifestyle it is helpful to go to the movies. The blockbuster film *Du Lala's Promotion Diary* (English name: "Go Lala Go!," 2010), which is based on an eponymous novel published in 2007, tells the story of a young woman pursuing her dream job in a company known simply as "DB," which is portrayed as an American Fortune 500 corporation trying to penetrate the Chinese market. The first half of the film charts Lala's advancement in DB as a metaphor for China shifting from national economic plans to enter the global market economy after it joined the WTO in 2001. Here the private-sector corporate world is a new environment of boundless possibilities and risks. Even the task of finding a job is relatively novel in China: until the end of the 1990s the party-state assigned jobs to most college graduates. So the details of applying for a job, interviewing, and job training that appear ordinary to Western viewers were still extraordinary to the Chinese audience. The film charts Lala's climb up the corporate ladder not simply through listing her new title and salary. Lala's meteoric rise is also reflected in her wardrobe. Her new colleagues not only teach Lala about office politics, but also give her advice on how to shop and what to wear. As Lala climbs the corporate ladder she not only gains self-confidence, but also gets more fashionable clothes, her first car, and her first apartment. Although it may not be remarkable to a Western audience, buying your first car and using a credit card were still exotic and exciting experiences for China's new middle class in the 2000s.

Du Lala's Promotion Diary is a successful example of the new genre of "workplace novels" that took China by storm. Some people read workplace novels for fun as "chick lit," but most saw *Du Lala's Promotion Diary* as a "reference book" of strategies for getting ahead in the corporate world and for how to be a global consumer. The film and the novel thus both tell people how to be modern: how to work, live—and succeed—in the ruthless global market economy that knits together Chinese and American individuals, rules, aspirations, and values.

China's economic growth in the 2000s was part of a continuous trend that began with Deng's new Reform and Opening policy in 1978. While this growth primarily benefited Chinese workers and consumers in the 1980s and 1990s, in the 2000s it shifted to benefit the global economy as well. One aspect of this is the expansion of the luxury goods market within China; famous European fashion shops have branches in China's major cities. It also works through international travel, as Chinese tourists travel to Europe, Japan, and the United States. These tourists not only take in the sights, but like Du Lala, spend much of their time shopping. What separates Chinese shopping tourists from earlier generations of Americans going to Europe and Japanese going to the West is the sheer scale of the PRC's middle class.

While the American consumer was the main engine of the world economy in the twentieth century, after 2008 China became the main engine of global economic growth, shifting the country from the margin of international society to the center of the world, economically at least.

Politics and foreign affairs

In the 2000s, however, not all news was good. China's rapid economic growth had a huge impact on society and the natural environment: growing corruption, pollution, inequality, regional polarization, a graying population, a housing bubble, a floating population of 100s of millions of workers, and a widespread sense of moral crisis. According to democratization theorists, we should expect China's new middle class to demand a greater say in political decision-making. The spread of free speech on the Internet was also seen as a harbinger of democratic change. Indeed, by the end of the novel, even Du Lala decides that material comfort is not enough: her fundamental goal changes to "be free to live life on her own terms." Even China's leaders were uneasy with the PRC's direction: in 2007 Premier

Wen Jiabao warned that China's economic growth was "unstable, imbalanced, uncoordinated and unsustainable."

In his 2001 book, American commentator Gordon G. Chang thus predicted *The Coming Collapse of China*, which would lead to a democratic revolution. On the other hand, the best-selling hyper-nationalist book *China's Road under the Shadow of Globalization*, published in 1999, described an international conspiracy to "Westernize and divide up China," predicting that the West was working to split up the PRC into a clutch of independent states including Tibet, Manchuria, Inner Mongolia, East Turkestan, and Taiwan.

China's Communist Party leadership took such predictions very seriously. We should remember that 1989 witnessed two important events: the June 4th massacre in China, and the collapse of Communism in Eastern Europe and the Soviet Union that eventually led to the dismemberment of the Soviet Union by 1992. To forestall the downfall of the PRC, the CCP engaged in a serious long-term study of the reasons for the Soviet Union's ideological and geopolitical collapse. The findings were that the CCP needed to embrace current global trends in economic and social affairs, while preserving its monopoly on political and coercive power. Indeed, by the end of the decade the trend among Western analysts was to describe the "authoritarian resilience" of the party-state.

In 2000, Jiang Zemin was coming to the end of his thirteen-year reign as Chinese leader. To cement his ideological legacy, he presented the idea of "The Three Represents": "Our Party must always represent the requirements for developing China's advanced productive forces, the orientation of China's advanced culture and the fundamental interests of the overwhelming majority of the Chinese people." Although much mocked—on the Internet "Three Represents-*daibiao*" became the homophone "Three Wrist Watches-*daibiao*" to criticize official corruption—Jiang's new slogan actually signaled a new flexibility in the CCP. By representing the majority of the people—rather than just the revolutionary proletarian class—Jiang shifted the CCP from being a revolutionary party to being a ruling party that could recruit members of China's new middle class, which used to be demonized as the class enemy. As a normal ruling party, Jiang suggested, the CCP needed to govern the country through the rule of law. This would involve a greater institutionalization of the CCP, and the expansion of political participation through "inner-party democracy."

"The Three Represents" was a response to the ideological gap created by the erosion of the legitimacy of socialism during the Reform Era. Although Jiang's goal was probably to forestall the development of liberal democracy, the vague flexibility of "The Three Represents" allowed space for officials and intellectuals to use it for economic and social reform projects, including the expansion of the scope of the rule of law and civil rights. Indeed, while political space was still quite narrow in the 2000s, there was a flowering of social and cultural life.

"The Three Represents" was enshrined in the CCP constitution at the Sixteenth Party Conference in 2002, which also witnessed the relatively smooth handover of power from Jiang Zemin to Hu Jintao, the successor who had been hand-picked by Deng Xiaoping in 1992. This was important because succession processes were always vexed in earlier periods of PRC history, as first Mao (with

Lin Biao) and then later Deng (with Hu Yaobang, whose death helped trigger the 1989 protests, and Zhao Ziyang, who was placed under house arrest for being too soft on those demonstrations) had presumptive heirs who were purged before they had a chance to assume power.

The handover in 2002, however, was not complete. While Jiang yielded his political power as the General Secretary of the CCP and his state power as the President of the PRC, he held onto his military power as the chairman of the Central Military Commission (CMC). This led to jokes about the weakness of the new leadership of President Hu and Premier Wen Jiabao: the Hu-Wen (i.e. Who? When?) regime.

By 2004, Hu had hit his stride as leader, taking over the chairmanship of the CMC and developing his own strategy through three slogans: "Scientific Development Perspective," "Harmonious Society," and "Harmonious World." Scientific Development Perspective describes the development strategy that resulted in the fantastic economic growth described above. Hu and Wen were both engineers; this generation of technocratic rulers measured their achievements in terms of "big things," the large projects of the party-state: the Three Gorges Dam, the Olympics and the World Expo, and the high-speed rail network. The Scientific Development Perspective also was developed to deal with the fall-out from rapid economic development and social change: it promoted sustainable development, social welfare and a more humanistic society. The 2008 Summer Games, for example, was billed as the "Green Olympics, the High-tech Olympics and the People's Olympics," and the slogan for the Shanghai World Expo 2010 was "Better City, Better Life."

The Scientific Development Perspective here overlaps with "Harmonious Society," which describes a set of government policies that sought to rebalance China's economic and social polarization. New funds were made available, for example, to provide free public education and subsidized health care to the people that had been left behind in the economic boom, especially those in rural areas. Harmonious Society's detailed set of policies, which look to the party-state to solve China's economic and social problems, appeal to a particular blend of socialist modernity and Chinese tradition. While English-language descriptions of the policy stress its Confucian roots, in Chinese it is called "Harmonious Socialist Society."

To celebrate the sixtieth anniversary of the founding of the United Nations in September 2005, Hu Jintao introduced "Harmonious World" as a new way of thinking about global politics. He explained to the UN General Assembly that his goal was to "build a harmonious world of lasting peace and common prosperity." In this new world order, different civilizations would coexist in the global community, making "humanity more harmonious and our world more colorful." At the CCP's Seventieth Party Conference in 2007, Hu stressed that building a harmonious world was necessary because of the "ever closer interconnection between China's future and destiny and those of the world.... The Chinese people will continue to work tirelessly with the people of other countries to bring about a better future for humanity." Hu stressed that China's goal was to build a more democratic and egalitarian harmonious world because "We maintain that all countries, big and small, strong and weak, rich and poor, are equal."

When we remember what was going on in 2005—the US–UK war in Iraq was spiraling into insurgency and civil war—it is easy to see why global opinion may well have welcomed Hu's new concept. Hence, to a world weary of American unilateralism and incensed at the Bush Doctrine of regime change, Hu's policy of world harmony was compelling. Beijing had been trying to change China's global image for years; Hu was finally successful because he was able to draw a clear distinction between a bellicose America and a peace-loving China.

As Hu was formulating his Harmonious World strategy, his main intellectual adviser Zheng Bijian floated the idea of "Peaceful Rise" to explain why China's rise was not a threat, but an opportunity to people around the world. This was a development of Deng Xiaoping's "Peace and Development" foreign policy announced in the 1980s, which prioritized economic over political goals, reasoning that China's development required a peaceful global environment to facilitate the international trade and investment necessary for economic growth. After the June 4th Massacre in 1989, Deng supplemented this Peace and Development policy with instructions that China should lay low diplomatically, bide its time, and hide its capabilities.

Once the PRC became a global player in the 2000s, many of its Asian neighbors and the United States were concerned that China was becoming a threat simply because of its rapidly expanding economy and military. China's double-digit economic growth was accompanied by double-digit growth in its defense budget. Many also were shocked at the virulence of 2005's anti-Japanese protests throughout urban China (which were sparked by Tokyo's quest to become a permanent member of the UN

Security Council, which Beijing vetoed). It was in this context that Zheng reassured the international community that China was a status quo power. The gist of Peaceful Rise is that China would concentrate on its own economic development in ways that would also benefit other countries, rather than pursue a military expansion that would challenge the international system. China, after all, is the main beneficiary of economic globalization.

Although the official name of the policy quickly changed to "Peaceful Development," the policy itself was quite successful. US–China relations were relatively stable, and focused primarily on economic issues such as how China's undervalued currency was harming the US economy. In East and Southeast Asia, Beijing's clout increased in the wake of the 1997 Asian Financial Crisis. While the International Monetary Fund and the West were criticized for using the crisis to force unpopular neoliberal policies on South Korea, Thailand, and Indonesia, China was credited for not devaluing its currency (which would have undermined the economic recovery of its neighbors). The result of the 1997 economic crisis was a regional agreement signed in 2000, which became the Chiang Mai Initiative in 2010, where Asian countries agreed to support each other's currencies in future financial crises. China and the Association for Southeast Asian Nations (ASEAN) also signed a treaty in 2002 to create the China–ASEAN Free Trade Area in 2010; once again, Beijing was credited with being generous in its terms. China likewise was an active member of the ASEAN Regional Forum and ASEAN Plus Three, and was a founding member of the East Asia Summit in 2005. China thus was welcomed into the regional system in Southeast Asia and East Asia. Such multilateral diplomatic actions were taken as evidence of China's peaceful rise, and its goal of building a harmonious world.

Things changed quite dramatically in 2009, however. China went from being very popular around Asia and the world, to being seen as a new threat. After the successful Olympics and the global financial crisis occurred in swift succession in 2008, policy-makers and opinion-makers in Beijing were convinced that they had entered a new era not just of the rise of China, but also of the decline of the United States and the West. Whereas Peaceful Rise and Harmonious World are "win-win" positive sum policies, Chinese hawks, who formulate international politics in terms of the zero-sum geopolitical game of winners and losers, gained influence. It was no longer enough to be accepted into the mainstream of the international community; from 2008 China wanted to be recognized as a new center of global power, and ultimately as the new center of the world.

China's global popularity, however, peaked in 2008. The world stood in awe at the Summer Olympic Games, which showcased China as the top gold medal winner and Beijing as the new center of global prosperity and order. This grand shift from west to east worked itself out in new foreign policy agendas in Asia and the United States. In 2009, Tokyo's newly elected Democratic Party of Japan government decided to rebalance its ties towards a growing China, and away from what it saw as a declining United States. In Washington, the newly elected Obama administration likewise extended a hand of friendship to Beijing in hopes of building more positive and productive bilateral relations.

But rather than following the Peaceful Rise policy that stressed mutual respect, Beijing saw these expressions of friendship as signs of weakness. Now that China was strong, it was time to settle scores. In a mad rush to surpass the United States and become the world's number one power, in 2009 Beijing shifted its policy to seek aggrandizement in military, economic, and diplomatic power. In so doing, Beijing revived long-dormant territorial disputes with South Korea, Japan, Vietnam, the Philippines, and India.

While in 2007 President Hu declared that "all countries, big and small, strong and weak, rich and poor, are equal," in 2010 Chinese foreign minister Yang Jiechi told his Southeast Asian counterparts that "China is a big country and other countries are small countries, and that's just a fact." An editorial in Beijing's semi-official newspaper, the *Global Times*, fleshed this out when it warned "small countries"—South Korea and the Philippines—to stop challenging China in the Yellow Sea and the South China Sea: "If these countries don't want to change their ways with China, they will need to prepare for the sounds of cannons."

In two short years China shifted from being admired for its peaceful rise to be the main regional threat that convinced many Asian governments—including Vietnam—to seek diplomatic and military support from the United States, which in turn led to Obama's Asian pivot in 2011.

While Hu Jintao was in power, he was seen as largely successful, presiding over China's emergence from the margins, first to the mainstream, and finally into the center of world attention. He responded quite well to the global financial crisis in 2008, instituting a massive US$586 billion stimulus package that kept China's economy chugging along at an enviable annual GDP growth rate of over

7 percent. During the 2000s, Hu presided over China's political and economic shift from the margins to the mainstream of the international community, and laid the groundwork for China's emergence as an alternative center of the world.

After he left power in 2012, however, critics were not so generous. Surprisingly, it was not for his move to a more aggressive foreign policy in 2008–09. The criticism, rather, focused on his domestic policies. Many described Hu's rule as a series of missed opportunities for economic, social, and even political reform. The Hu-Wen regime was essentially a caretaker government that witnessed no major scandals in the first decade of the twenty-first century. Yet problems were festering just below the surface: the Bo Xilai scandal of murder, official corruption, and the abuse of power, which erupted in 2012, providing the greatest challenge to the CCP's legitimacy since 1989, was brewing in Chongqing.

Society and culture

The first decade of the twenty-first century was also a time of optimism for China's growing civil society. Whereas before 2000, it was easy to divide intellectuals into two groups—establishment intellectuals who represented official culture and disestablished intellectuals who criticized the party-state as dissidents—in the new century a cadre of intellectuals emerged who operated between officialdom and dissent. This new group of "citizen intellectuals" emerged as an unintended consequence of Deng Xiaoping's reform and opening up policy. While Deng's goal was economic reform, the "opening up policy" has gone far beyond liberalizing markets to create a wide variety of cultural opportunities, ranging from elite literature to the popular culture of China's *American Idol*-like show *Go! Oriental Angel*.

Yet the optimism sparked in this new social and cultural space often took pessimistic forms, in what I have elsewhere called China's "pessoptimist" identity politics. After three decades of economic reform, many intellectuals felt that China was facing a moral crisis. In other words, China's New Left, traditionalists, and liberals are all worried about the "values crisis" presented by what they called the PRC's new "money-worship" society. For such people, Du Lala's materialist lifestyle symbolized China's moral problem: she is the epitome of an individual consumer who lacks Chinese values (for traditionalists), socialist values (for China's New Left), the martial spirit (for military intellectuals), and democratic values (for liberals). For different reasons, these citizen intellectuals all felt that Lala's "money-worship" lifestyle offered a ruinous scenario for the PRC's future.

Intellectuals from across the political spectrum thus were engaged in what Chinese call "patriotic worrying"; they felt that it was their job to ponder the fate of the nation, and to find the correct formula to solve China's problems. During the 2000s, many citizen intellectuals moved from relative obscurity on the margins to be at the center of mainstream debate in China. Yet, as we will see, prominent liberals also were pushed from the mainstream debate into the marginal existence of a dissident. Thematically, the main shift was very much like that in economic and political affairs: Chinese discussions generally shifted from universal ideals (e.g. socialism or democracy) to a new brand of Chinese exceptionalism that promoted socialism and Confucianism as Chinese traditions.

Among liberal citizen intellectuals, two people stand out: Liu Xiaobo and Ai Weiwei. Liu, who won the Nobel Peace Prize in 2010, is a well-known government critic who was imprisoned on-and-off by the party-state, starting after his activism at Tiananmen Square in May–June 1989. During the 2000s, Liu was a well-known essayist. He emerged from the margins to the mainstream with his co-authored manifesto, "Charter 08," which was published on the Internet on December 10, 2008—i.e. Human Rights Day. Charter 08 asks the central question that vexed China's citizen intellectuals: "Where is China headed in the twenty-first century? Will it continue with 'modernization' under authoritarian rule, or will it embrace universal human values, join the mainstream of civilized nations, and build a democratic system?" Charter 08 then set down the principles necessary to achieve the goal of a liberal democratic China, where people have political, civil, and economic rights and are entrusted with the responsibility to govern themselves.

This manifesto, which recalls Czechoslovakia's famous "Charter 77" declaration, was signed by hundreds—and eventually more than 10,000—Chinese intellectuals and activists. For drafting Charter 08, Liu was sentenced in 2009 to eleven years in jail for "inciting subversion of state power." The party-state thought that it had banished Liu to the margins by imprisoning him; but when he won the Nobel Peace Prize in 2010 for his "long and non-violent struggle for fundamental human rights in China," Liu was thrust into the center of world attention.

Ai Weiwei is an artist who became an activist in the 2000s. Like Liu, he is a liberal who sees China's authoritarian state as the problem. As Ai wrote in *The Guardian*, "every day in China, we put the state on trial." He stressed that China can only be saved if the government respects freedom of expression and the rule of law. Yet Ai's style and tactics are quite different from Liu's. Liu is a quintessential twentieth-century dissident. He drafts manifestos demanding radical change, and acts in rationally earnest ways. Charter 08 reads like a Five-Year Plan for the fifth modernization: democracy.

Ai, however, takes a twenty-first-century approach to dissent that blurs art, life, politics, and activism. Rather than writing earnest essays that demand rational governance, Ai appeals to people's outrage, mocks the government, and works primarily through the Internet. The year 2008 was a pivotal one for Ai. While he had always been political, his responses to the Olympics and the earthquake that year in Sichuan shifted his image from the political margins to the center of attention. Ai was the artistic consultant for Beijing's iconic Bird's Nest stadium; but in 2008 he refused to attend the Olympic opening ceremony because he was disgusted at how the stadium was being deployed by the party-state as China's "fake smile"—i.e. as part of an international propaganda campaign. He later Tweeted that "No outdoor sports can be more elegant than throwing stones at autocracy" (March 10, 2010).

Like many citizen intellectuals, Ai was critical of the official response to the earthquake in Sichuan in 2008. Noticing that public schools often suffered more damage than surrounding buildings, many people concluded that the schools collapsed due to substandard construction stemming from official corruption. After the party-state refused to investigate, Ai enlisted hundreds of volunteers in what he called a "Citizens' Investigation," which compiled and published a list of the names of the 5,212 children who were killed in the earthquake. Ai and his team eventually shamed the government into releasing its own list of 5,335 names.

Throughout the 2000s, Ai played cat-and-mouse with the party-state. His blog was hugely popular—until it was shut down in 2009 as a result of his posts on the Olympics and the Sichuan earthquake. Like with Liu Xiaobo, the party-state tried to control Ai by imprisoning him for eighty-one days in 2011; but this only served to thrust Ai onto the global stage where he was declared the most powerful artist in the world. Still, back in China, Liu's and Ai's political space was severely restricted: Liu was in jail and Ai's Internet posts were censored by China's Great Firewall.

Like Liu and Ai, filmmaker Jia Zhangke is worried about the lack of social justice in China, and argues that the PRC needs to have more freedom of speech and freedom of expression. But Jia's career trajectory gives an alternative example of how to be a citizen intellectual in China. He was well known in the 1990s for his "underground films" about people who were marginalized in China's transition to a market economy. Since his films could not be shown in the PRC, his main audience was the international film festival circuit, where he was very successful.

In 2004, however, Jia decided to work within China's propaganda system because he wanted a large Chinese audience for his films. He thus submitted his fourth feature film, The World, to the PRC's censors, who approved it for distribution in China. Unlike dissident directors who produce "packaged dissent" with an elite and often foreign audience in mind, Jia's target audience is the Chinese public because, as he told the *New Yorker*, he "believes his social critique is strongest not as a protestor on the sidelines but as a legal—and marketable—filmmaker." In this way, Jia hopes to raise public consciousness about the problems facing China's underclass. The result was a decade full of creatively critical films, that were popular in China and abroad, such as *Still Life* (2006), *24 City* (2008), and *I Wish I Knew* (2010).

Jia argues that the reason that his films now pass the censors is not because he has changed; rather, China's propaganda system itself has loosened up. As he later told the *New York Times*, after 2004

there was more discussion in the censorship process. In the past, no one came to talk to us. They would just say "yes" or "no" ... No one talked to the director about why they made the film or why they dealt with the subject in this manner. After 2004, directors began to have the opportunity to discuss and express their own views.

In the interview, Jia concluded that "I've always believed that we must encourage progress in China's system. If China makes progress, then we must recognize it. The censorship process has slowly become more relaxed." And Jia has been quite successful: his films, which still examine the underside of modernization and globalization in China, are now screened on the mainland, and they continue to win awards both in the PRC and in international film festivals. (Unfortunately, Jia's work was caught up in new General Secretary Xi Jinping's crackdown against critical views of China. His 2013 film, *A Touch of Sin*, was never released in the PRC.)

Still, it would be a mistake to conclude that China's citizen intellectuals are all liberal critics; this new trend also includes conservative voices. Colonel Liu Mingfu's *The China Dream* (2009) of building up the PRC's military power to challenge America was written as a personal commentary rather than an official statement from the People's Liberation Army. Peking University's Pan Wei even uses his position as a citizen intellectual to argue against civil society in China.

Liu's *The China Dream* is interesting because it is a direct critique of Deng Xiaoping's policy that prioritized the economy above all else, which was elaborated in Hu's Harmonious World and Zheng Bijian's Peaceful Rise. Liu warned that being an economic superpower like Japan is insufficient; as a trading state, China risked being gobbled up like a "plump lamb" by stronger military powers. To be a strong nation, Liu argued, a wealthy country needs to convert its economic success into military power. Rather than follow Deng's "Peace and Development" policy to beat swords into ploughshares, he tells us that China needed to "turn some 'money bags' into 'ammunition belts'." In this way, Liu refocuses China's ambitions from economic growth back to political-military power. Liu's goal is to "sprint to the finish" to beat the United States, and become the world's next superpower. His book was very influential, forming one of the key sources for Xi Jinping's catchphrase, "The China Dream," which emerged in 2012.

While military intellectuals like Col. Liu were worried about the growing power of economic liberalism, New Left intellectuals were worried about political liberalism. While for most the China model could be summarized as "authoritarian state + free market capitalism," Pan Wei was dissatisfied with this description. His 2009 edited volume, *The China Model*, was an influential attack on capitalism, liberal democracy, the West, and universal values. While at first the China model referred to the PRC's economic development strategy, with the rise of confidence in 2008–09 due to the successful Olympics and the PRC's sixtieth birthday celebration, it took on new life to describe a whole "Chinese system" of politics, economics, and society that is *unique*. Pan argued that for China to achieve its full potential it needed to jettison the "western model." Only then could China rediscover its own indigenous values, and craft a unique development model based on Chinese history and culture. Pan thus sees the China model less in terms of a set of policy prescriptions than as the sign of China's "cultural rejuvenation."

This was a shift for Pan. In the early 2000s, he was well known for his advocacy of political reform that promoted the rule of law and a neutral judiciary, although not necessarily liberal democracy. However, in the mid-2000s, as part of a broader trend among Chinese intellectuals, Pan started to draw on cultural arguments to explain Beijing's economic success. Looking to China's indigenous ideas to describe the China model, Pan argued that the PRC's strength is built on China's historical and cultural continuity. While many people criticize the Cultural Revolution as the "lost decade," Pan rehabilitated the Maoist period (1949–78) to praise the PRC's sixty years of success.

Alongside reaffirming the value of socialism, Pan also appealed to traditional Chinese village life to explain his organic social model. Here Chinese society is based on a "family theory" that values responsibility—unlike Western society that is based on individual rights—where the Party loves the people like a caring father, and the masses are loyal, grateful, and respectful, like well-behaved children. In Pan's view, China is neither a democracy nor an autocracy because the PRC is a "meritocracy." It has the rule of law and an independent judiciary, he claims, but little room for open debate in "civil society," which Pan sees as a battleground of special interests that divides the organic whole.

One of the main goals of China model discourse is to affirm and support Beijing's current system of governance that is dominated by the CCP. The China model involves tight state control of politics, economy, and society to promote the key values of stability, unity, and statism. It sees Chinese political-economic-cultural trends diverging from Western experience, and pits the China model against the "Western model," promoting Chinese exceptionalism against so-called "universal values."

This curious combination of egalitarian socialism and hierarchical tradition was popular among philosophers, social scientists, and international relations scholars in China. While Hu Jintao's Harmonious Society and Harmonious World appealed to socialist values, the invocation of "harmony" created opportunities for citizen intellectuals to explore how China's traditional values could be applied in the twenty-first century. Zhao Tingyang, a philosopher at the Chinese Academy of Social Sciences (CASS), wrote a series of influential books that revived China's imperial model of hierarchical governance as a model for global politics during the Chinese Century.

Historically, Chinese identity was defined according to cultural factors: civilization versus barbarism. Chinese civilization was seen as uniquely superior to everything else. As Pan's and Zhao's books show, the idea of exceptionalism re-emerged in postsocialist China as a response to the values crisis. Chinese exceptionalism looks to 5,000 years of uniquely continuous history to see China as the world's first ancient civilization, which is "inherently peaceful." They thus see their country as a peaceful and harmonious alternative to "American hegemony." This alternative is not merely different from the West; it provides a fundamentalist view of Chinese civilization that is organic, self-contained, and in a struggle with other civilizations. In his seminal 2003 essay "Chinese Exceptionalism," social philosopher Kang Xiaoguang argues that to be a true alternative, Chinese values have to be the "opposite of western individualism and a rejection of western culture," and grow out of a "resentment of American values and norms."

While Du Lala showed how China's new middle class likes to mix East and West, New Left intellectuals would criticize her as a "traitor to the Han race." According to Pan, Chinese critics who advocated deeper political reform actually wanted "to demolish the Forbidden City in order to build the White House" in Beijing, so "foreign forces can control China's military, politics, economy and society." China thus is at a "crossroads": "In the next 30 years, what direction will the Chinese nation take? Will it preserve China's rejuvenation? Or will it have superstitious faith in the Western 'liberal democracy' system, and go down the road of decline and enslavement?"

Citizen intellectuals here are "independent voices" not because they stand in opposition to state power, but because they take advantage of China's new social and economic opportunities to choose when to work with the state and when to work outside state institutions. Tsinghua University economist Hu Angang, for example, works within the system on the committee that draws up China's five-year economic and social development plans; but he also uses his status as a citizen intellectual to push a "green development model" that is often at odds with the political leadership in Beijing. While it is easy to dismiss people who work so closely with the party-state as establishment intellectuals, China's new social and economic freedoms mean that we need to take citizen intellectuals—and their new ideas—more seriously. While not political in the sense of always directly criticizing the party-state, public intellectuals are certainly political in the broader sense of probing the boundaries of what it means to be Chinese.

In this way, citizen intellectuals as a group have moved from the margins to the mainstream in China. Still, by end of the decade, cultural politics had moved to the right, from socialism to conservatism, from equality to hierarchy, and from cosmopolitan internationalism to exceptionalist nationalism.

Conclusion

The first decade of the twenty-first century was paradoxical for China. It was a very positive experience for many Chinese, who directly benefited from the PRC's economic growth and social and cultural flowering. Jiang Zemin and Hu Jintao took credit for China's fantastic rise as the PRC moved from the margins of international society first to the mainstream with the Olympics, and then to the center (of Asia at least) with its more aggressive foreign policy in 2008–09. Even so, these new economic, social, and cultural opportunities were accompanied by a tightening of political space.

Hence many Chinese had mixed feelings about the political, social, and environmental fall-out from the PRC's rapid economic growth. Political corruption and environmental degradation soared to become the main concerns of ordinary Chinese. Citizen intellectuals across the political spectrum were worried about how the market economy was eroding values, and felt that their society was facing a moral crisis. Liberals, militarists, the New Left, and traditionalists all critiqued the PRC's status quo, and provided detailed plans—depending on taste—for China's future direction as a liberal democracy, a strong military nation, a new China model, or a global Confucian civilization.

To understand how China's self-understanding changed in the 2000s, it is helpful to see how it shifted from "the rise of China" early in the decade, to "national rejuvenation" by the end of the decade. The rise of China is a geo-economic and geopolitical narrative that looks to material measures of national development: GDP growth, high-speed trains, Olympic Games, and so on. It is a medium-term measurement of how China joined the world after the isolation of the Cultural Revolution, and pursues the transnational goals of modernization and progress.

The rejuvenation of China, however, is a moral narrative that seeks to correct what is seen as the historical injustice of the century of national humiliation (1840–1949), and return China to its rightful place at the center of the world. It is a long-term narrative that looks back to the heyday of imperial China during the Han, Tang, and early Qing dynasties. According to this moral narrative, the world is a violent and unjust place under Pax Americana's liberal international system. The rejuvenation of the Chinese nation thus would bring peace and prosperity to the world. National rejuvenation appeals to a fundamentalist view of China and an exceptionalist view of its civilization. Any great power can rise; but in this particular narrative only China can experience "national rejuvenation." Hence while China can "rise" *within* the current international system, the narrative of "rejuvenation" generally *challenges* the system.

By the end of the 2000s, the PRC had emerged as a complex society that faced many challenges. Most Chinese were still optimistic that the twenty-first century would be their century, if only because, with all its problems, the PRC was still doing better than the United States and Europe. The mood at the time could best be described as characterized by a sense of anticipation: people wondered where the fifth generation of leaders, which was scheduled to take power early in the next decade, would take China.

As the following chapter shows, many of the trends of the 2000s came to fruition in the 2010s, when the China Model went global. For example, China's domestic infrastructure construction success was exported to the world through Xi Jinping's Belt and Road Initiative, which includes a globalization of technological standards and governance norms. Interestingly, this normative ambition grows out of China's reconsideration of the idea of "interdependence." Rather than see the outside world simply as a set of threats from "hostile foreign forces," Beijing now thinks that it can benefit from globalization. Instead of the West simply socializing China with liberal values, China can also socialize the Asian region (and beyond) with Chinese values. The Internet is another case in point. Whereas in the 2000s, the Chinese government treated the Internet as a source of Western influence that needed to be restricted, Beijing now promotes its own state-centric Cyber ideas, technologies, and policies around the world, and especially in the Global South.

While China's global influence expanded in the 2010s, the parameters of debate in civil society narrowed dramatically: Liu Xiaobo died in prison, Ai Weiwei fled into exile, Jia Zhangke's films were censored again, and Du Lala was repackaged into a television soap opera. As seen in the expanded influence of Liu Mingfu's militarist China Dream, Zhao Tingyang's hierarchical Tianxia system, and Pan Wei's illiberal China Model, a conservative exceptionalist version of Chinese culture and politics has spread from the margins to the mainstream, impacting both the PRC and the world. In many ways, these trends from the 2000s inform Xi Jinping's China Dream to "bring about the great rejuvenation of the Chinese nation."

12. *The People's Leader*

The Xi Jinping Era of Chinese Politics[1]

DIANA FU AND EMILE DIRKS

China's Illiberal Turn

WHEN Xi Jinping came to the helm of the Chinese Communist Party in 2012, leading commentators hoped he would usher in a new era of political liberalization. Among those was *New York Times* columnist Nicholas Kristof, who in January 2013 predicted that under Xi, "Mao's body will be hauled out of Tiananmen Square on his watch, and Liu Xiaobo, the Nobel Peace Prize-winning writer, will be released from prison." Kristof admitted he could be wrong. He was wise to include that caveat.

In 2017, Liu Xiaobo died while on medical parole, still under state custody while on his death bed. And far from being removed from his mausoleum in Beijing, Mao Zedong has found a worthy successor in Xi Jinping, the most powerful Chinese leader in decades. Like Mao, Xi has promoted a cult of personality. Xi's airbrushed face has

[1] This chapter draws partially on Fu, D. and Distelhorst, G. (2018). "Grassroots Participation and Repression under Hu Jintao and Xi Jinping." *The China Journal*, Vol. 79, (January), 100–22.

been imprinted on everything from billboards to ornamental gold plates. Books of his collected speeches are required reading for Party members. Initially, state propaganda anointed him as "Papa Xi" (*Xi Dada*), a humble man of the people. By 2020, a Maoist moniker was applied: "the People's Leader" (*renmin lingxiu*). But the clearest sign of Xi's strongman ambitions came in March 2018, when the National People's Congress voted to revise the constitution and remove term limits on the office of the presidency. The move, which paved the way for Xi to stay in power following the end of his second term in 2023, was one more step away from collective leadership towards personalistic rule.

Under Xi's watch, the Chinese party-state has implemented dramatic social reforms while increasing the reach of the security state. And with "Xi Jinping Thought on Socialism with Chinese Characteristics for a New Era" written into China's constitution in 2018, the party-state is increasingly indistinguishable from the man himself. How did tightening political controls under President Hu Jintao accelerate into a new era of authoritarian rule under Xi? This is the subject of this chapter.

Reforms under Xi Jinping

In 2012, Xi took over a country in need of reform. Despite years of high economic growth under his predecessors, China faced numerous internal problems. Among the most pressing: declining birth rates, growing social inequality, and persistent rural poverty. In his two terms in office, Xi has tackled these challenges, with mixed results.

One of the earliest targets of reform was China's one child policy. First implemented in 1979 as a population control measure, the policy limited couples to a single child, with some exceptions for rural and ethnic minority citizens. Over four decades, this policy—often coercively enforced—contributed to declining birth rates and an aging population. In 2019, the Chinese Academy of Social Sciences warned that China's population would peak at 1.44 billion in 2029, followed by "unstoppable decline." Seeking to address this, the Xi administration began to phase out the policy before officially replacing it with the two-child policy in 2016 and a three-child policy in 2021. Officials hoped the move would reverse China's demographic decline. However, the anticipated baby boom has not occurred. The expenses of raising a second child, combined with the fear of employment discrimination against expectant mothers, convinced many women that one child was enough. As a result, the 2019 birth rate fell to the lowest since the founding of the People's Republic in 1949.

Beyond reforming national birth policies, the Xi administration also tackled an equally challenging problem: the legal status of China's rural migrants. For decades, the Chinese government sought to control internal migration through the household registration (*hukou*) system. Under this system, rural residents could move to urban areas to work. However, neither they nor their family members enjoyed equal access to social services. These controls prevented the growth of large urban slums, but also created a permanent subaltern class locked out of many of the benefits of urban life. The growing calls for *hukou* reform were not only motivated by concern for the right of migrants to urban education and healthcare services, but also by economic considerations. Economists advised that granting housing rights to former migrants would deepen domestic consumption and build China's middle class.

In 2015, the Xi administration announced its ambitious *hukou* reform plan: relaxing or cancelling urban residence requirements for rural migrants. Many migrants have seized the opportunity to take up legal residency in small- and medium-sized cities. How many have done so, however, is disputed. The Chinese government claims urban residence permits were given to 100 million migrants between 2016 and 2020. Other estimates suggest only half this number were handed out. In either case, strict limits on internal migration remain, especially in first-tier cities. In Beijing, a point-based system was introduced, permitting only migrants under retirement age and without criminal records to settle down. In Shanghai, the children of lower-scoring applicants are prevented from attending top schools in the city center. This stratified system has also been accompanied by more repressive measures. Following a November 2017 fire that killed nineteen people in a migrant community in Beijing, police began a program of mass evictions that left tens of thousands homeless. Authorities justified the destruction of the migrant worker shanty-towns in the name of public health and sanitation. But many saw it as a reminder of the persistent social and legal discrimination China's migrant workers continue to face.

Outside of China's metropolises, Xi's administration pursued a major campaign to end rural poverty by the end of 2020. Launched in 2013, this campaign built upon the successes of his predecessors: between 1979 and 2015, the Chinese government estimates that 800 million Chinese citizens were lifted out of poverty. By some accounts, Xi's poverty eradication goal has been met. All 832 counties that had been identified by the government in 2014 as impoverished have been lifted out of extreme poverty. It also doubled as a propaganda tour for Xi, who regularly appeared on television chatting to peasants and inspecting crops. Local officials, never hesitant to congratulate themselves, decorated newly constructed homes with slogans praising the Party and photographs of Xi. Yet the campaign also reinforced central government control over these cadres, with the State Council's Poverty Alleviation Office conducting annual inspections to ensure that officials are not pocketing poverty alleviation funds.

These anti-graft measures are only one part of a massive anti-corruption campaign launched by the People's Leader against both Party insiders and outsiders. Corruption has long been the bane of the party-state. Despite periodic crackdowns, decades of economic growth in the post-Mao era produced ever greater and more flagrant graft. The public seethed at the lavish dinners, gold watches, imported cars, and luxury handbags of Party cadres. For some critics, the problem was structural: as long as the Party was above the law, it would never be free of corruption. For Xi Jinping, however, the problem was spiritual. Years of economic growth had softened the moral fiber of Party members and the Party had lost its ideological bearings. Without decisive action, the crisis at the heart of the Party would undermine the socialist system itself.

Hence, in November of 2012, Xi Jinping launched the largest campaign against corruption in decades. Hundreds of thousands of Party members have been targeted, including both low-level "flies" and high-level "tigers." Among those nabbed have been former "domestic security czar"

Zhou Yongkang, two vice chairmen of the Central Military Commission, Xu Caihou and Guo Boxiong, the Party Secretary of Chongqing and Politburo member Sun Zhengcai, and the former head of the Cyberspace Administration Lu Wei. Even the first Chinese citizen to lead Interpol, Meng Hongwei, was "disappeared" and eventually convicted on corruption charges. Other targets included the People's Liberation Army, with thousands of its officers investigated.

The campaign has also expanded beyond China's borders. Led by the Ministry of Public Security, Operation Fox Hunt and Operation Sky Net have repatriated hundreds of Chinese officials. Foreign intelligence services have expressed concern at Chinese agents covertly operating in their borders. In response, the Chinese government has presented its actions as part of a global fight against graft and as upholding the UN's Convention Against Corruption. The Chinese public has largely applauded these moves. Tallies of corrupt officials caught, charged, and convicted are regularly reported in the Chinese press. A popular 2017 television drama, *In the Name of the People*, about anti-corruption efforts in a fictitious Chinese province, was even financed by the Supreme People's Procuratorate.

Xi's expansive anti-corruption campaign, however, has also flouted the rule of law. In the beginning, the Central Commission for Discipline Inspection targeted only Party cadres, holding them for months without charge through the *shuanggui* (double designation) system. By 2018, the National Supervisory Commission expanded the campaign to target non-Party members, including state employees, which includes everyone from the State Council down to school teachers. Ranking above the Supreme People's Court and the People's Procuratorate, the National

Supervisory Commission can detain suspects for six months without access to a lawyer. In the subsequent trial, guilt is almost always assured. Government critics have also been targeted, including property tycoon Ren Zhiqiang, sentenced to eighteen years in prison in 2020 on corruption charges following his publication of a scathing public letter criticizing Xi's handling of the COVID-19 outbreak. Such moves are in keeping with the increasing centralization of power under Xi. Critics suspect that Xi has used the cover of fighting corruption to target his political rivals. Without institutional checks on the power of the Party, the long-term success of anti-corruption efforts ultimately rests on the moral rectitude of Party members, or on their fear of Xi.

Those Who have Been Sacrificed

Xi Jinping's rule has not only been characterized by social reforms and Party rectification. Alongside these moves, he has also extended the reach of the party-state's security apparatus. Upon assuming office, Xi wasted no time in initiating campaigns against targeted populations, from rights activists to ethnic minorities. State repression, of course, pre-dated Xi. But more so than his predecessors, Xi's administration has moved pre-emptively against groups the Party views as latent threats to social stability. Aided by new forms of surveillance and control, the result has been a chilling clamp-down on civil society.

Among the first targets were a handful of labor activists working to promote the legal rights of China's 260 million migrant workers. During the Hu Jintao era, these activists and their informal labor organizations were tolerated, so long as they contained the scale of their activism. However, this tacit agreement ended during Xi Jinping's first term in office. Before, these organizations had largely promoted individual rather than collective action—"mobilizing without the masses." In 2013, however, a number began supporting worker strikes in South China. In December 2015, the party-state launched an unprecedented crackdown of labor organizations in Guangdong Province, arresting at least twenty-five staff members from five different organizations and charging three—including the director of the province's largest labor NGO—with embezzlement and "organizing a crowd to disrupt social order."

This crackdown was only the beginning. Three years later, when a group of university students attempted to organize in solidarity with striking factory workers in Shenzhen, they were arrested. This crackdown was particularly notable due to the students belonging to Marxist student groups. Congregating in the southern city of Huizhou in support of their proletarian comrades, the students chanted the *Internationale* and carried portraits of Mao Zedong. Their actions symbolically aligned them with the Communist Party's own origins in organizing workers and peasants. Their crime, however, was translating their interpretation of Marxism into contentious action. Authorities swiftly cracked down on this student–worker alliance by disappearing student leaders and compelling the parents to dissuade their children from further activism. Detained student leaders were made to confess to their supposed crimes on videos later shown to other university students. Between the 2015 crackdown on labor activists and the 2018 repression of Marxist students, the Xi administration uprooted entire networks of grassroots labor organizations that had taken years to build.

Labor activists were not the only ones targeted. Beginning in July 2015, more than 200 rights lawyers and legal aides were rounded up in the largest mass detainment of legal practitioners in China since the 1990s. Several lawyers were charged with inciting subversion of state power, a serious charge reserved for people accused of challenging the party-state's rule. Using amendments to China's Criminal Procedure Law, police held suspects under residential surveillance for up to six months without formal changes or access to legal counsel. In what has become a routine feature of state repression under Xi, authorities created a spectacle of these arrests by compelling some detainees to issue public confessions on television. Part and parcel with the Chinese government's long-standing criminalization of dissent, these confessions are reminiscent of the public shaming of counter-revolutionaries during the Cultural Revolution, and criminals during the "strike hard" anti-crime campaigns of the 1980s and 1990s.

Arguably, none have felt the sting of deepening state control more than some of the country's religious communities. In a speech at the Communist Party's 2015 National Conference on Religious Work, Xi Jinping set the tone for state religious policy under his watch. Religious groups were to "sinicize" and align themselves with China's socialist system and the party-state. In turn, the Party would deepen direct management over religious affairs. Legislation embodying these changes followed, with regulations released in 2018 and 2020 requiring religious organizations to seek government approval for all activities and leadership changes. In addition, religious groups were instructed to help implement Party policies. Whereas previously, religious groups were to keep out of politics, they were now expected to be the handmaidens of the party-state.

This closer relationship with religious communities worked to the benefit of many Daoist, Buddhist and folk religious organizations, seen by authorities as promoting "traditional" values. For other religious communities, it meant tightened state controls, tinged by Xi's preoccupation with national security. Under Xi, the party-state is increasingly suspicious of unmonitored religious activity among Muslims and Christians. While both faiths have been features of Chinese spiritual life for centuries, authorities have subjected many Muslim and Christian communities to increasing surveillance due to their suspected links with their fellow faithful overseas. Such fears are not new. Even before Xi, China's Christian house churches were alternately tolerated and repressed. Under Xi, these trends have accelerated, with local authorities across China removing crucifixes from church steeples and domes, and minarets from mosques, all in an effort to demonstrate party-state power over these faiths.

These religious controls reached their grim peak in Xinjiang, where a campaign of mass state repression and surveillance has devastated the lives of the region's Muslims since 2017. In hundreds of re-education camps across the Xinjiang Uyghur Autonomous Region, authorities have detained hundreds of thousands of Uyghur, Kazakh, and other Muslim Chinese citizens without charge. Describing them as "vocational training" centers, the Chinese government claims these centers provide job training and Chinese language and cultural education for Muslims at risk of religious radicalization. Yet leaked government documents published by the *International Consortium of Investigative*

Journalists and *The New York Times* suggest the reasons for detention are more mundane. Their reports show that people can be detained for growing a beard or wearing a head covering; communicating with Muslim relatives overseas; violating government birth policies; "excessive" praying. Reports of abuse and forced labor within and outside these camps are numerous and credible.

Meanwhile, authorities across Xinjiang have demolished Islamic cemeteries and surveilled mosques. Internal checkpoints dot Xinjiang, while biometric data, like fingerprints, facial scans, and DNA samples of Xinjiang residents, are hoovered up by state authorities. Communications with relatives outside the country are monitored. And for those released from re-education, regular visits by government minders allow the state to peer into their private lives. The Chinese government has dismissed criticisms of these actions. A 2020 *Economist* special issue on the plight of Uyghurs inspired the Chinese embassy in London to write a letter to defend its actions as part of the global fight against terrorism. The Chinese government has long justified settler-colonialism in Xinjiang as a pacifying and civilizing mission, while the United States' post-9/11 war on terror gave China a cover for their own anti-Muslim policies. And despite growing international attention, in a September 2020 speech Xi Jinping declared that the policies in Xinjiang are "completely correct." Meanwhile, Xinjiang Party Secretary Chen Quanguo, the architect of the current campaign of repression, retains his seat on the Politburo.

Elsewhere, the Xi administration is recalibrating decades of preferential policies for ethnic minorities. Under China's constitution, the Chinese government promises to grant the right to limited autonomy within areas where ethnic minority peoples are concentrated. Members of China's fifty-five non-Han ethnic minorities are partially exempted from birth policy restrictions, while minority students are given bonus marks on their national college exams (the *gaokao*). While some Han Chinese complain these preferential policies are unfair, their grumbling ignores persistent inequalities. Many ethnic minority areas remain among the poorest places in China, despite receiving major government investments. And while making up roughly 8 percent of China's population, Han Chinese officials continue to dominate leadership positions in ethnic minority areas of the country.

For Party hardliners, a failure to fully assimilate ethnic minorities into Han society could send China down the same path of national disintegration as the Soviet Union. Following unrest in Tibet in 2008 and Xinjiang in 2009, some scholars and officials began discussing abandoning decades of ethnic minority policies. These proposed "second generation" ethnic policies would end the preferential treatment of ethnic minority people and instead encourage a melting pot approach to Chinese citizenship. There are signs Xi is siding with this view. Since coming to power, Xi has promoted deepening identification with a common Chinese identity centered around patriotism, a common Mandarin Chinese language, and adherence to China's socialist system. Such views seem to point towards an assimilationist approach to ethnic minority policy.

The most marked indication of this shift is in language education. The Chinese constitution enshrines the right of ethnic minority peoples to use and develop their native languages. Since the 2000s, authorities have begun promoting "bilingual education" in certain minority areas, allowing students to receive instruction in both indigenous languages and Mandarin Chinese. Yet in Tibet, where until recently primary school students were taught solely in Tibetan, authorities have begun pressuring teachers to use Mandarin Chinese as the primary language of instruction. Such moves—already rolled out in other provinces—are seen by some as a step towards the slow erasure of the unique linguistic identities of China's ethnic minorities. Some communities have pushed back. In August and September 2020, parents and students took to the streets of Inner Mongolia to protest a bilingual education program that would replace Mongolian with Mandarin Chinese in key elementary school classes. These protests were quickly suppressed and participants cowed into silence.

Hong Kong: A Lost Beacon

The Xi administration has also fundamentally altered politics in another of its frontier regions—Hong Kong. When Britain returned Hong Kong to China in 1997, China agreed to grant the Special Administrative Region limited political autonomy. Under the principle of "one country, two systems," Beijing would manage the defense and foreign affairs of Hong Kong. In return, Hong Kong would retain its quasi-democratic political system, free press, and independent judiciary, while its residents would enjoy political freedoms not granted to Mainland Chinese citizens.

The territory's special status, however, was always precarious and subject to the will of Beijing. Beijing's efforts to erode the territory's autonomy were met with fierce resistance by Hong Kongers, who prized their political freedoms. In 2012, the proposed addition of material seen as pro-Communist Party into Hong Kong's public-school curriculum triggered massive protests against this perceived encroachment on academic freedom. Two years later, in 2014, protesters again took to the streets in what became known as the Umbrella Movement. Carrying yellow umbrellas to shield themselves from police pepper spray and tear gas, protestors occupied the city's central business district in an ultimately fruitless effort to compel the government to implement direct elections for the city's leader, the Chief Executive. The idea that Hong Kong deserved greater autonomy from Beijing gained wide public support. At times, such demonstrations took on nativist tones. Public opprobrium was often directed at the city's Mainland Chinese residents, unfairly blamed for the Special Administrative Region's rising inequality and soaring housing prices.

Against this backdrop, an extradition agreement between Hong Kong and Mainland China, proposed in February 2019, was greeted with widespread anger. Under the agreement, Hong Kong residents charged with serious offenses could be extradited to Mainland China to face trial in its judicial system. This extradition proposal came in the wake of the 2015 kidnapping and detention by Chinese security agents of five Hong Kong booksellers who had distributed books on taboo political topics. As the Beijing-backed Hong Kong government pushed forward with the bill, protests spread. Within months, popular resistance had grown into the largest uprising in Hong Kong's history, with millions taking to the streets to protest in the summer of 2019.

The massive protests initially seemed to yield results. In July of 2019, Chief Executive Carrie Lam suspended the much-derided extradition bill. By then, state violence had inflamed public opinion. Police routinely assaulted protesters, passersby, and journalists. In response to the police's water cannons, rubber bullets, and batons, protesters responded by vandalizing government facilities. Under the slogan "Liberate Hong Kong, Revolution of Our Time," the movement demanded Lam's resignation, universal suffrage, and an apology for police violence. Lam categorically refused. For many, her refusal to give into protestors' demands highlighted their belief that she was a puppet of Beijing, rather than an autonomous Chief Executive.

Meanwhile, Beijing's propaganda apparatus kicked into gear. Initially, China's central government refrained from acknowledging the depth of public anger in Hong Kong. Yet as resistance escalated in the summer and fall of 2019, state media began to frame the movement as the work of dangerous radicals. Mainland media portrayed meetings between Hong Kong activists and foreign government officials as evidence that radicals were fomenting a "color revolution" intent on dividing Hong Kong from China.

In June 2020, a year after the massive protests against the extradition bill gained traction in Hong Kong, the Chinese government responded with the imposition of a new National Security Law. Passed by China's National People's Congress without public consultation or input by Hong Kong's Legislative Council, the Law criminalizes secession, subversion, sedition, terrorism, and collusion with foreign forces. While none of these offenses are clearly defined, all carry a maximum sentence of life in prison. Moreover, under Article 38, even offenses committed outside of Hong Kong by non-Chinese citizens are open to prosecution. Foreigners who espouse support for Hong Kong's protest movement could be prosecuted under the Law upon entering the Special Administrative Region.

Beijing claims the National Security Law will not impact the majority of Hong Kong's residents and is meant to punish only a small handful of radicals threatening national security. In the words of a deputy director of the central Chinese government office for Hong Kong, the law would be "a sharp sword hanging high over their heads that will serve as a deterrent against external forces meddling in Hong Kong." Yet the Law's effect on civil society has been immediate and chilling. Pro-democracy organizations have been disbanded and leading activists have been arrested or fled overseas. In January 2021, more than fifty activists and lawmakers were arrested under the Law for taking part in primaries for Hong Kong's opposition Democratic Party in July of the previous year. Teachers have been warned against lecturing on topics that could contravene the Law. In response, Hong Kong protesters have largely abandoned mass protests in favor of smaller acts of public defiance, such as holding up blank pieces of paper in lieu of banners to decry the imposition of state censorship. As in Xinjiang, the Chinese government saw unrest on its periphery in starkly Manichean terms: either order would be restored or the nation would succumb to chaos. Beijing chose the former, at a high cost to the people of Hong Kong.

COVID-19 *and the Threat of Chaos*

If Xi Jinping's rule has been characterized by his pre-occupation with maintaining order, no challenge proved as defining as the COVID-19 pandemic. First reported in Wuhan, Hubei Province in December 2019, in a matter of months the novel coronavirus had spread across the globe. National governments worried about the virus's impact on public health and its attendant social and economic effects. For the Chinese government, the epidemic represented another threat: that of chaos. In China, an unchecked viral outbreak could throw into question the political legitimacy of the Communist Party, China's sole ruling party.

When doctors in Wuhan first identified a novel coronavirus spreading among the public in late 2019, local authorities cowed them into silence. As rumors of the illness began to circulate online, censors deleted posts and suspended social media accounts. Dr. Li Wenliang, one of the whistleblowers who had first revealed the outbreak, was muffled by local authorities who accused him of "rumor mongering." Quickly, however, the cover up became untenable as the virus spread in Hubei and beyond. Public anger, especially in the wake of Dr. Li's death in February 2020, incited the government to action.

That month, Xi Jinping declared an all-out people's war on the virus. Facing the greatest public health crisis in a generation, the party-state moved swiftly to mobilize state and society. Authorities ordered Wuhan and other cities in Hubei into lockdown and urged citizens to report neighbors suspected of breaking quarantine. Tech companies worked with municipal governments to implement tracking apps for people at risk of contracting the virus. Wuhan built entire emergency hospitals for COVID patients in mere days. Citizen journalists who attempted to report openly about earlier government failures were disappeared and, in some cases, given harsh prison sentences.

By the summer of 2020, the domestic spread of COVID-19 had been largely brought under control. The cost had been high: more than 4,000 had lost their lives. Yet beyond China, other countries experienced rising case counts that dwarfed anything China had faced. In the United States alone, thousands were dying every week. The Chinese government touted its own success in combatting the virus. Among many Chinese citizens, there was a sense that the government's response to the outbreak, however initially inept and subsequently harsh, had saved China from the fate of many democratic states. In the eyes of many Chinese citizens the utter failure of the administration of US President Donald Trump to deal effectively with the pandemic, coupled with its Sino-phobic language around the virus, made the Chinese government's approach appear even more enlightened. Rather than undermining the legitimacy of the Communist Party, the party-state's response to the pandemic seemingly buttressed state power.

Wolf Warriors: China's Advance on the World Stage

On the world stage, deepening authoritarianism at home also unleashed a more bellicose foreign policy abroad. In the Hu era, China's Ministry of Foreign Affairs had followed Deng Xiaoping's dictum, "keep a low profile and bide your time." Issued during China's emergence from the devastation of the Cultural Revolution, Deng's advice was sage. But by the turn of the twenty-first century, China's place on the world stage had shifted. Many Chinese felt the country had risen from its "one hundred years of humiliation" and felt that the country's Foreign Ministry lacked the backbone to defend a strong China's interests abroad.

In a memo sent to diplomats in 2019, Xi reportedly urged Chinese diplomats to develop their "fighting spirit."

Enter a new breed of Chinese diplomat: the wolf warriors. The name derives from the 2017 Chinese blockbuster "Wolf Warrior 2," which featured a Chinese special forces soldier (a Chinese "Rambo") fighting Western mercenaries in Africa. China's wolf-warrior diplomats, unlike their staid predecessors, publicly defend China's interests without equivocation, as did China's ambassador to Sweden who in 2019 infamously remarked "we treat our friends with fine wine, but for our enemies we have shotguns." Such pugilistic rhetoric was once found only in the pages of the state tabloid *Global Times*. Now under this new brand of diplomacy, Chinese diplomats have taken to Twitter to defend their country's interests without politesse. Their efforts have also been fueled by China's rivalry with the United States. Explicit anti-China rhetoric from President Donald Trump's administration, accompanied by the Sino–US trade war, fueled nationalist sentiments in China and in turn spurred further undiplomatic language.

This wolf-warrior approach, however, also caused a decline in China's global reputation. China now spoke to governments in Europe and North America in hectoring tones it had previously reserved for smaller states. As a result, a 2020 Pew survey found record levels of public hostility towards China in fourteen developed economies. American public opinion towards China reached a fifteen-year low in the summer of 2020, with 73 percent of respondents harboring negative attitudes towards China. In China, public views of the United States were also increasingly bleak. While foreign attitudes soured towards China, domestic support for Xi Jinping soared in the aftermath of the government's handling of the Coronavirus pandemic. China's wolf-warrior diplomacy abroad, coupled with strong-man rule at home, appeared to garner significant support among much of the Chinese populace.

China: A Tech Competitor

China's global presence has not only been set by its Foreign Ministry. Increasingly, China is known worldwide for its rapid technological rise. For many outside the country, this ascent was unanticipated. As recently as the mid-2010s, Western observers commonly remarked that China could not innovate. At the time, China was seen as the factory of the world, manufacturing everything from toys and textiles to Apple computers and Samsung smartphones. China's export-based economy was driven by sales of these manufactured goods, not by domestically designed high-tech products.

Yet, a state-subsidized technological revolution catapulted China to the place of a world competitor in high-tech. A mixture of industrial policy, protectionism, and a large domestic market helped propel China's rise as a potential tech superpower. Some of these measures resemble economic policies implemented earlier by countries like Japan and South Korea, including an aggressive push to domestically produce the components needed for high-tech manufacturing. State support also catapulted the development of China's high-tech sector. Platforms like Baidu and Weibo were able to flourish in large part because the Chinese government blocked foreign competitors like Google and Twitter. Under Xi, these trends have continued. Through extensive state support for public and private research and development, China became a world leader in supercomputing and artificial intelligence. Alibaba's e-commerce sites and social media platforms like TikTok and WeChat are used by hundreds of millions in China and worldwide. So pervasive are the fruits of China's tech boom that it is now impossible to imagine the country without the omnipresence of mobile payment systems and social media apps like WeChat. These technologies have also connected China's rural hinterland to its cities.

China's rise as a technological competitor to the United States stirred suspicion among some foreign governments. Underlying these concerns was the Party's close relationship with tech companies and a belief that these firms would, if pressured, hand over user data—including that of dissidents and critics—to the Chinese government. Such worries do not exist in a vacuum: Edward Snowden's revelations in 2013 of massive US government surveillance efforts, and the growing power of tech giants like Facebook and Amazon, animated fierce debate in countries worldwide. The links between China's tech sector and the party-state added a deeper resonance to these concerns. Some of China's leading tech companies created the tools of surveillance and social control instrumental to the Chinese government's campaign of anti-Muslim repression in Xinjiang.

As the Trump administration's hardline policies on China increased, so too did the targeting of Chinese tech companies. Between 2019 and 2020, dozens of Chinese firms were placed on a Department of Commerce's blacklist due to the supposed threat they posed to US national security. One particular company stood out: telecommunications giant Huawei. Throughout the 2010s, the company, led by Party member and billionaire Ren Zhengfei, had expanded its global reach. By the middle of the decade, it was competing in North America and European markets to build 5G telecommunications infrastructure. The United States claimed that working with Huawei would be tantamount to placing telecommunications security in the hands of the Chinese state—conveniently ignoring that in the early 2010s the US's own National Security Agency had attempted to create backdoors in telecommunications networks maintained by Huawei. US pressure led to Huawei being effectively shut out of constructing 5G networks in the Five Eyes intelligence-sharing alliance of the United States, Canada, Australia, New Zealand, and the United Kingdom. In the face of this pushback, Huawei has retained the Chinese government's unflappable support.

The rise of China as a tech superpower has been facilitated by the Belt and Road Initiative (BRI), Xi Jinping's landmark project. Announced in 2013, the Belt and Road is presented as a successor to the Silk Road, the name given to trade routes which, beginning in the Han Dynasty (206 BCE—220 CE), connected what is now China to Central Asia and Europe. The expansive trade routes under the BRI encompass an economic "belt" running through Central Asia to Europe and a maritime "road" winding around the South China Sea and the Indian Ocean. As of 2020, more than sixty countries, accounting for two-thirds of the world's population, have signed onto the initiative, making the BRI a global project of staggering scale. Chinese companies, many of them state-owned enterprises, have helped build networks of railways, highways, and pipelines which connected China to neighboring countries, such as the China–Pakistan Economic Corridor launched in 2015. The hope was that these vast networks would bolster China's trade and expand the international use of the

Chinese currency, the Renminbi. In addition to infrastructure, China also plans to build special economic zones along the BRI, modeled after its own zones in southern China, which catapulted the country's economic reforms in the 1980s.

A technological dimension of the BRI has also emerged. This "Digital Silk Road," announced by Beijing in 2015, encourages Chinese companies to export technological infrastructure, including 5G, cloud services, and digital surveillance tools. Major Chinese companies have found eager buyers around the world. Huawei's "safe city" products, which include facial and license plate recognition cameras and social media monitoring, have been sold to cities in dozens of countries in Europe, Africa, the Middle East, and Asia. And despite the ire of the US government and human rights campaigners, dozens of countries along China's Belt and Road Initiative have purchased Chinese surveillance equipment. Such deals have played the dual role of helping to grow these companies and expand China's global footprint as a tech superpower.

Conclusion: A Dominant China

China's turn to authoritarianism under Xi Jinping has been unsettling. Under his rule, domestic repression has deepened and some pundits predict that China and the United States are heading towards a new cold war. Was this inevitable? In retrospect, Nicholas Kristof's rosy assessment of Xi Jinping appears naive. But if we return to early 2013, his optimism was not unfounded. Hu Jintao's rule was characterized by growing social inequality, party corruption, and public detachment from the country's socialist creed. But it had also witnessed a flowering of Chinese civil society, and the country's growing middle class was increasingly connected to the global community. Hu may not have ushered in a Chinese perestroika. Perhaps, though, he could have laid the groundwork for Xi Jinping, the first president to be born after 1949, to push forward with even bolder political reforms.

Yet Hu was hardly a liberal. Under his rule, the Chinese government jailed dissidents like Liu Xiaobo, blocked foreign websites, arrested journalists, and furthered repression in Tibet and Xinjiang. Rather than reversing course, Xi accelerated these trends as part of his drive to realize "the great rejuvenation of the Chinese nation." To this end, he drew on many of the tools of repression inherited from his predecessor. What differed between Hu and Xi was not the latter's willingness to use coercion to maintain the authority of the party-state. Rather, it was Xi's expansion of the party-state's repressive reach. And as under Hu, the victims of Xi's repression are the country's most vulnerable citizens and the party-state's most vocal critics.

Kristof's prediction of Xi as a potential reformer, while wrong, is illustrative. Political forecasting is a fool's errand, especially when the political system in question is as complex as China's. What shape Chinese politics will take under Xi's continuing rule or that of his unnamed successor is unclear. Should he serve as core leader beyond his second term, Xi Jinping may enforce a degree of policy and ideological continuity that buttresses the power of the party-state. It is also possible that Xi's increasingly autocratic rule will become one of his greatest weaknesses as it closes off dissenting viewpoints. Perhaps the only certainty is that under Xi Jinping, Mao's body will continue to rest by Tiananmen, the Gate of Heavenly Peace...

The Presence of the Past–A Coda

IAN JOHNSON

WHEN I first went to China in 1984, my fellow foreign classmates and I at Peking University used to play a game with an old guidebook. Called *Nagel's Encyclopaedia Guide: China*, it was first published in 1968 in Switzerland and featured descriptions of important cultural sites visited by French diplomats and scholars. The key for us was that they had gathered the information in the 1950s and 1960s— before the Cultural Revolution. We would look up a temple or a historical site in Beijing and set off on our bikes to find it. I remember one trip to find the Five-Pagoda Temple, which was built in the late fifteenth century and featured five small pagodas on top of a massive stone platform. *Nagel's* said most had been destroyed in the turmoil of the late nineteenth and early twentieth centuries, but that the five pagodas were still there. Our 1980s maps of Beijing showed nothing, but *Nagel's* intrigued us. Did it still exist?

We rode down Baishiqiao Street and tried to superimpose *Nagel's* maps of old "Pékin" on our maps of an exhausted, post-Cultural Revolution Beijing. Eventually we had to stop and ask. After many fruitless efforts, we were led through the gates of a factory and into the temple, which was hidden in the back. All that was left was the large stone platform topped by five stone pagodas. Tiles had fallen off the roof, and steles lay smashed on the ground. Weeds grew everywhere. Still, we walked the grounds with a sense of wonder: here was something that had vanished off today's maps, and yet it existed. In one structure we had the story of China's cultural grandeur, foreign invasions, auto-cultural destruction, but also of survival. Here, thanks to our odd guidebook, we had Chinese history in a nutshell—the past and the present.

Observing China sometimes requires a lens like *Nagel's*. Walking the streets of China's cities, driving its country roads, and visiting its centers of attraction can be disorienting. On the one hand, we know this is a country where a rich civilization existed for millennia, yet we are overwhelmed by a sense of rootlessness. China's cities don't look old. In many cities there exist cultural sites and tiny pockets of antiquity amid oceans of concrete, most of it just ten to twenty years old. When we do meet the past in the form of an ancient temple or narrow alleyway, a bit of investigation shows much of it to have been recreated. If you go back to the Five-Pagoda Temple today, you will find a completely renovated temple, not a brick or tile out of place. The factory has been torn down and replaced by a park, a wall, and a ticket booth. We might be on the site of something old, but the historical substance is so diluted that it feels as if it has vanished.

What does this tell us about a country? Optimists feel a sense of dynamism—here, at last, is a country getting on with things while the rest of the world stagnates or plods forward. This is always said with amazement and awe. The apex of this era of wonder came shortly before the 2008 Olympics, when the Western media tripped over itself trying to trot out the most effusive praise for China's rise/transformation/rejuvenation—pick your cliché. Typical was a *New York Times* architectural critic, who raved upon arrival in Beijing in 2008 about "the inescapable feeling that you're passing through a portal to another world, one whose fierce embrace of change has left Western nations in the dust" and concluded that "one wonders if the West will ever catch up."

Other emotions are more ambiguous. The bluntest I have experienced is this: a country that has so completely obliterated and then recreated its past—can it be trusted? What eats at a country, or a people, or a civilization, so much that it remains profoundly uncomfortable with its history? History is lauded in China. Ordinary people will tell you every chance they get that they have 5,000 years of culture: *wuqiannian de wenhua*. And for the government, it is the benchmark for legitimacy in the present. But it is also a beast that lurks in the shadows.

It is hard to overstate history's role in a Chinese society run by a Communist Party. Communism itself is based on historical determinism: one of Marx's points was that the world was moving inexorably toward Communism, an argument that regime-builders like Lenin and Mao used to justify their violent rises to power. In China, Marxism is layered on top of much older ideas about the role of history. Each succeeding dynasty wrote its predecessor's history, and the dominant political ideology—what is now generically called "Confucianism"—was based on the concept that ideals for ruling were to be found in the past, with the virtuous ruler emulating them. Performance mattered, but mainly as proof of history's judgment.

That means history is best kept on a tight leash. Shortly after taking power in 2012 as chairman of the Communist Party, Chinese leader Xi Jinping re-emphasized this point in a major speech on history published in *People's Daily*. Xi is the son of a top Communist official who helped found the regime, but who fell out with Mao, and suffered during the Cultural Revolution. Some thought that Xi might take a more critical view toward the Mao era, but in his speech, which was published on January 6, 2013, he said that the thirty years of reform should not be used to "negate" the first thirty years of Communist rule. In other words, Xi, who added President to his list of titles in March 2013, was stating that China's current policy of opening to the outside world and economic development could not be supported while also criticizing the Mao era. Both, he said, are one and the same, two sides of a coin.

The unstated reason for Xi's unwillingness to disavow the Mao era is that Mao is not just China's Stalin—someone who the Soviet Union could discard because it still had Lenin to fall back on as its founding father. For the Communist Party of China, Mao is Stalin and Lenin combined; attack Mao and his era and you attack the foundations of the Communist state. Five years after the Cultural Revolution ended with Mao's death in 1976, the Party issued a statement that condemned that era and Mao's role in it, but which also ended further discussion of Mao by declaring that "his contributions to the Chinese revolution far outweigh his mistakes. His merits are primary and his errors secondary."

But on a broader level, history is especially sensitive because change in a Communist country often starts with history being challenged. In the 1980s, for example, groups like the historical-research society Memorial morphed into a social movement that undermined the Soviet Union by uncovering its troubled past. Today's China is more robust than the Gorbachev-era Soviet Union, but memory is still escaping the government's grasp, posing challenges to a regime for which history is legitimacy. Even though history is by definition past, it is the present of China, and its future. In this chapter, we will look at some examples of how history has been suppressed, recreated, and revived.

History suppressed?

Chinese cities are ghost towns. Not in the sense of real estate boondoggles—vast complexes built prematurely, lying empty, and crumbling—though there are some of those. Instead, the country's urban centers are built on an obliterated past, which only sometimes seeps into the present through odd-sounding names for streets, parks, and subway stops.

In Beijing, like scores of cities across the country, streets are very often named after their relationship to things that no longer exist, ghostly landmarks, such as city gates, temples, memorial arches, and forgotten historical events. In the capital, for example, the Foreign Ministry is located on *Chaoyangmenwai*, or the Street Outside the Chaoyang Gate. Just a few hundred meters west, the street changes name to *Chaoyangmennei*, or the Street Inside the Chaoyang Gate. In between is the Second Ring Road. The streets' names only make sense if you realize that the ring road was built on the site of the city walls, which had a passageway right here, *Chaoyangmen*, the Chaoyang Gate. The wall has become a highway and the gate an interchange. Nothing beyond the street names exists in the neighborhood to remind you of either spectral structure.

One stop further north on the Second Ring is *Dongsishitiao*, or the Tenth Street (north of) the Fourth Eastern (*Pailou*). A *pailou* was a memorial archway spanning a road that commemorated an event or person. Beijing once had hundreds of *pailous*. Most notable were those lining two north–south streets, one to the east and one to the west of the Forbidden City. To the south of the Forbidden City is Beijing's main east–west axis, Chang'an Avenue. At the intersection of Chang'an and the big north–south street to the east was a *pailou*, known as Dongdan, which means "first east (*pailou*)." On the intersection of Chang'an with the big north–south street to the west of the Forbidden City was another pailou called Xidan, or "first west (*pailou*)." These *pailous* gave the north–south streets their names: Dongdan and Xidan. As you went north up Dongdan, you came to a second and a third *pailou* and then one of the most famous, the fourth, which was called Dongsi, or East Fourth. The alleys, or *tiao*, running north of the Dongsi *pailou* were numbered, so the first one was Dongsi First Alley, then Dongsi Second Alley, and so on until Dongsi Tenth Alley. This was at the intersection of a major east–west street that intersected the city walls and gave the gate there its name. Yet none of this is apparent today because virtually all of Beijing's *pailous*, like almost all of its city walls, were torn down in the early years of Communist rule. This was because they were seen as vestiges of an imperial, "feudal" order, a designation that opened up a majority of traditional China's infrastructure to demolition.

It is always possible when generalizing about a culture for a skeptic to relativize a phenomenon by saying, but wait, that exists elsewhere too. So one could say that all cities have neighborhoods or streets named after people or events long since forgotten to all but history buffs. This is of course true, but in China the cultural dislocation is greater, and the barriers to memory are higher. China does have online encyclopedias, as well as books that explain the city's history. Some even sell well, such as the path breaking work *City Record*, by the Xinhua news agency journalist Wang Jun. But these are heavily edited, and require cultural knowledge that most Chinese today lack. Back in the 1990s, it was still possible to find citizen activists who fought to preserve the old city because it meant something to them—they had grown up in the city when it had *pailous* and walls. Nowadays, real Beijingers no longer live in the old city; they have been relocated to suburbs and replaced by migrants (poor ones from China's hinterland, or rich expats) with no link to the city's past. The city has its stories, but to most residents they are mysterious.

Another difference is that efforts to commemorate the past are often misleading or so fragmentary as to be meaningless. Almost all plaques at historical sites, for example, tell either partial histories or outright lies. A few steps east of the Foreign Ministry along Dongzhimenwai, for example, is the Temple of the East Peak. Out front is a stone marker, which states that since 1961 it has been a nationally protected monument. A second plaque on the wall gives a few more details, explaining how the temple was built in the Yuan dynasty and is a key Daoist temple.

In reality, the temple was completely gutted in the Cultural Revolution, and statues burned or carted off to warehouses, where they were to be destroyed. Of the roughly fifty statues now in the temple, all but five are new. The five older statues belonged to another temple, Sanguanmiao (Temple to the Three Officials). After the Mao era ended in the late 1970s and temples reopened, the East Peak Temple's statues could not be located so it was given the statues from the Three Officials' Temple.

In addition, the temple's area was greatly reduced during the Cultural Revolution because it was occupied by military and public security agencies. When the Mao era ended, they vacated the central core of the temple—the three courtyards and buildings that one sees today. The rest was occupied by the Public Security Bureau until the 1990s, and eventually torn down and turned into commercial real estate in the early 2000s. As for the temple that one sees today, it is only partially functioning. The Ministry of Culture took over the temple and turned it into a museum of folk culture. It was only after a protracted struggle that the China Daoist Association retook partial control of the temple in the early 2000s, but still must share the space.

Of course, the plaques explain none of this. Instead, one gets the misleading impression that the temple is as it always was—an 800-year-old relic of China's great past. This history that I have sketched out is not definite or grounded in solid documentary evidence, but rather something that I have reconstructed by observing the temple over two decades and talking to Daoist priests who now work there. Until municipal archives on the Cultural Revolution are opened, however, or a systematic oral history is conducted, it may capture as much of truth as any account.

Obliterated or sanitized memory is common across China. At best, if you are persistent, you can find a specialized local historical publication known as a *difangzhi*, or gazetteer, that can help reconstruct the past. For example, I have looked closely at the history of a Daoist mountain east of Nanjing called Maoshan. The official history on the plaques is fragmentary: it says the temple complex was completely destroyed by the Japanese at the onset of World War II. The local gazetteers and interviews with older residents, however, show that the temple was functioning as late as 1962. It was only when the 1963 Socialist Education Movement began, and then the Cultural Revolution three years later, that the temples were truly destroyed. The Japanese had indeed set fire to some of the temples in 1937 (mainly to root out Communist guerrillas who had hidden there), but it was Chinese people who razed the scores of buildings to the ground.

But one shouldn't focus solely on China's material culture. Also suppressed are intangible events. One of the most complicated is the events surrounding the holiday of Pure Brightness, or Qingming, the Tomb Sweeping Festival. It was a day to honor ancestors and clean up their tombs, while performing rituals, such as burning paper money, offering food, and kowtowing in front of the tombstone or mound of earth that marked the graves of one's parents, grandparents, or even mythical ancestor. In some parts of China it is a simple trip to a cemetery or mountainside funeral home. In others it is a complex series of rituals in a family shrine. The holiday was largely banned or downplayed in the Mao period but began making a revival in the 1990s. By 2008 it had become a national holiday, with the date no longer set by the lunar calendar, which varies year by year in relationship to the solar calendar, but fixed as April 5. This was paralleled by increasing participation by senior leaders. Almost every year, they are shown on national television visiting the shrines of Communist martyrs. Some also plant trees because the day is also associated traditionally with tree planting. The clearest link between politics and ancestral worship is a ceremony held on Qingming in Shaanxi province to honor the Yellow Emperor, a mythical founder of the Han Chinese race. The enormous event takes place at the emperor's tomb, which was rebuilt in the early 1990s for $39.7 million. Events regularly involve an army honor guard, attendance by senior officials, as well as thousands of onlookers.

The holiday, however, is also dangerous for the government. The dead are not always happy and remembering them can be risky—a point not lost on those in power. Many of them remember, as earlier chapters have shown, how mourning and protest came together in 1976 after Zhou Enlai's death and 1989 after that of Hu Yaobang. These commemorations exist on a smaller, personal scale as well. Xu Jue, for example, is the mother of a young man who died trying to prevent the army from entering Beijing on the night of June 3, 1989. He was crushed by a tank at Muxidi, an intersection about a mile west of Tiananmen Square, one of the many who died that night and early the next morning. Along with many relatives of the dead, Mrs. Xu tries to go to Muxidi on Qingming to honor their dead children.

This is something the government doesn't want to happen, and yet it seems unwilling to completely prevent her from honoring her dead family members. So every year about a week ahead of Qingming, police escort her to the Babaoshan People's Cemetery and watch her pay her respects.

One year I waited outside the cemetery and watched the strange ritual unfold. It was a blustery day, the blue sky slightly covered by a film of dust that was being whipped up by the Mongolian winds. Xu Jue arrived in a black Audi, escorted by four plain-clothed policemen.

Two of the officers stood out front while she went in with the other two. She walked in the west gate and first turned right to her husband's grave. She always goes there first, she had earlier told me, because they had been married for over thirty years and she felt that his grave was less problematic—if something went wrong at her son's grave, at least she'd have done her husband's grave. When I talked to her later, she told me how she felt: *Qisile,* she said to herself as she looked at the tomb—he had died of anger. Soon after her son had been killed, her husband's hair had gone white. He had begun to curse the government regularly. Within five years of the massacre he was dead, of anger, and leukemia.

The front of the tombstone was engraved with his name and the back carried a poem written by a friend. Four of the middle lines were crucial, listing the flowers to be laid out in front of the grave:

> *Eight calla lilies*
> *Nine yellow chrysanthemums*
> *Six white tulips*
> *Four red roses*

Even though her husband had not participated in the protests, the numbers explained what had killed him: 8 9 6 4, or June 4, 1989. The two police officers stood well back and she laid down the chrysanthemums. As always, she added one red rose, for the blood and her love.

Then she walked back to the main path and straight over to her son's grave, the two officers trailing her by a dozen feet. The stone was small and simple, indistinguishable from the other graves. Obtaining it had been a small feat. She and her husband had to plead to get his corpse from the hospital. Worried doctors had told them they were under orders that corpses had to be surrendered to the army for a mass cremation. Yet doctors had turned a blind eye to the couple when they brought a flat-bed rickshaw to the back door of the morgue to load their son's body. Others had quietly bowed their heads and processed the paperwork when they registered for the grave. A young man who had been crushed to death on June 4. Who could not know what it meant? Yet no one asked any questions and the body was quickly buried.

Between every fifth or sixth tombstone, pine trees had grown, giving the area a quiet, shady feel. She stepped into the grove and found his tombstone: row 3, number 13. One of the rituals many Chinese perform is to use red paint to fill in the engraved characters to make them stand out. She pulled a jar of red paint and a brush out of her bag and stooped over to fill in the three characters of her son's name, which ran down the center:

Wu Xiangdong

Then she went to fill in the smaller lines to the left and right, giving his birth and death dates. But as she stooped down, she grimaced. Her back was sore and she put a hand on her hip, blowing out a sigh of pain and weariness. One of the plain-clothed officers stepped forward and reached out for the jar and the brush. She did not resist, and handed them over. He crouched down and carefully painted in the lines to the upper right:

Born: Year of 1968, August 13
Died: Year of 1989, June 4

And then to the bottom left:

Father: Wu Xuehan
Mother: Xu Jue

The police officer then painted the top and sides of the tombstone red. Not everyone did this but she wanted it to stand out, and if the symbolism of dark red paint was more than a little obvious, the officer did not argue. Maybe he wanted to get home, or maybe he was willing to grant her this bit of dignity—the right to paint her son's tombstone the way she wanted. He liberally slathered red paint over the top and sides, making it pop out of the row of whitish stones. The demands of the past had won.

History recreated

History is not just suppressed: it is also recreated to serve the present, appropriated to further overt ideological ends. In China, this has followed the CCP's near self-destruction in the Cultural Revolution, which led to a desperate search for ideological legitimacy. At first, this was mainly economic, although already in the 1980s the Party encouraged veneration and respect for national symbols, such as the Great Wall. Yet following the June 4th Massacre, the Party began to promote itself more aggressively as the defender of Chinese culture and tradition.

One way the Party has begun to do this has been to position itself as a protector of "Intangible Cultural Heritage," a term most widely associated with the United Nations Educational and Scientific Organization, or UNESCO, which keeps a country-by-country list of traditions important to a specific nation. As opposed to World Heritage Sites, which are physical structures like the Great Wall or Forbidden City, intangible heritage includes music, cuisine, theater, and ceremonies. As late as 1990s China, some of these were still being labeled "feudal superstition," a derogatory term in the Communist lexicon, denoting cultural practices deemed backward. For example, traditional funeral practices were widely discouraged but now funeral rites are on the government list of intangible culture. So, too, religious music that is performed exclusively in Daoist temples during ceremonies. This music is virtually never performed in a secular setting, so the support—which can be over 10,000 yuan a year—essentially subsidizes traditional religion.

Since taking power as Communist Party General Secretary in November 2012 and then assuming the title of President in March 2013, Xi Jinping has increased this turn to traditions. Indeed, it might not be too much of a stretch to say that Xi has cloaked himself in the mantle of tradition more thoroughly than any Chinese leader since the imperial system collapsed in 1911. His only rival, Chiang Kai-shek, often portrayed himself as a great traditionalist when fighting Japan or when in exile in Taiwan. But during the ten years from 1927 to 1937 when he had effective control over China, his Kuomintang party regularly launched attacks on traditional religion, destroying temples, banning the use of the lunar calendar, and declaring that many traditional religious practices were superstitious. Chiang and many of his key allies were Christians and, although some Confucian rites were reintroduced during his rule, he was by and large suspicious of traditions, especially the political-religious system that had dominated local Chinese society under the imperial system.

Xi, by contrast, has fewer qualms about the past. As a good Communist, he and his government still push Communist heroes, such as Lei Feng, and he appeals to Communist ideals when calling on Party cadres to be more honest and less corrupt. But these are almost de rigueur appeals to Communist ethics, and are overshadowed by his embrace of traditional terminology. Building on the work of his predecessors, especially Hu Jintao and his call for a Daoist-sounding "harmonious society" (*hexie shehui*), Xi's ideological program includes a much more explicit embrace of traditional ethical and religious imagery. Taken as a whole, it may well be seen as an effort to create a "civil religion" not unlike that described by the famous sociologist of religion Robert Bellah regarding the United States, or indeed that which existed in China prior to the collapse of the imperial system.

In 2013, according to a news report on December 5 of that year, Xi visited Confucius' hometown of Qufu, picked up a copy of *The Analects*, as well as a biography of the great sage, and declared that "I want to read these carefully." He also coined a Confucianesque aphorism, stating that "a state without virtue cannot endure." The next year, he became the first Communist Party leader to participate in a commemoration of Confucius' birthday. Speaking at the International Confucian Association, Xi said, "to understand today's China, today's Chinese people, we must understand Chinese culture and blood, and nourish the Chinese people's grasp of its own cultural soil." Indeed, so numerous have his classical allusions become, that on May 8, 2014, *People's Daily* published a full-page spread explaining them.

Not all of his rhetoric has been Confucian. In 2014, he visited the UNESCO offices in Paris and praised Buddhism, saying that after it had indigenized it made great contributions to Chinese culture. He also has made a point of meeting Buddhist leaders, such as the Taiwanese Buddhist Hsing Yun, and calling for greater morality in Chinese life. Tellingly, he has never spoken positively about Christianity or Islam. Indeed Protestant churches in the province he used to rule, Zhejiang, have suffered an unprecedented campaign that forced them to remove crosses from atop their steeples.

Xi has never spoken publicly about his faith—all eighty-plus million Communist Party members are supposed to be atheist—but his family has long been seen as sympathetic to Buddhism. His father, the senior Party leader Xi Zhongxun, was a personal friend of a key spiritual leader of Tibet, the tenth Panchen Lama, and wrote his obituary in 1989.

Maybe most tellingly, when Xi took his first major assignment, as Party chief of Zhengding County between 1983 and 1985, he made a point of cultivating close ties with local religious leaders. He was especially friendly with Shi Youming, a famous Buddhist monk who lived in the Linji Monastery. It had been a famous center of Chan, or Zen, Buddhism but had been mostly destroyed during the Cultural Revolution. These were the early days of economic reforms, when few temples were being rebuilt, but Xi made a point of visiting the temple on several occasions and approving its reconstruction. Shi Youming's former apartments are now a small museum, and include a photo of the 31-year-old Xi shaking his hand. In 2012, shortly before Xi took power, I visited the temple and the current abbot, Shi Huichang, told me: "Xi did a great service for Buddhism."

Perhaps this background makes it less surprising that soon into Xi's tenure as Party chief, traditional rhetoric came to dominate the public space of China's cities. A dramatic example concerns one of the biggest propaganda campaigns of recent years, which began in mid-2013. Posters began going up across China almost overnight whose appeal lay in their clever appropriation of traditional Chinese art, such as woodblock printing, paper cuts, and especially clay figurines by a well-known artisan, coupled with references to the "China Dream." The "China Dream" was to be Xi Jinping's contribution to national sloganeering— every top leader has to have at least one—but instead of being something esoteric and incomprehensible, as was the case with Jiang Zemin's "Three Represents," this was an easily understood idea. Although it would become associated with many goals, including nationalism and China's surge to global prominence, in public propaganda campaigns its imagery was almost always linked to traditional culture and virtues.

The posters were ubiquitous for many months, adorning the main squares of several big cities, overpasses, highway billboards. They were even printed on wooden barriers around construction sites, and impregnated on synthetic tarps used as windshields next to agricultural fields. Most traditional propaganda has a tired feel, usually touting someone like Lei Feng, the model citizen and soldier who became the subject of a nationwide posthumous campaign in 1963. And the form of this propaganda is boring: often red banners with white or gold lettering exhorting people to follow a Party policy, comply with a census, or make their local district more beautiful. The China Dream posters, however, were colorful, bright, and cute. Many of the posters featured paintings of clay figurines fashioned by "Niren Zhang" (Clay-man Zhang), a national-level intangible cultural heritage practitioner. Traditionally, these figurines show scenes from daily and religious life, or entertainment, such as characters from Peking Opera, or gods like Lord Guan or Zhang Gui. Sets of the figures were given to the Dowager Empress Cixi on her birthday and sent to world's fairs during the Qing dynasty as examples of Chinese arts.

In the propaganda campaign, the figures included many cute figures, such as a dreamy-eyed girl, or little boys practicing calligraphy. These are augmented by special creations for the campaign, such as a couple of upright cadres or a diorama of People's Liberation Army soldiers helping in disaster relief or a couple of upright cadres. The latter had in brash calligraphy "Great Love for China" and below it a poem that referred to an earthquake:

> *Such a short time, the ground cleaves and the land slides*
> *Such a short time, struck with fear*
> *Racing, pounding toward life*
> *Writing the harmony for Great Love of China!*

The most famous of the posters is a clay figurine of a chubby little girl, dreamily resting her head. Below it is a poem that conflates personal and national dreams:

> *Ah China*
> *My Dream*
> *A fragrant dream*

The author of these poems was Yi Qing, the pen-name of Xie Liuqing. Xie is an editor of the magazine "The World of Chinese" published by The Commercial Press. He is also the head of "Salon Famous Blog of China," a blog registered under the Ministry of Propaganda's official website. Xie also writes dramas and musical plays. More than several dozen of his works based on big historical events have been published, made into movies or television shows, or put on in theatres. Some of his blog articles have been published by the Party's chief ideological magazine, "Seeking Truth."

On one level, Xie could simply be seen as a government apparatchik, cranking out material for the government's latest campaign. But when I went to visit him in 2013, his story turned out to be more interesting, and revealing of the sophisticated propaganda techniques used by the Party during the 2010s to create an ideology that can link traditional Communism with traditional values. After we got in touch through a popular Chinese online messaging service called QQ, he invited me to his office. This turned out to be a hotel room at the Ordos Hotel, named after a small Inner Mongolian city famous for its cashmere and for having built an elaborate new center that was now a ghost town. I was surprised to learn that Xie lacked a proper government office as he was not the government official I had imagined, but instead a free-lancer.

"I like to work here because it's more convenient," he said, sitting on one of the twin beds in the room. "I don't have an office and it's easier to work here than at home. And they give me a long-term rate, store my material when I'm not here, and wash my clothes."

We chatted for a while and he told me he was from Mao Zedong's home province, Hunan, and that he wrote for a variety of publications, as well as operas, theater plays, and television shows. Most were about Mao, who he said was a hero of modern China.

"You can criticize him but you can't deny that he was important. This is my firm belief; it's something maybe due to me being Hunanese, I don't know. But I honestly believe it."

We were joined by Zhang Jiabin, an editor at Red Flag Publishing House, a Communist Party company that had just published a collection of the posters, and also of Xie's poetry. Xie turned on his computer and called up a recording of an event that had been held the day before. It was a ceremony honoring the China Dream posters and we watched the seven-minute segment.

The show honored a new government creation, "public service advertisements," that were displayed on the host website. A hostess called Xie onto the stage to explain how he had seen the signature statue of the chubby girl while at an exhibition in the Beijing suburb of Huairou. He posted pictures online with a few couplets of poetry.

In early 2013, when the civilization office, a government body, was planning a campaign to promote Xi Jinping's idea of a China Dream, they saw Xie's poems and the pictures of the figures. He met with officials and they brainstormed, coming up with the idea of broadening the campaign to include many forms of traditional culture, including papercuts, peasant paintings, and woodblock prints.

"They said, hey we need more poems, so I just dashed them off quickly and now they're up," he said as the video segment ended. "It's supposed to be a sixty-thousand-kilometer campaign. That's how many kilometers of highways there are in China—we joke that every meter of every road will be covered with it."

That was hardly an exaggeration. It was hard to avoid the posters, which covered billboards, and were even made into murals that lined some Beijing streets. They sometimes advocated traditional values like filial piety ("honesty and consideration, handed down through the generations"), other times outright admiration for the Communist Party ("feet shackled, hands cuffed | sturdy grass withstands strong winds | the Communist Party members on the road | the mountains can shake; their will is unshakeable | hot blood and spring flowers will write today's history"), and sometimes just patriotism or nationalism ("Our country is beautiful" and "It's springtime for our father's future"). All showed how for today's government, there was no better ally than history.

History recovered

Sometimes the resurfacing of history into the public consciousness is inadvertent and apolitical. This was driven home to me one day in 2014 when I went to hear a talk at the main office of the National Archives next to Beihai Park. The archives are located in 1950s-era buildings, built in the then-fashionable mixture of foreign and Chinese styles. The walls are high and of brick but the roofs are sloping and the eaves curved. When it was built, many roundly condemned the structure as a kitschy pastiche of styles, but today they are among the few buildings in the capital that bridge the past with the present.

The archives have a big auditorium with red velour-covered walls and enormous windows that overlook Beihai Park. On this February day the sun flooded in, making the winter seem less harsh and the polluted grey skies less oppressive. The speaker was Liu Guozhong, a Hunanese professor at Tsinghua University with a heavy accent and small eyes that often disappeared when he laughed. Liu spoke freely without notes for ninety minutes about something that might seem obscure but which was slowly shaking China's intellectual world: the discovery of long-lost texts from 2,500 years ago.

Liu began to talk generally, making his points understandable for lay people. He said that the Egyptians wrote on papyrus, while in Babylon there was no papyrus so they used clay tablets. In China, an early form of writing was found on tortoise shells, which were heated with pokers until they cracked. The lines were used in divination, much like the lines on people's hands might tell their future. On the tortoise bones, the questions and answers were written down, giving them their name: oracle bones. Those are the earliest known Chinese writing, but mainly about very narrow topics: should the crops be planted on such-and-such a day, should the king launch a war? Marry? Travel? Through them, the nitty gritty concerns of a Shang king's life could be fathomed. It was useful but limited.

The texts we were here to learn about had been written later on flat strips of bamboo. The slips were only the size of chopsticks. From the desk where he sat, Liu demonstrated how researchers think the texts were composed: a strip was placed on the left forearm and the writer used the right hand to hold a writing brush and compose the text. This, he said, is presumably why for millennia Chinese wrote their script top to bottom, right to left.

Even more significant were the topics. These were not the miscellanea of court life, but the ur-texts of Chinese culture. Over the past twenty years, three batches of bamboo slips from this era have been unearthed. One cache was discovered in 1998 in Guodian and has 800 slips. Another discovered in 2000 and held by the Shanghai Museum, has 1,200 slips. The discovery Liu was introducing has a whopping 2,500 slips. (The exact number of slips is open to debate. Twenty-five hundred include some fragments. At least 2,000 are full slips.) The trove came to light because of grave robbers who were likely working in Hubei. The slips ended up in Hong Kong and were to be auctioned off when a donor stepped in, bought the lot, and gave it to his alma mater, Tsinghua University, in 2008.

The Communists made Tsinghua into China's most famous science and technology university, but before 1949 it also had a famous liberal arts tradition. The slips are now at the center of Tsinghua's efforts to revive this past and it did so by recruiting the country's most famous historian, Li Xueqin, to head the project to catalog and study the slips.

Born in 1933, Li has headed numerous key projects, including an effort in the 1990s to date semi-mythical dynasties from roughly 5,000 years ago, such as the Xia and Shang, which are seen as the earliest dynasties in Chinese civilization. For millennia, their existence was taken for granted, even though no texts or archaeological material relating to some were traceable (the historicity of the Xia in particular remains in doubt). In the early twentieth century, historians in China started a "doubt antiquity" movement that challenged the existence of these dynasties, positing that they were merely myths. That was more than an intellectual dispute; it challenged the deeply cherished certainty among Chinese that they are one of the oldest civilizations on the planet, going back as far as ancient Egypt. Li's efforts essentially pushed back against this skepticism, marshaling evidence that these dynasties did indeed exist.

The bamboo slips are from a much later date, but they challenge certainties of Chinese culture in other, possibly more profound ways. The texts stem from the Warring States period, an era of turmoil in China that ran from the fifth to the third centuries BCE. It was a time when civilizations around the world, from the Yellow River in China to the Greek peninsula in Europe and the Indian subcontinent, were organizing new ways of political and philosophical order—a period so crucial to world history that the German historian Karl Jaspers called it the Axial Age. All major Chinese schools of thought that exist today stem from this era, especially Daoism and Confucianism, which has been the country's dominant political ideology, guiding kings and emperors—at least in theory—until the twentieth century.

The bamboo slips that Liu was describing change how we understand this era. Some have compared its impact on China's understanding of the past to how the past was viewed in Europe's Enlightenment, a period when Western core texts were for the first time analyzed as historical documents instead of texts delivered intact from antiquity.

"It's as though suddenly you had texts that discussed Socrates and Plato that you didn't know existed," Sarah Allan, a Dartmouth university professor who has worked with Liu and Li in the project, told me a few months before I heard Professor Liu speak. "People also say it's like the Dead Sea scrolls, but they're more important than that. This isn't Apocrypha. These texts are from the period when the core body of Chinese philosophy was being discussed. They are transforming our understanding of Chinese history."

Until now, most of this history was culled from the classic texts of Confucianism, which includes the *Analects* and the *Mencius* that also date from about 2,300 years ago. One of the surprising ideas that comes through in the new texts is that ideas that were only alluded to in the Confucian classics have now become full-blown schools of thought that challenge some Confucian ideas. One key text, for example, argues in favor of meritocracy much more forcefully than is found in currently known Confucian texts. Until now, the Confucian texts only allowed for abdication or replacement of a ruler as a rare exception; otherwise kingships were hereditary—a much more pro-establishment and anti-revolutionary standpoint. The new texts argue against this. For an authoritarian state wrapping itself in "tradition" to justify its never-ending rule, the implications of this new school are subtle but interesting. "This isn't calling for democracy," Allan, author of *Buried Ideas: Legends of Abdication and Ideal Government in Early Chinese Bamboo-Slip Manuscripts*, told me, "but it more forcefully argues for rule by virtue instead of hereditary rule."

Back in the auditorium next to Beihai Park, Liu continued to talk about the new findings. Some texts are curious—a chart for multiplying and dividing complex numbers, as well as new books of divination, perhaps showing that the magical and esoteric were as important to this era of Chinese as the more rational and this-worldly Confucians. That in itself is a challenge to a government trying to instrumentalize the past, but wary of unpredictable religious and spiritual outbursts.

Although the contents of the strips are known to most experts, they are being edited carefully and one volume is being released a year. Professor Li still comes in each day, Liu says, and helps guide the younger scholars.

Liu then flashed newspaper headlines on the screen. Media interest in China has been intense, he said. After each volume is released, the Chinese media rush to discuss the findings, while blogs and amateurs—like many of the people here this winter afternoon—try their own hands at interpreting these new finds. The audience listened carefully to Liu as he outlined their Tsinghua team's publishing schedule.

"We think we have another fifteen volumes, so that's another fifteen years—until I'm retired," Liu said, laughing. "But then you and others will be debating this for the rest of this century. The research is endless."

Liu concluded and bowed to the audience. He had gone on past the allotted ninety minutes and the janitorial staff was eager to go home. No sooner did he leave the podium than they began to turn off the lights. But the audience rushed the stage, peppering Liu with questions. There was a man from the "I Ching Research Society" asking how they should treat the new texts on divination. A graduate student from Peking University eagerly asked about the political implications of abdication. Liu answered them all, while handing out name cards. When the last of his stack was gone, people began to pass them around, snapping photos of his card with cell phones. The room was now lit only by the dim winter sun. The guards at the back waited to lock the door but the crowd of two dozen wouldn't let Liu leave. For them, he held a key to the present: the past.

TIMELINE OF MODERN CHINESE POLITICAL HISTORY

960–1279	Song Dynasty (ethnicity of rulers: Han Chinese)
1271–1368	Yuan Dynasty (ethnicity of rulers: Mongolian)
1368–1644	The Ming Dynasty (ethnicity of rulers: Han Chinese)
1644–1911	The Qing Dynasty (ethnicity of rulers: Manchus)
1654–1722	Kangxi Emperor (reigned 1661–1722)
1711–1799	Qianlong Emperor (reigned 1735–1796)
1793	Macartncy Mission
1794–1804	White Lotus Rebellion (Buddhist millenarian)
1839–42	The Opium War (Opponent of Qing: The British Empire)
1850–64	Taiping Uprising (Quasi-Christian Millenarian)
1856–60	Second Opium War/Arrow War (Opponents: Britain and France)
1868	Meiji Restoration in Japan
1894–95	War with Japan; China defeated; Treaty of Shimonoseki signed
1898	100 Days Reform; ends with conservatives taking control
1900	Boxer Uprising (anti-Christian)
1900–01	Invasion and occupation of North China by International Force
1905	Examination system ends
1911	Republican Revolution (Xinhai Revolution)
1912–49	Republican Era
1912	Sun Yat-sen serves (briefly) as China's president
1912–1916	Presidency of Yuan Shikai
1915–22	New Culture Movement
1916–27	Warlord Era

1919	May Fourth Movement
1921	Chinese Communist Party (CCP) founded
1924–27	First United Front: Communist/Guomindang Alliance
1925	May Thirtieth Movement
1927	Guomindang purge of Communists
1927–37	Guomindang in charge of country; capital at Nanjing
1931	Japan invades Manchuria
1934–35	The Long March
1936	Xi'an Incident
1937	Japan invades North China
1937–1945	Second United Front: Communist–Guomindang alliance
1942–1944	CCP Rectification Campaign
1945	Japan surrenders
1945–49	The Civil War between the Guomindang and the CCP
1947–52	Land reform
1949	Guomindang retreats to Taiwan
1949	People's Republic of China (PRC) founded; Beijing serves as capital
1949–76	Mao Era
1950	New Marriage Law
1950–53	Korean War
1956	100 Flowers Campaign
1957	Anti-Rightist Campaign
1958	Great Leap Forward and People's Communes
1959–61	Great Leap Famine
1962	Retreat from communal to collective production
1966–69	Great Proletarian Cultural Revolution
1966–76	The "Cultural Revolution Decade"
1969–78	Urban youth sent down to the countryside
1972	Nixon visits Beijing and Shanghai
1976	Mao Zedong dies, Hua Guofeng succeeds him
1978	Official reform policy announced; Deng Xiaoping rises to power
1979	Reform Era begins; stringent birth control policy initiated
1979–82	Dismantling of collective agricultural production
1986–88	Small-scale student movements

1989	Massive student-led movement, ends with massacres in June
1993	China's Olympic bid fails
1997–2003	Jiang Zemin leads the country as head of CCP and President
1997	Hong Kong becomes part of PRC
1999	Falungong crackdown; anti-NATO protests; Macao becomes part of PRC
2001	China's Olympic bid succeeds
2002–12	Hu Jintao leads the country as head of CCP and President
2008	Tibetan uprisings; Sichuan earthquake; Beijing Olympics
2009	Uyghur uprisings; 60th anniversary of PRC's Founding Celebrated
2010	Shanghai Expo held (China's first World Fair)
2012	Xi Jinping installed as head of CCP
2013	Xi Jinping selected to be President of PRC
2014	Umbrella Movement in Hong Kong
2017	repression in Xinjiang increases via the creation of an extensive network of camps
2018	constitution changed to remove term limits for the office of president
2019	first reports from Wuhan of a novel Coronavirus
2020	National Security Law imposed on Hong Kong

FURTHER READING

INTRODUCTION (AND GENERAL BACKGROUND)

Barmé, Geremie R. *The Forbidden City (Wonders of the World)* (London: Profile, 2009).

Brook, Timothy. *The Troubled Empire: China in the Yuan and Ming Dynasties* (Cambridge, MA: Harvard University Press, 2010).

Ebrey, Patricia Buckley. *The Cambridge Illustrated History of China*, 2nd edition(Cambridge: Cambridge University Press, 2010).

Fogel, Joshua. *Politics and Sinology: The Case of Naito Konan, 1866–1934* (Cambridge, MA: Harvard University Asia Center, 1984).

Hsia, Chih-tsing. *The Classic Chinese Novel: A Critical Introduction* (Ithaca, NY: East Asia Program, Cornell University, 1996).

Jensen, Lionel M. *Manufacturing Confucianism: Chinese Traditions and Universal Civilization* (Raleigh, NC: Duke University Press, 1998).

Kuhn, Dieter. *The Age of Confucian Rule: The Song Transformation of China* (Cambridge, MA: Harvard University Press, 2009).

Lewis, Mark Edward. *The Early Chinese Empires, Qin and Han* (Cambridge, MA: Harvard, 2010).

Mair, Victor, ed. *The Columbia Anthology of Traditional Chinese Literature* (New York: Columbia University Press, 1996).

Mote, Frederick W. *Imperial China, 900–1800* (Cambridge, MA: Harvard University Press, 2000).

Nyland, Michael and Thomas Wilson. *Lives of Confucius: Civilization's Greatest Sage through the Ages* (New York: Crown, 2010).

Pierson, Stacey. *From Object to Concept: Global Consumption and the Transformation of Ming Porcelain* (Hong Kong: Hong Kong University Press, 2013).

Pomeranz, Kenneth. *The Great Divergence: China, Europe, and the Making of the Modern World Economy* (Princeton: Princeton University Press, 2000).

Qian, Sima. *The First Emperor: Selections from the Historical Records*, trans. Raymond Dawson, edited and introduced by K. E. Brashier (Oxford: Oxford University Press, 2009).

Spence, Jonathan. *The Search for Modern China*, 3rd edition (New York: Norton, 2012).

Waldron, Arthur. *The Great Wall of China: From Myth to History* (Cambridge: Cambridge University Press, 1992).

Waley-Cohen, Joanna. *The Sextants of Beijing: Global Currents in Chinese History*. (New York: Norton, 2000).

CHAPTER 1

Clunas, Craig. *Superfluous Things: Material Culture and Social Status in Early Modern China*, 2nd edition (Honolulu: University of Hawai'i Press, 2004).

Elliott, Mark C. *Emperor Qianlong: Son of Heaven, Man of the World* (New York: Longman, 2009).

Elman, Benjamin A. *On their Own Terms: Science in China, 1550–1900* (Cambridge, MA: Harvard University Press, 2005).

Finlay, Robert. *The Pilgrim Art: Cultures of Porcelain in World History* (Berkeley: University of California Press, 2010).

Hsia, R. Po-chia. *A Jesuit in the Forbidden City: Matteo Ricci 1552–1610* (Oxford: Oxford University Press, 2012).

Ko, Dorothy. *Teachers of the Inner Chambers: Women and Culture in Seventeenth-Century China* (Stanford, CA: Stanford University Press, 1994).

Ko, Dorothy. *Cinderella's Sisters: A Revisionist History of Footbinding* (Berkeley: University of California Press, 2005).

Laven, Mary. *Mission to China: Matteo Ricci and the Jesuit Encounter with the East* (London: Faber, 2011).

Mann, Susan. *Precious Records: Women in China's Long Eighteenth Century* (Stanford, CA: Stanford University Press, 1997).

Naquin, Susan and Evelyn Rawksi. *Chinese Society in the Eighteenth Century* (New Haven: Yale, 1989).

Schäfer, Dagmar. *The Crafting of the 10,000 Things: Knowledge and Technology in Seventeenth-Century China* (Chicago: The University of Chicago Press, 2011).

Schneewind, Sarah, ed. *Long Live the Emperor! Uses of the Ming Founder across Six Centuries of East Asian History* (Minneapolis: Society for Ming Studies, 2008).

Wade, Geoff and Laichen Sun. *Southeast Asia in the Fifteenth Century: The China Factor* (Singapore: NUS Press, 2010).

EXHIBITION CATALOGUES

Clunas, Craig and Jessica Harrison-Hall. *Ming: 50 Years That Changed China* (London: The British Museum Press, 2014).

Rawski, Evelyn Sakakida and Jessica Rawson. *China: The Three Emperors, 1662–1795* (London: Royal Academy of Arts, 2005).

CHAPTER 2

Cranmer-Byng, J. L., ed. *An Embassy to China: Being the Journal Kept by Lord Macartney during his Embassy to the Emperor Ch'ien-lung, 1793–1794* (Hamden, CT: Longmans, 1962).

Dai Yingcong. "Civilians Go Into Battle: Hired Militias in the White Lotus War," *Asia Major*, 3rd Series, 22.2 (2009): 145–78.

Elliott, Mark C. *Emperor Qianlong: Son of Heaven, Man of the World* (New York: Pearson, 2009).

Grace, Richard J. *Opium and Empire: The Lives and Careers of William Jardine and James Matheson* (Montreal and Kingston: McGill-Queen's University Press, 2014).

Greenberg, Michael. *British Trade and the Opening of China* (Cambridge: Cambridge University Press, 1951).

Lovell, Julia. *The Opium War: Drugs, Dreams, and the Making of China* (London: Picador, 2011).

Macauley, Melissa. "Small Time Crooks: Opium, Migrants, and the War on Drugs in China, 1819–1860," *Late Imperial China* 30.1 (June, 2009): 1–47.

Platt, Stephen R. *Autumn in the Heavenly Kingdom* (New York: Atlantic Books, 2012).

Polachek, James M., *The Inner Opium War* (Cambridge, MA: Harvard University Press, 1992).

Pomeranz, Kenneth L. *The Great Divergence: China, Europe, and the Making of the Modern World Economy* (Princeton: Princeton University Press, 2000).

Spence, Jonathan D. *God's Chinese Son: The Taiping Heavenly Kingdom of Hong Xiuquan* (New York: W. W. Norton, 1996).

Wang Wensheng. *White Lotus Rebels and South China Pirates: Crisis and Reform in the Qing Empire* (Cambridge, MA: Harvard University Press, 2014).

Zheng Yangwen. *The Social Life of Opium in China* (Cambridge: Cambridge University Press, 2005).

CHAPTER 3

Bickers, Robert. *The Scramble for China: Foreign Devils in the Qing Empire, 1832–1914* (London: Allen Lane, 2011).

Cohen, Paul A. *China and Christianity: The Missionary Movement and the Growth of Chinese Antiforeignism, 1860–1870* (Cambridge, MA: Harvard University Press, 1963).

Fogel, Joshua A. *Articulating the Sinosphere: Sino-Japanese Relations in Space and Time* (Cambridge, MA: Harvard University Press, 2009).

Frodsham, J. D. *The First Chinese Embassy to the West: The Journals of Kuo-Sung-T'ao, Liu Hsi-Hung and Chang Te-yi* (Oxford: Clarendon Press, 1974).

Platt, Stephen R. *Autumn in the Heavenly Kingdom: China, the West, and the Epic Story of the Taiping Civil War* (London: Atlantic, 2012).

Rennie, D. F. *Peking and the Pekingese during the First Year of the British Embassy at Peking* (London: John Murray, 1865).

Smith, Richard J., John K. Fairbank, and Katherine F. Bruner, eds. *Robert Hart and China's Early Modernization: His Journals, 1863–1866* (Cambridge, MA: Harvard University Asia Center, 1991).

Wasserstrom, Jeffrey N. *Global Shanghai, 1850–2010* (New York: Routledge, 2008).

Westad, Odd Arne. *Restless Empire: China and the World Since 1750* (London: Vintage, 2013).

Yangwen Zheng. *The Social Life of Opium in China* (Cambridge: Cambridge University Press, 2005).

CHAPTER 4

Chang, Hao. *Liang Ch'i-ch'ao and Intellectual Transition in China, 1890–1907* (Cambridge, MA: Harvard University Press, 1971), is an insightful and contextualized analysis of Liang's evolving thought.

Chang, Hao. *Chinese Intellectuals in Crisis: Search for Order and Meaning, 1890–1911* (Berkeley: University of California Press, 1987), describes the tumultuous intellectual evolution of four key figures.

Chow, Tse-tsung. *The May Fourth Movement: Intellectual Revolution in Modern China* (Cambridge, MA: Harvard University Press, 1960), begins with a magisterial introduction to the New Culture Movement.

Esherick, Joseph W. *Reform and Revolution in China: The 1911 Revolution in Hunan and Hubei* (Berkeley: University of California Press, 1976), isolates the social forces and individuals who led the Wuchang Uprising and took control of the 1911 Revolution.

Esherick, Joseph W. *The Origins of the Boxer Uprising* (Berkeley: University of California Press, 1988), is an insightful analysis of the conditions leading to the formation of the Boxers.

Gasster, Michael. *Chinese Intellectuals and the Revolution of 1911: The Birth of Modern Chinese Radicalism* (Seattle: University of Washington Press, 1969), is still the best overview of the intellectual change of the period.

Judge, Joan. *Print and Politics:* Shibao *and the Culture of Reform in Late Qing China* (Stanford, CA: Stanford University Press, 1997), highlights the institutional and cultural bases of reform thought.

Karl, Rebecca E. *Staging the World: Chinese Nationalism at the Turn of the Twentieth Century* (Durham, NC: Duke University Press, 2002), demonstrates the role of internationalism in the growth of nationalist discourse.

Rhoads, Edward J. M. *Manchus and Han: Ethnic Relations and Political Power in Late Ch'ing and Early Republican China, 1861–1928* (Seattle: University of Washington Press, 2000), highlights the role of ethnic consciousness in the fall of the Qing and beyond.

Strand, David. *An Unfinished Republic Leading by Word and Deed in Modern China* (Berkeley: University of California Press, 2011), is an outstanding study of the political culture created by the 1911 Revolution.

Wong, Young-tsu. *Search for Modern Nationalism: Zhang Binglin and Revolutionary China, 1869–1936* (Oxford: Oxford University Press, 1989), is the standard intellectual biography of Zhang.

Young, Ernest P. *The Presidency of Yuan Shih-k'ai: Liberalism and Dictatorship in Early Republican China* (Ann Arbor: University of Michigan Press, 1977), is a careful and balanced study of Yuan's presidency.

Zarrow, Peter. *After Empire: The Conceptual Transformation of the Chinese State, 1885–1924* (Stanford, CA: Stanford University Press, 2012), focuses on the development of statist forms of nationalism in the late Qing.

CHAPTER 5

Carter, James H. *Creating a Chinese Harbin* (Ithaca, NY: Cornell University Press, 2000).

Chen, Janet. *Guilty of Indigence: The Urban Poor in China, 1900–1953* (Princeton: Princeton University Press, 2012).

Field, Andrew David. *Shanghai's Dancing World: Cabaret Culture and Urban Politics, 1919–1954* (Hong Kong: The Chinese University Press, 2011).

Honig, Emily. *Sisters and Strangers: Women in the Shanghai Cotton Mills, 1919–1949* (Stanford, CA: Stanford University Press, 1992).

Lee, Leo Ou-fan. *Shanghai Modern: The Flowering of a New Urban Culture in China, 1930–1945* (Cambridge, MA: Harvard University Press, 1999).

Lipkin, Zwia. *Useless to the State: "Social Problems" and Social Engineering in Nationalist Nanjing, 1927–1937* (Cambridge, MA: Harvard University Asia Center, 2006).

Lu, Hanchao. *Beyond the Neon Lights: Everyday Shanghai in the Early Twentieth Century*, 2nd edition (Berkeley and Los Angeles: University of California Press, 2004).

Stapleton, Kristin. *Civilizing Chengdu* (Cambridge, MA: Harvard University Press, 2000).

Strand, David. *Rickshaw Beijing: City People and Politics* (Berkeley and Los Angeles: University of California Press, 1993).

Wakeman, Frederic W. *Policing Shanghai, 1927–1937* (Berkeley and Los Angeles: University of California Press, 1996).

REVOLUTIONARIES AND REFORMERS

Dirlik, Arif. *The Origins of Chinese Communism* (Oxford: Oxford University Press, 1989).

Gilmartin, Christina. *Engendering the Chinese Revolution: Radical Women, Communist Politics, and Mass Movements in the 1920s* (Berkeley and Los Angeles: University of California Press, 1995).

Schoppa, R. Keith. *Blood Road: The Mystery of Shen Dingyi in Republican China* (Berkeley and Los Angeles: University of California Press, 1995).

WARLORDS

Lary, Diana. *Warlord Soldiers: Chinese Common Soldiers 1911–1937* (Cambridge: Cambridge University Press, 1990).

McCord, Edward. *The Power of the Gun: The Emergence of Modern Chinese Warlordism* (Berkeley and Los Angeles: University of California Press, 1993).

MAY FOURTH

Ding Ling. *I Myself Am Woman: Selected Writing of Ding Ling*, ed. and trans. Tani Barlow and Gary J. Bjorge (Boston: Beacon Press, 1990).

Jones, Andrew. *Developmental Fairy Tales* (Cambridge, MA: Harvard University Press, 2011).

Lu Xun. *The Real Story of Ah-Q and Other Tales of China: The Complete Fiction of Lu Xun*, trans. Julia Lovell (New York: Penguin, 2010).

Rahav, Shakar. *The Rise of Political Intellectuals in Modern China: May Fourth Societies and the Roots of Mass-Party Politics* (Oxford: Oxford University Press, 2015).

Schwarcz, Vera. *The Chinese Enlightenment: Intellectuals and the Legacy of the May Fourth Movement of 1919* (Berkeley and Los Angeles: University of California Press, 1990).

CHAPTER 6

Eastman, Lloyd et al. *The Nationalist Era in China, 1927–1949* (Cambridge: Cambridge University Press, 1991) has two excellent overview essays, by Lloyd Eastman on the Nationalists and Lyman van Slyke on the Communists, that cover the wartime period.

Hsiung James and Steven Levine, eds. *China's Bitter Victory: The War with Japan, 1937–1945* (Armonk, NY: Routledge, 1992), covers key topics on wartime China.

Mitter, Rana. *Forgotten Ally: China's World War II, 1937–1949* (Boston: Houghton Mifflin, 2013), covers the political and social history of the war.

BIOGRAPHIES

Boyle, John Hunter. *China and Japan at War, 1937–1945: The Politics of Collaboration* (Stanford, CA: Stanford University Press, 1972).

Pantsov, Alexander and Steven Levine. *Mao: The Real Story* (New York: Simon and Schuster, 2012).

Short, Philip. *Mao: A Life* (London; Owl Books, 2001).

Taylor, Jay. *The Generalissimo: Chiang Kai-shek and the Struggle for Modern China* (Cambridge, MA: Harvard University Press, 2007), gives comprehensive coverage of Chiang's whole life, including his period on Taiwan.

THE NATIONALISTS: POLITICAL, SOCIAL, AND MILITARY HISTORY OF WARTIME

Garver, John. *Chinese–Soviet Relations, 1937–1945: The Diplomacy of Chinese Nationalism* (Oxford: Oxford University Press, 1988), deals ably with the diplomacy of the period between China and the USSR.

Moore, Aaron William. *Writing War: Soldiers Record the Japanese Empire* (Cambridge, MA: Harvard University Press, 2013), has powerful new material from Nationalist soldiers.

Peattie, Mark, Edward Drea, and Hans van de Ven, eds. *The Battle for China: Essays on the Military History of the Sino-Japanese War of 1937–1945* (Stanford, CA: Stanford University Press, 2011), is essential on individual campaigns.

van de Ven, Hans J. *War and Nationalism in China, 1925–1945* (London: Routledge, 2003), important overall account of wartime.

THE COMMUNISTS AND THEIR REVOLUTION

Benton, Gregor. *Mountain Fires: The Red Army's Three-Year War in South China, 1934–1938* (Berkeley and Los Angeles: University of California Press, 1992), monumental analysis of CCP base areas other than Yanan.

Benton, Gregor. *New Fourth Army: Communist Resistance Along the Yangtze and the Huai, 1938–1941* (Berkeley and Los Angeles: University of California Press, 1999).

Goodman, David. *Social and Political Change in Revolutionary China: The Taihang Base Area in the War of Resistance to Japan, 1937–1945* (Lanham, MD: Rowman and Littlefield, 2000).

Hartford, Kathleen and Steven M. Goldstein, eds. *Single Sparks: China's Rural Revolutions* (Armonk, NY: Routledge, 1989).

Johnson, Chalmers. *Peasant Nationalism and Communist Power: The Emergence of Revolutionary China, 1937–1945* (Stanford, CA: Stanford University Press, 1962), a classic.

Pepper, Suzanne. "The Political Odyssey of an Intellectual Construct: Peasant Nationalism and the Study of China's Revolutionary History: A Review Essay," *Journal of Asian Studies* 63.1 (2004).

Selden, Mark. *The Yenan Way in Revolutionary China* (Cambridge, MA: Harvard University Press, 1971), an important response to Johnson's thesis.

Yung-fa, Chen. *Making Revolution: The Communist Movement in Eastern and Central China, 1937–1945* (Berkeley and Los Angeles: University of California Press, 1986).

COLLABORATION WITH THE JAPANESE

Barrett, David, ed. *Chinese Collaboration with Japan, 1932–1945: The Limits of Accommodation* (Stanford, CA: Stanford University Press, 2001), very useful.

Brook, Timothy. *Collaboration: Japanese Agents and Chinese Elites in Wartime China* (Cambridge, MA: Harvard University Press, 2005), pathbreaking.

THE CIVIL WAR

Lary, Diana. *China's Civil War: A Social History, 1945–1949* (Cambridge: Cambridge University Press, 2014), major recent social historical perspective.

Pepper, Suzanne. *Civil War in China: The Political Struggle, 1945–1949* (Berkeley and Los Angeles: University of California Press, 1978), significant overall account, especially on politics.

Westad, Odd Arne. *Decisive Encounters: The Chinese Civil War, 1946–1950* (Stanford, CA: Stanford University Press, 2004), important on political history.

CHAPTER 7

Brown, Jeremy and Matthew D. Johnson, eds. *Maoism at the Grassroots: Everyday Life in China's Era of High Socialism* (Cambridge, MA: Harvard University Press, 2015).

Brown, Jeremy and Paul Pickowicz, eds. *Dilemmas of Victory: The Early Years of the People's Republic of China* (Cambridge, MA: Harvard University Press, 2007).

Dikötter, Frank. *The Tragedy of Liberation: A History of the Chinese Revolution, 1945–57* (London: Bloomsbury, 2013). A hostile view.

Friedman, Edward, Paul Pickowicz, and Mark Selden. *Revolution, Resistance, and Reform in Village China* (New Haven: Yale University Press, 2007).

Meisner, Maurice. *Mao's China and After: A History of the People's Republic of China*, third edition (New York: Free Press, 1999). A sympathetic but not uncritical view.

Spence, Jonathan. *The Search for Modern China* (New York: W. W. Norton, 1991).

MAO ZEDONG

Benton, Gregor and Lin Chun, eds. *Was Mao Really a Monster?* (London: Routledge, 2009).

Chang, Jung and Jon Halliday. *Mao: The Unknown Story* (London: Vintage, 2005).

Leese, Daniel. *Mao Cult: Rhetoric and Ritual in China's Cultural Revolution* (Cambridge: Cambridge University Press, 2011).

Pantsov, Alexander with Steven Levine. *Mao: the Real Story* (New York: Simon and Schuster, 2007).

Short, Philip, *Mao: A Life* (London: Owl Books, 1999).

POLITICS

Eddy, U. *Disorganizing China: Counter-Bureaucracy and the Decline of Socialism* (Stanford, CA: Stanford University Press, 2007).

Lü, Xiaobo. *Cadres and Corruption: the Organizational Involution of the Chinese Communist Party* (Stanford, CA: Stanford University Press, 2000).

MacFarquhar, Roderick. *The Origins of the Cultural Revolution: The Coming of the Cataclysm, 1961–1966* (Oxford: Oxford University Press, 1997).

Mei, Zhi. *F: Hu Feng's Prison Years*, trans. Gregor Benton (London: Verso, 2013).

Smith, S. A. "On not Learning from the Soviet Union: Religious Policy in China, 1949–65," *Modern China Studies* 22.1 (2015): 70–97.

Strauss, Julia C. "Paternalist Terror: The Campaign to Suppress Counterrevolutionaries and Regime Consolidation in the People's Republic of China, 1950–1953," *Comparative Studies in Society and History* 44.1 (2002): 80–105.

Teiwes, Frederick C. with Warren Sun. *China's Road to Disaster: Mao, Central Politicians and Provincial Leaders in the Unfolding of the Great Leap Forward* (Armonk, NY: Routledge, 1999).

ECONOMICS

Bramall, Chris. *Industrialization of Rural China* (Oxford: Oxford University Press, 2007).

Li, Hua-Yu. *Mao and the Economic Stalinization of China, 1948–1953* (Lanham, MD: Rowman and Littlefield, 2006).

Naughton, Barry. *The Chinese Economy: Transitions and Growth* (Cambridge, MA: Harvard University Press, 2007).

THE GREAT LEAP FORWARD AND THE FAMINE

Bernstein, Thomas P. "Mao Zedong and the Famine of 1959–60: A Study in Wilfulness," *China Quarterly* 186 (2006): 421–45.

Chan, Alfred L. *Mao's Crusade: Politics and Policy Implementation in China's Great Leap Forward* (Oxford: Oxfrd University Press, 2001).

Dikötter, Frank. *Mao's Great Famine: The History of China's Most Devastating Catastrophe, 1958–1962* (London: Bloomsbury, 2010).

Manning, Kimberley Ens and Felix Wemheuer, eds. *Eating Bitterness: New Perspectives on China's Great Leap Forward and Famine* (Vancouver: University of British Columbia Press, 2011).

Thaxton, Ralph. *Catastrophe and Contention in Rural China: Mao's Great Leap Forward Famine and the Origins of Righteous Resistance in Da Fo Village* (Cambridge: Cambridge University Press, 2008).

Zhou, Xun. *Forgotten Voices of Mao's Great Famine, 1958–1962: An Oral History* (New Haven: Yale University Press, 2014).

RURAL SOCIETY

Brown, Jeremy. *City and Countryside in Mao's China* (Cambridge: Cambridge University Press, 2012).

Hershatter, Gail. *The Gender of Memory: Rural Women and China's Collective Past* (Berkeley and Los Angeles: University of California Press, 2011).

Li, Huaiyin. *Village China under Socialism and Reform: A Micro-history, 1948–2008* (Stanford, CA: Stanford University Press, 2009).

Ruf, Gregory. *Cadres & Kin: Making a Socialist Village in West China, 1921–91* (Stanford, CA: Stanford University Press, 1998).

Yang, Dali. *Calamity and Reform in China: State, Rural Society, and Institutional Change since the Great Leap Famine* (Stanford, CA: Stanford University Press, 1996).

URBAN SOCIETY

Diamant, Neil J. *Revolutionizing the Family: Politics, Love, and Divorce in Urban and Rural China, 1949–1968* (Berkeley and Los Angeles: University of California Press, 2000).

Frazier, Mark W. *The Making of the Chinese Industrial Workplace: State, Revolution and Labor Management* (Cambridge: Cambridge University Press, 2002).

Howard, Joshua. *Workers at War: Labor in China's Arsenals, 1937–1953* (Stanford, CA: Stanford University Press, 2010).

Perry, Elizabeth J. "Shanghai's Strike Wave of 1957," *China Quarterly* 137 (1994): 1–27.

Sheehan, Jackie. *Chinese Workers: A New History* (London: Routledge, 1998).

Ye, Weili and Ma Xiaodong. *Growing Up in the People's Republic* (Basingstoke: Palgrave, 2005).

CULTURE AND EDUCATION

Hung, Chang-tai. *Mao's New World: Political Culture in the Early People's Republic.* (Ithaca, NY: Cornell University Press, 2010).

Kraus, Richard Curt. *The Party and the Arty: The New Politics of Culture* (Lanham, MD: Rowman and Littlefield, 2004).

Pepper, Suzanne. *Radicalism and Educational Reform in 20th Century China* (Cambridge: Cambridge University Press, 1996).

Perry, Elizabeth J. *Anyuan: Mining China's Revolutionary Tradition* (Berkeley and Los Angeles: University of California Press, 2012).

Peterson, Glen. *The Power of Words: Literacy and Revolution in South China, 1949–95* (Vancouver: University of British Columbia Press, 1997).

430 Further Reading

SINO-SOVIET RELATIONS

Bernstein, Thomas P. and Hua-yu Li, eds. *China Learns from the Soviet Union: 1949–Present* (Lanham, MD: Rowman and Littlefield, 2010).

Chen, Jian. *Mao's China and the Cold War* (Chapel Hill, NC: University of North Carolina Press, 2001).

Jersild, Austin. *The Sino-Soviet Alliance: An International History* (Chapel Hill, NC: University of North Carolina Press, 2014).

Kaple, Debora, ed. "China and the USSR: A Retrospective Look at the 1950s." Special Issue, *Modern China Studies* 22.1 (2015).

Lüthi, Lorenz. *The Sino-Soviet Split: Cold War in the Communist World* (Princeton: Princeton University Press, 2008).

Westad, O. A., ed. *Brothers in Arms: The Rise and Fall of the Sino-Soviet Alliance, 1945–1963* (Washington, DC: Stanford University Press, 1998).

CHAPTER 8

Brady, Anne-Marie. *Making the Foreign Serve China: Managing Foreigners in the People's Republic* (Lanham, MD: Rowman and Littlefield, 2003).

Bramall, Chris. *Chinese Economic Development* (London: Routledge, 2009).

Chan, Anita, Richard Madsen, and Jonathan Unger. *Chen Village: The Recent History of a Peasant Community in Mao's China* (Berkeley and Los Angeles: University of California Press, 1984).

Chang, Jung. *Wild Swans: Three Daughters of China* (New York: Simon and Schuster, 1991).

Cheng, Nien. *Life and Death in Shanghai* (New York: Grove, 1987).

Clark, Paul. *The Chinese Cultural Revolution: A History* (Cambridge: Cambridge University Press, 2008).

Esherick, Joseph W., Paul G. Pickowicz, and Andrew G. Walder, eds. *The Chinese Cultural Revolution as History* (Stanford, CA: Stanford University Press, 2006).

Gao Mobo. *Gao Village* (Honolulu: University of Hawaii Press, 1999).

Gao Yuan. *Born Red: A Chronicle of the Cultural Revolution* (Stanford, CA: Stanford University Press, 1987).

Goldstein, Melvyn, Ben Jiao, and Tanzen Lhundrup. *On the Cultural Revolution in Tibet: The Nyemo Incident of 1969* (Berkeley and Los Angeles: University of California Press, 2009).

Han, Dongping. *The Unknown Cultural Revolution* (New York: Monthly Review Press, 2008).

Jiang Yang. *A Cadre School Life: Six Chapters* (Hong Kong: Joint Publication Company, 1982).

Joseph, William A., Christine P. W. Wong, and David Zweig, eds. *New Perspectives on the Cultural Revolution* (Cambridge, MA: Harvard University Press, 1991).

Kraus, Richard Curt. *Pianos and Politics in China: Middle-Class Ambitions and the Struggle over Western Music* (New York: Oxford University Press, 1989).

Kraus, Richard Curt. *The Cultural Revolution: A Very Short Introduction* (Oxford: Oxford University Press, 2012).

Law, Kam-yee, ed. *The Chinese Cultural Revolution Reconsidered: Beyond Purge and Holocaust* (Houndmills: Palgrave Macmillan, 2003).

Leese, Daniel. *Mao Cult: Rhetoric and Ritual in China's Cultural Revolution* (Cambridge: Cambridge University Press, 2011).

Li Zhisui. *The Private Life of Chairman Mao* (New York: Random House, 1994).

Liang Heng and Judith Shapiro. *Son of the Revolution* (New York: Knopf, 1983).

Ma Jisen. *The Cultural Revolution in the Foreign Ministry of China* (Hong Kong: Chinese University Press, 2004).

Meisner, Maurice. *Mao's China and After: A History of the People's Republic* (New York: Free Press, 1986).

Milton, David, and Nancy Dall Milton. *The Wind Will Not Subside: Years in Revolutionary China* (New York: Pantheon, 1976).

Min, Anchee. *Red Azalea* (New York: Pantheon, 1994).

Mittler, Barbara. *A Continuous Revolution: Making Sense of Cultural Revolution Culture* (Cambridge, MA: Harvard University Asia Center, 2012).

Naughton, Barry. *The Chinese Economy: Transitions and Growth* (Cambridge, MA: MIT Press, 2007).

Perry, Elizabeth and Li Xun. *Proletarian Power: Shanghai in the Cultural Revolution* (Boulder, CO: Westview Press, 2000).

Rae Yang. *Spider Eaters: A Memoir* (Berkeley and Los Angeles: University of California Press, 1997).

Riskin, Carl. *China's Political Economy: The Quest for Development since 1949* (Oxford: Oxford University Press, 1987).

Schoenhals, Michael. *China's Cultural Revolution, 1966–1969: Not a Dinner Party* (Armonk, NY: M. E. Sharpe, 1996).

Schoenhals, Michael and Roderick MacFarquhar. *Mao's Last Revolution* (Cambridge, MA: Harvard University Press, 2006).

Su, Yang. *Collective Killings in Rural China during the Cultural Revolution* (Cambridge: Cambridge University Press, 2011).

Teiwes, Frederick C. and Warren Sun. *The End of the Maoist Era: Chinese Politics during the Twilight of the Cultural Revolution, 1972–1976* (Armonk, NY: M. E. Sharpe, 2007).

Walder, Andrew G. *Fractured Rebellion: The Beijing Red Guard Movement* (Cambridge, MA: Harvard University Press, 2009).

Wang Ban, ed. *Words and their Stories: Essays on the Language of the Chinese Revolution* (Leiden: Brill, 2010).

White, Lynn T. III. *Policies of Chaos: The Organizational Causes of Violence in China's Cultural Revolution* (Princeton, NJ: Princeton University Press, 1989).

Woei Lien Chong, ed. *China's Great Proletarian Cultural Revolution* (Lanham, MD: Rowman and Littlefield, 2002).

Yan Jiaqi and Gao Gao. *Turbulent Decade: A History of the Cultural Revolution* (Honolulu: University of Hawai'i Press, 1996).

Yue Daiyun and Carolyn Wakeman. *To the Storm: The Odyssey of a Revolutionary Chinese Woman* (Berkeley and Los Angeles: University of California Press, 1985).

WEBSITES

Morning Sun: A Film and Website about Cultural Revolution <www.morningsun.org>.

Chinese Posters: Propaganda, Politics, History, Art <chineseposters.net>.

Posters from the collections of International Institute of Social History Amsterdam, and Stefan R. Landsberger.

Videos, photos, and interviews related to the documentary film of the same title, from the Long Bow Group.

CHAPTER 9

Barmé, Geremie and Linda Javin, eds. *New Ghosts, Old Dreams: Chinese Rebel Voices* (New York: Times Books, 1992).

Binyan, Liu. "People or Monsters?" in *People or Monsters?and Other Stories and Reportage from China After Mao* (Bloomington: Indiana University Press, 1983).

Brugger, Bill and David Kelly. *Chinese Marxism in the Post-Mao Era* (Stanford, CA: Stanford University Press, 1991).

Cheek, Timothy. *The Intellectual in Modern Chinese History.* (Cambridge: Cambridge University Press, 2016).

Clark, Paul. *Reinventing China: A Generation and its Films* (Hong Kong: Chinese University Press, 2006).

Garside, Roger. *Coming Alive: China After Mao* (New York: Signet, 1982).

Gittings, John. *The Changing Face of China: From Mao to Market* (New York: Oxford University Press, 2005).

Gold, Thomas B. "Guerrilla Interviewing Among the *Getihu*," in Perry Link, Richard Madsen, and Paul G. Pickowicz, eds, *Unofficial China: Popular Culutre and Thought in the People's Republic* (Boulder, CO: Westview Press, 1989).

Goldman, Merle. *Sowing the Seeds of Democracy in China: Political Reform in the Deng Xiaoping Era* (Cambridge, MA: Harvard University Press, 1994).

Goldman, Merle, Timothy Cheek, and Carol Hamrin, eds. *China's Intellectuals and the State: The Search for a New Relationship* (Cambridge, MA: Harvard Contemporary China Series, 1989).

Greenhalgh, Susan. *Just One Child: Science and Policy in Deng's China* (Berkeley: University of California Press, 2008).

Kelly, David A. "Wang Ruoshui and Socialist Humanism," in Merle Goldman, Timothy Cheek, and Carol Hamrin, eds, *China's Intellectuals and the State: The Search for a New Relationship* (Cambridge, MA: Harvard Contemporary China Series, 1989).

Lizhi, Fang. *Bringing Down the Great Wall: Writings on Science, Culture, and Democracy in China*, trans. James H. Williams (New York: W. W. Norton, 1992).

Meisner, Maurice. *The Deng Xiaoping Era: An Inquiry into the Fate of Chinese Socialism, 1978–1994* (New York: Hill & Wang, 1996).

Naughton, Barry. *Growing Out of the Plan: Chinese Economic Reform, 1978–1993* (New York: Cambridge University Press, 1995).

Potter, Pitman. *From Leninist Discipline to Socialist Legalism: Peng Zhen on Law and Political Authority in the PRC* (Stanford, CA: Stanford University Press, 2003).

Saich, Tony. *Governance and Politics of China*, 3rd edition (New York: Palgrave Macmillan, 2011).

Shambaugh, David. *Modernizing China's Military: Progress, Problems, and Prospects* (Berkeley and Los Angeles: University of California Press, 2004).

Shuo, Wang. *Playing for Thrills*, trans. Howard Goldblatt (New York: Penguin Books, 1998).

Wasserstrom, Jeffrey N. and Elizabeth J. Perry, eds. *Popular Protest and Political Culture in Modern China: Learning from Tiananmen* (Boulder, CO: Westview Press, 1992).

Williams, James H. "Fang Lizhi's Expanding Universe," *China Quarterly* 123 (1990): 458–83.

Zheng, Yongnian. *Contemporary China: A History Since 1978.* (Oxford: Wiley-Blackwell, 2014).

Zweig, David. *Freeing China's Farmers: Rural Restructuring in the Reform Era* (Armonk, NY: M. E. Sharpe, 1997).

CHAPTER 10

Bandurski, David. "The Shishou Riots and the Uncertain Future of Control 2.0," China Media Project, June 29, 2009.

Barmé, Geremie R. and Linda Jaivin, eds. *New Ghosts, Old Dreams: Chinese Rebel Voices* (New York: Random House, 1992).

Brook, Timothy. *Quelling the People: The Military Suppression of the Beijing Democracy Movement* (Stanford, CA: Stanford University Press, 1998).

Chan, Kam Wing and Li Zhang. "The Hukou System and Rural–Urban Migration in China: Processes and Changes," *China Quarterly* 160 (1999): 831–5.

Cunningham, Philip J. *Tiananmen Moon: Inside the Chinese Student Uprising of 1989.* (New York: Rowman & Littlefield, 2010).

Davis, Deborah. "Chinese Social Welfare: Policies and Outcomes," *China Quarterly* 119 (1989): 577–97.

Davis, Deborah, ed. *The Consumer Revolution in Urban China* (Berkeley and Los Angeles: University of California Press, 2000).

Guidi, Chen and Wu Chuntao. *Will the Boat Sink the Water? The Life of China's Peasants*, trans. Zhu Hong (New York: Public Affairs, 2006).

He, Rowena Xiaoqing. *Tiananmen Exiles: Voices of the Struggle for Democracy in China* (Basingstoke: Palgrave Macmillan, 2014).

Jeremy Brown, *June Fourth: The Tiananmen Protests and Beijing Massacre of 1989*. (Cambridge: Cambridge University Press, 2021).

Lim, Louisa. *The People's Republic of Amnesia: Tiananmen Revisited* (Oxford: Oxford University Press, 2014).

Naughton, Barry. "The Impact of the Tiananmen Crisis on China's Economic Transition," *China Perspectives* 2 (2009): 63–78.

Naughton, Barry. "China's Economy: Complacency, Crisis & the Challenge of Reform," *Daedalus* spring 2014.

O'Brien, Kevin J. "Rural Protest," *Journal of Democracy* 20.3 (2009): 25–8.

Ownby, David. "China's War Against Itself," *New York Times,* February 15, 2001.

Ownby, David. *Falun Gong and the Future of China* (New York: Oxford University Press, 2008).

Unger, Jonathan and Geremie Barmé, eds. *Pro-Democracy Protest in China* (London: M. E. Sharpe, 1991).

Zhang, Liang, Andrew J. Nathan, and Perry Link, eds. *The Tiananmen Papers* (New York: PublicAffairs, 2002).

FILMS AND WEBSITES

"The Gate of Heavenly Peace"

"Tank Man"

Posters from the 1950s–1980s held in the University of Westminster Chinese Poster Collection <http://chinaposters.westmister.ac.uk/zenphoto/>.

CHAPTER 11

Callahan, William A. *China Dreams: 20 Visions of the Future* (New York: Oxford University Press, 2013).

Chan Koonchung. *The Fat Years*, trans. Michael S. Duke (London: Doubleday, 2011).

Hessler, Peter. *Oracle Bones: A Journey Between China's Past and Present* (New York: HarperCollins, 2006).

Scocca, Tom. *Beijing Welcomes You: Unveiling the Capital City of the Future* (New York: Riverhead Books, 2011).

Wasserstrom, Jeffrey N., with contributions by Maura Elizabeth Cunningham. *China in the 21st Century: What Everyone Needs to Know*, 2nd edition (New York: Oxford University Press, 2013).

Xu Guoqi. *Olympic Dreams: China and Sports, 1895–2008* (Cambridge, MA: Harvard University Press, 2008).

ECONOMY

Barabantseva, Elena. "In Pursuit of an Alternative Model? The Modernisation Trap in China's Official Development Discourse," *East Asia: An International Quarterly* 29 (2012): 63–79.

Chang, Gordon G. "The Coming Collapse of China: 2012 Edition," <Foreign Policy.com> (December 29, 2011).

Gerth, Karl. *As China Goes, So Goes the World: How Chinese Consumers are Transforming Everything* (New York: Hill and Wang, 2010).

He Chuanqi, et al. *China Modernization Report Outlook (2001–2010)* (Beijing: Peking University Press, 2010).

Hessler, Peter. *Country Driving: A Journey Through China from Farm to Factory* (New York: Harper, 2010).

Hu Angang. *China in 2020: A New Kind of Superpower* (Washington, DC: Brookings Institution Press, 2011).

Lin, Justin Yifu, Fang Cai, and Zhou Li. *The China Miracle: Development Strategy and Economic Reform*, revised edition (Hong Kong: Chinese University Press, 2003).

Pan Wei. "The Chinese Model of Development" (London: Foreign Policy Centre, 2007).

Ramo, Joshua Cooper. *The Beijing Consensus* (London: Foreign Policy Centre, 2004).

World Bank. *China 2030: Building a Modern, Harmonious and Creative High-Income Society* (Washington, DC: World Bank, 2012).

Xu Jinglei, dir. "Go Lala Go!" (2010).

Yang Yao. "The End of the Beijing Consensus: Can China's Model of Authoritarian Growth Survive?" *Foreign Affairs* (February 2010).

POLITICS

Brady, Anne-Marie. *Marketing Dictatorship: Propaganda and Thought Work in Contemporary China* (New York: Rowman & Littlefield Publishers, 2008).

Callahan, William A. *China: The Pessoptimist Nation* (Oxford: Oxford University Press, 2010).

Glaser, Bonnie and Evan S. Medieros. "The Changing Ecology of Foreign Policy-Making in China: The Ascension and Demise of the Theory of 'Peaceful Rise'," *China Quarterly* 190 (2007): 291–310.

Gries, Peter Hays. *China's New Nationalism: Pride, Politics and Diplomacy* (Berkeley and Los Angeles: University of California Press, 2004).

Jiang Zemin. *On the "Three Represents"* (Beijing: Foreign Languages Press, 2002).

Johnston, Alastair Iain. "Is China a Status Quo Power?" *International Security* 27.4 (2003): 5–56.

Leonard, Mark, ed. *China 3.0*. London: European Council on Foreign Relations, 2012.

Miller, Alice, ed. *China Leadership Monitor* (2002–present).

Pieke, Frank N. *The Good Communist: Elite Training and State Building in Today's China* (Cambridge: Cambridge University Press, 2009).

Zhao, Suisheng. *A Nation-State by Construction: Dynamics of Modern Chinese Nationalism* (Stanford, CA: Stanford University Press, 2004).

FOREIGN AFFAIRS

Callahan, William A. and Elena Barabantseva, eds. *China Orders the World: Normative Soft Power and Foreign Policy* (Baltimore: Johns Hopkins University Press, 2011).

Deng, Yong. *China's Struggle for Status: The Realignment of International Relations* (New York: Cambridge University Press, 2008).

Hughes, Christopher R. "Reclassifying Chinese Nationalism: The *Geopolitik* Turn," *Journal of Contemporary China* 20.71 (2011): 601–20.

Kurlantzick, Joshua. *Charm Offensive: How China's Soft Power Is Transforming the World* (New Haven: Yale University Press, 2007).

Shambaugh, David. *China Goes Global* (New York: Oxford University Press, 2013.

Shirk, Susan. *China: Fragile Superpower* (New York: Oxford University Press, 2007).

Yan Xuetong. *Ancient Chinese Thought, Modern Chinese Power*, ed. Daniel A. Bell and Sun Zhe (Princeton: Princeton University Press, 2011).

Zhao, Tingyang. "Rethinking Empire from a Chinese Concept 'All-under-Heaven' (Tian-xia)," *Social Identities* 12.1 (2006): 29–41.

Zheng Bijian. *China's Peaceful Rise* (Washington, DC: Brookings Institution Press, 2005).

SOCIETY AND CULTURE

Ai Weiwei. *Ai Weiwei's Blog: Writings, Interviews, and Digital Rants, 2006–2009* (Cambridge, MA: MIT Press, 2011).

Bandurski, David. "Zhang vs. Yang on the China Model." *China Media Project*. March 29, 2011.

Berry, Michael. *Jia Zhangke's "Hometown Trilogy": Xiao Wu, Platform, Unknown Pleasures* (London: British Film Institute, 2009).

Callahan, Bill, dir. Documentary "Border Crossings." (2014).

Davies, Gloria. *Worrying about China: The Language of Chinese Critical Inquiry* (Cambridge, MA: Harvard University Press, 2007).

Goldman, Merle. *From Comrade to Citizen: The Struggle for Political Rights in China* (Cambridge, MA: Harvard University Press, 2005).

Han Han. *This Generation*, trans. Allan Barr (London: Simon & Schuster, 2012).

Jia Zhangke, dir. "The World" (2004).

Liu Xiaobo. *No Enemies, No Hatred: Selected Essays and Poems*, ed. Perry Link, Tianchi Martin-Liao, and Liu Xia (Cambridge, MA: Harvard University Press, 2012).

Osnos, Evan. *Age of Ambition* (New York: FSG, 2014).

Ownby, David. "Kang Xiaoguang: Social Science, Civil Society, and Confucian Religion," *China Perspectives* 4 (2009): 101–11.

Woeser, Tsering and Wang Lixiong. *Voices from Tibet*, ed. and trans. Violet S. Law (Honolulu: University of Hawaii Press, 2012).

Wu, Cheng'en, *Monkey King: Journey to the West*, translation by Julia Lovell. (London: Penguin Classics, 2021).

Zha, Jianying. *Tide Players: The Movers and Shakers of a Rising China* (New York: New Press, 2011).

CHAPTER 12

Dirks, Emile, and James Leibold. (2020). *Genomic Surveillance: Inside China's DNA Dragnet*. Barton, Australia: Australian Strategic Policy Institute.

Economy, Elizabeth. (2018). *The Third Revolution: Xi Jinping and the New Chinese State*. New York: Oxford University Press.

Fu, Diana. (2018). *Mobilizing Without the Masses: Control and Contention in China*. New York: Cambridge University Press.

Huang, Yanzhong. (2020). *Toxic Politics: China's Environmental Health Crisis and Its Challenge to the Chinese State*. New York: Cambridge University Press.

Lee, Ching Kwan. (2018). *The Specter of Global China: Politics, Labor, and Foreign Investment in Africa*. Chicago, IL: The University of Chicago Press.

Li, Cheng. (2016). *Chinese Politics in the Xi Jinping Era: Reassessing Collective Leadership*. Washington, DC: Brookings Institution Press.

Liu, Sida and Terrence Halliday. (2016). *Criminal Defense in China: The Politics of Lawyers at Work*. New York: Cambridge University Press.

Mattingly, Daniel. (2020). *The Art of Political Control in China*. New York: Cambridge University Press.

Millward, James (2021). *Eurasian Crossroads: A History of Xinjiang*, Revised Edition. London: Hurst.

Perry, Elizabeth, Grzegorz Ekiert, and Xiaojun Yan (Eds.) (2020). *Ruling by Other Means: State-Mobilized Movements*. New York: Cambridge University Press.

Roberts, Dexter. (2020). *The Myth of Chinese Capitalism*. New York: St. Martin's Press.

Roberts, Molly. (2018). *Censored: Distraction and Diversion Inside China's Great Firewall*. Princeton, NJ: Princeton University Press.

Wasserstrom, Jeffrey N. (2020). *Vigil: Hong Kong on the Brink*. New York: Columbia Global Reports.

Weiss, Jessica Chen. (2014). *Powerful Patriots: Nationalist Protest in China's Foreign Relations*. New York: Oxford University Press.

CODA

Allan, Sarah. "Not the Lun yu: The Chu Script Bamboo Slip Manuscript, Zigao, and the Nature of Early Confucianism," *Bulletin of the School of Oriental and African Studies* 72.1 (2009): 115–51.

Allan, Sarah. "On Shu 書 (Documents) and the Origin of the Shang shu 尚書 (Ancient Documents) in Light of Recently Discovered Bamboo Slip Manuscripts," *Bulletin of the School of Oriental and African Studies* 75.3 (2012): 547–57.

Barmé, Geremie R., et al. *Yearbook 2012: Red Rising, Red Eclipse* Canberra: Australia National University, 2012).

Barmé, Geremie R., et al. *Yearbook 2013: Civilising China* (Canberra: Australia National University, 2013).

Barmé, Geremie R., et al. *Yearbook 2014: Shared Destiny* (Canberra: Australia National University, 2015).

Bellah, Robert. *The Robert Bellah Reader*, ed. Steven Tipton (Durham, NC: Duke University Press, 2006).

Goosaert, Vincent and David A. Palmer. *The Religious Question in Modern China* (Chicago: University of Chicago Press, 2010).

Liao Yiwu. *God is Red: The Secret History of How Christianity Survived and Flourished in Modern China*, trans. Wenguang Huang (New York: Harper One, 2011).

Lim, Louisa. *The People's Republic of Amnesia: Tiananmen Revisited* (Oxford: Oxford University Press, 2014).

Perry, Elizabeth J., ed. *Growing Pains in a Rising China*. Special issue of *Daedalus*, Spring 2014.

Schell, Orville and John Delury. *Wealth and Power: China's Long March to the Twenty-First Century* (New York: Random House, 2013).

Yang, Jisheng. *Tombstone: The Great Chinese Famine, 1958–1962*, trans. Stacy Mosher and Guo Jian, edited and with an introduction by Edward Friedman (New York: FSG, 2012).

Yu Hua. *China in Ten Words*, trans. Allan H. Barr (London: Duckworth, 2012).

INDEX